Insight Through Computing

Insight Through Computing

A MATLAB Introduction to
Computational Science and Engineering

Charles F. Van Loan
K.-Y. Daisy Fan
Cornell University
Ithaca, New York

 Society for Industrial and Applied Mathematics

Library of Congress Cataloging-in-Publication Data

Van Loan, Charles F.
Insight through computing : a MATLAB introduction to computational science and engineering / Charles F. Van Loan, K.-Y. Daisy Fan.

   p. cm.
  Includes index.
  ISBN 978-0-898716-91-7
  1. Numerical analysis--Data processing. 2. Science--Computer simulation.
  3. Engineering mathematics--Data processing. 4. MATLAB. I. Fan, K.-Y. Daisy. II. Title.
  QA297.V25 2010
  005.1--dc22   2009030277

 is a registered trademark.

To our families

Contents

Preface

As the title suggests, this book is both an introduction to MATLAB® programming and to the computational side of science and engineering. We target college freshman intending to major in engineering (including computer science) or a natural science (including mathematics). Given the quantitative abilities of this group of students, we do not shy away from trigonometry and elementary notions of approximation as seen in Calculus I. Indeed, it is against the grain of liberal education not to intermingle introductory programming with continuous mathematics if the student clientele is capable of handling the mix. Liberal education is all about acquiring an appreciation for different modes of thought. Why squander the opportunity to contrast digital thinking with continuous thinking?

Our approach is simple. Each section begins with the posing of a problem that points to some larger computational story. The solution is carefully derived and along the way we introduce whatever new MATLAB is required. This is followed by a brief "talking point" that emphasizes some aspect of the larger story. This pattern resonates with our belief that a first course in programming should be taught through examples. Every section culminates in the production of a working MATLAB script and (usually) a few MATLAB functions. The section exercises include straightforward "M-problems" that focus on the developed code and whatever new MATLAB is developed. More involved "P-problems" are designed to reinforce the section's computational message.

We use the MATLAB environment because of its friendliness to the first-time programmer <u>and</u> because it supports the idea of playing with computational ideas through experimentation. This is central to the development of computational intuition.

> *Playing with programs builds computational intuition.*

Intuition is a sense of direction no different from the sense of direction that enables you to find your way around an old childhood neighborhood without a map. The key is that you have been there before. If intuition is a sense of direction, then computational intuition is a sense of computational direction. Those who have it will be able to find their way around science and engineering in the 21st century. Navigation requires five keen senses. Through examples and problems we aim to do the following:

1. *Develop eyes for the geometric.* The ability to visualize is very important to the computational scientist. Of course, computer graphics plays a tremendous role here, but the visualization tools that it offers do not obviate the need to reason in geometric terms. It is critical to be familiar with sines and cosines, polygons and polyhedra, metrics and proximity, etc.

2. *Develop an ear that can hear the "combinatoric explosion."* Many design and optimization problems involve huge search spaces with an exponential number of possibilities. It is important to anticipate this complexity and to have the wherewithal to handle it with intelligent heuristics.

3. *Develop a taste for the random.* Science and engineering is populated with processes that have a random component. Having a sense of probability and the ability to gather and interpret statistics with the computer is vital.

4. *Develop a nose for dimension.* Simulation is much more computationally intensive in three dimensions than in two dimensions—a hard fact of life that is staring many computational scientists right in the face. An accurate impression of how computers assist in the understanding of the physical world requires an appreciation of this point. Moreover, being able to think at the array level is essential for effective, high-performance computing.

5. *Develop a touch for what is finite, inexact, and approximate.* Rounding errors attend floating point arithmetic, computer displays are granular, analytic derivatives are approximated with divided differences, a polynomial is used in lieu of the sine function, and the data acquired in a lab may only be correct to three significant digits. Life in computational science is like this and the practitioner must be resolute enough to face such uncertainties. Steady footwork is required on the balance beam that separates the continuous and the discrete.

While the development of these five senses is an explicit priority, our overarching ambition is to communicate the excitement of computing together with an appreciation for its constraints and its connections to other methodologies. The interplay between computing, theory, and experimentation is particularly important.

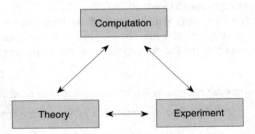

Each vertex represents a style of research and provides a window through which we can view science and engineering in the large. The vibrancy of what we see inside the triangle depends upon the ideas that flow around its edges. A good theory couched in the language of mathematics may be realized in the form of a computer program, perhaps just to affirm its correctness. Running the program results in a simulation that may suggest a physical experiment. The experiment in turn may reveal a missed parameter in the underlying mathematical model, and around we go again.

There are also interesting dynamics in the other direction. A physical experiment may be restricted in scope for reasons of budget or safety, so the scene shifts to computer simulation. The act of writing the program to perform the simulation will most likely have a clarifying influence, prompting some new mathematical pursuit. Innovative models are discovered, leading to a modification of the initial set of experiments, and so forth.

In thinking about these critical interactions we are reminded of the great mathematical scientist Richard Hamming, who stated in the 1960s that "the purpose of computing is insight, not numbers." We are in obvious agreement with this point of view. The takeaway message from a first programming course should be "Insight Through Computing" instead of just "Output Through Computing." The next generation of computational scientists and engineers needs to think broadly and creatively, and we hope that our book is a contribution in that direction.

Acknowledgments

This book is derived from many years of experience teaching CS 100M (now CS 1112) at Cornell University. We are indebted to the many graduate student teaching assistants who, through their hard work, have given us the time to refine our course notes and to develop interesting assignments. In particular, we would like to thank Mr. Tim Condon for coauthoring Appendix C.

More generally, we are fortunate to have our academic home defined by two of Cornell's great academic units: the College of Engineering and the Faculty of Computing and Information Science. Location is everything if you want to be energized by both colleagues and students. We have the best.

K.-Y. Daisy Fan
Charles F. Van Loan
Ithaca, New York

Programming Topics

The computational topics in this book easily map to the programming topics of a typical introductory programming course. Our "programming tetris" below shows the organization by programming topics. Each block depends on the block(s) immediately underneath. Chapters 1–7 cover programming basics (white blocks), including control flow, functions, and one- and two-dimensional arrays. Chapters 8, 9, and 14 present algorithmic topics (dark gray blocks) such as sorting, bisection, and recursion. Data structure ideas, strings, and file processing (light gray blocks) are discussed in Chapters 9, 10, and 11. Applications and more advanced examples appear in Chapters 12, 13, and 15 (black blocks).

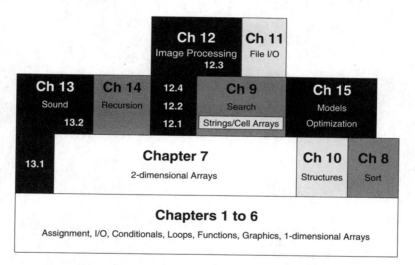

Upon completion of the first six chapters, there is considerable freedom in arranging the remaining topics to fit the needs of your course. In fact, there is some flexibility in how you can use the early chapters as well. The discussion of loops is divided into three chapters: simple loops in Chapter 2, nested loops in Chapter 3, and loops for vectors in Chapter 4. If getting to vectors is a priority, Chapter 4 can be covered before Chapter 3. If you wish to use procedural abstraction as early as possible, then you can go to §5.1 after covering simple loops in Chapter 2. Traveling on our "computational landscape" is really quite similar to navigating the more familiar "programming landscape."

Software

Playing with the programs and models that we present is an important element in developing the first-time programmer's computational intuition. Such "play" checks for comprehension of the presented programs, elicits questions on ideas that require closer study, and, we hope, motivates further exploration in the field of computational science and engineering. A good starting point is to the "M-problems" in the section exercises which typically involve some modification of the presented code. This book contains more than 120 MATLAB scripts and functions, all of which are available electronically.

If a picture is worth a thousand words, how many words is a video worth? MatTV is a series of short videos—from 3 to 9 minutes each—that cover specific MATLAB language features and programming tools. In general the videos review and demonstrate MATLAB language syntax, or rules.

The availability of the programs in "play"—electronic—format and the animation of MATLAB topics in MatTV complement the rich discussion in this book. All three parts are essential to the student's first journey through a programming course. Enjoy our computational science and engineering playground!

Getting the m-Files and Watching MatTV

All the files and videos are available on the Web at

www.siam.org/books/ot117

To watch a video you need to sign in with a Cornell University "NetID" or as a guest. If you are a guest, create a guest account *the first time only*. For subsequent video viewing simply sign in with your guest account name and password.

Using the m-Files—Setting the Path

Create a directory (folder) on your memory device to store the downloaded files. You may want to create subdirectories to keep the files organized. MATLAB needs to know where to find the files in order to execute them. Here are two options:

1. Set the MATLAB *Current Directory* to be the directory holding the file(s) that you want to execute. The Current Directory is indicated in a bar near the top middle of the MATLAB window. You can type in the directory name or browse to it by pressing the ⋯ button next to the Current Directory bar. *This is a good option if you use MATLAB in a computer lab and your files are on a portable memory device.*

2. Put your directory on the MATLAB *search path*. In MATLAB, choose *File → Set Path* and click the *Add with Subfolders* button. Then you can browse to the folder that you want to add and change its rank in the search path. MATLAB searches first in the Current Directory and then according to the rank in the search path. *This is a convenient option if you have MATLAB on your own computer.*

MatTV Listings

Chapter 1

From Formula
to Program

1.1 Just Plug It In!

Surface Area of a Sphere

1.2 Check and Evaluate

Minimum of a Quadratic on an Interval

After we become thoroughly at home with the four arithmetic operations in grade school, we begin to play around with formulae. At first it is fun. The simplicity of "plugging in" and letting the formula "do the work" is appealing. It seems that we are in charge of a powerful machine. But then along comes the dreaded "word problem" and we discover that problem solving is not quite so mechanical. Which formula is relevant and must it be rearranged? Should it be combined with some other formula? And what—actually—is the question being posed?

The situation is similar with computer-based problem solving. A program is a formula and the act of writing a program is the act of describing its steps in such a way that the computer can carry them out. What takes us beyond the world of simple math book recipes is complexity and length. The logic behind a computer program, even a very short one, is typically more intricate than what we encounter in elementary mathematics. Reasoning about a computer program whose evaluation involves a billion steps is very different than checking over the arithmetic associated with $F = (9/5)C + 32$. We clearly need to expand our problem-solving skill set if we are to write and use computer programs.

A good way to begin is to practice the conversion of simple mathematical formulae into computer programs, and the two examples that make up this chapter each has a "message." We develop a program that computes how much the surface area of a sphere increases if its radius increases by a small amount. Three different strategies are explored, previewing the importance of approximation and providing a clue that there is more to programming than simply transcribing some formula from a math book. We also consider the problem of finding the minimum value of a quadratic on an interval. In this case the "formula" to invoke depends upon the location of the quadratic's "turning point." Is it inside the interval or beyond its endpoints? The method requires a single decision midway through the solution process. Soon, we will entertain algorithmic formulae that involve billions of decisions all along the solution path. Let us get ready!

Programming Preview

Concepts

Program, formula, algorithm, variables, assignment, initialization, arithmetic expressions, input, output, strings, types of error, program fragment, conditionals, boolean expressions, logical reasoning.

Language Features

Script: A program, i.e., a sequence of instructions (called statements) written in the MATLAB language.

disp, fprintf: Functions for printing text, e.g., results, to the screen.

input: A function that solicits and accepts user input.

sin, cos, abs: Examples of elementary mathematical functions in MATLAB.

pi: The MATLAB built-in value for π.

Boolean Expression: An expression that has the value true or false.

if else: Keywords for specifying conditional execution of statements.

MatTV

Video 1. The MATLAB Desktop

How to use and manage the MATLAB Desktop.

Video 2. Script

How to write and run MATLAB scripts.

Video 3. Input, Output, Help

How to use input, how to produce formatted output using fprintf, and how to use the *help* facilities.

Video 4. Conditional Statement

How to use the conditional statement, including elseif. The relational and logical operators, as well as "shortcircuiting," are discussed.

Video 5. Nested ifs

How to "nest" conditional statements and how nesting relates to elseif.

Video 6. Path

How to set the MATLAB search path.

1.1 Just Plug It In!

Problem Statement

The surface area of a sphere having radius r is given by

$$A(r) = 4\pi r^2.$$

We wish to explore how the surface area increases when the radius is increased by a tiny amount δr:

$$\delta A = 4\pi(r + \delta r)^2 - 4\pi r^2 \tag{1.1}$$

$$\delta A = 4\pi(2r + \delta r) \cdot \delta r \tag{1.2}$$

$$\delta A = 8\pi r \cdot \delta r. \tag{1.3}$$

The first two formulae are exact, and the third is an approximation that ignores the $(\delta r)^2$ term.

Write a script that solicits the sphere radius r (in kilometers), the increase amount δr (in millimeters), and then displays the surface area increase (in square meters). What is the increase when the radius of a spherical Earth ($r = 6367$km) is increased by a few millimeters? Explore the answer to this question using each of the above formulae.

Program Development

Let us begin by writing a program that computes just the surface area. Given pencil and paper, we would most likely start by writing down something like this:

$$A = 4(3.1416)(6367)^2. \tag{1.4}$$

Calculator in hand, we would then button-push our way to the solution:

$$12.56640000e + 000 \leftarrow (4)(3.1416) \tag{1.5}$$

$$8.001026880e + 004 \leftarrow (12.56640000e + 000)(6367) \tag{1.6}$$

$$5.094253814e + 008 \leftarrow (8.001026880e + 004)(6367). \tag{1.7}$$

Notice that to use the calculator, the "high-level" recipe (1.4) has to be broken down into the sequence of more elementary subcomputations (1.5)–(1.7). This is how plug-into-the-formula-problem-solving works.

If we switch from the Earth (and kilometers) to a baseball (and inches), then it is exactly the same process but with a different input. Instead of (1.4)–(1.7) we have

$$A = 4(3.1416)(1.455)^2$$

and

$$12.56640000e + 00 \leftarrow (4)(3.1416)$$

$$18.28411200e + 00 \leftarrow (12.56640000e + 00)(1.455)$$

$$26.60338296e + 00 \leftarrow (18.28411200e + 00)(1.455).$$

The computation of surface area for a golf ball or a basketball would be similar. However, we are getting bored! It would be nice to automate the sequence of button-pushes once the input radius is specified.

MATLAB allows us to do this. Before we see how, we need to nail down a few concepts that are best illustrated by using MATLAB as a calculator from the *command window*. The starting point is to get the value of the input radius into the memory of the computer:

```
>> r = 6367;
```

The ">>" symbol is a prompt and we responded with an instruction that assigns the value 6367 to a *variable* named r. Although the instruction "r = 6367" looks like an equation, it really prescribes an action. The proper way to talk about the action is to say "the value of 6367 has been assigned to r," or "r gets 6367," not "r equals 6367." Visualize a variable such as r as a named box with a value "inside":

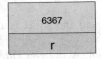

Because the variable r has been *initialized*, it can be referenced by subsequent instructions that require its value. Indeed, corresponding to (1.5)–(1.7) we have

```
>>   T1 = 4*3.1416;
>>   T2 = T1*r;
>>   A  = T2*r;
```

A sequence of instructions like this is called a *script*. This particular script creates three new variables: T1, T2, and A. Together with r, they each house a value:

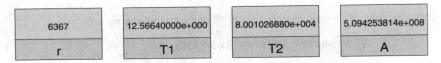

Our 3-line script looks a little different from the more informal sequence (1.5)–(1.7). Multiplication is indicated with an asterisk "*". We dropped all the parentheses, but that was optional. The script

```
>>   T1 = (4)*(3.1416);
>>   T2 = (T1)*(r);
>>   A  = (T2)*(r);
```

is equivalent. However, the main distinction between our MATLAB script and (1.5)–(1.7) is the precise management of the subcomputations. Each operation produces a result that must be stored in a variable.

The naming of the variables is our choice and does not affect the results. Thus,

```
>>   radius = 6367;
>>   Temp1 =  4*3.1416;
>>   Temp2 = Temp1*radius;
>>   Sphere_Area  =  Temp2*radius;
```

involves the same four assigned values:

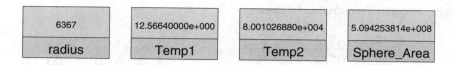

Variable names must begin with a letter and must be composed solely of letters, numbers, and the underscore character "_". Upper-lowercase is acceptable.

The concept of verbosity, which exists in the pencil and paper world, also applies to the writing of MATLAB scripts. Just as (1.4) is "equivalent" to the more verbose (1.5)–(1.7), so too is

```
>> A = 4*3.1416*r^2;
```

equivalent to our original 3-line script. We do not have to manage personally the storage of every single intermediate result—MATLAB takes care of that behind the scenes.

A disappointing feature of our 1-line solution is that it does not display the answer! MATLAB displays the result of an assignment statement only if it is <u>not</u> followed by a semicolon, e.g.,

```
>> r = 6367
r =
        6367
>> A = 4*3.1416*r^2
A =
      5.094253814496000e+008
```

Because the value of A is so large, its value is displayed using scientific notation. Ordinarily it would be conventionally displayed with 4 digits of precision:

```
>> A = 4*3.1416*.6367^2
A =
     5.0943
```

The `format` command can be used to alter how MATLAB displays results in the command window:

```
>> format long
>> A = 4*3.1416*.6367^2
A =
     5.094253814496001
```

There are other possibilities, e.g., `format short`, `format short e`, etc.

We now turn our attention to a convenience issue and an aesthetic issue. The convenience issue revolves around having to keystroke the input radius and the surface area formula for each application (Earth, baseball, golf ball, etc.) The aesthetic issue concerns the sloppy output of the computed surface area.

To address both of these issues we create an "m-file" and place within it a script that solicits the input radius, performs the surface area computation, and "pretty prints" the results. It can be visualized as follows:

```
SurfArea.m
   % The Script SurfArea
   r = input('Enter radius r:');
   A = 4*3.1416*r^2;
   fprintf('r = %10.3f A = %10.3e\n', r, A)
```

There are four things to discuss: comments, the input statement, the fprintf statement, and the m-file itself.

Comments begin with the percent symbol % and are a very important part of a well-written script. We shall make it a habit to begin each script with a comment that specifies the name of the script.

The input statement is an effective way to prompt the MATLAB user for data. The prompt includes a message which is enclosed in quotes. The script waits until the data value is acquired before proceeding. A sequence of characters delimited by single quotes is called a *string*.

The fprintf command also includes a string. Here the string is a message with special character sequences that specify the display format for the numerical values that are to be incorporated into the string as shown in Figure 1.1. Ten spaces are allocated for the display of r with three spaces used for values to the right of the decimal point. The f format displays numbers in standard decimal notation. Because of the e format, A is displayed in scientific notation. Ten spaces are allocated with three to the right of the decimal point. The "\n" generates a carriage return, ensuring that subsequent output appears on a new line.

An m-file must have a name, e.g., SurfArea. In the MATLAB environment m-files are used to store scripts. Once an m-file is set up, we can initiate the execution of the script it contains by simply entering the name of the m-file, e.g.,

```
>> SurfArea
Enter radius r:6367
r =    6367.000  A = 5.094e+008
```

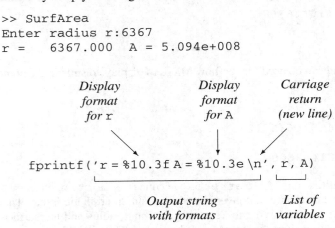

Figure 1.1. *The* fprintf *Statement.*

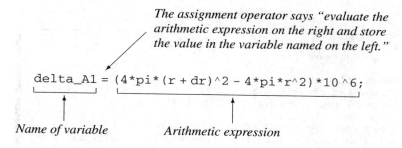

The assignment operator says "evaluate the arithmetic expression on the right and store the value in the variable named on the left."

```
delta_A1 = (4*pi*(r + dr)^2 - 4*pi*r^2)*10^6;
```

Name of variable   *Arithmetic expression*

Figure 1.2. *The Assignment Statement.*

We are now set to address the surface area increase problem posed at the beginning of this section. The three formulae (1.1)–(1.3) are easy to encode using the MATLAB built-in constant pi:

```
delta_A1 = (4*pi*(r+delta_r)^2) - (4*pi*r^2)
delta_A2 = 4*pi*(2*r + delta_r)*delta_r
delta_A3 = 8*pi*r*delta_r
```

The script Eg1_1 (shown below) is structured to compute the surface area increase according to these three recipes. It makes some assumptions about units to facilitate the inputting of values for the skim-coat-the-Earth problem. In particular, it solicits the radius r in kilometers and the increase δr in millimeters. The value of δA is reported in square meters. The clc command clears the command window before the results are displayed.

A high point of the script is the use of the assignment statement. The assignment operator "=" prescribes an action. See Figure 1.2. It is important to keep this in mind when developing a program. Avoid thinking of the assignment operator "=" as a statement about algebraic equality.

The use of comments in Eg1_1 is important. *It will be our policy to always begin a script with a pair of comments—one that specifies its name and another that describes what it does.* Comments should also be used to herald the beginning of important *code fragments*. In Eg1_1 we highlight with comments the acquisition and display of the data and each of the three area computations.

Talking Point: Error and More Error

Even though script Eg1_1 is short and simple, it prompts us to think about error. There is a model error associated with the assumption that the Earth is a perfect sphere. The fact is, the shape of the Earth is better modeled by an oblate spheroid, i.e., an ellipse of revolution. Second, if the Earth radius value r is obtained via satellite, then measurement error will contaminate the results. The value of r that we hand over to the program will not be exact. Third, there is a mathematical error associated with the built-in constant pi which has the value 3.14159265358979. This does not quite equal the true value of π, which is a never-ending decimal. Finally, there is roundoff error associated with the actual computation. Computers do not perform exact real arithmetic. Just as the division of 1 by 3 on a calculator produces something like .333333, so should we expect the computer

The Script Eg_1

```
% Script Eg1_1
% Surface Area Increase

% Acquire and display the input data...
r = input('Enter radius (kilometers):');
delta_r = input('Enter increase (millimeters):');
clc
fprintf('Sphere radius   = %12.6f kilometers\n',r)
fprintf('Radius increase = %12.6f millimeters\n\n',delta_r)
disp('Surface Area Increase:')

dr = delta_r/10^6;

% Method 1
delta_A1 = (4*pi*(r + dr)^2 -  4*pi*r^2)*10^6;
fprintf('\n   Method 1: %15.6f square meters\n',delta_A1)

% Method 2
delta_A2 = (4*pi*(2*r + dr)*dr)*10^6;
fprintf('   Method 2: %15.6f square meters\n',delta_A2)

% Method 3
delta_A3 = (8*pi*r*dr)*10^6;
fprintf('   Method 3: %15.6f square meters\n',delta_A3)
```

Sample Output from the Script Eg1_1

```
Sphere radius   =   6367.000000 kilometers
Radius increase =      1.234000 millimeters

Surface Area Increase:

    Method 1:   197464.823723 square meters
    Method 2:   197464.881659 square meters
    Method 3:   197464.881640 square meters
```

to make a small error every time an arithmetic operation is performed. This explains why Methods 1 and 2 produce different results even though they are equivalent mathematically. The imprecisions of computer arithmetic are discussed in §4.3.

Intelligent numerical computing always requires an honest assessment of error. The computer does not give us the right to waive the traditions of good science.

MATLAB Review

Script

A script is a program, i.e., a sequence of instructions such as Eg1_1. The order of the instructions is important.

Executing a Script

This is the same as "running a script" or "executing a program." To execute a script, in the MATLAB *command window* type the name of the script *without* the extension .m. For example, type Eg1_1 to run the script with the filename Eg1_1.m. The script should be stored in the *Current Directory*.

Current Directory

The Current Directory (also known as the current working directory or current folder) is indicated in a textbox at the top of the MATLAB window. You can type the appropriate directory (folder) name in the bar or browse to the correct folder by pressing the .... button next to the Current Directory bar.

Code Fragment

Any contiguous part of a script, e.g.,

```
r = input('Enter radius (kilometers):');
delta_r = input('Enter increase (millimeters):');
```

Variable

A variable is a storage location (a "box") that holds a value. Letters, numbers, and the underscore may be used in the name of a variable. Upper- and lowercase are distinguished. The first character in a variable name must be a letter. Example: delta_A1.

Arithmetic Expression

A recipe that produces a number, e.g., (4*pi*(r + dr)^2 - 4*pi*r^2)*10^6. The usual arithmetic operators are allowed including $+, -, *, /,$ and $\hat{} $.

Simple Numerical Assignment

The assignment statement has the following form:

$$\text{variable name} = \text{arithmetic expression}$$

For example,

```
delta_A1 = (4*pi*(r + dr)^2 - 4*pi*r^2)*10^6
```

In an assignment statement, the right-hand side is evaluated first and then the value obtained is assigned to the variable named on the left-hand side. The variables on the right-hand side must be *initialized* before they can be used in an expression, i.e., every participating variable must have a value at the time the statement is executed.

Echo Control and the Semicolon

If a semicolon is left off the end of an assignment statement, then the value assigned is displayed in the command window.

format

A command used to control the display of assignment statement output in the command window. Here are some of the more widely used options:

`format short`	decimal notation, 5 digits
`format long`	decimal notation, 15 digits
`format short e`	scientific notation, 5-digit mantissa
`format long e`	scientific notation, 15-digit mantissa

The `short` format is in force when MATLAB is started. Whenever a `format` command is entered, the designated format remains in effect until the next `format` command.

Strings

A string is a sequence of characters enclosed by single quotes, e.g., `'ei@2>.%k'`. If you need a string that includes a single quote, double it: `'ei''@2>.%k'`.

Comments

Except within a string, everything that follows the "%" symbol is a comment. Comments facilitate the reading and understanding of the script. They should be clear and concise. There should always be a comment at the beginning of a script indicating what it does. As programs get more complicated, comments should be used to clarify the mission of critical code fragments and variables.

Multiple Statements per Line

It is legal to have more than one statement per line in a script, but the statements must be separated by either a semicolon or comma. Thus,

```
x = 3;
fprintf('x = %5.3f\n',x)
y = x^2 + 4;
```

is equivalent to

```
x = 3; fprintf('x = %5.3f\n',x), y = x^2 + 4;
```

Continuing a Statement on the Next Line

Use the ellipsis (...) to indicate that a statement continues on the next line. Thus,

```
delta_A1 = (4*pi*(r + dr)^2 - 4*pi*r^2)*10^6;
```

is equivalent to

```
delta_A1 = (4*pi ...
           *(r + dr)^2 - 4*pi*r^2) ...
           *10^6;
```

clc

The command `clc` clears the command window, a typical thing to do prior to displaying the results.

input

The `input` function can be used to solicit keyboard input:

$$\boxed{\text{variable name}} = \text{input}(\boxed{\text{string}})$$

The string should be an informative prompt, e.g.,

```
r = input('Enter radius (kilometers): ')
```

disp

The `disp` function has the form

$$\text{disp}(\boxed{\text{string}})$$

and is used to display a string in the command window, e.g.,

```
disp('Surface Area Increase:')
```

fprintf

The `fprintf` function is used to display formatted strings that incorporate values of specified variables. It has the form

$$\text{fprintf}(\boxed{\text{string with format controls}} , \boxed{\text{list of variables}})$$

Examples:

```
fprintf('Temperature = %4d degrees\n',T)
fprintf('Temperature = %6.3d degrees\n',T)
fprintf('Temperature = %4d   Pressure = %10.3e\n',T,P)
fprintf('\nTemperature = %4d\nPressure = %8.2f\n',T,P)
```

To display values as integers, use the d format. The f and e formats are for conventional decimal format and scientific notation format. The integers that precede the d, f, and e are used to specify the "width" of the displayed value. Thus, `%10.6f` allocates ten characters for the display: six for the decimal part, one for the decimal point, and three for the integer part (including the sign). To initiate printing on a new line, use `\n`.

pi

At the start of a MATLAB session, the value of `pi` is `3.14159265358979`. It is legal (but usually unwise) to change the value of this "built-in constant," e.g., `pi = 22/7`.

Square Root

The `sqrt` function can be applied to any arithmetic expression. If the arithmetic expression evaluates to a negative number, then an imaginary value is produced. Examples: `sqrt(3)`, `sqrt(-3)`, `sqrt(x)`, and `sqrt(b^2 - 4*a*c)`.

Logs and Exponentials

The exp function can be applied to any arithmetic expression and returns the value e^v where v is the value of the expression. The natural logarithm, base-10 logarithm, and base-2 logarithm can be computed using log, log10, and log2, respectively.

Trigonometric Functions

The sin, cos, and tan functions can be applied to any arithmetic expression and return the value of $\sin(v)$, $\cos(v)$, and $\tan(v)$ where v is the value of the expression in radians.

Inverse Trigonometric Functions

The asin, acos, and atan functions can be applied to any arithmetic expression and return the value of $\arcsin(v)$, $\arccos(v)$, and $\arctan(v)$ where v is the value of the expression.

Exercises

M1.1.1 Modify Eg1_1 to calculate and print the original surface area before calculating the area increase.

M1.1.2 Modify Eg1_1 to print the area increases in exponential notation. The original script specifies the print format of variable delta_A to be fixed point notation using the specifier f in the substitution sequence %15.6f in the fprintf statement. Change the specifier to e to specify exponential notation. Experiment with the numbers in the substitution sequence to print the value of delta_A to fewer decimal places.

M1.1.3 A temperature can be converted from the Fahrenheit scale into Celsius using the formula $c = (5/9)(f - 32)$, where f is a temperature given in °F and c is the resulting temperature in °C. Write a script to prompt the user for a temperature in °F, convert the temperature into °C, and print it.

P1.1.4 An *oblate spheroid* such as the Earth is obtained by revolving an ellipse about its minor axis. In everyday terms, it is the shape of a slightly compressed beach ball. The Earth's equatorial radius is about 20km longer than its polar radius.
        The surface area of an oblate spheroid is given by

$$A(r_1, r_2) = 2\pi \left(r_1^2 + \frac{r_2^2}{\sin(\gamma)} \log\left(\frac{\cos(\gamma)}{1 - \sin(\gamma)} \right) \right),$$

where r_1 is the equatorial radius, r_2 is the polar radius, and

$$\gamma = \arccos\left(\frac{r_2}{r_1} \right).$$

We assume $r_2 < r_1$. Write a script that inputs the equatorial and polar radii and displays both $A(r_1, r_2)$ and the approximation $4\pi((r_1 + r_2)/2)^2$. Apply the script to the Earth data $(r_1, r_2) = (6378.137, 6356.752)$. Display enough digits so that the discrepancy is revealed.

P1.1.5 A solid is a *Platonic solid* if each face is identical in size and shape. There are only five:

Solid	Faces	Face Shape
Tetrahedron	4	equilateral triangle
Cube	6	square
Octahedron	8	equilateral triangle
Dodecahedron	12	regular pentagon
Icosahedron	20	equilateral triangle

Key attributes of a given Platonic solid P include its edge length E, *inradius* r, *outradius* R, surface area S, and volume V. The inradius of P is the distance from its center to the centroid of any face. It is the radius of the largest sphere that fits inside P. The outradius of P is the distance from its center to any vertex. It is the radius of the smallest sphere that encloses P. Here is a table that specifies, for each Platonic solid, the values of r, R, S, and V as a function of E:

Solid	r	R	S	V
Tetrahedron	$\frac{\sqrt{6}}{12}E$	$\frac{\sqrt{6}}{4}E$	$\sqrt{3}E^2$	$\frac{\sqrt{2}}{12}E^3$
Cube	$\frac{1}{2}E$	$\frac{\sqrt{3}}{2}E$	$6E^2$	E^3
Octahedron	$\frac{\sqrt{6}}{6}E$	$\frac{\sqrt{2}}{2}E$	$2\sqrt{3}E^2$	$\frac{\sqrt{2}}{3}E^3$
Dodecahedron	$\frac{\sqrt{250+110\sqrt{5}}}{20}E$	$\frac{\sqrt{15}+\sqrt{3}}{4}E$	$3\sqrt{25+10\sqrt{5}}E^2$	$\frac{15+7\sqrt{5}}{4}E^3$
Icosahedron	$\frac{\sqrt{42+18\sqrt{5}}}{12}E$	$\frac{\sqrt{10+2\sqrt{5}}}{4}E$	$5\sqrt{3}E^2$	$\frac{15+5\sqrt{5}}{12}E^3$

Using the entries in this table, it is possible to solve various Platonic solid problems. For example, here is a fragment that assigns to `Vol20` the volume of the largest icosahedron that fits inside the unit sphere:

```
E = 1/(sqrt(10 + 2*sqrt(5))/4);
Vol20 = ((15 + 5*sqrt(5))/12)*E^3;
```

Define T, C, O, D, and I as follows:

> T: the largest tetrahedron that fits inside the unit sphere
> C: the largest cube that fits inside T
> O: the largest octahedron that fits inside C
> D: the largest dodecahedron that fits inside O
> I: the largest iscosahedron that fits inside D.

Write a script that prints a table showing the inradius, outradius, and edge length of these (nested) Platonic solids. The table should have a heading, and numerical values should be displayed through the fifteenth decimal place.

P1.1.6 An ellipse with semiaxes a and b is specified by

$$\left(\frac{x}{a}\right)^2 + \left(\frac{y}{b}\right)^2 = 1.$$

If $r = a = b$, then this defines a circle whose perimeter is given by $P = 2\pi r$. Unfortunately, if $a \neq b$, then there is no simple formula for the perimeter and we must resort to approximation. Numerous possibilities have been worked out:

$$P_1 = \pi(a+b) \qquad\qquad P_5 = \pi(a+b)\left(1 + \frac{3h}{10 + \sqrt{4 - 3h}}\right)$$

$$P_2 = \pi\sqrt{2(a^2 + b^2)}$$

$$P_6 = \pi(a+b)\frac{64 - 3h^2}{64 - 16h}$$

$$P_3 = \pi\sqrt{2(a^2 + b^2) - \frac{(a-b)^2}{2}} \qquad P_7 = \pi(a+b)\frac{256 - 48h - 21h^2}{256 - 112h + 3h^2}$$

$$P_4 = \pi(a+b)\left(1 + \frac{h}{8}\right)^2 \qquad\qquad P_8 = \pi(a+b)\left(\frac{3 - \sqrt{1-h}}{2}\right).$$

Here,

$$h = \left(\frac{a-b}{a+b}\right)^2$$

can be regarded as a departure from "circlehood." Write a script that solicits a and b and prints the values of $P_1, \ldots, P_8$ in a way that facilitates comparison. The value of h should also be displayed. Try input values $(a,b) = (1,1)$, $(1,.9), \ldots, (1,.1)$. What can you say about the discrepancies among the perimeter formulae as the ellipse becomes more oblong in shape?

P1.1.7 It is known that $\cos(60°) = 1/2$ and $\cos(72°) = (\sqrt{5} - 1)/4$. Using some or all of the trigonometric identities found in Appendix C, write a script that prints both $\cos(3°)$ and $\sin(3°)$.

1.2   Check and Evaluate

Problem Statement

A quadratic function of the form $f(x) = x^2 + bx + c$ attains its minimum value at the critical point $x_c = -b/2$. Computing the minimum value of f on an interval $[L, R]$ requires some checking. If x_c is in the interval, then $f(x_c)$ is the answer. Otherwise, f is minimized either at $x = L$ or at $x = R$.

Write a script that inputs real numbers L, R, b, and c and prints the minimum value of the quadratic function $f(x) = x^2 + bx + c$ on the interval $[L, R]$. The script should also display the value of x where the minimum occurs.

Program Development

To acquire a geometric sense of the problem we depict the three alternatives:

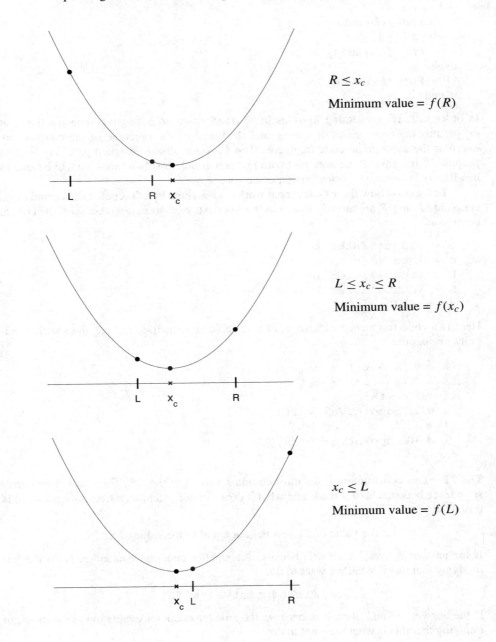

$R \leq x_c$

Minimum value $= f(R)$

$L \leq x_c \leq R$

Minimum value $= f(x_c)$

$x_c \leq L$

Minimum value $= f(L)$

Given these three possibilities, here is a *pseudocode* plan that identifies and processes the correct alternative:

$$
\begin{aligned}
&\text{if } x_c < L \\
&\qquad \text{Print } f(L) \text{ and } L \\
&\text{else if } L \le x_c \le R \\
&\qquad \text{Print } f(x_c) \text{ and } x_c \\
&\text{else} \\
&\qquad \text{Print } f(R) \text{ and } R \\
&\text{end}
\end{aligned}
\tag{1.8}
$$

In order to "say" something like this in MATLAB we need a language construction that (a) permits the comparison of values, and (b) based on the outcome of the comparison, executes the appropriate code fragment. The if-statement is designed precisely for this purpose. It has several variants, and with this new problem-solving tool we will be able to handle any "alternative" situation that comes our way.

To focus on how the if-statement works, we assume that the coefficients b and c and endpoints L and R are already stored in the MATLAB workspace together with the critical point, e.g.,

```
b = input('Enter b: ');
c = input('Enter c: ');
L = input('Enter L: ');
R = input('Enter R (L < R): ');
xc = -b/2;
```

Here is a code fragment that assigns to a variable minEndpointVal the smaller endpoint evaluation:

```
fL = L^2 + b*L + c;
fR = R^2 + b*R + c;
if fL <= fR
    minEndpointVal = fL;
else
    minEndpointVal = fR;
end
```

The if-else construction is the most common variant of the if. There is a close correspondence between how it reads and what it does. In our example, a true-false question is posed:

> Is the value of fL less than or equal to the value of fR?

If the answer is "yes," then it is because the smaller endpoint evaluation is on the left implying that this is what we want to do:

> minEndpointVal = fL

If the answer is "no," then it is because the smaller endpoint evaluation is on the right implying that this is what we want to do:

> minEndpointVal = fR

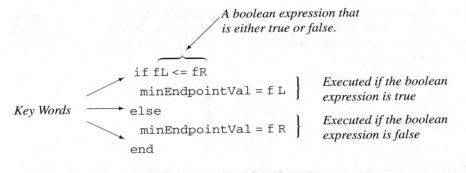

Figure 1.3. *The* `if-else` *Statement.*

This fully illustrates the general idea behind an `if-else`. The truth value of a comparison is obtained. The "true" code fragment follows immediately after the `if` and the "false" code fragment follows just after the `else`. See Figure 1.3. The comparison `fL <= fR` is a *boolean expression*. Just as arithmetic expressions produce a numerical value when evaluated, boolean expressions evaluate to either "true" or "false." The less-than-or-equal-to operator "`<=`" is a *relational operator*. Other relational operators that can be used to build up a boolean expression are "`<`" (less than), "`>`" (greater than), "`>=`" (greater than or equal to), "`==`" (equal to), and "`~=`" (not equal to).

Conditionals may involve more complicated tests. Suppose that we want to print x_c and $f(x_c)$ if the former is in the interval $[L, R]$, and to print an informative message if it is not. Note that two comparisons are required to check if x_c is the interval. We must have x_c to the right of L <u>and</u> to the left of R. Here is how to carry out such a test-and-print computation:

```
% Solution 1
if L <= xc && xc <= R
   xc = -b/2;
   fc = c - (b/2)^2;
   fprintf(' f(xc) = %6.3f xc = %6.3f\n',fc,xc)
else
   disp('Either xc < L or R <xc')
end
```
(1.9)

The essential difference between this and the previous example is that the true-false test is more complicated. Two conditions need to be satisfied if we are to conclude that x_c is in $[L, R]$:

$$x_c \text{ must be to the right of } L$$

<u>and</u> (1.10)

$$x_c \text{ must be to the left of } R.$$

The "and" operator `&&` is used to assemble the two criteria:

```
L <= xc  &&  xc <= R
```

The && operator is an example of a *boolean operator*. Just as arithmetic operations $(+, -, \times, /)$ combine numbers to produce other numbers, boolean operators combine true-false values to produce other true-false values. The && operation is completely defined by the following truth table:

a	b	a && b
F	F	F
F	T	F
T	F	F
T	T	T

Here, a and b are boolean expressions. Note that a&&b is true if and only if both a and b are true.

The || operation is another example of a boolean operator. Just like &&, it is completely defined by a truth table:

a	b	a||b
F	F	F
F	T	T
T	F	T
T	T	T

Thus, $a \mid\mid b$ is true if at least one of a or b is true.

It is instructive to rewrite (1.9) using the <u>or</u> operator and reversing the sense of the conditional:

```
% Solution 2
if xc < L || xc > R
   disp('Either xc < L or R <xc')
else
   xc = -b/2;
   fc = c - (b/2)^2;
   fprintf(' f(xc) = %6.3f xc = %6.3f\n',fc,xc)
end
```

The theory behind this version is that x_c is <u>not</u> in the interval $[L, R]$ if

$$x_c \text{ is to the left of } L$$

$$\underline{\text{or}} \hspace{6cm} (1.11)$$

$$x_c \text{ is to the right of } R.$$

Note the duality between (1.10) and (1.11).

The "not" operator $\sim$ is a third boolean operator that is occasionally useful when putting together boolean expressions:

a	$\sim a$
F	T
T	F

With the $\sim$ operator we can formulate yet another if-else solution to the problem:

```
% Solution 3
if ~(L <= xc && xc <= R)
    disp('Either xc < L or R <xc')
else
    xc = -b/2;
    fc = c - (b/2)^2;
    fprintf(' f(xc) = %6.3f xc = %6.3f\n',fc,xc)
end
```

Thus, we have three different if-else solutions to the same logical problem. As with algebraic computation, there is usually more than one way to organize a logical calculation.

A more general version of the if statement is useful whenever there are more than two alternatives from which to choose. This is the case for the problem posed at the start of this section, and the pseudocode solution (1.8) needs but a minor adjustment to become legal MATLAB code. Notice that the challenge in our problem is to discover which of three situations prevails. After the "discovery" is made, then a particular code fragment is executed. The checking is carried out sequentially and the first "hit" is processed. Here is the MATLAB refinement of (1.8):

```
if xc < L
    % Fragment 1...
    fL = L^2 + b*L + c;
    fprintf('L = %6.3f f(L) = %6.3f\n',L,fL)
elseif L <= xc && xc <= R
    % Fragment 2...
    fxc = c - (b/2)^2;
    fprintf('xc = %6.3f f(xc) = %6.3f\n',xc,fxc)
else
    % Fragment 3...
    fR = R^2 + b*R + c;
    fprintf('R = %6.3f f(R) = %6.3f\n',R,fR)
end
disp('On to the next thing!')
```

We have inserted comments and an extra print statement to help explain how it works.

- If the expression xc < L is true, then Fragment 1 is executed and control passes on to the disp instruction.

- Otherwise the boolean expression L <= xc && xc <= R is evaluated. If it is true, then Fragment 2 is executed and control passes on to the disp instruction.

- Otherwise, Fragment 3 is executed after which control again passes on to the disp instruction.

In an if-elseif-else construction, exactly one of the alternative fragments is executed.

The complete solution to the section problem is given below together with sample output. Notice how important it is to include comments to help the reader step through the logical alternatives.

The Script Eg1_2

```
% Script Eg1_2
% Minimum of the quadratic x^2 + bx + c on the interval [L,R].

% Acquire and display the input data...
b = input('Enter b:');
c = input('Enter c:');
L = input('Enter L:');
R = input('Enter R (L<R):');
clc
fprintf('Quadratic: x^2 + bx + c,  b = %5.2f, c = %5.2f\n',b,c)
fprintf('Interval : [L,R], L = %5.2f, R = %5.2f\n\n',L,R)
% The critical point...
xc = -b/2;
if xc < L
    % Minimum at the left endpoint...
    fL = L^2 + b*L + c;
    fprintf('Minimizing x     = %5.2f\n',L)
    fprintf('Minimum f value = %5.2f\n',fL)
elseif L <= xc && xc <= R
    % Minimum at the critical point...
    fxc = c - (b/2)^2;
    fprintf('Minimizing x     = %5.2f\n',xc)
    fprintf('Minimum f value = %5.2f\n',fxc)
else
    % Minimum at the right endpoint...
    fR = R^2 + b*R + c;
    fprintf('Minimizing x     = %5.2f\n',R)
    fprintf('Minimum f value = %5.2f\n',fR)
end
```

Sample Output from the Script Eg1_2

```
Quadratic: x^2 + bx + c,  b =  2.00, c =   4.00
Interval : [L,R], L =  1.00, R =   5.00

Minimizing x     =   1.00
Minimum f value =   7.00
```

In closing we mention a variant of the if statement that is useful when there is just "one thing to do" should the result of the boolean-valued test be true—no action is to take place should the boolean value be false. Here is an example:

```
if L > R
    temp = L;
    L = R;
    R = temp;
end
```

The idea is to swap the contents of variables L and R if the value in L is greater than the value in R. An else-branch is not necessary. One can imagine placing this fragment in Eg1_2 just after the input statements as a way of guarding against the situation where (inadvertently) the value of R is less than the value of L.

Talking Point: The Boolean Way

Problem solving in science and engineering requires an ability to reason logically. When the computer is involved, the challenge is greater because it suddenly becomes possible to piece together boolean expressions that have great complexity. Computing with or's and and's must become as routine as computing with additions and multiplications. Just as algebra comes equipped with an associative law and a distributive law, boolean logic comes equipped with analogous rules. For example, if a, b, and c are boolean expressions, then

$$a \,\&\&\, (b \,||\, c)$$

is equivalent to

$$(a \,\&\&\, b) \,||\, (a \,\&\&\, c).$$

Here is a truth table "proof" of this fact:

a	b	c	$b \,||\, c$	$a \,\&\&\, (b \,||\, c)$	$a \,\&\&\, b$	$a \,\&\&\, c$	$(a \,\&\&\, b) \,||\, (a \,\&\&\, c)$
F	F	F	F	F	F	F	F
F	F	T	T	F	F	F	F
F	T	F	T	F	F	F	F
F	T	T	T	F	F	F	F
T	F	F	F	F	F	F	F
T	F	T	T	T	F	T	T
T	T	F	T	T	T	F	T
T	T	T	T	T	T	T	T

There are eight ($= 2^3$) possible true-false configurations for a, b, and c, and in each case, $a \,\&\&\, (b \,||\, c)$ has the same value as $(a \,\&\&\, b) \,||\, (a \,\&\&\, c)$.

Note the similarity between the above distributive law and the arithmetic rule $a(b+c) = ab + ac$ which we all learn in grade school. As you progress through the text, you will become as "boolean savvy" as you are currently "algebraically savvy."

MATLAB Review

max and min

The value of

$$\texttt{max (}\ \boxed{\text{arithmetic expression 1}}\ \texttt{,}\ \boxed{\text{arithmetic expression 2}}\ \texttt{)}$$

is the larger of the two values obtained by evaluating the expressions. The function min is analogous.

floor, ceil, round

These functions are used to obtain nearby integer values. If the value of x is real, then `floor(x)` is the largest integer less than or equal to the value of x, `ceil(x)` is the smallest integer greater than or equal to the value of x, and `round(x)` is the closest integer to the value of x. In the case of a tie, rounding is away from zero.

rem

If x and y have positive integer values, then `rem(x,y)` is the remainder when x is divided by y. Thus, the value of `rem(22,7)` is 1. The function `rem` can also be applied to real values of arbitrary sign.

Boolean Expressions

Their value is either true or false. Boolean expressions are made up of comparisons that are either true or false, and they are connected by the logical operators and, or, not.

Relational Operators

These operators are used to compare values, resulting in either true or false:

<	Less than
<=	Less than or equal to
==	equal to
>=	greater than or equal to
>	greater than
˜=	not equal to

Logical "and" Operation

The && (and) operation has the form

> boolean expression 1 && boolean expression 2

and is "true" if and only if both boolean expressions are true. Here is the corresponding truth table:

&&	T	F
T	T	F
F	F	F

Logical "or" Operation

The || (or) operation has the form

> boolean expression 1 || boolean expression 2

and is "true" if either boolean expression is true. Here is the corresponding truth table:

||	T	F
T	T	T
F	T	F

Logical "not" Operation

The ~ (not) operation has the form

$$\sim \text{boolean expression}$$

and is "true" if the boolean expression is false, and false if the boolean expression is true.

Shortcircuiting

When MATLAB evaluates

$$\text{boolean expression 1} \;\&\&\; \text{boolean expression 2}$$

it only evaluates the second expression if the first expression is true. This is useful when there can be possible "trouble" during the second evaluation, e.g.,

```
if d>0 && abs(log(d))>1
```

Likewise, when MATLAB evaluates

$$\text{boolean expression 1} \;||\; \text{boolean expression 2}$$

it only evaluates the second expression if the first expression is false. To use the nonshortcircuit version of "and" and "or", use & instead of && and | instead of ||.

Precedence

Relational and logical operators have precedence levels just like arithmetic operators do. Negation (~) has the highest precedence, followed by relational operations (e.g., <, ==, ~=, etc.), then the "and" operation, and finally the "or" operation. Within the same level of precedence the operators are evaluated left to right, but the order of evaluation may be changed using parentheses. One must use logical operators to "chain up" individual relational expressions. For example, to determine whether x is between 3 and 7 you must connect the two individual comparisons with the "and" operator:

$$3 < x \;\&\&\; x < 7$$

Writing 3<x<7 is wrong because given left-to-right evaluation, 3<x is evaluated first giving *true* or *false*. Then this resulting *boolean* value, not x, would be compared to 7.

if-else

This construct is used in situations where the decision to choose between a pair of alternative computations is based upon a single boolean expression:

```
if  boolean expression
        fragment to execute if the boolean expression is true
else
        fragment to execute if the boolean expression is false
end
```

if-elseif

This construct is used in situations where the decision to choose from a number of possible computations is based upon a sequence of boolean expressions. For example,

```
if  boolean expression

        fragment to execute if the boolean expression is true

elseif  boolean expression

        fragment to execute if this boolean expression is the first to be true

elseif  boolean expression

        fragment to execute if this boolean expression is the first to be true

else

        fragment to execute if none of the boolean expressions are true

end
```

The last "else" is not required.

if

This construct is used in situations where the decision to carry out a particular computation is based upon a single boolean expression:

```
if  boolean expression

        fragment to execute if the boolean expression is true

end
```

Exercises

M1.2.1 Suppose the value of x is a positive integer. Write a boolean expression that is true if x is divisible by 2, 5, and 7.

M1.2.2 Suppose a, b, and c have positive integer values. Write a boolean expression that is true if it is possible to form a Pythagorean triangle whose three sides have lengths given by these integers.

M1.2.3 Suppose the value of theta is a positive radian value. Write a boolean expression that is true if the underlying angle is in the second quadrant.

M1.2.4 Assume that a, b, and c are initialized with positive integer values and that their sum is 180. Regard these values as the angles of a given triangle. Complete the following fragment so that it prints the appropriate message.

```
if (_____)
    disp('Scalene triangle')
else
    if (_____)
        disp('Equilateral triangle')
    else
        disp('Isosceles triangle')
    end
end
```

Recall that a triangle is scalene if all three angles are different, isosceles if exactly two of the angles are equal, and equilateral if all three angles are equal.

M1.2.5 Modify Eg1_2 to first check that L is less than or equal to R. Switch the values of L and R if necessary before computing the minimum of the quadratic.

M1.2.6 Refer to Eg1_2. Reorder the three branches of the conditional statement to first check whether the critical point is inside the interval.

P1.2.7 Modify Eg1_2 so that it also prints the maximum value of $f(x) = x^2 + bx + c$ on $[L, R]$.

P1.2.8 Write a script that solicits real numbers L, R, a, b, and c and prints the minimum value and maximum value of $f(x) = ax^2 + bx + c$ on the interval $[L, R]$. Assume $a \neq 0$ and $L < R$.

P1.2.9 Write a script that solicits real numbers L and R and prints the maximum value of $f(x) = \cos(x)$ on the interval $[L, R]$. Assume $L < R$. Recall that the cosine achieves a maximum value of 1 at integral multiples of 2π.

P1.2.10 Write a script that solicits real numbers L, R, and α and prints the maximum value of $f(x) = \cos(\alpha x)$ on the interval $[L, R]$. Assume $L < R$. Recall that the cosine achieves a maximum value of 1 at integral multiples of 2π.

P1.2.11 Consider the cubic function

$$q(x) = ax^3 + bx^2 + cx + d \qquad a \neq 0.$$

We say that q is *simple* if its three roots are real and distinct. We say that q is *monotone* if it is either always increasing or always decreasing. If

$$q_1(x) = (x-1)(x-2)(x-3) = x^3 - 6x^2 + 11x - 6$$
$$q_2(x) = (x-1)(x-2)(x-3) + 100 = x3 - 6x^2 + 11x + 94$$
$$q_3(x) = -x(x^2 + 1) = -x^3 - x$$

then q_1 is simple but not monotone, q_2 is neither simple nor monotone, and q_3 is monotone but not simple. In this problem you are to write a script that can be used to check for these situations. It turns out that the derivative $q'(x)$ and its roots r_1 and r_2 are important.

The script should start by prompting the user for the four coefficients a, b, c, and d. These four values should then be printed using 10.6f format. If $q'(x)$ does not have distinct real roots, then q is monotone and the message "Monotone" should be printed. Otherwise, the values of r_1, $q(r_1)$, r_2, and $q(r_2)$ should be printed. In this latter case q is not monotone and we can deduce from the output whether or not it is simple. In particular, q is simple if and only if $q(r_1)q(r_2) < 0$.

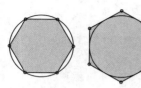

Chapter 2

Limits and Error

2.1 Tiling a Disk
Summation

2.2 Inside/Outside Polygons
Sequences

The number π is a never-ending decimal:

```
3.141592653589793238462643383279502884197169399375105 8...
  944592307816406286208998628034825342117067982148086 5...
  306647093844609550582231725359408128481117450284102 7...
  521105559644622948954930381964428810975665933446128 4...
```

In this chapter we compute more modest π-approximations using two different ideas.

Our first approach is to cover the circle $x^2 + y^2 = n^2$ with 1-by-1 "tiles." If N is the number of tiles that are completely within the circle, then from the approximation $\pi n^2 \approx N$ we conclude that $\pi \approx N/n^2$. In this case the problem of estimating π reduces to a count-the-tiles problem. We will see that the error goes to zero as $n \to \infty$.

Alternatively, we can approximate the unit circle with a polygon and regard the polygon area as an approximation to π. For a given n, a good approximating polygon is the regular n-gon whose vertices are on the unit circle. This area will underestimate π. If we use the regular n-gon whose edges are tangent to the unit circle, then its area will be an overestimation of π. The "inner" and "outer" polygon areas converge to π as $n \to \infty$ and the difference between the two estimates bounds the error.

These π-approximation examples illustrate how iteration can be used to approximate limits. Indeed, it is through iteration that we are able to bridge the gap between the discrete (finite) world of digital computing and the continuous (infinite) world of calculus. Integrals and derivatives give way to summations and divided differences. In many ways, computational science and engineering is all about "choosing n." Hardware limitations and economic constraints motivate the search for better algorithms, i.e., methods that run quicker because n does not have to be quite so large. Intuition and analysis are required to assess the difference between what is computed and the real thing.

Programming Preview

Concepts

Iteration, termination criteria, top-down development, edge effects, sequences, summation, approximation, error.

Language Features

`for`-loop: A construct to repeatedly execute statements. Repetition is controlled by setting the loop index values. It has the form

```
for <loop index values>
      <repeat these statements>
end
```

`while`-loop: A construct to repeatedly execute statements. Repetition is controlled by setting the termination criterion. It has the form

```
while <termination criterion not met>
      <repeat these statements>
end
```

`floor`: A function for rounding down to the nearest integer value.

MatTV

Video 7. The for-Loop

How to design a `for`-loop.

Video 8. The while-Loop

How to design a `while`-loop.

2.1 Tiling a Disk

Problem Statement

Suppose n is a positive integer and we draw the circle $x^2 + y^2 = n^2$ on graph paper that has 1-by-1 squares. Figure 2.1 displays the case $n = 10$. Note that the area of the disk is πn^2 and that each "uncut" tile has unit area. If there are N uncut tiles, then we conclude that

$$N \approx \pi n^2$$

since the uncut tiles almost cover the disk. Write a script that inputs an integer n and displays the π-approximation

$$\rho_n = \frac{N}{n^2}$$

together with the error $|\rho_n - \pi|$.

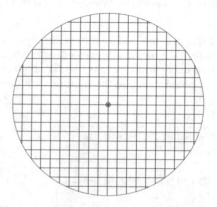

Figure 2.1. *Tiling the Circle $x^2 + y^2 = n^2$.*

Program Development

The first thing to observe is that by symmetry, each quadrant has exactly the same number of uncut tiles. Thus, we need only count the number of uncut tiles in the first quadrant as displayed by Figure 2.2. If N_1 is the number of uncut tiles in the first quadrant, then $\rho_n = 4N_1/n^2$.

To compute N_1 we sum the number of uncut tiles that are located in each horizontal row. Referring to Figure 2.2, we see that there are nine uncut tiles in row 1, nine uncut tiles in row 2, etc. For general n, we may proceed as follows:

Initially set $N_1 = 0$

Repeat for rows 1 through n (2.1)

    Compute the number of uncut tiles in the row.
    Add that number to N_1.

Set $\rho_n = 4N_1/n^2$

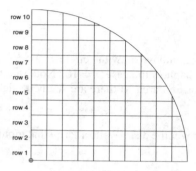

Figure 2.2. *Tiling the First Quadrant ($n = 10$).*

The pseudocode solution exposes a new and important concept: iteration. The central action of updating the running sum N_1 is iterated (repeated) n times. For a specific value of n we can implement a solution using what we know so far about the MATLAB language. For example, if $n = 10$, then we could structure the solution as follows:

Initially set $N_1 = 0$

Compute the number of uncut tiles in row 1.
Add that number to N_1.

Compute the number of uncut tiles in row 2.
Add that number to N_1.

$\vdots \quad \vdots \quad \vdots \quad \vdots \quad \vdots \quad \vdots \quad \vdots$

Compute the number of uncut tiles in row 10.
Add that number to N_1.

Set $\rho_{10} = 4N_1/10^2$

Note that in this example we need $n = 10$ repetitions of the boxed action. We can say two things about this strategy. First, it is boring, and second, it is not an effective strategy for large n. The solution fragment would be over two million lines long for n equal to one million! Fortunately, MATLAB has a construction that is tailor made for this situation and it is called the "for-loop." Using a for-loop, the pseudocode (2.1) transforms into

Assume n is initialized and set N_1 to zero
```
for k = 1:n
```

Compute the number of uncut tiles in row k.
Add that number to N_1.

(2.2)

```
end
```
Set $\rho_n = 4N_1/n^2$

The amount of repetition is specified in the `for`-statement which identifies k as the *loop variable*. If the value of n is 10, then during the course of the iteration, k takes on the values $1, 2, 3, \ldots, 10$, one at a time. The mechanics of how the whole thing works is more effectively described after we complete the refinement of all the boxed actions in (2.2).

We first develop a recipe for the number of uncut tiles in the kth row. Note that $y = k$ along the top "edge" of the kth row of tiles and that

$$x = \sqrt{n^2 - k^2}$$

at the intersection of $y = k$ and $x^2 + y^2 = n^2$. Thus, the number of uncut tiles in the kth row is the largest integer less than or equal to this value. The built-in function `floor` is handy for this. It takes any real value and returns the largest integer less than or equal to the value. Thus,

```
m = floor(sqrt(n^2 - k^2))
```

assigns to m the number of uncut tiles in the kth row.

We next consider the updating of N_1, which can be regarded as a "running sum." Using a variable N1 for this purpose, we start with the initialization

```
N1 = 0;
```

before the loop. Inside the loop and just after the assignment to m, we update as follows:

```
N1 = N1 + m
```

The fact that the target variable N1 also appears in the arithmetic expression to the right of the "=" does not involve anything new vis-à-vis the mechanics of the assignment statement. The expression N1 + m says "add the values in N1 and m." <u>After</u> that action is completed, the result is stored in the variable named to the left of the "=" as usual. The left-hand side variable just happens to be N1. This is an opportune moment to stress again that an assignment statement like N1 = N1 + m specifies an action—the right-hand side is evaluated to a value and then that value is stored in the variable named on the left—*not* an algebraic equation.

With these observations about the recipe for m and the updating of N1, we obtain the following refinement of (2.2) in which we store the final estimate of π in a variable `rho_n`:

```
N1 = 0;
for k = 1:n
    m = floor(sqrt(n^2 - k^2));
    N1 = N1 + m;
end
rho_n = 4*N1/n^2;
```

To facilitate the discussion of this `for`-loop's execution, we identify its key parts in Figure 2.3. The `for`-statement defines the entire set of values that the loop variable will take on during the "life" of the loop. We read the `for`-statement in Figure 2.3 as "for k going from 1 to 10 in steps of one." This means that the set of values for k is $1, 2, 3, \ldots, 10$. In each iteration, the loop variable takes on *one* value from the set in order and then executes the loop body. This loop variable update followed by loop body execution is repeated until

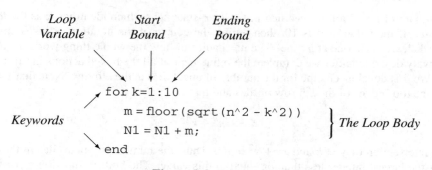

Figure 2.3. *The* `for`*-loop.*

all the loop variable values have been used. Control then passes to the statement after the `end`. Inside the loop body, the value of the loop variable can be involved in an arithmetic expression, e.g., `floor(sqrt(n^2 - k^2))`.

Assuming that $n = 10$, let us track the changes in k, m, and N1 as the loop progresses. Deducing the value of m from Figure 2.2, here are some snapshots of these three variables taken just *after* the N1 updates:

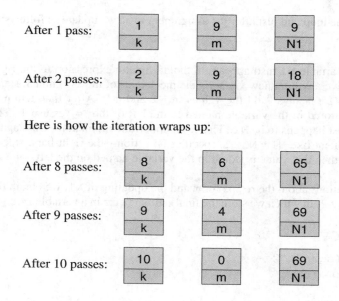

Notice how the value assigned to m decreases as the iteration progresses and that the "mission" of N1 is to maintain the current summation of uncut tiles. The solution script `Eg2_1` is given below with sample output. Notice that the ending bound in the `for`-statement is specified by the variable n. This permits maximum flexibility—the script works for any input value that is a positive integer. Finally, we mention that it is very important that `for`-loops be sufficiently commented. In `Eg2_1`, the "mission" of the *k*th pass through the loop is spelled out in a comment.

The Script `Eg2_1`

```
% Script Eg2_1
% Pi Via Tiling

% Enter the disk radius...
clc
n = input('Enter an  integral radius n: ');

% Tile just the first quadrant, then multiply by four...
N1 = 0;
for k = 1:n
    % Add in the number of uncut tiles in row k...
    m = floor(sqrt(n^2 - k^2));
    N1 = N1 + m;
end

% Display the estimate...
rho_n = 4*N1/n^2;
clc
fprintf('n      = %1d\n',n)
fprintf('rho_n  = %12.8f\n',rho_n)
fprintf('Error  = %12.8f\n',abs(pi-rho_n))
```

Sample Output from the Script `Eg2_1`

```
n      = 10000
rho_n  =    3.14119052
Error  =    0.00040213
```

Talking Point: Working on the Edge

The error associated with our method for computing π is precisely the sum of the areas of the "cut" tiles. This suggests that we might get a better approximation if we do more than simply discard the cut tiles. Here are some ideas.

- Assume that a cut tile has area one-half. If B is the number of cut tiles, then the approximation

$$\pi n^2 \approx N + B/2$$

  leads to $\pi \approx (N + B/2)/n^2$. Whether or not this renders a better approximation would depend on the assumption that the average cut tile has area one-half.

- Replace the curved edge of the cut tile with a straight line. Depending upon the intersection points of the circle with the graph paper grid, this would result in a "replacement tile" that has the shape of a triangle, quadrilateral, or pentagon. In any case, we could compute its area from well-known area formulae.

- Refine the graph paper on those grid squares that intersect the circle. For example, we could tile such a grid square with four half-size grid squares. The area of a smaller tile inside the circle would be incorporated into the overall summation.

In the tiling problem, things go bad near the boundary of the disk, so that is where we should focus our attention if we are to improve upon Eg2_1. This is a metaphor for many applications where the overall success of a computation depends upon how clever we are along the "edge" of the underlying problem.

MATLAB Review

for-Loop (Simplest Case)

This construct is used in situations where a fragment needs to be repeatedly executed and the number of repetitions is known in advance.

for   loop variable = 1:   arithmetic expression

      code fragment
end

The number of repetitions is specified by the arithmetic expression which evaluates to a positive integer. The code fragment is referred to as the *loop body*. The loop variable is also called the loop index. The value of the loop variable should *never* be modified in the loop body. Examples:

```
for k = 1:3
    fprintf('k = %1d\n',k)
end

itMax = 100;
for k = 1:itMax
    fprintf('k = %1d\n',k)
end

itN = input('Enter number of iterations: ');
for k = 1:min(itN,100)
    fprintf('k = %1d\n',k)
end
```

Exercises

M2.1.1 By playing around with Eg2_1, how would you expect the error to change if n is increased by a factor of 10? How would you expect the execution time to increase if n is increased by a factor of 10?

M2.1.2 Notice that ρ_n is always less than π. If M is the total number of tiles (cut and uncut), then $\mu_n = M/n^2$ is always bigger than π. Modify Eg2_1so that it prints ρ_n, μ_n, and $\mu_n - \rho_n$.

M2.1.3 Modify Eg2_1 so that it inputs a small number $h < 1$ and produces an estimate of π based on the number of h-by-h tiles that fit inside the unit circle $x^2 + y^2 = 1$. Assume that (0,0) is the center of the "innermost" tile. Exploit symmetry.

M2.1.4 Modify `Eg2_1` so that it displays the value of $|\pi - \rho_n|$ for $n = 10^j$, $j = 1:8$.

P2.1.5 For large n,

$$R_n = 1 - \frac{1}{3} + \cdots - \frac{(-1)^{n+1}}{2n-1} = \sum_{k=1}^{n} \frac{(-1)^{k+1}}{2k-1} \approx \frac{\pi}{4}$$

$$T_n = 1 + \frac{1}{2^2} + \cdots + \frac{1}{n^2} = \sum_{k=1}^{n} \frac{1}{k^2} \approx \frac{\pi^2}{6}$$

$$U_n = 1 + \frac{1}{2^4} + \cdots + \frac{1}{n^4} = \sum_{k=1}^{n} \frac{1}{k^4} \approx \frac{\pi^4}{90}$$

giving three different ways to estimate π:

$$\rho_n = 4R_n$$

$$\tau_n = \sqrt{6T_n}$$

$$\mu_n = \sqrt[4]{90U_n}.$$

Write a script that displays the value of $|\pi - \rho_n|$, $|\pi - \tau_n|$, and $|\pi - \mu_n|$ for $n = 100, 200, 300, \ldots, 1000$.

P2.1.6 It is possible to find real numbers a, b, c, d, and e so that

$$\sum_{k=1}^{n} k^3 = an^4 + bn^3 + cn^2 + dn + e$$

for all n. Note that if n is large enough, then

$$\sum_{k=1}^{n} k^3 \approx an^4.$$

By dividing both sides by n^4 and assuming that n is large, we see that

$$a \approx \left(\sum_{k=1}^{n} k^3 \right) / n^4.$$

Write a program that estimates a using this approximation for $n = 1, \ldots, 50$.

P2.1.7 Write a script that verifies the inequalities

$$\frac{2}{3}n\sqrt{n} \leq \sum_{k=1}^{n} \sqrt{k} \leq \frac{4n+3}{6}\sqrt{n}$$

for $n = 1, \ldots, 100$.

P2.1.8 Define

$$E_n = \left(\sum_{k=1}^{n} \frac{1}{k} \right) - \ln(n).$$

It is known that E_n converges to the *Euler constant* for large n. Write a script that prints E_{100k} for $k = 1, \ldots, 100$.

P2.1.9 Refer to a regular hexagon with unit edge length as a unit hexagon. Write a script that inputs a positive real number r and prints the number of unit hexagons that are entirely inside the circle $x^2 + y^2 = r^2$. Assume that the tiling is organized as follows:

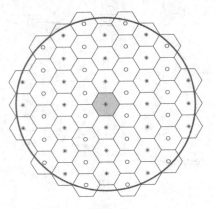

In designing your summation process, it might be handy to identify "*" tiles and "o" tiles.

2.2 Inside/Outside Polygons

Problem Statement

Suppose we have n equally spaced points around the unit circle $x^2 + y^2 = 1$. If we connect these points in order, then we obtain a *regular inscribed polygon* with n sides. If we connect the tangent lines at those points, then we obtain a *regular circumscribed polygon* with n sides. Figure 2.4 displays these constructions for the case $n = 6$. The area of the unit circle is π. The inscribed and circumscribed polygon areas are given by

$$A_n = \frac{n}{2} \sin\left(\frac{2\pi}{n}\right) \tag{2.3}$$

$$B_n = n \tan\left(\frac{\pi}{n}\right) \tag{2.4}$$

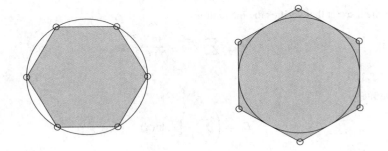

Figure 2.4. *Inscribed and Circumscribed Hexagons.*

respectively. It is clear that for all n

$$A_n < \pi < B_n.$$

Using Figure 2.4 as an intuition guide, we conclude that the average of the two polygon areas

$$\rho_n = \frac{A_n + B_n}{2} \tag{2.5}$$

is an approximation to π with absolute error that satisfies

$$|\rho_n - \pi| < B_n - A_n. \tag{2.6}$$

Clearly the error converges to zero as $n \to \infty$.

Write a script that solicits a positive real tolerance δ and displays the value of ρ_{n_*} where n_* is the smallest integer such that

$$|A_{n_*} - B_{n_*}| \le \delta.$$

This guarantees that ρ_n is within δ of π.

Program Development

It is useful to start out by writing a short script that reveals the quality of the approximation ρ_n as n increases, e.g.,

```
n = 10;
for k=1:8
    A_n = (n/2)*sin(2*pi/n);
    B_n = n*tan(pi/n);
    rho_n = (A_n + B_n)/2;
    n = 10*n;
end'
```

The trial values are $n = 10, 100, 1000, \ldots, 10,000,000$, and if we add appropriate print statements to the script, then here is what we find:

n	A_n	B_n	|rho_n - pi|
1.00e+001	2.9389262614623659	3.2491969623290631	4.75e-002
1.00e+002	3.1395259764656687	3.1426266043351152	5.16e-004
1.00e+003	3.1415719827794755	3.1416029890561563	5.17e-006
1.00e+004	3.1415924468812859	3.1415927569440529	5.17e-008
1.00e+005	3.1415926515227079	3.1415926546233357	5.17e-010
1.00e+006	3.1415926535691225	3.1415926536001288	5.17e-012
1.00e+007	3.1415926535895866	3.1415926535898966	5.15e-014
1.00e+008	3.1415926535897909	3.1415926535897944	4.44e-016

It appears that for a given n, the error is about $1/n^2$.

While this `for`-loop investigation is interesting, it does not help us directly with the problem at hand. Our job is to keep checking the quality of ρ_n until it is "good enough" as measured by the area discrepancy $B_n - A_n$. The search for n_* must proceed as follows:

If $B_3 - A_3 > \delta$, then ρ_3 is not good enough and $n_* > 3$. Otherwise $n_* = 3$.

If $B_4 - A_4 > \delta$, then ρ_4 is not good enough and $n_* > 4$. Otherwise $n_* = 4$.

If $B_5 - A_5 > \delta$, then ρ_5 is not good enough and $n_* > 5$. Otherwise $n_* = 5$.

$$\vdots \quad \vdots \quad \vdots \quad \vdots \quad \vdots \quad \vdots$$

This is clearly an iterative process, but it is an open-ended iteration because we do not know the exact number of repetitions. Here is a more precise formulation of the search-for-n_* process:

> Input the positive error tolerance δ and set $n = 3$.
>
> Compute A_3, B_3, and the error bound $B_3 - A_3$.

(2.7)

> Repeat while the error bound is larger than δ:
>
> > Increase n by one.
> >
> > Update A_n, B_n, and the error bound.
>
> Set $n_* = n$ and display ρ_{n_*}.

Notice that a `for`-loop cannot be used to oversee this kind of conditional repetition. `for`-loops are applicable in situations where the number of required iterations is known before the iteration starts. In our problem, the number of required iterations is "discovered" during the iteration process itself.

An alternative loop mechanism known as the `while`-loop is designed to handle open-ended iterations such as (2.7). Whereas in a `for`-loop the iteration terminates after a predetermined set of loop variable values have been used up, in a `while`-loop the iteration terminates as soon as a prescribed boolean-valued condition becomes false. Here is a `while`-loop implementation of (2.7):

```
delta = input('Enter delta:  ')
n = 3; A_n = (n/2)*sin(2*pi/n); B_n = n*tan(pi/n);
ErrorBound = B_n - A_n;
while ErrorBound > delta
    n = n+1;
    A_n = (n/2)*sin(2*pi/n);
    B_n = n*tan(pi/n);
    ErrorBound = B_n - A_n;
end
nStar = n; rho_nStar = (A_n + B_n)/2;
```

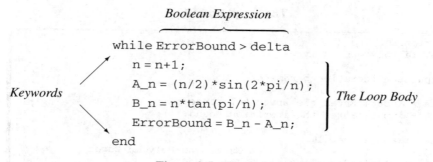

Figure 2.5. *The* while-*loop.*

To understand how this works, we identify key features of the while-loop construction in Figure 2.5.

As with a for-loop, a while-loop has a loop body. If the boolean expression is true, then the loop body is executed. This check-and-execute ritual is repeated as long as the boolean expression is true. If a check of the boolean expression reveals that it is false, then the loop terminates and control passes to the next statement after the end.

In a for-loop, the loop variable controls the iteration and it is automatically initialized to the first value in the set of possible loop variable values. In a while-loop, the boolean expression controls the iteration, and the variables that participate in the expression must be initialized *before* the loop is entered.

The final solution script Eg2_2 is given below together with sample output. Several features of Eg2_2 are worthy of discussion. A danger associated with while-loops is that they may never terminate. In our application we happen to know that for any positive δ, eventually $B_n - A_n$ will be smaller than δ which "guarantees" that the loop will terminate.[1] We are not always so lucky. For that reason it often makes sense to guard against the situation when the loop runs too long. This is easily done by adjusting the boolean condition so that it "turns false" as soon as the iteration count exceeds some predefined value. In Eg2_2 we use the variable nMax for this purpose. Note that the iteration continues as long as the error bound is too large <u>and</u> n has not yet reached nMax.

When designing a while-loop, it is very useful to "define" the variables that are affected. In our application they are

n:	The number of sides possessed by the current polygon.
A_n:	The area A_n of the current inscribed polygon.
B_n:	The area B_n of the current circumscribed polygon.
ErrorBound:	The area discrepancy $B_n - A_n$.

With these definitions in hand, the initializations and loop body implementations are much more straightforward.

---

[1] Not exactly. See problem P2.2.5.

The Script Eg2_2

```
% Script Eg2_2
% Pi Via Polygons

% Input the iteration parameters...
clc
delta = input('Enter the error tolerance: ');
nMax  = input('Enter the iteration bound: ');

% The triangle case...
n = 3;                            % Number of Polygon Edges
A_n = (n/2)*sin(2*pi/n);          % Inscribed Area
B_n = n*tan(pi/n);                % Circumscribed Area
ErrorBound = B_n - A_n;           % The error bound

% Iterate while error too big and n sufficiently small...
while (ErrorBound > delta  && n < nMax)
    n = n+1;
    A_n = (n/2)*sin(2*pi/n);
    B_n = n*tan(pi/n);
    ErrorBound = B_n - A_n;
end

% Display the final approximation...
nStar = n;
rho_nStar = (A_n + B_n)/2;
clc
fprintf(' delta = %10.3e\n nStar = %1d\n nMax  = %1d\n\n',...
                                   delta,nStar,nMax)
fprintf(' rho_nStar = %20.15f\n Pi          = %20.15f\n',...
                                   rho_nStar,pi)
```

Sample Output from the Script Eg2_2

```
delta = 1.000e-006
nStar = 5569
nMax  = 10000

rho_nStar =      3.141592486963389
Pi        =      3.141592653589793
```

Talking Point: Reasoning about Repetition

For novice programmers, the design of for-loops and while-loops is one of the most challenging aspects of computer problem solving. We offer a number of tips.

- Learn how to "spot" a computation that calls for iteration. Sometimes this is obvious, e.g, print $\rho_3, \ldots, \rho_{100}$. On other occasions, the underlying repetition needs to be exposed as in the problem we considered in this section.

- Decide whether the iteration is best handled by a `for`-loop or a `while`-loop. If the number of required repetitions is known in advance, then a `for`-loop is appropriate.

- Define precisely through program comments all the variables that are to participate in the iteration. Make sure these variables are properly initialized before the iteration begins and then proceed to develop the loop body. As you do this, keep the variable definitions foremost in your mind.

- For a `for`-loop, make sure that the loop variable range is correct. Often, a small example can affirm correctness. In a `while`-loop, write a comment that states the conditions for the iteration to continue and then design accordingly the boolean expression that is to control the loop.

- Test your loop-based code on small examples with enough intermediate output to affirm correctness.

Iteration is an excellent venue for refining your programming skills. Our goal is to develop an approach to computer problem solving that is methodical and respects the traditions of "good science" and "good engineering." Now is the time to dismiss ad hoc, trial-and-error program development.

MATLAB Review

while-Loop

This construct is used in situations where a fragment needs to be repeatedly executed and the number of repetitions is *not* known in advance:

```
while  boolean expression

        code fragment
end
```

The boolean expression is the *continuation criterion* and the code fragment is the *loop body*. At the start, the continuation criterion is evaluated and, if it is true, then the loop body is executed. If it is false, then the flow of control passes to the next statement after the `end`. After each loop body execution, the boolean expression is evaluated and, if it is true, then the loop body is executed once again. Examples:

```
k = 1; n = 10;
while k<=n
    fprintf('k = %1d\n',k)
    k = k+1;
end


k = 1;
while 4^k < 1000000
    k = k+1;
end
fprintf('k = %1d\n',k)
```

Panic Button

Now that we have loops there is the spectre of a program that runs too long. It is possible to terminate the execution of a script by pushing Ctrl-c, i.e., hold the "Ctrl" key down while pressing the "c" key. Make sure the cursor is in the command window before you do this.

break

This command can be used to terminate a loop, but we strongly discourage its use. Typically, it is used to make a for-loop act like a while-loop. For example, the fragment

```
s = 0;
for k=1:1000
    s = s + k;
    if s>100
        break
    end
end
fprintf('s = %1d',s)
```

is equivalent to

```
s = 0;
k = 1;
while s <=100
    s = s+k;
    k = k+1;
end
fprintf('s = %1d',s)
```

Exercises

M2.2.1 Modify Eg2_2 so that it terminates as soon as $|A_{n+1} - A_n| \le \delta$ or $|B_{n+1} - B_n| \le \delta$, whichever comes first.

M2.2.2 Modify Eg2_2 so that the program prompts the user for a larger value of δ if the entered value is less than 10^{-12}.

M2.2.3 It can be shown that $|\rho_n - \pi| \le (B_n - A_n)/2$. Rerun Eg2_2 with this "half-sized" error bound and comment on how the output is affected.

M2.2.4 Add appropriate print statements to the for-loop fragment at the beginning of this section so that it produces the displayed output.

M2.2.5 Change the while-loop condition in Eg2_2 to

```
while ErrorBound > delta
```

Run the modified script inputting $\delta = 10^{-20}$. After you get bored, terminate the script by pushing the "panic button" Ctrl-c. (In §4.3 we explain why the loop fails to terminate if the value of delta is very small.)

P2.2.6 From the `for`-loop experiment at the beginning of this section we may conclude that $|\rho_n - \pi| \leq 10/n^2$. Thus, if $10/n^2 \leq \delta$, then $|\rho_n - \pi| \leq \delta$. This says that

$$n_* \leq \text{ceil}\left(\sqrt{\frac{10}{\delta}}\right) \equiv n_+.$$

Use this fact to develop a `for`-loop version of `Eg2_2`. Explain why it is less efficient to use a `for`-loop instead of a `while`-loop.

P2.2.7 Note that the implementation of `Eg2_2` requires the built-in constant `pi`. By repeatedly using the half-angle formulae

$$\cos(\theta/2) = \sqrt{\frac{1 + \cos(\theta)}{2}} \qquad \sin(\theta/2) = \sqrt{\frac{1 - \cos(\theta)}{2}}$$

we can avoid this dependency and produce a genuine method that "discovers" π. Note that the case $n = 3$ involves $\cos(\pi/3) = \sqrt{3}/2$, $\sin(\pi/3) = 1/2$, and $\sin(2\pi/3) = 1/2$. The necessary cosine and sine evaluations for A_6 and B_6 can be obtained from these values via the half-angle formulae. Using these updated trig evaluations, we can obtain the necessary cosine and sine values for A_{12} and B_{12}, etc. Using this idea, write a script that inputs a positive number $\delta > 10^{-12}$ and computes an estimate of π with error less than δ.

P2.2.8 Each of the following sequences converges to π:

$$a_n = \frac{6}{\sqrt{3}} \sum_{k=0}^{n} \frac{(-1)^k}{3^k(2k+1)}$$

$$b_n = 16 \sum_{k=0}^{n} \frac{(-1)^k}{5^{2k+1}(2k+1)} - 4 \sum_{k=0}^{n} \frac{(-1)^k}{239^{2k+1}(2k+1)}.$$

Write a single script that prints $a_0, \ldots, a_{n_a}$ where n_a is the smallest integer so $|a_{n_a} - \pi| \leq .000001$ and prints $b_0, \ldots, b_{n_b}$ where n_b is the smallest integer so $|b_{n_b} - \pi| \leq .000001$.

P2.2.9 Here are the n-*stars* of size 5 and 8:

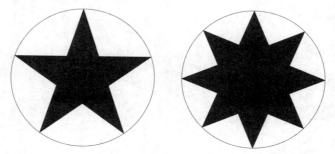

Figure 2.6. *n-Stars* ($n = 5$, $n = 8$).

The precise definition of an n-star is not important. Suffice it to say that the area of an n-star that is inscribed in the unit circle is given by

$$A(n) = \begin{cases} n \dfrac{\sin((n-1)\theta)\sin(\theta)}{\sin(\theta) + \sin((n-2)\theta)} & \text{if } n \text{ is odd,} \\[4mm] n \dfrac{\sin((n-2)\theta)\sin(\theta)}{\sin(\theta) + \sin((n-3)\theta)} & \text{if } n \text{ is even,} \end{cases}$$

where $\theta = \pi/n$. Write a program that prints a table whose kth line has the values n, $A(n)$, and $A(n+1)$ where $n = 10k$. The value of k should range from 1 to 20.

P2.2.10 Refer to the definitions in the previous problem. Write a script that inputs δ and prints the smallest integer n_* such that

$$|A(n_* - 2) - A(n_*)| \le \delta$$

and

$$|A(n_* - 1) - A(n_* + 1)| \le \delta.$$

Chapter 3

$$\frac{22}{7}, \frac{245}{78}, \frac{355}{113}, \dots$$

Approximation with Fractions

3.1 22/7ths and Counting
Proximity to Pi

3.2 Not Quite Perfect
Fibonacci Quotients and the Golden Ratio

We continue with the theme of approximation by looking at how well we can approximate π and the *golden ratio*

$$\phi = \frac{1+\sqrt{5}}{2}$$

with quotients of integers. Of course, π needs no introduction. It is the most famous and important number in all of mathematics. But right up there in the "top 3" along with $e = 2.71828182845905\dots$ is the golden ratio. All of these numbers have the property that they cannot be expressed as a ratio of two whole numbers. However, they can be closely approximated by fractions, e.g., $\pi \approx 22/7$. In mathematics, a quotient of integers is referred to as a *rational number* and in this chapter we develop a computational taste for rational approximation. Along the way we deepen our understanding of iteration and enhance our ability to write programs with loops.

Starting with π, we derive a script that computes the best rational approximation p/q subject to "size constraints." In particular, we will insist that $p \le M$ and $q \le M$, where M is a given (presumably large) integer. A "brute force" search procedure would simply check all possible quotients and identify the best. Note that if $M = 10^6$, then this would require the checking of a trillion quotients. We show with a little analysis that the number of necessary trial fractions can be dramatically reduced. This will be the first of several examples in the book that highlight the importance of efficiency.

Rational approximation of the golden ratio turns out to involve the Fibonacci number sequence. This sequence of integers is interesting from the computational point of view because it is recursively defined; i.e., the nth Fibonacci number is defined in terms of its predecessors. Recursive definitions/formulae are extremely important and our golden ratio problem serves as a nice introduction. A more detailed treatment of recursion is given in Chapter 14 where we discuss various "divide-and-conquer" solution strategies.

45

Programming Preview

Concepts

Nested loops, top-down development, efficiency, benchmarking, running time, big-O notation, approximation, recursive definitions, explicit versus implicit formula.

Language Features

`tic`, `toc`: Commands for timing the execution of a program fragment.

`abs`: A function that returns the absolute value of an expression.

`floor`, `ceil`: Functions for rounding down or up to the nearest integer value.

`factorial(n)`: A function that returns $n!$.

`nchoosek(n,k)`: Binomial coefficient $\binom{n}{k}$.

MatTV

Video 9. Troubleshooting Loops

Avoiding common mistakes with iteration.

3.1 22/7ths and Counting

Problem Statement

The quotient 22/7 is the closest rational approximation to π with both numerator and denominator less than 100. Write a script that inputs a positive integer M and then prints the best approximation to π of the form p/q, where p and q are integers that satisfy $1 \le p \le M$ and $1 \le q \le M$.

Program Development

This problem provides an opportunity for us to illustrate a program development strategy known as *top-down design*. Top-down programming is an approach to complex problem solving that compensates for the limitations of the human mind. By hiding unnecessary detail, the top-down methodology keeps our mental desktop neat and tidy as we systematically transform pseudocode into MATLAB.

The starting point is to rough out the overall strategy in words. For the problem at hand, such a beginning might be

> Generate all possible quotients p/q and select the one that minimizes $|p/q - \pi|$.   (3.1)

This modest rephrasing of the problem provides a clue as to what to do next: generate all possible quotients. One way to hit all the possibilities is to step through all the allowable denominators. Then, for each denominator q, we must step through all possible numerators p, searching for the one that minimizes the error. This leads to the following refinement of (3.1):

> Get M and perform other initializations.   (3.2)

```
% Check out all possible denominators...
for q = 1:M
```

> Find the best numerator p to go along with q, i.e., the p-value that minimizes $|\pi - p/q|$. Remember this quotient if it is the best one found so far.   (3.3)

```
end
```

> Print the best p/q and its error.   (3.4)

The boxed actions (3.2)–(3.4) are hardly finished MATLAB code. However, by ignoring the syntactical details we are able to focus on a "top-level" overall solution. The next task is to *refine* (3.2), (3.3), and (3.4), one by one.

The bit about "remembering" the best p/q so that subsequent quotients can be assessed requires variables to house the relevant information. Our plan is to store in pBest

and qBest the numerator and denominator of the most accurate quotient that has so far
been discovered. We use err_pq to store the associated error. These variables must be
initialized before the loop begins. Thinking of 1/1 as the "first" quotient, we obtain the
following by refining (3.2):

```
% Clear the command window and acquire M...
clc
M = input('Enter M: ');
% Best numerator "found so far"...
pBest = 1;
% Best denominator "found so far"...                              (3.2')
qBest = 1;
% Error in current best fraction...
err_pq = abs(pBest/qBest - pi);
```

Notice the use of comments to clearly delineate the mission of these variables.
    Next, we turn our attention to the loop body (3.3), splitting it into two parts:

> Find the best numerator p to go along with q, i.e.,
> the p-value that minimizes $|\pi - p/q|$.   (3.3a)

> Remember this quotient if it is the best one found
> so far.   (3.3b)

As we set out to refine these boxed actions, remember that we are working with just one
value of q. The mechanics of the for-loop is not a concern as we transform (3.3a) and
(3.3b) into MATLAB.
    Likewise, (3.3b) is "off the table" while we work on (3.3a). Regarding this boxed
action, it is clear that another for-loop is required to oversee the checking of all possible
numerators:

> Initialize variables p0 and e0 to keep track of the
> best numerator found so far and its error.   (3.3a(i))

```
% For this q, find the best numerator p0...
for p=1:M
```
> If the error in p/q is less than e0, then revise
> p0 and e0 and its error.   (3.3a(ii))
```
end
```

At the start, the "first" quotient $1/q$ is the best and so (3.3a(i)) refines to

```
% Initializations for the p-search...
p0 = 1;    % Best p so far
e0 = abs(pi - p0/q);
```

while the translation of the loop body (3.3a(ii)) is equally straightforward:

```
if abs(pi - p/q) < e0
   % A new best numerator has been found for this q...
   p0 = p;
   e0 = abs(pi - p/q);
end
```

This completes the implementation of (3.3a):

```
% Initializations for the p-search...
p0 = 1; e0 = abs(pi - p0/q);
% For this q, find the best numerator p0...
for p=1:M                                                               (3.3a′)
   if abs(pi - p/q) < e0
      % Found a new best numerator for this q...
      p0 = p; e0 = abs(pi - p/q);
   end
end
```

Regarding (3.3b), we have to compare the value of e0 with the value of err_pq to see if we have a new best quotient:

```
% Check if we have a new best quotient for this q...
if e0 < err_pq
   pBest = p0; qBest = q;                                               (3.3b′)
   err_pq = e0
end
```

Sequenced one after the other, (3.3a′) and (3.3b′) is the MATLAB version of (3.3).

Our last task is to implement the boxed action (3.4). We display the input value M, the best numerator and denominator, the resulting quotient, the exact value of π, and the error:

```
MyPi = pBest/qBest;
clc
fprintf('M = %1d\npBest = %1d\nqBest = %1d\n', ...                      (3.4′)
        M,pBest,qBest)
fprintf('MyPi = %17.15f\npi = %17.15f\nerror = %17.15f\n\n',...
        MyPi,pi,err_pq)
```

This completes the derivation of the solution script Eg3_1 which is displayed below with the sample output. Observe that we ended up with *nested loops*, i.e., one loop is completely enclosed in another. For the first value of q, all values of p are checked. Then q takes on its second value and all values of p are checked again. This continues until q takes on its last value, M. The end result is that the script can take a long time to execute if M is large because there are M^2 fractions to check.

We can speed things up dramatically by observing that for a given q, we need only check the p-values $p_- = \text{floor}(q\pi)$ and $p_+ = \text{ceil}(q\pi)$. This is because values of p that are

The Script Eg3_1

```
% Script Eg3_1
% Rational Approximation of pi

% Clear the command window and acquire M...
clc
M = input('Enter M: ');
% Best numerator ``found so far''...
pBest = 1;
% Best denominator ``found so far''...
qBest = 1;
% Error in current best fraction...
err_pq = abs(pBest/qBest - pi);
% Check out all possible denominators...
for q = 1:M
    % Initializations for the p-search...
    p0 = 1; e0 = abs(pi - p0/q);
    % For this q, find the best numerator p0...
    for p=1:M
        if abs(pi - p/q) < e0
            % A new best numerator has been found for this q...
            p0 = p; e0 = abs(pi - p/q);
        end
    end
    % Check to see if we have a new best quotient for this q...
    if  e0 < err_pq
        pBest = p0; qBest = q; err_pq = e0;
    end
end
MyPi = pBest/qBest;
clc
fprintf('M     = %1d\npBest = %1d\nqBest = %1d\n',...
        M,pBest,qBest)
fprintf('MyPi= %17.15f\npi =%17.15f\nerror =%17.15f\n\n',...
        MyPi,pi,err_pq)
```

Sample Output from the Script Eg3_1

```
M     = 1000
pBest = 355
qBest = 113
MyPi  = 3.141592920353983
pi    = 3.141592653589793
error = 0.000000266764189
```

less than p_- render less accurate approximations than p_-/q. Likewise, values of p greater than p_+ are less accurate than p_+/q. Thus, instead of checking M possible numerators we need only check two. This reduces the number of quotient checks by a factor of $2/M$. Another economy results if we realize that q need only range from one to ceil(M/pi) since larger values would involve checking numerators that are bigger than M. By incorporating these changes in Eg3_1 we obtain a much more efficient implementation.

The Script `FasterEg3_1`

```
% Script FasterEg3_1
% Rational Approximation of pi

% Clear the command window and acquire M...
clc
M = input('Enter M: ');
% Best numerator ''found so far''...
pBest = 1;
% Best denominator ''found so far''...
qBest = 1;
% Error in current best fraction...
err_pq = abs(pBest/qBest - pi);
% Check out all possible denominators...
for q = 1:ceil(M/pi)
    pMinus = floor(pi*q); errMinus = abs(pi - pMinus/q);
    pPlus  = ceil(pi*q);  errPlus  = abs(pi - pPlus/q);
    if errMinus < errPlus
        p0 = pMinus; e0 = errMinus;
    else
        p0 = pPlus; e0 = errPlus;
    end
    % Check to see if we have a new best quotient for this q...
    if  e0 < err_pq
        pBest = p0; qBest = q; err_pq = e0;
    end
end
MyPi = pBest/qBest;
clc
fprintf('M     = %1d\npBest = %1d\nqBest = %1d\n',M,pBest,qBest)
fprintf('MyPi = %17.15f\npi = %17.15f\nerror =%17.15f\n\n',...
        MyPi,pi,err_pq)
```

Sample Output from the Script `FasterEg3_1`

```
M     = 10000000
pBest = 5419351
qBest = 1725033
MyPi  = 3.141592653589815
pi    = 3.141592653589793
error = 0.000000000000022
```

We mention that the script Eg3_1 with input $M = 10^8$ would require *weeks* to run on a typical computer.

The MATLAB functions `tic` and `toc` can be used to time how long it takes for a code fragment to execute. They work like a stopwatch:

```
tic
```

> The fragment to be timed.

```
T = toc
```

This assigns to `T` the time required for the fragment to execute. We can use the following technique to compare `Eg3_1` and `FasterEg3_1`.

The Script Benchmark

```
% Script Benchmark
% Compares the efficiency of the scripts Eg3_1 and FasterEg3_1.
% For the results to make sense, the input statements and fprintf
% statements in both scripts should be commented out.

% Clear the command window and acquire M...
clc
M = input('Enter M: ');

% Benchmark Eg3_1...
tic
Eg3_1A
T1 = toc;

% Benchmark FasterEg3_1...
tic
FasterEg3_1A
T2 = toc;

% Report the results...
clc
timeRatio = T1/T2;
fprintf('M = %1d\n',M)
fprintf('Eg3_1 Time / FasterEg3_1 Time = %10.1f\n',timeRatio)
```

Sample Output from the Script Benchmark

```
M = 10000
Eg3_1 Time / FasterEg3_1 Time =      10712.5
```

Talking Point: Programs That Run a Long Time

Fragments that involve nested loops can take a long time to execute. In this section the difference between a double-loop and a single-loop solution was an order of magnitude.

The script `FasterEg3_1` involves $O(M)$ quotient checks while `Eg3_1` requires $O(M^2)$ comparisons. The "big-O" notation is a way of capturing the essential running time behavior of an algorithm. If M is multiplied by 100, then we expect that the $O(M^2)$ method would take 100^2 times as long to run while the $O(M)$ technique would just take 100 times longer. A nesting of the form

```
for i1=1:n1
    for i2=1:n2
        for i3=1:n3
            etc
```

involves executing "the box" $N = n_1 n_2 n_3 \cdots$ times. With even modest values for the loop bounds, it is easy to see why deep loop nestings can pose a problem for even the fastest computers.

Being able to look at a computation and anticipate how long it will take to execute is an important skill to acquire. It enables you to focus attention on those parts of a calculation that may be sped up through program adjustments and algorithm modification.

MATLAB Review

tic and toc

To find out (approximately) how long it takes your computer to execute a fragment, use `tic` and `toc` as follows:

```
tic
    Fragment to be Timed
T = toc;
```

This will assign to `T` the time (in seconds) that has elapsed during the execution of whatever code is situated between the `tic` and `toc` statements. Clock granularity is around a millisecond, so for the sake of getting a reliable benchmark, it is important for the code fragment to take a second or two to execute. This rule can always be enforced through repetition:

```
tic
for k=1:nRepeat
    Fragment to be Timed
end
T = toc/nRepeat;
```

Here, `nRepeat` is initialized to some suitably large integer value.

abs

Function `abs` returns the absolute value of an expression. Example: `abs(cos(pi))` is 1.

Exercises

M3.1.1 Modify `FasterEg3_1` so that the script displays the total number of "`p_minus` improvements" and the total number of "`p_plus` improvements." To avoid an excessive amount of output, the script should display a maximum of 10 improvements including the last one.

M3.1.2 Explain why the fraction `pBest/qBest` displayed by `Eg3_1` is reduced to lowest terms.

M3.1.3 Regarding the check for possible numerators to go along with q, would the same output be obtained if we just checked `round(pi/q)` instead of both `floor(pi/q)` and `ceil(pi/q)`?

M3.1.4 Modify `Eg3_1` so that it displays `pBest` and `qBest` every time they are updated. Display the associated error as well in a table like this

```
        p      q   | p/q  - pi |
        ----------------------------
        3      1      0.14159265
       13      4      0.10840735
       16      5      0.05840735
       19      6      0.02507401
       22      7      0.00126449
      179     57      0.00124178
      201     64      0.00096765
      223     71      0.00074758
      245     78      0.00056701
      267     85      0.00041618
      289     92      0.00028831
      311     99      0.00017851
      333    106      0.00008322
      355    113      0.00000027
```

P3.1.5 Write a script that inputs a positive integer d satisfying $1 \le d \le 15$ and prints the smallest integers p and q for which $|p/q - \pi| \le 10^{-d}$.

P3.1.6 Remember the *times table* from grade school days? Below is the times table for the numbers 2 to 5:

```
    4      6      8     10
    6      9     12     15
    8     12     16     20
   10     15     20     25
```

Write a script to input positive integers p and q where $p < q$ and print the times table for the numbers p to q.

P3.1.7 Write a script that "draws" the figure below in the *command window* using `fprintf` statements. Prompt the user to input an integer n for the number of asterisks on each side of the square. Assume $n > 3$.

```
    * * * * *
    * *     *
    *   *   *
    *     * *
    * * * * *
```

Recall that `fprintf(' ')` prints a single blank (space) while `fprintf('\n')` starts a new line.

P3.1.8 Write a script to display the following figure in the *command window* using `fprintf` statements:

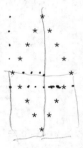

Your script should prompt the user to input an integer n for the number of asterisks on each side of the diamond. In the above example, $n = 5$. You may assume that $n > 3$.

P3.1.9 As a function of n, explore how long it takes to execute the following fragment on your computer:

```
k = 0;
for i1 = 1:n
    for i2 = 1:n
        for i3 = 1:n
            for i4 = 1:n
                k = k+1;
            end
        end
    end
end
```

Use `tic` and `toc`. How is execution time affected if the value of n is doubled? What if a fifth nested loop `for i5=1:n` is added? Compared to the above fragment, how long does it take to execute

```
k = 0;
for i1 = 1:n
    for i2 = i1:n
        for i3 = i2:n
            for i4 = i3:n
                k = k+1;
            end
        end
    end
end
```

P3.1.10 For all positive n, define

$$a_n = \sum_{j=1}^{n^2} \frac{n}{n^2 + j^2}.$$

Write a script that prints $a_2, \ldots, a_n$ where n is the smallest integer such that $|a_{n-1} - a_n| \leq .01$.

3.2 Not Quite Perfect

Problem Statement

The Fibonacci numbers $f_0, f_1, \ldots$ are defined *recursively*. We start off by setting $f_0 = 0$ and $f_1 = 1$. Now assume that n is greater than or equal to one and refer to f_n and f_{n-1} as the "current" and "old" Fibonacci numbers, respectively. The "next" Fibonacci number f_{n+1} is given by

$$f_{n+1} = f_n + f_{n-1}. \tag{3.5}$$

It can be shown that the quotients $r_n = f_{n+1}/f_n$ converge to the golden ratio

$$\phi = \left(1 + \sqrt{5}\right)/2. \tag{3.6}$$

Write a script that displays the values of n, f_n, r_n, and $|\phi - r_n|$ for $n = 1:n_*$ where n_* is the smallest value of n such that $|r_n - r_{n+1}| \leq 10^{-15}$.

Program Development

The golden ratio is one of the most interesting numbers in all of mathematics. For example, the Greeks regarded an L-by-W rectangle with $L/W = \phi$ as the most aesthetically appealing rectangle. See Figure 3.1. With a recipe of the form (3.5) it is not a simple matter of just plugging n into the right-hand side and getting f_n. We need to have the previous two Fibonacci numbers "on tap." If we start off with f_0 and f_1, then we can repeatedly apply

W = 1

L = (1 + sqrt(5))/2

Figure 3.1. *The Golden Rectangle.*

the recursive formula (3.5):

$$
\begin{array}{rclcrclcl}
f_0 &=& 0 & & & & & & \\
f_1 &=& 1 & & & & & & \\
f_2 &=& f_1 &+& f_0 &=& 1 + 0 &=& 1 \\
f_3 &=& f_2 &+& f_1 &=& 1 + 1 &=& 2 \\
f_4 &=& f_3 &+& f_2 &=& 2 + 1 &=& 3 \\
f_5 &=& f_4 &+& f_3 &=& 3 + 2 &=& 5 \\
f_6 &=& f_5 &+& f_4 &=& 5 + 3 &=& 8
\end{array}
$$

etc.

A triplet of variables can be used to carry out these updates. For any positive integer n, assume that f_old, f_cur, and f_new contain the values of f_{n-1}, f_n, and f_{n+1}, respectively. Here is how these variables are modified as we transition from $n = 1$ to $n = 2$ to $n = 3$ to $n = 4$:

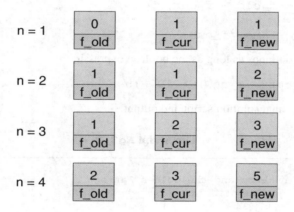

Thus, the code fragment

```
f_old = f_cur
f_cur = f_new
f_new = f_old + f_cur
```

can be used to carry out these updates. The order of the updates is crucial: we must update f_old before f_cur.

Noting that the iteration is to proceed until r_n and r_{n+1} are very close, we organize the solution script with a while-loop:

Initializations

while r_n and r_{n+1} not close enough

      Get the next Fibonacci number and the next ratio

end

Since the termination criterion involves the ratios r_n and r_{n+1}, we use variables `r_cur` and `r_new` to house these values. Thus, the required initializations are

```
tol = 10^-15;
n = 2;
f_old = 1;                    % (n-1)st   Fibonacci number
f_cur = 1;                    % nth       Fibonacci number
f_new = 2;                    % (n+1)st   Fibonacci number
r_cur = f_cur/f_old;
r_new = f_new/f_cur;
```

The loop oversees the updates

```
n = n+1;
f_old = f_cur;
f_cur = f_new;
f_new = f_old + f_cur;
r_cur = r_new;
r_new = f_new/f_cur;
```

and the iteration continues as long as the boolean expression

```
abs(r_cur - r_new) > 10^-15
```

is true. Here is the final solution script and output.

The Script Eg3_2

```
% Script Eg3_2
% Fibonacci numbers and the Golden Ratio
clc
disp('    n            f_n                  r_n  ')
disp('------------------------------------------------')
% Initializations
tol = 10^-15;
n = 2;
f_old = 1;                    % (n-1)st   Fibonacci number
f_cur = 1;                    % nth       Fibonacci number
f_new = 2;                    % (n+1)st   Fibonacci number
r_cur = f_cur/f_old;
r_new = f_new/f_cur;
fprintf('  %2d    %8d    %20.15f \n',n,f_cur,r_cur)

while (abs(r_new - r_cur)>tol)
      % Increase n and update...
      n = n+1;
      f_old = f_cur;
      f_cur = f_new;
      f_new = f_old + f_cur;
      r_cur = r_new;
      r_new = f_new/f_cur;
      fprintf('  %2d    %8d    %20.15f \n',n,f_cur,r_cur)
end
```

Sample Output from the Script Eg3_2

n	f_n	r_n
2	1	1.000000000000000
3	2	2.000000000000000
4	3	1.500000000000000
5	5	1.666666666666667
6	8	1.600000000000000
7	13	1.625000000000000
8	21	1.615384615384615
:	:	:
35	9227465	1.618033988749909
36	14930352	1.618033988749890
37	24157817	1.618033988749897
38	39088169	1.618033988749894
39	63245986	1.618033988749895

Talking Point: The Explicit versus the Implicit

Explicit formulae are attractive because they support the plug-it-in mentality. It turns out that the Fibonacci numbers can be defined explicitly, but the formula is counter intuitive:

$$f_n = \frac{1}{\sqrt{5}} \left(\left(\frac{1+\sqrt{5}}{2} \right)^n - \left(\frac{1-\sqrt{5}}{2} \right)^n \right). \tag{3.7}$$

It is not at all obvious that this complicated recipe defines integers.

On the other hand, the recursive formula for the Fibonacci sequence is aesthetically more appealing because it is so simple—f_{n+1} is just the sum of its two predecessors f_n and f_{n-1}. Of course, we had to work a bit during the derivation of Eg3_2 to make sure that enough "history" was preserved to generate f_new. It was not a matter of just plugging the value of n into an explicit formula for f_n.

Thus, there is sometimes tension between the mathematical comfort of an explicit formula and the algorithmic simplicity of an update strategy. With practice, the transition from an implicit, recursive formula to a program will become as straightforward as the routine encoding of an explicit formula.

MATLAB Review

Factorial

If n is a nonnegative integer, then the value of factorial(n) is $n! = 1 \cdot 2 \cdots n$. Convention: The value of factorial(0) is one.

Binomial Coefficients

If r and m are nonnegative integers and $r \leq m$, then the value of nchoosek(m,r) is the binomial coefficient

$$\binom{m}{r} = \frac{m!}{r!(m-r)!} = \frac{m(m-1)\cdots(m-r+1)}{1 \cdot 2 \cdots r}.$$

Convention: The value of nchoosek(m,0) is one.

Exercises

M3.2.1 Refer to `Eg3_2`. At the end of program execution, which Fibonacci numbers do the variables `f_old`, `f_cur`, and `f_new` represent?

M3.2.2 Modify `Eg3_2` to print the percent difference between `r` and `r_n` as an additional column of the output table.

P3.2.3 Write a script that prints a table showing the first 32 Fibonacci numbers computed in two ways. In the first column of the table should be the values produced by the recursive formula (3.5). The second column should be the results when (3.7) is applied. Choose output formats that reveal discrepancies between the two formulae.

P3.2.4 The factorial of a number k, $k!$, is the product $k(k-1)(k-2)\cdots 1$. For example, $4! = 4\cdot 3\cdot 2\cdot 1$. An alternative way to define the factorial is $k! = k(k-1)!$. Write a script to prompt the user for a positive integer k and calculate and print $k!$ without using built-in function `factorial`.

P3.2.5 The number of base-10 digits required to represent a positive integer `x` is given by `floor(log10(x))+1`. Write a script that prints the smallest n such that $n!$ requires at least one million digits to represent. Use the fact that $\log(ab) = \log(a) + \log(b)$.

P3.2.6 Develop a recursive formula for the binomial coefficient

$$B(m,r) = \begin{pmatrix} m \\ r \end{pmatrix}.$$

Hint: How would you compute $B(m,r)$ given $B(m,r-1)$? Write a script that inputs the value of m and r and displays $B(m,0), B(m,1), \ldots, B(m,m)$. Make effective use of the recursive formula.

P3.2.7 Define

$$
\begin{cases}
t_0 = \sqrt{1+0} \\
t_1 = \sqrt{1+1} \\
t_2 = \sqrt{1+2} \\
t_3 = \sqrt{1+2\sqrt{1+3}} \\
t_4 = \sqrt{1+2\sqrt{1+3\sqrt{1+4}}} \\
t_5 = \sqrt{1+2\sqrt{1+3\sqrt{1+4\sqrt{1+5}}}}.
\end{cases}
$$

Pick up the pattern and develop a program that prints $t_1, \ldots, t_{26}$. A loop is required for each t_k.

P3.2.8 Let m be a positive integer and consider the sequence

$$t_1 = \sqrt{m}$$

$$t_2 = \sqrt{m - \sqrt{m}}$$

$$t_3 = \sqrt{m - \sqrt{m + \sqrt{m}}}$$

$$t_4 = \sqrt{m - \sqrt{m + \sqrt{m - \sqrt{m}}}}$$

$$t_5 = \sqrt{m - \sqrt{m + \sqrt{m - \sqrt{m + \sqrt{m}}}}}.$$

Pick up the pattern and write a script that helps you determine the limit of t_n as n gets large. For your information, the limit is an integer if $m = 7, 13, 21, 31$, or 43.

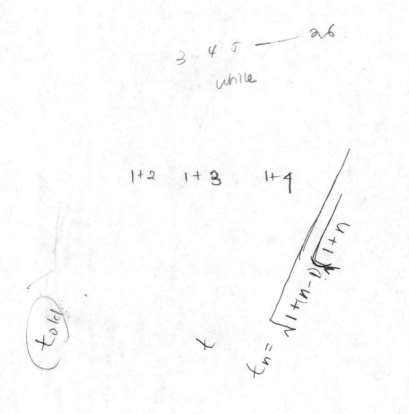

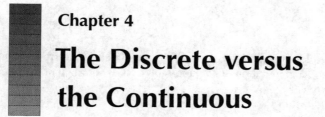

Chapter 4

The Discrete versus the Continuous

4.1 Connect the Dots
Plotting Continuous Functions

4.2 From Cyan to Magenta
Color Computations

4.3 One Third Plus One Third Is Not Two Thirds
The Floating Point Environment

There is an interesting boundary between continuous mathematics and digital computing:

- Display monitors are an array of dots. However, the dots are so tiny that the depiction of a continuous function like $\sin(x)$ actually looks continuous on the screen.

- The number of possible display colors is limited. However, the number is so large that for all practical purposes, it looks like we are free to choose from anywhere in the continuous color spectrum.

- Computer arithmetic is inexact. However, the hardware can support so many digits of numerical precision that there is the appearance of perfect computation. We begin to think that one third *is* .333333333333333.

In this chapter we build respect for these scientifically based illusions and an appreciation for what they can hide.

The stakes are high. In many applications, the volume of data that make up "the answer" is too big for the human mind to assimilate. Increasingly, we must rely upon quality graphics to help us spot patterns that would otherwise be hidden. Will the critical discontinuities of a function be exposed? Will the shading of an object from hot pink to deep purple look real or fake? Regarding arithmetic, if we think of the computer as a kind of telescope, then rounding errors affect what we can distinguish in deep "computational" space. Double stars will look like single stars if we are not careful.

Part of being a good computational scientist or engineer is to recognize professionally (not cynically) that seeing is not always believing.

Programming Preview

Concepts

Visualization, plotting functions, granularity, one-dimensional arrays, vectors, vector operations, vector notation, subvectors, color, RGB, interpolation, floating point arithmetic, error.

Language Features

`vector`: A one-dimensional list of values. May be a row or a column.

`length`: Returns the number of components in a vector.

`zeros, ones`: Return an array of 0's or an array of 1's.

`linspace, logspace`: Return an array of values that are equally spaced on a linear scale or a logarithmic scale.

Colon notation: Specifies a set of values with a fixed increment, e.g., 1:2:9 is the set "1 to 9 in steps of 2".

`for`-loop: The loop index can count up or down with a fixed increment, e.g., 9:−2:1, or take on the values in an arbitrary vector, e.g., [5, −2.5, 1].

`plot, fill`: Draw an xy plot or a colored polygon.

`eps, inf, NaN, realmax, realmin`: Several MATLAB predefined constants.

MatTV

Video 10. Creating Arrays

How to create arrays of numbers.

Video 11. Array Addressing

How to access subarrays.

Video 12. Basic Mathematical Operations on Arrays

How to write simple expressions that perform a mathematical operation on all elements of a vector. *Vectorized code* performs arithmetic (and relational and logical) operations on multiple elements of an array in one statement.

Video 13. Script

How to write and run MATLAB scripts that create simple graphics.

4.1 Connect the Dots

Problem Statement

Write a script that displays a plot of the function

$$f(x) = \frac{\sin(5x)\exp(-x/2)}{1+x^2}$$

across the interval $[-2, 3]$.

Program Development

Let us first consider a much simpler problem: the plotting of the sine function across the interval $[0, 2\pi]$. Even more, let us consider how we would approach such a problem "by hand." First, we would produce a table of values, e.g.,

x	0.000	1.571	3.142	4.712	6.283
$\sin(x)$	0.000	1.000	0.000	-1.000	0.000

We would then connect the five points

$$P_1 = (0.000, 0.000)$$
$$P_2 = (1.571, 1.000)$$
$$P_3 = (3.142, 0.000)$$
$$P_4 = (4.712, -1.000)$$
$$P_5 = (6.283, 0.000)$$

obtaining the simple plot that is illustrated in Figure 4.1. It is hard to be happy with such a coarse depiction of such a smooth function. Five evenly distributed sample points means an x-spacing of $\pi/2$ and that is just too crude. If we reduce the spacing from $\pi/2$ to $\pi/4$, then the table of values expands to

x	0.000	0.785	1.571	2.356	3.142	3.927	4.712	5.498	6.283
$\sin(x)$	0.000	0.707	1.000	0.707	0.000	-0.707	-1.000	-0.707	-0.000

$$(4.1)$$

and we obtain the plot shown in Figure 4.2. The graph still has "kinks" but there is definitely an improvement.

Obviously, we can repeat this process of refining the graphs by checking out plots that are based on more and more sample points. Eventually, the kinks disappear and our eyes

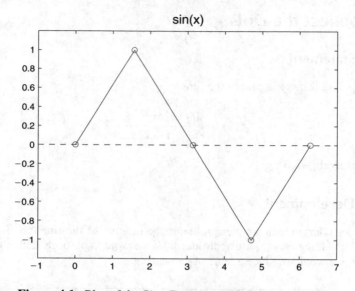

Figure 4.1. *Plot of the Sine Function with 5 Sample Points.*

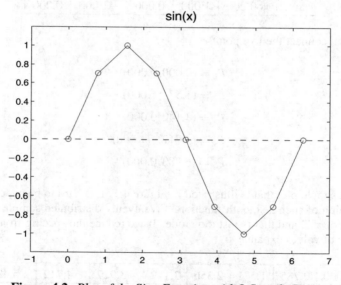

Figure 4.2. *Plot of the Sine Function with 9 Sample Points.*

are "fooled" into seeing a smooth function. Just how much sampling is required to produce an acceptable plot depends on human perception factors (How good are your eyes?), screen granularity (Are there 100 pixels per inch or 500 pixels per inch?), and the underlying application (How wild is the underlying function?). Let us write a script that sheds light on the quality of our sine plot as a function of n, the number of sample points.

The graphing of a given function $y = f(x)$ across a given interval $[L, R]$ involves three basic steps:

Step 1. The production of a table of x-values chosen from the interval.

Step 2. The production of a table of y-values that correspond to the evaluation of f at the x-values.

Step 3. A mechanism that connects the dots defined by the xy-pairs and displays the resulting polygonal line.

To illustrate, here is a "rough draft" of the script that produced the plot shown in Figure 4.2:

```
x = linspace(0,2*pi,9);
y = sin(x);
plot(x,y)
```

The built-in function `linspace` is used to generate a table of equally spaced values across the given interval. The syntax for `linspace` is as follows:

linspace(Left Endpoint , Right Endpoint , Number Sample Points)

The assignment `x = linspace(0,2*pi,9)` is the assignment of an array to `x`:

x:	0.000	0.785	1.571	2.356	3.1412	3.927	4.712	5.498	6.283

A table of values like this is a one-dimensional *array*. In MATLAB this assembly of data is also known as a *vector*. Higher-dimensional arrays will be discussed later. For now, we use the terms "array," "vector," and "table" interchangeably.

The statement `y = sin(x)` looks familiar enough, only now the `sin` function is handed a table of values instead of just a single number as is more customary. The result is that `y` is assigned the array of sine evaluations that correspond to `x`:

y:	0.000	0.707	1.000	0.707	0.000	−0.707	−1.000	−0.707	−0.000

Notice that `x` and `y` house the top and bottom half, respectively, of the table of values (4.1).

The last line in the above script involves the `plot` function. If `x` and `y` are vectors with the same length, then they define a set of points in the plane and the command `plot(x,y)` simply "connects the dots."

With these preliminaries we can address the question of how many function evaluations are necessary to produce a smooth sine plot. A script of the form

```
for n=25:25:500
    % Show sin(x) with n points
    x = linspace(0,2*pi,n);
    y = sin(x);
    plot(x,y)
    title(sprintf('n = %3d',n))
    pause
end
```

reveals that $n = 100$ is "good enough" given typical screen granularity and average eyesight. See Figure 4.3.

The `title` command is used to display the string `sprintf('n = %3d',n)` across the top of the plot window. The function `sprintf` is just like `fprintf`, except that it returns the specified string message instead of writing it to the command window.

The `pause` command halts the program until the user strikes a key. With this feature, we can study the sequence of plots at our own pace.

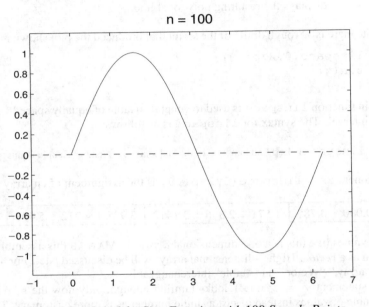

Figure 4.3. *Plot of the Sine Function with* 100 *Sample Points.*

Let us return to the problem posed at the beginning of the section. Two features of MATLAB make the task of function plotting easy. First, built-in functions like `sin`, `cos`, `exp`, and `log` can accept an input argument that is a vector. When this is the case, they return the corresponding array of function evaluations, e.g.,

| 1.234 | 5.678 | 9.123 | $\longrightarrow$ | Built-In Function f | $\longrightarrow$ | $f(1.234)$ | $f(5.678)$ | $f(9.123)$ |

A second feature of MATLAB that is very handy in plot situations is its support of vector-level operations. To illustrate, suppose variables a and b are initialized as follows:

a: | 10 | 8 | −5 |

b: | 2 | 4 | 1 |

These vectors can be

scaled(*)	c = 5*a	⇒ c:	50	40	−25
scaled(/)	c = a/2	⇒ c:	5	4	−2.5
negated	c = -a	⇒ c:	−10	−8	5
reciprocated	c = 1./a	⇒ c:	.100	.125	−.200
shifted	c = 5+a	⇒ c:	15	13	0
exponentiated	c = a.^2	⇒ c:	100	64	25
added	c = a+b	⇒ c:	12	12	−4
subtracted	c = a-b	⇒ c:	8	4	−6
multiplied	c = a.*b	⇒ c:	20	32	−5
divided	c = a./b	⇒ c:	5	2	−5

With this repertoire, we can easily build a table of values for more complicated functions. For example, the script

```
x = linspace(-2,3,100);
y1 = 5*x;              % vector scaling
y2 = sin(y1);          % vector of sine evaluations
y3 = -x;               % vector negation
y4 = y3/2;             % vector scaling
y5 = exp(y4);          % vector of exp evaluations
y6 = y2.*y5;           % vector multiplication
y7 = x.^2;             % vector exponentiation
y8 = 1 + y7;           % vector shifting
y  = y6./y8;           % vector division
plot(x,y)
```

results in the plotting of the function

$$f(x) = \frac{\sin(5x)\exp(-x/2)}{1+x^2}$$

across the interval $[-2,3]$. The code for y can be collapsed down to a single assignment statement:

```
y = (sin(5*x).*exp(-x/2))./(1 + x.^2);
```

Notice how this looks just like a typical scalar assignment except for the "dot operations" that designate vector multiplication, vector division, and vector exponentiation. Here is the full solution script and the plot that it produces.

The Script Eg4_1

```
% Script Eg4_1
% Plots the function f(x) = sin(5x)*exp(x/2)/(1 + x^2)
% across [-2,3].

L = -2;    % Left endpoint
R =  3;    % Right endpoint
N = 200;   % Number of sample points

% Obtain the vector of x-values and f-values...
x = linspace(L,R,N);
y = sin(5*x) .* exp(-x/2) ./ (1 + x.^2);

% Plot and label...
plot(x,y,[L R],[0 0],':')
title('The function f(x) = sin(5x) * exp(x/2) / (1 + x^2)')
ylabel('y = f(x)')
xlabel('x')
```

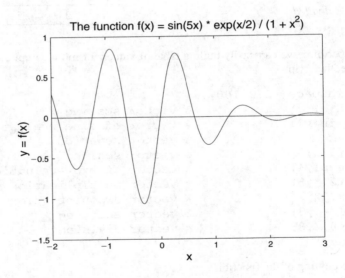

Figure 4.4. *Sample Output from the Script* Eg4_1.

The support of vector-level operations is a rich feature of the MATLAB language that enables us to write more readable and efficient code. To appreciate this point we need to look more carefully at the vector structure and how particular components can be accessed through the use of *subscripts*.

Consider the assignment x = linspace(15,30,4) which establishes x as a length-4 row vector:

x:

15	20	25	30

Here is a better way to visualize x:

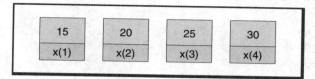

This schematic reinforces the idea that x is an array variable having four components that are (traditional) simple variables. The names of the component variables are x(1), x(2), x(3), and x(4). The numbers within the parentheses are *subscripts*. Subscripted variables can be involved in assignment statements. For example, the fragment

```
x(1) = x(1) + 2;
x(2) = x(3) + x(4);
x(4) = x(4)/2;
```

transforms the vector x above into

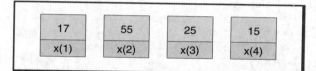

The value of a subscript can be specified by a variable or an arithmetic expression. Thus,

```
x(1) = x(1) + 2;
```

is equivalent to

```
k = 1;
x(k) = x(k) + 2;
```

while

```
x(2) = x(3) + x(4);
```

is equivalent to

```
i = 1;
x(i) = x(i+2) + x(i+3);
```

When a subscript is specified by an arithmetic expression, the expression must evaluate to a "legal" subscript. Thus

```
i = 3;
x(i) = x(i+1) + x(i+2);
```

will result in an error because i+2 evaluates to 5 and there is no x(5).

To further our ability to reason about subscripts, let us use a `for`-loop to set up the vector x = `linspace(15,30,4)`. Of course, for such a short vector we can do this "by hand":

```
x(1) = 15;
x(2) = 20;
x(3) = 25;
x(4) = 35;
```

But the recipes for the component values are simple functions of the subscript: the value of `x(k)` is `10+5*k` for k = 1, 2, 3, and 4. Thus,

```
for k=1:4
    x(k) = 10 + 5*k;
end
```
                                                                                     (4.1)

does the job. Knowing that the loop counter k steps from 1 to 2 to 3 to 4, this is equivalent to

```
k = 1;
x(k) = 10 + 5*k;
k = 2;
x(k) = 10 + 5*k;
k = 3;
x(k) = 10 + 5*k;
k = 4;
x(k) = 10 + 5*k;
```

When using a loop to set up a vector, it is a good habit to establish the size and orientation of the vector using the `zeros` function before beginning the iteration. The command

```
x = zeros(1,4);
```

establishes x as a length-4 row vector with components initialized to zero:

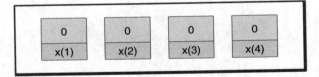

Let us trace the execution of (4.1) now that x has this form. The first time through the loop, k has the value of 1. The dynamics of the assignment `x(k) = 10 + 5*k` is very similar to what we learned for simple variable assignments. The right-hand side is a recipe for a value, in this case 15. The left-hand side names the target variable, but now the name of the target variable is computed: `x(1)`. After the first pass the x array looks like this

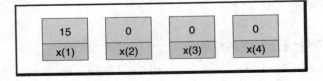

The processing is similar during the second pass when k is 2:

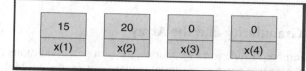

And during the third pass when k is 3:

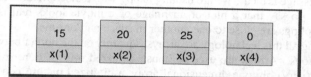

And during the fourth pass when k is 4:

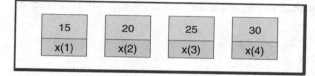

As a more general illustration of vector setup using a for-loop, here is a fragment that is equivalent to x = linspace(a,b,n) assuming that the variables a, b, and n (positive integer greater than one) are initialized:

```
% The spacing factor...
h = (b-a)/(n-1);
% A length-n row vector...
x = zeros(1,n);
for k=1:n
   x(k) = a + (k-1)*h;
end
```
(4.2)

The recipe for the spacing factor h is derived from the fact that linspace generates *n* equally spaced sample points across the interval [*a*,*b*] *including* both endpoints *a* and *b*. Thus, the value of x(1) is a and the value of x(n) is b.

The above loop implementation requires the derivation of an explicit recipe for the value of x(k). Here is an equivalent solution that avoids this:

```
% The spacing factor...
h = (b-a)/(n-1);
% A length-n row vector...
x = zeros(1,n);
x(1) = a;
for k=2:n
   x(k) = x(k-1) + h;
end
```
(4.3)

The idea behind this approach is that the kth sample point is h plus the $(k-1)$st sample point.

Talking Point: Granularity and the Array

With a sufficient number of function evaluations, the plot of a continuous function appears smooth. With enough pixel support, a digital camera can produce a high-resolution wall poster. With a sufficient number of frames per second a video can create the illusion of motion. The message is clear: we are usually happy with a discretization if it is sufficiently "fine grained." To say that a plot or an image or a movie looks real is to say that the underlying samplings are close to one another in space and/or time.

Underlying all this technology are arrays, squarely on the border between the discrete and the continuous. Arrays are used to house digitized information. As we will see, a music CD is a (very) big one-dimensional array, a digitized picture is a (very, very) big two-dimensional array, and a DVD, being a sequence of still images, is a (very, very, very) big three-dimensional array. Problem solving in these venues requires having a facility with subscripts and an ability to reason at the vector level. It will take practice. Lots of practice!

MATLAB Review

Vector Orientation and Subscripts

A vector is a one-dimensional array. Vectors have a length and can be row oriented or column oriented. If x is a vector, then y = x' has the opposite orientation and we say that x has been *transposed*. Subscripts start at one and must be integers. An error results if the value of a subscript is less than one or is not an integer. A *scalar* variable is a length-1 vector.

Creating Short Vectors

To specify explicitly a short row vector, enclose the component values with square brackets and separate the component values with spaces or with commas, e.g., v = [19 2 -3] or v = [19, 2, -3]. The same rules apply for column vectors, except that the component values are separated by semicolons, e.g., v = [19; 2; -3].

Concatenating Vectors

It is possible to make longer vectors by "gluing together" shorter vectors. If x is a length-n row vector and y is a length-m row vector, then z = [x y] is a length $n+m$ row vector obtained by augmenting x with values from y. Thus,

```
x = [10 20];   y = [30 40 50];   z = [x y];
```

is equivalent to z = [10 20 30 40 50]. Column vectors may also be concatenated, but the column vectors that make up the concatenation must be separated by semicolons, e.g.,

```
x = [10; 20];   y = [30; 40; 50];   z = [x; y];
```

length

If x is a vector, then n = length(x) assigns its length to n.

Addressing an Array Component

If x is a vector, then x(k) is the kth component of x. To *access* an existing component, k is an integer satisfying $1 \leq k \leq$ length(x), e.g.,

```
x = [10 25 20];   y = x(2);
```

To *create* a vector component, k can be any positive integer, e.g.,

```
x = [10 25 20];   y(4) = x(2);
```

creates a vector y with the values [0 0 0 25].

linspace

Use linspace to construct row vectors with equally spaced values. For example, the assignment x = linspace(0,3,7) is equivalent to

```
x = [0.0   0.5   1.0   1.5   2.0   2.5   3.0]
```

In general, if a and b are real-valued scalars and n is an integer with $n \geq 2$, then the assignment x = linspace(a,b,n) is equivalent to

```
h = (b-a)/(n-1);
for k=1:n
    x(k) = a + (k-1)*h;
end
```

Note that the spacing between components is $(b - a)/(n - 1)$ and not $(b - a)/n$.

logspace

Use logspace to construct vectors with values that are equally spaced logarithmically. For example, x = logspace(-1,-6,6) is equivalent to

```
x = [10^-1   10^-2   10^-3   10^-4   10^-5   10^-6]
```

More generally, x = logspace(a,b,n) is equivalent to

```
e = linspace(a,b,n);
for k=1:n
    x(k) = 10^e(k);
end
```

Colon Notation

The colon notation can be used to generate a row vector of equally spaced values with a prescribed spacing. For example, x = 1:.3:2 is equivalent to x = [1.0 1.3 1.6 1.9], i.e., read x = 1:.3:2 as "x goes from 1 up to 2 in steps of 0.3." Note that the last component has the value 1.9, not 2. In general, if $a < b$ and $s > 0$ or if $b < a$ and $s < 0$, then x = a:s:b is equivalent to

```
n = floor((b-a)/s) + 1;   % Number of components
for k = 1:n
    x(k) = a + (k-1)*s;
end
```

The value of s is referred to as the *stride*. Use linspace(a,b,n) if it is handier to reason about the number of sample points rather than their spacing or if it is critical to "land" on the "target" b. If the stride in the colon expression is "missing," then it is assumed to be one. Thus, 2:5 is the same as 2:1:5 and the vector of integers [2 3 4 5].

zeros and ones

If n is an initialized positive integer, then x = zeros(1,n) assigns to x a length-n row vector of zeros. Similarly, x = zeros(n,1) assigns to x a length-n column vector of zeros. The ones function behaves the same way except that the components are assigned the value one instead of zero.

Vector Operations

If x is a vector and s is a scalar, then x*s multiplies each component by s, x+s adds s to each component, x/s divides each component by s, s./x reciprocates each component and then multiplies by s, and x.^s raises each component to the power of s. If y has the same length and orientation as x, then x+y, x-y, x.*y, x./y, x.^y produce vectors by combining components in the indicated fashion.

for-Loops (Again)

for-loops have the form

> for   loop variable =   vector of loop values
>
>   code fragment
> end

where the loop variable successively takes on the values in the vector of loop values. The number of loop body repetitions is therefore the length of this vector. In the simplest case, the vector of loop values has the form 1:n. Other possibilities include 0:.1:10, [1 -2 3 -4], n:-1:1,..., etc.

pause

pause stops the program and waits for the user to press any key before continuing. pause(t) stops the program for t seconds before continuing; t can be a fraction.

plot

Use plot to display the data points (x_k, y_k) defined by a pair of vectors that have equal length and orientation. The command plot(x,y) "connects the dots," thereby displaying the graph of y versus x in a figure window. It is possible to display more than one graph with a single plot command, e.g., plot(x,y1,x,y2,x,y3,...) plots y1 versus x, y2 versus x, y3 versus x, etc.

Line and Marker Formats

It is possible to specify how the dots are connected in a plot command, e.g.,

```
plot(x,y1,'-',x,y2,':',x,y3,'-.',x,y4,'--')
```

Use '–' for solid lines, use ':' for dotted lines, use '–.' for dash-dot lines, and use '– –' for dashed lines. Instead of connecting the dots, it is possible just to put a specified marker at the dots, e.g.,

```
plot(x,y1,'.',x,y2,'o',x,y3,'+',x,y4,'x',x,y5,'*')
```

Use '.' for point marks, use 'o' for circle marks, use '+' for plus marks, use 'x' for x-marks, and '*' for star marks.

Line and Marker Colors

Lines and markers can be colored using these mnemonics:

w	white	c	cyan	b	blue	m	magenta
r	red	y	yellow	g	green	k	black

For example,

```
plot(x,y1,'r',x,y2,'*b',x,y3)
```

colors the first plot red (line) and the second plot blue (star marks). The color of the third plot (line) is automatically selected since no color is specified.

title, xlabel, ylabel

It is possible to place a title over a plot and to label the axes:

title(string)

xlabel(string)

ylabel(string)

sprintf

The sprintf function, like fprintf, is used to produce formatted strings that incorporate values of specified variables. It has the form

sprintf(string with format controls , list of variables)

Example:

```
title(sprintf('Temperature = %4d degrees',T))
```

sprintf returns a string that can be stored in a variable or used as the argument to a function, as shown in the example above with function title.

semilogx, semilogy, loglog

A plot with logarithmic scaling along the x-axis, y-axis, or both can be achieved by using semilogx(a,b), semilogy(a,b), or loglog(a,b), where a and b are vectors of the same length.

More Refined Graphics

Appendix A covers line width, font size, special characters, legends, axis labelling, coloring, and other features that can be used to produce professional-looking graphics.

Exercises

M4.1.1 Experiment with Eg4_1 by changing the number of sample points in the interval $[-2,3]$. If you double N, is the graph visibly smoother? If you halve N, is the shape of the function still clear? For this function in the given range, roughly how small can N be and still give a reasonable graph?

M4.1.2 Modify Eg4_1 so that it places a green x marker at the point (z,o) if z is a zero, a blue circle marker at $(z, f(z))$ if z is a local minimum, and a red circle marker at $(z, f(z))$ if z is a local maximum.

M4.1.3 Modify Eg4_1 to solicit user input values of L and R. The plot should be a red dashed line across $[L,c]$, a black solid line across $[c,d]$, and a red dashed line across $[d, R]$, where $c = (2L+R)/3$ and $d = (L+2R)/3$.

P4.1.4 Modify Eg4_1 to use the colon expression instead of the built-in function linspace to create the vector of x-values. linspace allows you to specify the number of points, while the colon expression allows you to specify the increment between points. Write a colon expression that matches the linspace function call in Eg4_1 exactly.

P4.1.5 Write a script that inputs three values a, b, c and then prints the length of a:c:b and the distance from the last vector component to b.

P4.1.6 How long is the vector x after the following script is executed?

```
x = 1:10:100;
while length(x) < 1000
    x = [x x(1) x];
end
```

P4.1.7 Write a script that uses semilogy to display the function $f(x) = 3^x + (2+\sin(x))2^x$ across $[0,10]$.

P4.1.8 Recall that the cosine function has period 2π. In the following fragment, complete the plot statement so that the cosine function is displayed across the interval $[-2\pi, 6\pi]$:

```
x = linspace(0,2*pi);
y = cos(x);
plot( ??? )
```

Your solution should not involve any additional cosine evaluations.

P4.1.9 Write a script that displays in a single figure window a plot of the functions x, x^2, x^3, x^4, and x^5 across the interval $[0,1]$.

P4.1.10 Plot the function

$$f(x) = 1 + \cfrac{x}{1 - \cfrac{x/2}{1 + \cfrac{x/6}{1 - \cfrac{x/6}{1 + \cfrac{x/10}{1 - x/10}}}}}$$

across the interval $[-2,5]$.

P4.1.11 Write a script that inputs a positive integer n and then generates a length-10 row vector f according to the following formula:

$$f_k = \begin{cases} n & \text{if } k = 1 \\ 3f_{k-1} + 1 & \text{if } 10 \geq k > 1 \text{ and } f_{k-1} \text{ is odd} \\ f_{k-1}/2 & \text{if } 10 \geq k > 1 \text{ and } f_{k-1} \text{ is even.} \end{cases}$$

Your script should plot the points $(1, f_1), \ldots, (10, f_{10})$ using the star marker.

4.2 From Cyan to Magenta

Problem Statement

The idea of interpolating values in a table is familiar. Consider this excerpt from a sine table:

$x°$	$\sin(x°)$
⋮	⋮
44	0.6947
45	0.7071
46	0.7193
47	0.7314
⋮	⋮

To estimate $\sin(45.2)$, $\sin(45.4)$, $\sin(45.6)$, and $\sin(45.8)$, we take appropriate linear combinations of $\sin(45)$ and $\sin(46)$:

$$\sin(45.2) = \sin(45) + \frac{1}{5}(\sin(46) - \sin(45)) = \frac{4}{5}\sin(45) + \frac{1}{5}\sin(46) = 0.7096$$

$$\sin(45.4) = \sin(45) + \frac{2}{5}(\sin(46) - \sin(45)) = \frac{3}{5}\sin(45) + \frac{2}{5}\sin(46) = 0.7120$$

$$\sin(45.6) = \sin(45) + \frac{3}{5}(\sin(46) - \sin(45)) = \frac{2}{5}\sin(45) + \frac{3}{5}\sin(46) = 0.7144$$

$$\sin(45.8) = \sin(45) + \frac{4}{5}(\sin(46) - \sin(45)) = \frac{1}{5}\sin(45) + \frac{4}{5}\sin(46) = 0.7169.$$

The idea is that if we "walk" from $x = 45$ to $x = 46$ and have completed fraction f of the journey, then we should see the same fractional change in the sine value, e.g.,

$$\frac{2}{5} = \frac{45.4 - 45.0}{46.0 - 45.0} = \frac{\sin(45.4) - \sin(45)}{\sin(46) - \sin(45)}.$$

This is *linear interpolation*.

Linear interpolation can be used to interpolate between "known" colors just as it can be used to interpolate between known numerical values. Colors in the MATLAB graphics environment are represented by length-3 vectors whose first, second, and third components specify the amounts of red, green, and blue that makes up the color, e.g.,

cyan = = [0.0 1.0 1.0]

magenta = = [1.0 0.0 1.0]

We refer to vectors that represent colors as *rgb* vectors. Each component value is between 0 and 1. Thus, cyan is an equal mix of green and blue while magenta is an equal mix of red and blue. We can generate an interpolation of these two colors by applying linear interpolation to each component. Thus, we can compute the rgb vector for a color that is 3/5 cyan and 2/5 magenta as follows:

$$\frac{3}{5}[\ 0.0 \quad 1.0 \quad 1.0\ ] + \frac{2}{5}[\ 1.0 \quad 0.0 \quad 1.0\ ] = [\ 0.4 \quad 0.6 \quad 1.0\ ].$$

Here is what it looks like:

= [0.4 0.6 1.0]

Write a script that displays eleven "paint chips" that range from cyan to magenta:

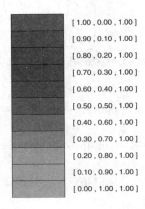

[1.00 , 0.00 , 1.00]

[0.90 , 0.10 , 1.00]

[0.80 , 0.20 , 1.00]

[0.70 , 0.30 , 1.00]

[0.60 , 0.40 , 1.00]

[0.50 , 0.50 , 1.00]

[0.40 , 0.60 , 1.00]

[0.30 , 0.70 , 1.00]

[0.20 , 0.80 , 1.00]

[0.10 , 0.90 , 1.00]

[0.00 , 1.00 , 1.00]

Figure 4.5. *Cyan to Magenta.*

The nine "in between" colors should be equally spaced. Use linear interpolation.

Program Development

The `fill` command can be used to display a "tile" of a particular color. For example,

```
x = [0 3 3 0];    y = [0 0 1 1];    v = [0.0 1.0 1.0];
fill(x,y,v)
```

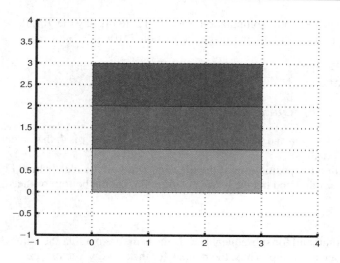

Figure 4.6. *Three Colored Rectangles.*

produces a rectangle with vertices (0,0), (3,0), (3,1), and (0,1) and fills it with the color specified by the rgb vector v (cyan).

The following fragment displays in a single window a cyan rectangle, a magenta rectangle, and a rectangle that has the interpolated color that we derived above:

```
x = [0 3 3 0];
y = [0 0 1 1];
hold on
fill(x,y,[0.0 1.0 1.0])
fill(x,y+1[0.4 0.6 1.0])
fill(x,y+2,[1.0 0.0 1.0])
```

See Figure 4.6. The `hold` command ensures that all subsequent plots are added to the current figure window.

The problem we are to solve requires a similar display, only there are to be eleven rectangles. Using a loop to oversee this, we obtain the following pseudocode solution:

```
n = 10;
```

Other Initializations

```
for j=0:n
    % Display rectangle j
```

    Compute the rgb vector v for the jth tile's color.   (4.4)

    Compute the x and y vectors that locate the position of the jth tile.

```
    fill(x,y,v)
end
```

Let us start with the color computation. Our plan is to display the jth tile with a color that has cyan fraction $(1 - j/10)$ and magenta fraction $j/10$:

```
cyan = [0 1 1];
magenta = [1 0 1];                                               (4.5)
f = j/n;
v = (1-f)*cyan + f*magenta;
```

Note that tile 0 is cyan and tile 10 is magenta. If the value of j is 4, then v defines the mixed color displayed above.

Regarding the positioning of the tiles, we build on the idea behind Figure 4.6 where each tile has width 3 and height 1. We position tile 0 at the bottom of the stack, e.g.,

```
fill([0 3 3 0],[0 0 1 1],v).
```

The fill command for subsequent tiles is the same except that the values in the y vector increase by one each step. Thus, the recipes for the x and y vectors are

```
x = [0 3 3 0];                                                  (4.6)
y = [0 0 1 1] + j;
```

Substituting (4.5) and (4.6) into (4.4) and doing a little rearranging, we obtain

```
cyan = [0 1 1];       % rgb of the "bottom" color
magenta = [1 0 1];    % rgb of the "top" color
n = 10;               % the number of "in between" colors is n-1
x = [0 3 3 0];        % locates the x-values in the tiles
y = [0 0 1 1];        % locates the y-values in the tiles

for j=0:n
   % Display the jth tile ...
   f = j/n;
   v = (1-f)*cyan + f*magenta
   fill(x,y+j,v)
end
```

This essentially completes the solution. However, we add a few features so that the overall graphic looks better and is more informative.

For starters, next to each tile we display its rgb value using the text command. This command expects an xy location and a string that is to be displayed at that location. Inserting the statement

```
text(3.5,j+.5,sprintf('[ %4.2f , %4.2f , %4.2f ]',v(1),v(2),v(3)))
```

just after the fill statement results in the display of the rgb values. Notice how individual components of the rgb vector v are referenced by the sprintf command. The xy position is just to the right of the tiles. It usually takes a bit of trial and error to get the location of a "text message" exactly right.

At the beginning of the script we prepare the figure window with

```
close all
figure
axis equal off
hold on
```

These commands (a) close any open figure windows, (b) create a new figure window, (c) hide the axes and force the scaling in the x and y directions to be the same, and (d) hold the current figure window in place so that the results of the subsequent `fill` commands are added to the current window. After the loop we add the statements

```
hold off
shg
```

which turns off the `hold` toggle (good programming) and ensures that the figure window is displayed on the screen (on top of the command window instead of being hidden by it). Here is the finished script:

The Script Eg4_2

```
% Script Eg4_2
% Displays interpolants of the colors cyan and magenta

% Prepare the figure window...
close all
figure
axis equal off
hold on

% Initializations...
cyan    = [0 1 1];   % rgb of the "bottom" color
magenta = [1 0 1];   % rgb of the "top" color
n = 10;              % the number of "in between" colors is n-1
x = [0 3 3 0];       % locates the x-values in the tiles
y = [0 0 1 1];       % locates the y-values in the tiles

% Add colored tiles to the figure window...
for j=0:n
    % Display the jth tile and its rgb value...
    f = j/n;
    v = (1-f)*cyan + f*magenta;
    fill(x,y+j,v)
    text(3.5,j+.5,sprintf('[ %4.2f , %4.2f , %4.2f ]',...
                          v(1),v(2),v(3)))
end
hold off
shg
```

It produces the "paint chip" graphic that is displayed in Figure 4.5.

Talking Point: Interpolation

Interpolation is a way of inferring the value of a function from known, surrounding values of the function. We have examined the notion in the context of color.

An interesting step up from linear interpolation is *cubic* interpolation where the interpolant is a cubic polynomial rather than a linear polynomial. Whereas a linear interpolant is based upon a pair of data points, a cubic interpolant is based on four.

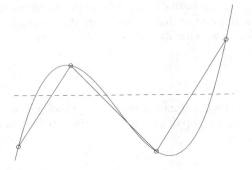

Cubic interpolants do a better job of capturing nonlinearity. Moreover, they have a "smoothness" about them that can translate into graphical renditions that are more pleasing to the human eye.

Because it serves as a bridge between the discrete and the continuous, interpolation has a central role to play in computational science and engineering. There is a never-ending search for clever new ways to estimate what is going on in between the dots (or colors).

MATLAB Review

fill

Use fill to display colored polygons. It works like plot except that in fill(x,y,c) the last point specified by vectors x and y is connected to the first point and the enclosed area is colored according to c. Examples:

```
fill(x,y,'r')
fill(x,y,[.3 .1 .9])
fill(x1,y1,'k',x2,y2,'w',x3,y3,[.5 .5 .5])
```

The perimeter of fill(x,y,c) is displayed by plot([x x(1)],[y y(1)],'k').

rgb Vectors

A 3-vector c with component values chosen from [0,1] can be used to represent a color. The red intensity value is c(1), the green intensity value is c(2), and the blue intensity value is c(3). Here are the rgb values for the eight basic colors that have MATLAB mnemonics:

Color	Mnemonic	rgb
black	k	[0 0 0]
blue	b	[0 0 1]
green	g	[0 1 0]
cyan	c	[0 1 1]
red	r	[1 0 0]
magenta	m	[1 0 1]
yellow	y	[1 1 0]
white	w	[1 1 1]

text

Use text to display strings in the figure window. A text command has the form

text(x-coordinate ,   y-coordinate ,   string) .

figure

This opens up a new figure window and makes it the "current" figure window. Figure windows are indexed. Thus, figure(3) makes the third figure window the current figure window, if it exists, or creates a figure window that is indexed 3 if it does not already exist. The fragment

```
x = linspace(0,2*pi,100);
figure
plot(x,sin(x))
figure
plot(x,cos(x))
```

creates two figure windows; one displays the sine function and the other the cosine function.

close all

This closes (deletes) all open figure windows.

hold on, hold off

Following a hold on command, subsequent executions of plot and fill are placed in the current figure window. To turn off this feature use hold off. It is good to set the hold toggle to off at the end of a script. Otherwise, the next script that you run might exhibit strange behavior if it involves graphics.

shg

This brings the current figure to the front, eclipsing the command window and all other open figure windows. It is often handy to place an shg at the end of an important graphical computation that requires an immediate evaluation.

axis off, axis equal, axis square

These commands adjust the default axis properties. Use axis off to hide the axes. (In this case title still works but xlabel and ylabel do not.) Use axis equal to force equal scaling along the x- and y-axes. (Otherwise, a circle will appear as an ellipse.) Use axis square if you want the plot window to be square instead of the default rectangular shape. Note that

        axis off equal

is equivalent to

        axis equal
        axis off

Exercises

M4.2.1 Modify Eg4_2 so that instead of cyan and magenta the "endpoint" colors are [x x x] and [1 1 1] (white) where the value of x satisfies $0 \le x \le 1$ and is obtained via input. How small must x be before you see a distinct levels of grayness across the 11 tiles?

M4.2.2 Modify Eg4_2 so that it produces three figures. The first should display the tiles with endpoint colors red and green, the second with endpoint colors red and blue, and the third with endpoint colors green and blue.

P4.2.3 Consider the regular n-gon with vertices

$$\left(\cos\left(\frac{2\pi k}{n}\right), \sin\left(\frac{2\pi k}{n}\right) \right) \qquad k = 1{:}n.$$

Write a script that inputs n and draws a regular n-gon that is colored yellow and has a red perimeter.

P4.2.4 Write a script that draws an 8-by-8 checkerboard with red and black tiles.

P4.2.5 Write a script that draws an equilateral triangle that is partitioned into four smaller equilateral triangles by connecting the midpoints of its sides. The four little triangles should be colored differently.

P4.2.6 Define the ellipse $E(\theta,a,b)$ by

$$x(t) = a\cos(t)\cos(\theta) - b\sin(t)\sin(\theta)$$

$$y(t) = b\sin(t)\cos(\theta) + a\cos(t)\sin(\theta),$$

where $0 \le t \le 2\pi$ and θ is the "tilt angle." Write a script that displays $E(0,3,1)$, $E(\pi/6,3,1)$, $E(\pi/3,3,1)$, and $E(\pi/2,3,1)$ in four separate figures. Paint the ellipses magenta.

P4.2.7 Write a script that draws a bullseye with n concentric rings. The kth ring should have inner radius $k-1$ and outer radius k. (Thus, the innermost ring is just a radius-1 disk.) The kth ring should be colored white if k is odd and red if k is even.

P4.2.8 Write a script that draws the 5-ring Olympic symbol. Get the colors and proportions right!

P4.2.9 Look up the design parameters for the flags of Japan, Switzerland, France, and Sweden and write a script that produces accurate renditions in four separate figures.

P4.2.10 Write a script that draws an 11-by-11 checkerboard with the property that the tile in row i and column j has color [$(i-1)/11$ 0 $(j-1)/11$]. Assume that row 1 is the bottom row and column 1 is the leftmost column.

4.3 One Third Plus One Third Is Not Two Thirds

Problem Statement

Consider the following command window interaction:

```
>> format long
>> x = 1/3
x =
   0.333333333333333
>> y = x+x
y =
   0.666666666666667
```

The computer is doing what we do with never-ending decimals: it rounds. Rounding is necessary because the hardware that is used to store numbers is finite.

The finiteness of computer arithmetic has other ramifications. For sufficiently large values of k, $1 + 1/2^k$ will equal 1 and $1/2^k$ will equal zero. Moreover, there is a limit to the size of 2^k. These features distinguish computer arithmetic, which is discrete, from real arithmetic, which is continuous.

Write a script that showcases the finiteness of computer arithmetic and sheds light on how much memory the computer allocates for the storage of a real value.

Program Development

Let us first confirm that there are indeed issues with computer arithmetic. At first glance, it sure looks like the following script would never terminate:

```
k = 0;
while (1 + 1/2^k) > 1                                    (4.7)
    k = k+1
end
```

However, it does terminate and the last value of k that it reports is 53. This is because the computer does *floating point arithmetic*, a system of calculation that basically represents numbers in a "constrained" scientific notation. The constraints are necessary because computer memory is finite—there is not enough room to store never-ending decimals like π or $\sqrt{2}$ or 1/3.

Recall that any nonzero number x can be expressed in the form

$$x = \pm m \times 10^e$$

where m satisfies $1 \leq m < 10$ and e is an integer.[2] Here are some examples:

$$1230 = +1.23 \times 10^{+3} \qquad -.000083615 = -8.3615 \times 10^{-5}.$$

---

[2] "Classical" scientific notation restricts m to the range $1/10 \leq m < 1$. The style we are adopting is sometimes referred to as "engineering notation."

The representation is unique. (A special convention is required for the representation of zero, e.g., 0.0×10^0.)

Floating point arithmetic systems represent real numbers in this style with limits placed on the precision of m and the size of e. To illustrate, let us consider a "toy" system in which three digits are allocated for m and one digit is allocated for e. Here are some numbers and their representations in this environment:

$a \;=\; 12.3$ a: $\boxed{+\;|\;1\;|\;2\;|\;3\;\|\;+\;|\;1}$

$b \;=\; .000000123$ b: $\boxed{+\;|\;1\;|\;2\;|\;3\;\|\;-\;|\;7}$

$c \;=\; -12.3$ c: $\boxed{-\;|\;1\;|\;2\;|\;3\;\|\;+\;|\;1}$

Note that with 3-digit precision, some numbers can only be stored approximately:

$x \;=\; 12.34$ x: $\boxed{+\;|\;1\;|\;2\;|\;3\;\|\;+\;|\;1}$

$y \;=\; 12.37$ y: $\boxed{+\;|\;1\;|\;2\;|\;4\;\|\;+\;|\;1}$

$z \;=\; \pi$ z: $\boxed{+\;|\;3\;|\;1\;|\;4\;\|\;+\;|\;0}$

A reasonable thing to do if there is not enough room to store a value is to *round*. Since 12.37 is closer to 1.24×10^1 than 1.23×10^1, the former value is stored. A tie-breaking rule is required in the event that the value to be represented is midway between two floating point numbers.

Rounding is a necessary feature of just about every floating point calculation because the mantissa, m, of the answer is almost always bigger than the mantissas of the operands, e.g.,

evaluates to 5.6088×10^2. The mantissa must be rounded. The official floating point product becomes

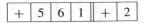

In general, when two floating point numbers are combined through addition, subtraction, multiplication, or division, the floating point result is the rounded version of the correct answer.

A consequence of having limited precision is that a small number can have zero impact when it shows up in an arithmetic operation. For example, in our toy system, $1 + 10^{-1}$ and $1 + 10^{-2}$ can be computed exactly:

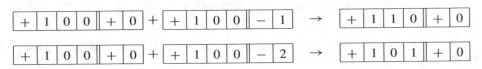

while the floating point addition of 1 and 10^{-3} is 1:

$$\boxed{+\,|\,1\,|\,0\,|\,0}\;\boxed{+\,|\,0}\;+\;\boxed{+\,|\,1\,|\,0\,|\,0}\;\boxed{-\,|\,3}\quad\rightarrow\quad\boxed{+\,|\,1\,|\,0\,|\,0}\;\boxed{+\,|\,0}$$

This is because the floating point representation of 1.001 requires four digits which is beyond the capability of our toy system. Notice that if we were able to execute the script

```
k = 0;
while 1 + 1/10^k > 1
    k = k+1
end
```

on a computer with our toy floating point number system, then the last value of k displayed would be three—precisely the number of digits allocated to m.

    We are now set to explain why on a "real computer" 53 is the smallest integer value of k for which the floating point addition of 1 and $1/2^k$ is 1. Computers encode information with 0's and 1's. This is why the base-2 system is used to represent numerical information. With a base-2 place value system, 1.0101 represents $1+5/16$ because

$$1\cdot 2^0 + 0\cdot 2^{-1} + 1\cdot 2^{-2} + 0\cdot 2^{-3} + 1\cdot 2^{-4} = 1\frac{5}{16}.$$

Just about every computer manufacturer implements the *IEEE floating point standard*. In this standard, 52 base-2 bits are allocated for the fraction part of m. Thus, the number 1 has the representation

$$1.\underbrace{000\cdots 000}_{52\text{ bits}}$$

On the other hand, because the sum of 1 and $1/2^{53}$ has the form

$$1.\underbrace{000\cdots 0001}_{53\text{ bits}}$$

it evaluates to 1 because there is not enough room to store the 53-bit fraction part.[3] This explains the output of the script (4.7).

    Let us turn our attention to the floating point behavior of $1/2^k$ and 2^k, again using our toy system for motivation. It is natural to think that 10^{-9} is the smallest positive number that can be represented:

$$x = 10^{-9}\qquad x:\boxed{+\,|\,1\,|\,0\,|\,0}\;\boxed{-\,|\,9}$$

However, if the system permits *unnormalized* representations, then we can encode even smaller values, e.g.,

$$x = 10^{-11}\qquad x:\boxed{+\,|\,0\,|\,0\,|\,1}\;\boxed{-\,|\,9}$$

Thus, in our toy floating point environment it makes sense to regard any number smaller than 10^{-11} as zero.

---

[3] A "round-to-even" tie-breaking rule is used.

At the other extreme, the largest number our miniature system can represent is

$$x = 9.99 \times 10^9 \qquad x: \boxed{+} \boxed{9} \boxed{9} \boxed{9} \; \boxed{+} \boxed{9}$$

It is natural to regard any number larger than this as infinite.

How does the IEEE floating point standard treat these extreme situations? To answer this question we need to understand the overall IEEE representation. Altogether, 64 bits are used to represent a floating point number: one bit for the sign, 52 bits for the fraction part of m, and 11 bits for e including its sign. Analogous to why the smallest positive floating point number in the toy system is $10^{-2} \cdot 10^{-9} = 10^{-11}$, we find that the smallest positive number in the IEEE system is about $2^{-52} \cdot 2^{-2^{10}} \approx 2^{-1076}$. That is why 1075 is the last value of k displayed by the script

```
k = 0;
while 1/2^k > 0
    k = k+1
end
```

For very large numbers, the IEEE standard assigns the special value of `inf` if an expression evaluates to a quantity that is larger than the largest representable floating point number. The threshold is approximately $2^{2^{10}}$ and that explains why the last value of k reported by the script

```
k = 0;
while 2^k < inf
    k = k+1
end
```

is 1024.

The script `Eg4_3` illustrates all these features of the IEEE floating point standard. It is listed below together with its output.

Talking Point: Xeno Revisited

The ancient Greek Xeno of Elea posed a number of paradoxes that have bothered philosophers for centuries. The most famous can be framed in the context of trying to reach a wall through a succession of steps, each of which halves the remaining distance. If $d = 1$ at the start, then $d = 1/2$ after one step, $d = 1/2^2$ after two steps, $d = 1/2^3$ after three steps, etc. The paradox is that you apparently will never reach the wall. However, in the floating point context, you do arrive at your destination even though it may require 1075 steps! Apologies to Xeno.

In computational science and engineering we have to appreciate the finiteness of computer arithmetic. Rounding errors and exponent limits force a departure from business-as-usual mathematics. *Full machine precision* in the IEEE setting means approximately 16 significant (base-10) digits, and it is almost always a challenge to attain such small relative error in a calculation. The floating point scene is rife with less-is-more paradoxes, situations where an approximate algorithm can yield more accurate results than an allegedly

The Script Eg4_3

```
% Script Eg4_3
% Floating Point Number Facts

clc
% p = largest positive integer so 1+1/2^p > 1.
x=1; p=0; y=1; z=x+y/2;
while x~=z
     y = y/2;
     p = p+1;
     z = x+y/2;
end
fprintf(...
'p = %2.0f    is the largest positive integer so 1+1/2^p > 1.\n',p)

% q = smallest positive integer so 1/2^q = 0.
x = 1; q = 0;
while x>0
     x = x/2;
     q = q+1;
end;
fprintf(...
   'q = %2.0f is the smallest positive integer so 1/2^q == 0.\n',q)

% r = smallest positive integer so 2^r = inf.
x = 1; r = 0;
while x~=inf
     x = 2*x;
     r = r+1;
end
fprintf(...
   'r = %2.0f is the smallest positive integer so 2^r == inf.\n',r)
```

Sample Output from the Script Eg4_3

```
p = 52    is the largest positive integer so 1+1/2^p > 1.
q = 1075 is the smallest positive integer so 1/2^q = 0.
r = 1024 is the smallest positive integer so 2^r = inf.
```

exact algorithm. Xeno with a digital computer would have been the author of numerous paradoxes!

MATLAB Review

eps

This built-in constant is the machine precision, i.e., the smallest number ϵ such that $1+\epsilon > 1$ in floating point arithmetic. For the IEEE standard, it has the value $2^{-52} \approx 10^{-16}$.

inf

This is a special floating point number that behaves like infinity. The following expressions have value inf: `1/0`, `tan(pi/2)`, `abs(log(0))`, `sqrt(inf)`, `inf/10000`. If x = `inf`, then a = `1/x` is assigned the value of zero and a = `-x` is assigned the value of `-inf`. The boolean expression `x==inf` is true if the value of x is `inf`.

realmax, realmin

This is the largest positive floating point number and smallest positive floating point number, respectively.

NaN

This is a special floating point number that is referred to as *not-a-number*. If x = `0/0`, then x has the value `NaN`. If a variable has value `NaN`, then any expression involving the variable has value `NaN`.

Exercises

M4.3.1 Consider the following script:

```
x = input('Enter a positive number:');
z = x;
while x+z>x
    z = z/2;
end
```

What is the connection between the last value of z, the value of x, and `eps`?

M4.3.2 What is the value of `1/0 - 1/0`? What is the value of `2/0 - 1/0`? What is the value of `(1/0)/(1/0)`?

P4.3.3 Calculus tells us that for very small positive values of h,

$$e_h(x) = \left| \frac{\sin(x+h) - \sin(x)}{h} - \cos(x) \right| = O(h).$$

Write a script that inputs x in the range $[0, 2\pi]$ and prints out the value of $e_h(x)$ for $h = 1/10, 1/100, \ldots, 1/10^{16}$. What value of h minimizes the error? Note that in the evaluation of the divided difference, any errors in the evaluation of $\sin(x+h) - \sin(x)$ are magnified by $1/h$. Thus, as h goes to zero the "calculus" error goes to zero but the roundoff error goes to infinity. Thus, the "optimum" choice of h reflects the need to compromise these two tendencies.

P4.3.4 Plot the functions $f(x) = (1-x)^6$ and

$$g(x) = x^6 - 6x^5 + 15x^4 - 20x^3 + 15x^2 - 6x + 1$$

across the interval $[.995, 1.005]$. Even though $f = g$, the plots will look very different. This is because the g-evaluation attempts to compute very small values through the "lucky cancellation" of large values while the f-evaluation computes very small values through repeated multiplication of modestly small values.

P4.3.5 Horner's scheme rearranges a polynomial as follows:

$$a_n x^n + a_{n-1} x^{n-1} + \cdots + a_0 = ((a_n x + a_{n-1})x + \cdots)x + a_0.$$

Evaluating the polynomial in this order helps reduce the cancellation error discussed in P4.3.4. Plot the function $g(x) = x^6 - 6x^5 + 15x^4 - 20x^3 + 15x^2 - 6x + 1$ across the interval [.995,1.005] using Horner's scheme and using the "typical" evaluation order ($g(x)$ exactly as shown above). You will see that the cancellation error using Horner's scheme is smaller.

P4.3.6 What is the smallest value of n such that the value of `factorial(n)` is `inf`?

P4.3.7 How many base-10 digits are there in 1000!?

Chapter 5

Abstraction

There are a number of reasons why the built-in `sin` function is so handy. To begin with, it enables us to compute sines *without having a clue* about the method used. The design of an accurate and efficient sine function is somewhat involved, but by taking the "black box" approach, we are able to be effective `sin` users while being blissfully unaware of how the built-in function works. All we need to know is that `sin` expects a real input value and that it returns the sine of that value interpreted in radians. Another advantage of `sin` can be measured in keystrokes and program readability. Instead of disrupting the "real business" of a program with lengthy compute-the-sine fragments, we merely invoke `sin` as required. The resulting program is shorter and harmonizes better with our mathematical thinking.

Being able to write effective functions is central to the problem-solving process. It supports the top-down methodology, enabling us to hide lower-level details while we address higher-level design issues.

We start by developing a function for computing square roots that is based on a rectangle averaging process. The fact that `sqrt` is a built-in function gives us a standard against which we can measure the quality of our implementation. Next, we consider the problem of computing the perimeter of an ellipse. Two reasonable function-writing strategies emerge, providing an opportunity to discuss the tension that sometimes exists between clarity and efficiency. The challenge of designing the 13-star Colonial flag dramatizes the power of the top-down methodology and illustrates how function writing can crystallize our thinking during the design process. It forces us to identify the factors that characterize the design and to spot underlying hierarchies.

Programming Preview

Concepts

Functions, specification, implementation, local variables, parameters, output parameters, call-by-value, clarity, efficiency, level of abstraction, subfunctions, in-line code, top-down development, relative error, absolute error.

Language Features

Function: A named set of statements stored in an m-file. A function may have any number of input parameters and output parameters.

Subfunction: A function m-file may contain more than one function. The top function is the main function and is accessible by scripts and other functions on the Search Path (described below). The remaining functions are subfunctions and are accessible only by the top function.

function: A function m-file begins with this keyword. If there are multiple functions in a file, each function begins with the keyword function.

Search Path: A ranked set of directories (folders) from which MATLAB locates a function for execution.

Current Working Directory: The first directory on the Search Path.

MatTV

Video 14. User-Defined Function

How to define and call your own functions.

Video 15. Executing a Function

How a function executes and what happens in memory.

Video 16. Figure Editor

How to edit or format a figure from the Figure Editor Window.

5.1 Reshaping Rectangles

Problem Statement

The act of computing the square root of a positive number A is the act of "building" a square with area A. Thinking along these geometric lines, we make a pair of observations. First, if a square with side $\sqrt{A}$ has the same area as an L-by-W rectangle, then as illustrated in Figure 5.1, the square root of A is in between L and W. Second, we can make any given rectangle "more square" by replacing L with $L_{new} = (L+W)/2$ and W with $W_{new} = A/L_{new}$. The process can obviously be repeated:

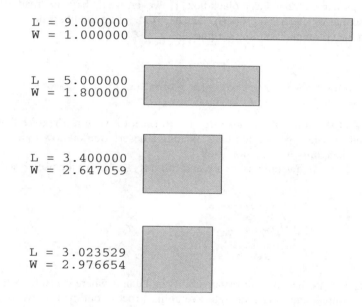

```
L = 9.000000
W = 1.000000


L = 5.000000
W = 1.800000


L = 3.400000
W = 2.647059


L = 3.023529
W = 2.976654
```

Write a function $s = \text{MySqrt}(A)$ that produces an estimate of $\sqrt{A}$ by repeating the rectangle averaging process a sufficient number of times. The relative error in the value MySqrt(A) should be less than 10^{-15}, i.e., MySqrt(A) should have 15 correct significant digits.

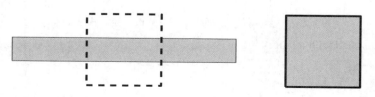

Figure 5.1. *Equal Area.*

Program Development

Before we develop MySqrt, let us think a little bit about the MATLAB built-in function
sqrt. It can be visualized as a "black box" with an input and an output:

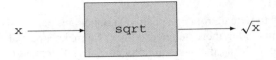

A nonnegative number arrives at the "front door," mysterious things happen, and out pops
the square root. As users of sqrt, we do not have to worry about the mysterious inner
workings of sqrt, i.e., it can be treated as a black box. However, we do have to "read the
manual" about sqrt so that we can use it properly. The MATLAB help facility is designed
for this purpose. From the command window we find

```
>> help sqrt
 SQRT    Square root.
     SQRT(X) is the square root of the elements of X. Complex
     results are produced if X is not positive.
```

The language here is a little confusing because sqrt can accept a vector, a feature that
we ignore for now. But the message is important. Writing a description on how to use a
function is as critical as designing the function itself.

Our plan is to write our own version of sqrt and call it MySqrt. To the user, it will
look the same:

The inner workings of MySqrt become our responsibility and that is where we start. After
code is developed that implements the rectangle averaging process outlined above, we
"package it up" as a function that can then be used just like sqrt.

Define L_i and W_i to be the length and width of the rectangle after i averagings. Let us
examine the quality of the approximation after ten iterations. The improvement sequence

$$
\begin{array}{llll}
L_0 & = & A & \qquad W_0 & = & 1 \\
L_1 & = & (L_0 + W_0)/2 & \qquad W_1 & = & A/L_1 \\
L_2 & = & (L_1 + W_1)/2 & \qquad W_2 & = & A/L_2 \\
& \vdots & & \qquad & \vdots & \\
L_{10} & = & (L_9 + W_9)/2 & \qquad W_{10} & = & A/L_{10}
\end{array}
$$

is nicely handled with a loop:

```
L = A; W = 1;
for i = 1:10
   L = (L+W)/2; W = A/L;
end
```

(We are assuming that A is initialized.) This implementation is fine except that it does not handle the case A = 0. Another concern is whether 10 iterations is enough. Anticipating that we may want to adjust the iteration limit, we introduce a variable iMax whose mission is to house this critical value:

```
iMax = 10;
if A==0
    s = 0;
else
    L = A; W = 1;
    for i = 1:iMax
        L = (L+W)/2; W = A/L;
    end
    s = L;
end
```

Assigned to s is the length of the final rectangle, our alleged square root.

Next in the derivation of MySqrt comes the packaging part. It involves prefacing the above implementation with a *function header* and placing everything in an m-file, MySqrt.m as shown in Figure 5.2. The various parts that make up a function are indicated in Figure 5.3.

```
MySqrt.m

function s = MySqrt(A)
% A is a nonnegative real number and
% s is an approximation to its square root.

iMax = 10;
if A==0
    s = 0;
else
    L = A; W = 1;
    for i = 1:iMax
        L = (L+W)/2; W = A/L;
    end
    s = L;
end
```

Figure 5.2. *The Function* MySqrt *(Preliminary Version).*

The function header begins with the keyword function. Every function must have a name and the naming conventions are the same as for variables. Admissible characters include letters (upper- or lowercase), digits, and the underscore, and the first character must be a letter. The specification consists of comments that communicate everything you need to know about using the function. The part of the function where the calculations

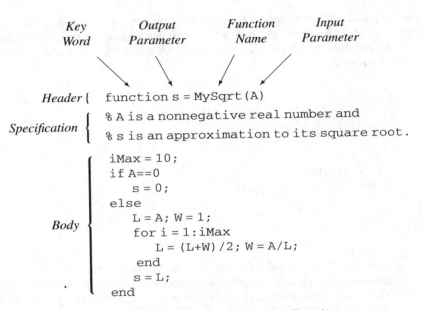

Figure 5.3. *The Structure of a Function.*

are performed is referred to as the *function body*. Function bodies have all the appearance of an ordinary script. MySqrt has one input parameter and one output parameter. (Later in the book we will see that a function can have more than one input parameter (or none) and more than one output parameter (or none).) To understand the role that the parameters play in a function, it is instructive to review how we (as human calculators) use a formula like

$$F = \frac{9}{5}C + 32$$

that converts a Centigrade temperature value into its Fahrenheit equivalent. When using the formula, the "input parameter" C serves as a placeholder into which we substitute a particular value. The formula produces a value which is communicated through the "output parameter" F. Although it would "look funny," we could also advertise

$$\theta = \frac{9}{5}\tau + 32$$

as a formula for Centigrade-to-Fahrenheit conversion, provided we clearly define τ as the Centigrade value and θ as its Fahrenheit counterpart. Except for readability concerns, the names are not important when specifying a formula.

All these observations apply to functions and their input/output parameters. However, because the substitution of the input value and the return of the output value are fully automated during program execution, there is a lot of formality behind the scenes. To understand these mechanisms, we consider the following script which compares `MySqrt(a)` and `sqrt(a)` over a range of input values.

The Script Eg5_1

```
% Script Eg5_1
% Examines the relative error in MySqrt

clc
disp('     a          Relative Error')
disp('                in MySqrt(a)')
disp('---------------------------')
for i = -6:6
    a = 10^i;
    y = sqrt(a);
    z = MySqrt(a);
    relErr = abs(y - z)/y;
    fprintf('%7.0e     %15.7e\n',a,relErr)
end
```

The relative error is the "percent error"—the absolute error divided by the "true" value. It turns out that the two functions essentially agree on the interval $[10^{-3}, 10^{+3}]$ but depart significantly from one another as a gets very large or small.

Sample Output from the Script Eg5_1

```
     a        Relative Error
              in MySqrt(a)
---------------------------
1e-006        2.9619159e-001
1e-005        3.0835354e-003
1e-004        2.5490743e-009
1e-003        0.0000000e+000
1e-002        0.0000000e+000
1e-001        0.0000000e+000
1e+000        0.0000000e+000
1e+001        1.4043334e-016
1e+002        0.0000000e+000
1e+003        0.0000000e+000
1e+004        2.5490743e-009
1e+005        3.0835354e-003
1e+006        2.9619159e-001
```

Thus, there is a real problem with the accuracy of `MySqrt`. We address this concern after first studying the highly structured interaction between `Eg5_1` and `MySqrt`. We do this by taking some "snapshots" of the variables in play during the course of program execution.

Snapshot 1:

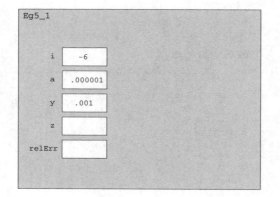

The script Eg5_1 starts executing. The command window is cleared and the table headings are displayed. The for-loop is entered and the loop variable is assigned the value of −6. The variable a is initialized as .000001. The function sqrt is called and returns the square root of .000001. That value, .001, is assigned to y.

Snapshot 2:

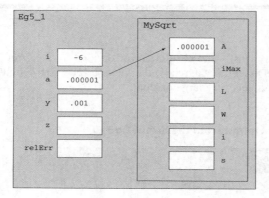

In Eg5_1, the statement z = MySqrt(a) is reached. With this reference, a new "context box" opens and the program control passes from the "calling script" Eg5_1 to the function MySqrt. The value in the *actual parameter* a in Eg5_1 is copied into the input parameter A inside MySqrt. The current context is now the function MySqrt and there are six variables in play: A, the *local variables* iMax, L, W, and i, and the output parameter s.

Snapshot 3:

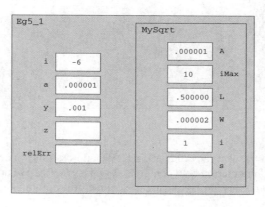

The body of the function MySqrt is now executed. Things are held up in Eg5_1 until the output value from MySqrt is received. While MySqrt is executing, only the six variables shown in the MySqrt context box can be referenced. The snapshot shows the state of affairs after the first pass through the loop is completed. *Note that references to i refer to the local variable i, not the variable i in Eg5_1.*

Snapshot 4:

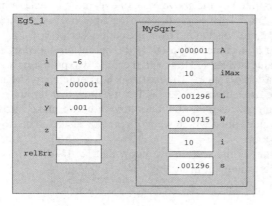

The loop in MySqrt runs to completion and the final value in L is assigned to s.

Snapshot 5:

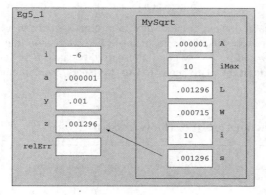

Since s is the output parameter, its value is passed back to Eg5_1 where the assignment z = MySqrt(a) can now be completed. The function call is over.

Snapshot 6:

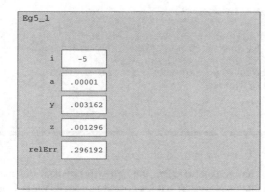

The context box associated with the call to MySqrt disappears and Eg5_1 resumes execution. With program control returning to Eg5_1, the relative error is calculated and assigned to relErr, a line of output is produced, the loop counter is updated, and new values are assigned to a and y. Eg5_1 is once again at the point of having to process the assignment z = MySqrt(a), etc.

Altogether, Eg5_1 calls MySqrt thirteen times, meaning that control passes back and forth thirteen times. The key ideas illustrated by the above trace of execution is that communication between MySqrt and Eg5_1 takes place only through the input and output parameters. The computations inside MySqrt are "insulated" from the calling script Eg5_1.

We now return to the issue of accuracy exposed by the output produced by Eg5_1. One solution is to increase the value of iMax. However, there are two problems associated with the approach of choosing a large iMax. The first concerns efficiency. Many more iterations than necessary will be carried out for "nice" input values that do not require a huge number of rectangle averagings. Second, no matter how large we make iMax, there will always be a range of input values upon which we will get poor results. The way out of this situation is to use a while-loop.

From our remarks at the start of the section, we know that $|\sqrt{A} - L| \leq |L - W|$. It follows that if we change the for-statement in MySqrt to

```
while abs(L-W) > 10^(-15)*sqrt(A)
```
(5.1)

then the relative error in MySqrt(A) will be 10^{-15} or less because

$$\frac{|\sqrt{a} - \text{MySqrt(A)}|}{\text{sqrt(A)}} \leq \frac{|L - W|}{\text{sqrt(A)}} \leq 10^{-15}.$$

The only problem with (5.1) is that it does not make sense to reference sqrt in a function that is designed to compute square roots itself. So instead of (5.1) we reason that while abs(L-W) > 10^(-15)*L would be a very good alternative because L is very close to $\sqrt{A}$ in the final stages of the iteration. This leads to our "finished" implementation of MySqrt.

The Function MySqrt (Final Version)

```
function s = MySqrt(A)
% A is a nonnegative real number and s is an approximation
% to its square root.

if A == 0
    % Nothing to do in this case...
    s = 0;
else
    % The initial rectangle is A-by-1...
    L = A; W = 1;
    % Iterate until the difference between L and W
    % is less than L/10^15...
    while abs(L-W) > (10^-15)*L
        % The new L is the average of the current L and W...
        L = (L+W)/2; W = A/L;
    end
    s = L;
end
```

Note that even though we made a change to MySqrt, we can still check it out using the original test script Eg5_1. A script that uses MySqrt does not care about its inner workings.

The results for the modified `MySqrt` suggest that indeed, the relative error condition is satisfied.

Sample Output from the Script `Eg5_1`

a	Relative Error in MySqrt(a)
1e-006	0.0000000e+000
1e-005	1.3714193e-016
1e-004	0.0000000e+000
1e-003	0.0000000e+000
1e-002	0.0000000e+000
1e-001	0.0000000e+000
1e+000	0.0000000e+000
1e+001	1.4043334e-016
1e+002	0.0000000e+000
1e+003	0.0000000e+000
1e+004	0.0000000e+000
1e+005	1.7975467e-016
1e+006	0.0000000e+000

Talking Point: Who Needs Calculus?

Newton's method for finding a zero of a function f is given by

$$x_{i+1} = x_i - \frac{f(x_i)}{f'(x_i)}.$$

The idea behind this calculus-based iteration is to model f at $x = x_i$ with the tangent line

$$\ell_i(x) = f(x_i) + (x - x_i)f'(x_i)$$

and then choose x_{i+1} so that $\ell_i(x_{i+1}) = 0$. If ℓ_i approximates f, then a zero of ℓ_i should approximate a zero of f. See Figure 5.4.

Noting that the square root of A is a zero of the function $f(x) = x^2 - A$, we can apply Newton's method to the square root problem:

$$x_{i+1} = x_i - \frac{x_i^2 - A}{2x_i} = \frac{1}{2}\left(x_i + \frac{A}{x_i}\right).$$

If $x_0 = A$, then the sequence of values obtained by this process is *precisely* the sequence of L_i that is generated by our rectangle averaging method. For this special problem, simple geometric considerations bring as much "to the table" as the heavy machinery of calculus. In more complicated root-finding situations, intuition certainly has a role to play, especially in the preliminary design of a numerical method. But there usually comes a time when we "run out of intuition" and at that point must turn to calculus or some other branch of mathematics for insight and analysis.

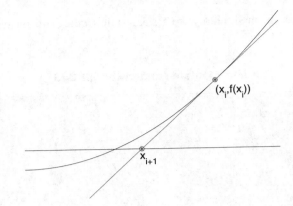

Figure 5.4. *Newton's Method.*

MATLAB Review

Functions

To specify a function, code of the form

function [output parameters] =   name (input parameters)

Specification

Function Body

has to be placed in an m-file whose name is the same as the name of the function. Function names follow the same rules as variable names. Functions may have zero, one, or more input parameters and zero, one, or more output parameters. Here are examples of what the function header looks like in these situations:

```
function   z = SimpleF(x)
function   z = Fof3Var(x,y,z)
function [h,t,m] = ElapsedTime(n)
function   ShowPoint(x,y)
function   MakeWindowGreen()
```

A value must be assigned to each output parameter. It is legal for an input or output parameter to be a vector. The specification is a set of comments that immediately follow the header statement. Its mission is to adequately describe how to *use* the function. It does *not* describe how the function works.

Local Variables

Variables used by the function that are not input parameters are *local*, i.e., recognized only in the function's memory space (local space). In the function MySqrt, L and W are two of the local variables. While parameters are not called local variables, they also have the "local property" in that they are recognized only in the function's space.

Function Execution

When a function is called, the actual values are assigned to the input parameters. Thus, if u and v are initialized and nonnegative, then to execute z = MySqrt(u) + MySqrt(v), the input parameter A in MySqrt is assigned the value of u in the first function call and the value of v in the second function call.

Current Working Directory

A user-defined function is accessible if its function file is in the *Current Directory*, also called the current *folder*. The Current Directory is indicated in a textbox near the top of the MATLAB window. You can type the appropriate directory (folder) name in the bar or browse to the correct folder by pressing the .... button next to the Current Directory textbox.

semilogx, semilogy, loglog

Logarithmic scaling along the x-axis, y-axis, or both can be achieved by using `semilogx(x,y)`, `semilogy(x,y)`, or `loglog(x,y)`. When using a logarithmic plotting function to display error, it is wise to "keep away from zero" by adding an inconsequential positive value to the data, e.g., `loglog(A,relErr+eps)`.

Complex Numbers

MATLAB supports complex arithmetic. The statement x = sqrt(-1) assigns to x the imaginary number i which satisfies $i^2 = -1$. If a = real(x) and b = imag(x), then a and b are assigned the real and imaginary parts of the value in x. The arithmetic operations $+$, $-$, $*$, and $/$ all work when the operands are complex.

Exercises

M5.1.1 Write a script that plots the number of required iterations in MySqrt as a function of the input value A. Use `semilogx`.

M5.1.2 Any positive real number A can be uniquely written in the form

$$A = m \times 4^e \qquad .25 \leq m < 1.$$

It follows that

$$\sqrt{A} = \sqrt{m} \times 2^e.$$

Implement MySqrt so that it first computes m and 2^e and then applies the rectangle averaging process to compute $\sqrt{m}$. How many iterations are necessary to compute the square root of a number in the interval [.25,1] with relative error less than or equal to 10^{-15}? Your implementation of MySqrt should iterate just enough to achieve this level of accuracy.

P5.1.3 Write a function `myFactorial` to compute $n!$. To illustrate the effect of finite computer arithmetic, write a script that displays the smallest n such that the value returned by `myFactorial` is not an integer.

P5.1.4 Write a function `relativeErr` to compute and return the relative error of an observed, or experimental, value. For example, if the "true" value is t and the observed value in an experiment is u, then the relative error of that observation is $|t - u|/t$. What should be the parameters of function `relativeErr`? Use it to print the relative error associated with the approximation $\sin(x) \approx x - x^3/6$ for $x = 2^k$ with $k = -20:1$.

P5.1.5 How could you make an L-by-W-by-H box more cubical? Devise a three-dimensional analogue of the rectangle averaging process. Implement and test a function `MyCubeRoot(A)` that incorporates your idea.

P5.1.6 For integers k and n that satisfy $0 \le k \le n$, the *binomial coefficient* $B(n,k)$ is defined by

$$B(n,k) = \frac{n \cdot (n-1) \cdots (n-k+1)}{1 \cdot 2 \cdots k} = \frac{n!}{k!(n-k)!}$$

with the convention that $B(n,0) = 1$. $B(n,k)$ is the number of ways that one can select k objects from a set of n objects. For example, there are $45 = B(10,2)$ possible chess matches where the players are selected from a 10-contestant pool. Note that $B(n,k) = B(n,n-k)$. Use this fact to write an efficient function `BinCoeff(n,k)`.

P5.1.7 Consider a lotto game where the winning ticket has d distinct numbers selected from the set $\{1,2,\ldots,r\}$. Let $P(m,d,r)$ be the probability that there are exactly m matches between a random ticket and the winning ticket. It can be shown that $P(m,d,r) = B(d,m)B(r-d,d-m)/B(r,d)$. Implement a function `ExactMatch(m,d,r)` that returns this value. You can compute binomial coefficients using the MATLAB function `nchoosek`. Write a script that prints a table for the choices $d = 3,4,5$, and 6. Each table should display the value of $P(m,d,r)$ for $m = 0{:}d$ and $r = 20{:}10{:}50$.

P5.1.8 If j and k are nonnegative integers that satisfy $j + k \le n$, then the coefficient of $x^k y^j z^{n-j-k}$ in $(x + y + z)^n$ is given by the *trinomial coefficient*

$$T(n,j,k) = \left(\begin{array}{c} n \\ j \end{array} \right) \left(\begin{array}{c} n-j \\ k \end{array} \right).$$

Write a function `TriCoeff(n,j,k)` that computes $T(n,j,k)$ and use it to print a list of all trinomial coefficients of the form $T(10,j,k)$ where $0 \le j \le k$ and $j + k \le 10$. Make use of `nchoosek`.

P5.1.9 The number of ways a set of n objects can be partitioned into m nonempty subsets is given by

$$\sigma_n^{(m)} = \sum_{j=1}^{m} \frac{(-1)^{m-j} j^n}{(m-j)!j!}.$$

It is not obvious, but the summation always renders an integer as long as $1 \le m \le n$. For example,

$$\sigma_4^{(2)} = \frac{(-1)^{2-1}1^4}{(2-1)!1!} + \frac{(-1)^{2-2}2^4}{(2-2)!2!} = -1 + 8 = 7.$$

Thus, there are 7 ways to partition a 4-element set like $\{a,b,c,d\}$ into two nonempty subsets:

$$
\begin{array}{ccl}
1 & : & \{a\},\{b,c,d\} \\
2 & : & \{b\},\{a,c,d\} \\
3 & : & \{c\}, \{a,b,d\} \\
4 & : & \{d\},\{a,b,c\} \\
5 & : & \{a,b\},\{c,d\} \\
6 & : & \{a,c\},\{b,d\} \\
7 & : & \{a,d\},\{b,c\}.
\end{array}
$$

Note that $\sigma_n^{(1)} = \sigma_n^{(n)} = 1$. Implement a function `Subset(n,m)` that returns the value of $\sigma_n^{(m)}$. Use `Subset` to print a table with 10 lines. On line n should be printed the numbers $\sigma_n^{(1)}, \sigma_n^{(2)}, \ldots, \sigma_n^{(6)}$.

P5.1.10 Write a script that displays the relative error associated with `MySqrt` in a plot like this:

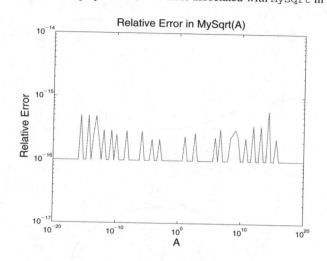

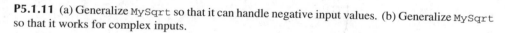

P5.1.11 (a) Generalize `MySqrt` so that it can handle negative input values. (b) Generalize `MySqrt` so that it works for complex inputs.

5.2 Oval Odometer

Problem Statement

The area $\mathcal{A}$ enclosed by the ellipse

$$
\begin{aligned}
x(t) &= a\cos(t) \\
y(t) &= b\sin(t)
\end{aligned}
\qquad 0 \le t \le 2\pi
\tag{5.2}
$$

is given by $\mathcal{A} = \pi ab$. Thinking of a and b as radii, we see that this is an obvious generalization of the circle area formula πr^2. Interestingly, there is no snappy, one-line analogue of $2\pi r$ for the perimeter $\mathcal{P}$ of an ellipse. See P1.1.6. Recipes like $\pi(a+b)$ and $2\pi\sqrt{ab}$ are just crude approximations. What if we want to compute $\mathcal{P}$ to high precision?

One idea is to distribute n points on the ellipse and compute the perimeter of the "inner" polygon that they define. Figure 5.5 illustrates the $n = 6$ case. For general n, the perimeter points are given by

$$
P_k = (a\cos(k\theta), b\sin(k\theta))
\tag{5.3}
$$

where $\theta = 2\pi/n$. If $\mathcal{P}_{inner}(n)$ denotes the perimeter of the inner polygon, then clearly $\mathcal{P}_{inner}(n) \rightarrow \mathcal{P}$ in the limit.

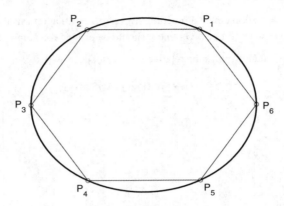

Figure 5.5. *The Inner Polygon (n = 6).*

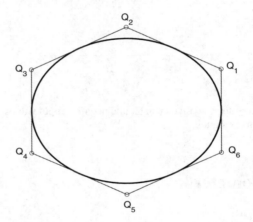

Figure 5.6. *The Outer Polygon (n = 6).*

An "outer" polygon approximation can be obtained by computing the perimeter of the polygon whose sides are tangent to the ellipse at $P_1, \ldots, P_n$. See Figure 5.6. The outer polygon vertices are given by

$$Q_k = (a(\cos(k\theta) - \gamma \sin(k\theta)), b(\sin(k\theta) + \gamma \cos(k\theta))) \tag{5.4}$$

where

$$\gamma = \frac{1 - \cos(\theta)}{\sin(\theta)}.$$

If $\mathcal{P}_{outer}(n)$ denotes the perimeter of the outer polygon, then it is obvious that $\mathcal{P}_{outer}(n) \to \mathcal{P}$ in the limit.

Let $\mathcal{P}_{ave}(n)$ be the average of the two perimeters:

$$\mathcal{P}_{ave}(n) = \frac{\mathcal{P}_{inner}(n) + \mathcal{P}_{outer}(n)}{2}.$$

Since the true perimeter is in between $\mathcal{P}_{inner}(n)$ and $\mathcal{P}_{outer}(n)$, it follows that

$$|\mathcal{P}_{ave}(n) - \mathcal{P}| \leq \frac{|\mathcal{P}_{outer}(n) - \mathcal{P}_{inner}(n)|}{2}. \tag{5.5}$$

Thus, the discrepancy between $\mathcal{P}_{inner}(n)$ and $\mathcal{P}_{outer}(n)$ is more than twice as big as the absolute error in $\mathcal{P}_{ave}(n)$. This fact can be used to obtain perimeter estimates of prescribed accuracy.[4]

Implement functions P_inner(a,b,n) and P_outer(a,b,n) that return the inner and outer perimeter approximations $\mathcal{P}_{inner}(n)$ and $\mathcal{P}_{outer}(n)$. Implement a function P_ave(a,b,tol) that returns perimeter estimate $\mathcal{P}_{ave}(n)$ where n is determined so that the relative error is approximately equal to tol, a small positive tolerance.

Program Development

Our plan is to (a) implement the functions P_inner and P_outer, (b) write a script that explores their accuracy as n increases, (c) figure out how to determine n so that the relative error in $\mathcal{P}_{ave}(n)$ is roughly equal to a prescribed tolerance, and (d) implement P_ave.

It is a good habit to begin the task of implementing a function by writing down the function header and the specification:

```
function P = P_inner(a,b,n)
% a and b are the semiaxes of an ellipse E.
% n is an integer bigger than 2.
% P is the perimeter of the inner polygon whose vertices are on E.
```

There is a "work order" advantage to doing this. The header and the specification together spell out what we must build as implementers. Perimeter computation is an iterative task—we must sum the lengths of the n sides. This suggests that the implementation of P_inner revolves around a for-loop:

> Initialize a running sum variable to zero.
>
> Other initializations. (5.6)

```
% Sum the side lengths...
for k = 1:n
```

> Compute the xy-coordinates of the kth vertex.
> Compute the xy-coordinates of the $(k+1)$st vertex. (5.7)
> Add the distance between them to the running sum.

```
end
```

> Assign to P the final sum. (5.8)

---

[4]We have seen "inner/outer" reasoning before. In §2.2 we used inner and outer regular polygons to approximate π.

For the running sum we use a variable innerSum. Thus, the initialization fragment (5.6) must include the assignment innerSum = 0. Another calculation to perform in the initialization fragment is theta = 2*pi/n. This quantity is used over and over again in the vertex computations, so it makes sense to compute it once and for all before the loop.

The xy-coordinates of the vertices are given in (5.3). Turning these recipes into MATLAB is straightforward and we obtain this refinement of the loop body (5.7):

```
xk = a*cos(k*theta);
yk = b*sin(k*theta);
xkp1 = a*cos((k+1)*theta);
ykp1 = b*sin((k+1)*theta);
dk = sqrt((xk-xkp1)^2 + (yk-ykp1)^2);
innerSum = innerSum + dk;
```

Notice the use of the well-known Euclidean distance formula. The update of innerSum involves adding in the value of the side distance dk. In a way, we are driving around the polygon and the odometer "ticks" after we complete the journey across each side.

Upon completion of the loop, innerSum houses the required perimeter value. Its value must be assigned to the output parameter P. Thus, (5.8) becomes P = innerSum. The final implementation of P_inner is given below. The derivation of P_outer is similar.

The Function P_inner

```
function P = P_inner(a,b,n)
% a and b are the semiaxes of an ellipse E.
% n is a positive integer bigger than 2.
% P is the perimeter of the inner polygon whose
% vertices are on E.

theta = 2*pi/n;
innerSum = 0;
% Sum the side lengths...
for k=1:n
    % Coordinates of vertex k...
    xk = a*cos(k*theta);
    yk = b*sin(k*theta);
    % Coordinates of vertex k+1...
    xkp1 = a*cos((k+1)*theta);
    ykp1 = b*sin((k+1)*theta);
    % Add in the distance between them...
    dk = sqrt((xk-xkp1)^2 + (yk-ykp1)^2);
    innerSum = innerSum + dk;
end
P = innerSum;
```

Using P_inner and P_outer we can write a brief script Eg5_2A that sheds light on how the relative error in $\mathcal{P}_{ave}(n)$ behaves as a function of n.

The Function P_outer

```
function P = P_outer(a,b,n)
% a and b are the semiaxes of an ellipse E.
% n is a positive integer bigger than 2.
% P is the perimeter of the outer polygon whose edges are
% tangent to E.

theta = 2*pi/n;
gamma = (1 - cos(theta))/sin(theta);
outerSum = 0;
% Sum the side lengths...
for k = 1:n
    % Coordinates of vertex k...
    xk = a*(cos(k*theta)-gamma*sin(k*theta));
    yk = b*(sin(k*theta)+gamma*cos(k*theta));
    % Coordinates of vertex k+1...
    xkp1 = a*(cos((k+1)*theta)-gamma*sin((k+1)*theta));
    ykp1 = b*(sin((k+1)*theta)+gamma*cos((k+1)*theta));
    % Add in the distance between them...
    Dk = sqrt((xk-xkp1)^2 + (yk-ykp1)^2);
    outerSum = outerSum + Dk;
end
P = outerSum;
```

The Script Eg5_2A

```
% Script Eg5_2A
% Explores the accuracy of P_inner and P_outer

% Acquire the semiaxes...
a = input('Enter a: ');
b = input('Enter b: ');
clc
fprintf('a = %5.3f  b = %5.3f\n\n',a,b)
disp('     n              RelErrEst')
disp('------------------------------')
for n = logspace(1,6,6)
    Inner = P_inner(a,b,n);
    Outer = P_outer(a,b,n);
    Ave = (Inner + Outer)/2;
    relErrEst = (Outer-Inner)/(2*Ave);
    fprintf('%6.2e    %10.6e\n',n,relErrEst)
end
```

The expression for the relative error estimate relErrEst is based on the absolute error result (5.5). Since the relative error in a computed quantity is its absolute error divided by its magnitude, we see that

$$\frac{|\mathcal{P}_{ave}(n) - \mathcal{P}|}{\mathcal{P}} \leq \frac{|\mathcal{P}_{outer}(n) - \mathcal{P}_{inner}(n)|}{2\mathcal{P}}. \tag{5.9}$$

Since we are in the business of *estimating* the relative error and since we do not know $\mathcal{P}$, we obtained the recipe for relErrEst by replacing $\mathcal{P}$ with $\mathcal{P}_{ave}(n)$ in the denominator. Checking Eg5_2A with the input $a = 5$ and $b = 3$ we find the following:

Sample Output from the Script 5_2A

```
a = 5.000   b = 3.000


    n               RelErrEst
------------------------------
1.00e+001       2.503433e-002
1.00e+002       2.467807e-004
1.00e+003       2.467405e-006
1.00e+004       2.467401e-008
1.00e+005       2.467344e-010
1.00e+006       2.431731e-012
```

After many trials, we conclude that these results are typical. Experimentally we conclude that the relative error in $\mathcal{P}_{ave}(n)$ is about $2.5/n^2$. Thus, if tol is a small positive tolerance and n = ceil(sqrt(2.5/tol)), then the relative error in $\mathcal{P}_{ave}(n)$ is about tol. This leads to the following implementation of P_ave.

The Function P_ave

```
function P = P_ave(a,b,tol)
% a and b are the semiaxes of an ellipse E.
% tol is a small positive error tolerance.
% P is an estimate of E's perimeter with relative error
% approximately equal to tol.

% Initializations...
n = ceil(sqrt(2.5/tol));
% Inner perimeter estimate...
Inner = P_inner(a,b,n);
% Outer perimeter estimate...
Outer = P_outer(a,b,n);
% Return the average of the two perimeters...
P = (Inner + Outer)/2;
```

Notice that it is perfectly legal for one user-defined function, e.g., P_ave, to call another user-defined function, e.g., P_inner. The same substitution dynamic that we discussed in §5.1 prevails.

As a way of affirming the correctness of P_ave, we test it with the script Eg5_2B given below. It reports the perimeter estimates for a range of tol values. The results suggest that the advertised level of relative error is achieved. (Recall that if a result has relative error 10^{-d}, then it will have approximately d correct significant digits.)

The Script Eg5_2B

```
% Script Eg5_2B
% Explores the performance of P_ave

% Acquire the semiaxes...
a = input('Enter a: ');
b = input('Enter b: ');
clc
fprintf('a = %5.3f  b = %5.3f\n\n',a,b)
disp('    tol              Perimeter')
disp('------------------------------')
for tol = logspace(-1,-12,12)
    P = P_ave(a,b,tol);
    fprintf('%6.2e    %18.12f\n',tol,P)
end
```

Sample Output from the Script Eg5_2B

```
a = 5.000  b = 3.000

    tol              Perimeter
------------------------------
1.00e-001     26.697542152973
1.00e-002     25.611738442292
1.00e-003     25.535425132737
1.00e-004     25.527829609136
1.00e-005     25.527082511737
1.00e-006     25.527007252332
1.00e-007     25.526999703203
1.00e-008     25.526998947372
1.00e-009     25.526998871796
1.00e-010     25.526998864238
1.00e-011     25.526998863482
1.00e-012     25.526998863407
```

Talking Point: Clarity, Efficiency, and Abstraction Level

The choice to encapsulate the computation of $P_{inner}(n)$, $P_{outer}(n)$, and $P_{ave}(n)$ in separate functions is a nice division of labor that mimics how we think about the problem mathematically. However, scrutiny of P_inner and P_outer reveals a great deal of redundancy. To quantify this, let us pretend that each cos and sin evaluation costs one dollar and that all other calculations are free.[5] The way they are implemented, we conclude that the evaluations of P_inner(n) and P_outer(n) cost about $4n$ dollars and $8n$ dollars, respectively. Appreciate the wasteful extravagance. In P_inner every sine and cosine is

---

[5]Although this is a silly assumption for these supercheap MATLAB functions, it is often the case that function evaluations make up the most expensive part of a computation. Thus, this make-believe accounting is a worthy exercise. It gets us thinking in the right way about function design and efficiency.

computed twice, while in P_outer the redundancy is fourfold. Noting that P_ave calls both P_inner and P_outer with the same value of n, we conclude that every cosine and sine is computed six times. Is it possible to reduce the cost of a P_ave evaluation from $12n$ dollars to $2n$ dollars?

The answer is "yes." The idea is to change its implementation so that (a) it starts out by precomputing all the necessary cosines and sines and storing them in a pair of arrays and (b) it does not delegate to P_inner and P_outer the computation of $\mathcal{P}_{inner}(n)$ and

The Function P_ave_Inline

```
function P = P_ave_Inline(a,b,tol)
% a and b are the semiaxes of an ellipse E.
% tol is a small positive error tolerance.
% P is an estimate of E's perimeter with relative error
% approximately equal to tol.

% Initializations...
n = ceil(sqrt(2.5/tol));
theta = 2*pi/n;
gamma = (1 - cos(theta))/sin(theta);
% Precompute the cosines and sines...
TheThetas = linspace(0,2*pi,n+1);
c = cos(TheThetas);
s = sin(TheThetas);
% Inner perimeter estimate...
Inner = 0;
% Sum the side lengths...
for k=1:n
    % Coordinates of vertex k...
    xk = a*c(k);
    yk = b*s(k);
    % Coordinates of vertex k+1...
    xkp1 = a*c(k+1);
    ykp1 = b*s(k+1);
    % Add in the distance between them...
    dk = sqrt((xk-xkp1)^2 + (yk-ykp1)^2);
    Inner = Inner + dk;
end
% Outer perimeter estimate..
Outer = 0;
% Sum the side lengths...
for k=1:n
    % Coordinates of vertex k...
    xk = a*(c(k)-gamma*s(k));
    yk = b*(s(k)+gamma*c(k));
    % Coordinates of vertex k+1...
    xkp1 = a*(c(k+1)-gamma*s(k+1));
    ykp1 = b*(s(k+1)+gamma*c(k+1));
    % Add in the distance between them...
    Dk = sqrt((xk-xkp1)^2 + (yk-ykp1)^2);
    Outer = Outer + Dk;
end
% Return the average of the two perimeters...
P = (Inner + Outer)/2;
```

$\mathcal{P}_{outer}(n)$. Refer to the revised implementation P_ave_Inline. If we assume that setting up the vectors c and s costs about n dollars each, then our modified P_ave is six times more cost efficient. The penalty is that we lose the nice crisp subdivision of the overall computation into three separate function implementation tasks.

The tension between efficiency and clarity is the issue of abstraction level. It is hard to reason about long complicated program fragments. Writing functions that take care of important subcomputations is critical to the process of problem solving and code debugging. Sometimes it is easy to identify fragments that are natural to write as functions. In more complicated applications, it can be very difficult to decide on the level of detail that is worth hiding through the implementation of a function.

MATLAB Review

Functions and Their m-files

Ordinarily, a user-defined function MyFun is stored by itself in an m-file with the same name, i.e., MyFun.m. Function MyFun can call other user-defined functions in the *Current Working Directory* or on the *search path*.

Search Path

The search path is a set of directories (folders) from which MATLAB locates a function for execution. The search path is preset to include the directories that contain the built-in function files. You can add your own directories to the search path: in MATLAB, choose *File → Set Path* and click the *Add Folder* button. Then you can browse to the folder that you want to add and change its rank in the search path. MATLAB searches first in the Current Directory and then according to the rank in the search path.

Subfunctions

Ordinarily, a user-defined function MyFun is stored by itself in an m-file with the same name. However, it is sometimes the case that the implementation of a particular function requires very special "helper functions" that only it needs to access. In this situation it is handy to include the helper functions in the same m-file. For example, instead of having separate m-files for P_ave, P_inner, and P_outer, we could have packaged them all in a single file as follows.

```
P_ave.m
    function P = P_ave(a,b,tol)
       Body

    function P = P_inner(a,b,n)
       Body

    function P = P_outer(a,b,n)
       Body
```

In this arrangement, P_inner and P_outer are said to be subfunctions of P_ave. A consequence of this is that these subfunctions can only be accessed by P_ave. With this strategy, the script Eg5_2A would not work in its current form.

Exercises

M5.2.1 Write a script that inputs a and b and prints the smallest value of n such that the discrepancy between P_inner(a,b,n) and P_inner(a,b,n+1) is less than .001.

M5.2.2 For $i = 1{:}5$ and $j = 1{:}5$, let $\mathcal{E}_{ij}$ be the ellipse $(x/i)^2 + (y/j)^2 = 1$. Write a script that displays, in a 5-by-5 table, the perimeter of all these ellipses. Use P_ave with tol set to .001.

M5.2.3 Modify P_ave so that it checks to see if tol is less than 10^{-15}. If it is, it should reset its value to 10^{-15}. Why does this make sense? Be sure to modify the function header comments as appropriate.

P5.2.4 Modify P_inner and P_outer so that they work by computing the first quadrant portion of the polygon perimeter and then multiplying the result by four.

P5.2.5 Write a script that creates in two separate figure windows the images shown in Figures 5.5 and 5.6.

P5.2.6 Using tic and toc, assess the actual efficiency difference between the two implementations of P_ave.

P5.2.7 Implement the following function without loops:

```
function L = PolyLine(u,v)
% u and v are column (n+1)-vectors with u(1) = u(n+1) and v(1) = v(n+1).
% L is the perimeter of the polygon with vertices
% (u(1),v(1)),...,(u(n),v(n))
```

Hint: Use vectorized arithmetic. If z is a length-5 vector, then

$$\text{alpha} = \text{sum(abs(z(1:4)-z(2:5)))}$$

assigns to alpha the value of

$$\alpha = |z_1 - z_2| + |z_2 - z_3| + |z_3 - z_4| + |z_4 - z_5|.$$

P5.2.8 As another exercise in vectorization, implement a loop-free version of P_ave_Inline.

P5.2.9 Do you think that $\mathcal{P}_{inner}(n)$ is more accurate than $\mathcal{P}_{outer}(n)$? Write a script that backs up your conjecture.

5.3 The Betsy Ross Problem

Problem Statement

During the American Revolutionary War, the Marine Committee of the Second Continental Congress passed a resolution on June 14, 1777, establishing a flag design:

> *Resolved, that the flag of the United States be thirteen stripes, alternate red and white; that the union be thirteen stars, white in a blue field, representing a new constellation.*

Neither the exact proportions nor the arrangement of the stars is specified. As a result, the earliest Colonial armies served under several different flags. One of the most recognizable flags is the 13-star "Betsy Ross" flag which arranges the thirteen stars in a circle so that "no one colony would be viewed above another."

The 13-star Colonial flag is characterized by five design parameters:

$$
\begin{aligned}
L_1 &= \text{The length of the flag} \\
W_1 &= \text{The width of the flag} \\
L_2 &= \text{The length of blue corner patch} \\
r_1 &= \text{The radius of the circle of stars} \\
r_2 &= \text{The radius of an individual star.}
\end{aligned}
$$

Various possibilities are displayed in Figure 5.7. The design parameters must satisfy certain constraints for the resulting flag to be "feasible." For example, we do not want the flag to be taller than it is wide or to have the stars extend outside of the blue area. Here are the rules:

- The flag is at most twice as long as it is wide, i.e., $L_1 \le 2W_1$.

- The flag has seven red stripes and six white stripes. They alternate in color and have uniform width.

- The flag has a blue rectangular area situated in the upper left corner. Its length must satisfy $(7/13)W_1 \le L_2 \le L_1/2$. Its width is exactly the width of seven stripes.

- The thirteen white stars are equally spaced around a circle that is centered in the blue area. One of the stars is located at the top of the circle. (There is a star at 12 o'clock.) The stars do not overlap and they are entirely within the blue area.

Implement a function `DrawFlag` that adds a 13-star Betsy Ross flag specified by the parameters L_1, W_1, L_2, r_1, and r_2 to the figure window at a specified location (a, b). Write a script that facilitates the review of various feasible flag designs.

Figure 5.7. *Betsy Ross Flags.*

Program Development

A graphics function like `plot` does not have any output parameters. This sounds strange because we are hardwired to think that all functions must "return something." However, graphics functions are not too much of an exception to this if we regard as their output the object that they add to the figure window. It is handy to write a graphics function whenever there is an important graphical computation that you wish to encapsulate for repeated use, e.g.,

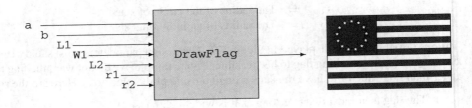

The first two input parameters locate the flag in the figure window while the last five determine its design. Here is the formal specification that we intend to follow:

```
function DrawFlag(a,b,L1,W1,L2,r1,r2)
% Adds a 13-star, 13-stripe Colonial flag to the current
% figure window.  Assumes hold is on.
% The flag is L1-by-W1 with lower left corner at (a,b).
% The length of the blue area is L2.  The ring of stars has
% radius r1 and its center is the center of the blue area.
% The radius of the individual stars is r2.
```

The reader of this specification has all the necessary information to draw Betsy Ross flags. Looking at the displayed examples in Figure 5.7, we see that the flag is "made up" of colored rectangles and stars. Thinking about the display process as a sequence of overlays, it makes sense to progress from stripes to blue area to stars:

Initializations	(5.10)
`for k = 1:13`	
Draw the kth stripe.	(5.11)
`end`	
Draw the blue corner patch	(5.12)
Initializations	(5.13)
`for k = 1:13`	
Draw the kth star.	(5.14)
`end`	

Starting with the stripes, a useful quantity to have available is the stripe width which must be one thirteenth of the flag width: `s = W1/13`. Assume that this initialization is part of (5.10) so that it is available during the stripe-drawing loop (5.11). Index the stripes from the bottom to the top and recall that the lower left corner of the flag is at (a,b). This is what we can say about the location and color of the kth stripe:

- If $k \leq 6$, its length is L_1 and the x-coordinate of its lower left corner is a. Otherwise, its length is $L_1 - L_2$ and the x-coordinate of its lower left corner is $a + L_2$.

- The y-coordinate of its lower left corner is $b_k = b + (k-1)s$.

- If k is odd, the stripe is red. Otherwise, it is white.

It follows that the `for`-loop (5.11) refines to

```
for k=1:13
    % Draw the kth stripe.
    if rem(k,2)==1 && k<=6
        Draw a red L1-by-s stripe, lower left corner at (a,bk)
    elseif rem(k,2)==0 && k<=6
        Draw a white L1-by-s stripe, lower left corner at (a,bk)
    elseif rem(k,2)==1 && k>6
        Draw a red (L1 - L2)-by-s stripe, lower left corner at (a + L2,bk)
    else
        Draw a white (L1 - L2)-by-s stripe, lower left corner at (a + L2,bk)
    end
end
```

The MATLAB function `fill` can be used to draw the stripes. For example, the first draw instruction in the pseudocode translates into

```
fill([a a+L1 a+L1 a], [b+(k-1)*s b+(k-1)*s b+k*s b+k*s], 'r')
```

Although absolutely correct, this `fill` command is cumbersome, because the displayed rectangle must be specified by its vertices and not by its length, width, and corner. To facilitate the implementation we create a function `DrawRect` that makes it easier for us to jump from "flag thinking" to code.

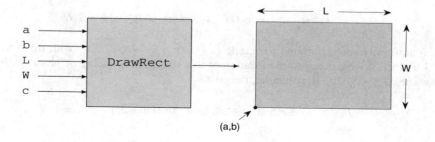

The Function `DrawRect`

```
function DrawRect(a,b,L,W,c)
% Adds a rectangle to the current window. Assumes hold is on.
% The rectangle has vertices (a,b),(a+L,b),(a+L,b+W), and (a,b+W)
% and color c where c is either an rgb vector or one of the
% built-in colors 'r', 'g', 'y', 'b', 'w', 'k', 'c', or 'm'.

x = [a a+L a+L a  ];
y = [b b    b+W b+W];
fill(x,y,c)
```

Using this function, the pseudocode fragment (5.10)–(5.11) for stripe drawing becomes

```
for k=1:13
    % Draw the kth stripe.
    bk = b + (k-1)*s;
    if rem(k,2)==1 && k<=6
        DrawRect(a,bk,L1,s,'r')
    elseif rem(k,2)==0 && k<=6
        DrawRect(a,bk,L1,s,'w')
    elseif rem(k,2)==1 && k>6
        DrawRect(a+L2,bk,L1-L2,s,'r')
    else
        DrawRect(a+L2,bk,L1-L2,s,'w')
    end
end
```

(5.15)

The next order of business concerns the blue area computation (5.12). But that just involves a single call to `DrawRect`:

```
DrawRect(a,b+7*s,L2,6*s,'b')
```

Regarding the stars, we need some facts about how to position equally spaced points around a circle with one of the stars at "12 o'clock." Assume that the number of points N is greater than 2 and define the spacing angle θ by $\theta = 2\pi/N$. The points

$$P_k = (x_c + r\cos(k\theta), y_c + r\sin(k\theta)) \qquad k = 1:N$$

are uniformly spaced around the circle $(x - x_c)^2 + (y - y_c)^2 = r^2$ with the Nth point at "3 o'clock." We can adjust the location of this star by introducing a "phase angle" ϕ that satisfies $0 \leq \phi \leq 2\pi$. In particular, the points

$$P_k = (x_c + r\cos(k\theta + \phi), y_c + r\sin(k\theta + \phi)) \qquad k = 1:N$$

are uniformly spaced around the same circle, but now the Nth point is at ϕ radians. In our application, $N = 13$, $r = r_1$, $x_c = a + L_2/2$, $y_c = b + 9.5s$, and $\phi = \pi/2$. The phase angle choice ensures that one of the stars is positioned at "12 o'clock" as required.

With these observations in mind, we are able to refine the star-generation pseudocode (5.13)–(5.14):

$$
\begin{aligned}
&\texttt{xc = a + L2/2;}\\
&\texttt{yc = b + 9.5*s;}\\
&\texttt{theta = 2*pi/13;}\\
&\texttt{phi = pi/2;}\\
&\texttt{for k=1:13}\\
&\quad\texttt{\% Draw the kth star.}\\
&\quad\texttt{angle = k*theta + phi;}\\
&\quad\texttt{xk = xc + r1*cos(angle);}\\
&\quad\texttt{yk = yc + r1*sin(angle);}\\
&\quad\text{Draw a white star with center at (xk,yk) and radius r2.}\\
&\texttt{end}
\end{aligned}
\tag{5.16}
$$

As with the drawing of the stripes, it makes sense to encapsulate the drawing of the stars:

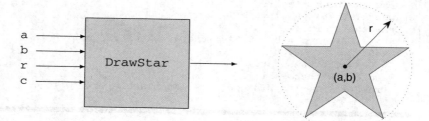

There is a modest amount of trigonometry involved which we suppress. We merely give the specification:

The Function DrawStar (**Specification Only**)

```
function DrawStar(xc,yc,r,c)
% Adds a 5-pointed star to the current window.
% Assumes hold is on.
% The star has radius r, center (xc,yc), and color c where c
% is either an rgb vector or one of the built-in colors
% 'r', 'g', 'y', 'b', 'w', 'k', 'c', or 'm'.
```

With DrawStar available, the command DrawStar(xk,yk,r2,'w') completes the refinement of pseudocode block (5.16). The complete implementation of DrawFlag is given below together with a test script Eg5_3 that generates Figure 5.7.

The Function `DrawFlag`

```
function DrawFlag(a,b,L1,W1,L2,r1,r2)
% Adds a 13-star, 13-stripe Colonial flag to the current window.
% Assumes hold is on. The flag is L1-by-W1 with lower left corner
% at (a,b). The length of the blue area is L2.  The ring of stars
% has radius r1 and its center is the center of the blue area.
% The radius of the individual stars is r2.

% Stripe width...
s = W1/13;
% Draw the stripes...
for k=1:13
    % Draw the kth stripe
    bk = b + (k-1)*s;
    if rem(k,2)==1 &&  k<=6
        DrawRect(a,bk,L1,s,'r')
    elseif rem(k,2)==0 && k<=6
        DrawRect(a,bk,L1,s,'w')
    elseif rem(k,2)==1 && k>6
        DrawRect(a+L2,bk,L1-L2,s,'r')
    else
        DrawRect(a+L2,bk,L1-L2,s,'w')
    end
end
% Draw the blue area...
DrawRect(a,b+6*s,L2,7*s,'b')
% Draw the stars...
xc = a + L2/2; yc = b + 9.5*s; theta = 2*pi/13; phi = pi/2;
for k=0:12
    % Draw the kth star...
    angle = k*theta+phi;
    DrawStar(xc+r1*cos(angle),yc+r1*sin(angle),r2,'w')
end
```

Talking Point: Top-Down Design

Functions are the vehicle for breaking up a large programming task into smaller, independent subtasks. In the flag problem, there was enough on our plate without having to worry about the details of stripe drawing and star drawing. We successfully derived `DrawFlag` without having to pay attention to the specific implementation details associated with `DrawRect` and `DrawStar`.

The idea is not new. The founders delegated the function of star making to Betsy Ross while they focused on other design issues. With independence comes creativity. Her single-snip method (implementation) for cutting (computing) the 5-pointed star was so impressive that it was adopted over the 6-pointed version favored by George Washington.

The Script Eg5_3

```
% Script Eg5_3
% Illustrates DrawFlag

% Initializations
close all
figure
axis equal off
hold on
SW = 1;                  % Stripe width
FW = 13*SW;              % Flag width
GR = (1+sqrt(5))/2;      % Golden ratio
FL = GR*FW;              % Flag length
RR = 2.5*SW;             % Ring radius
SR = 0.5*SW;             % Star radius
% Display four flags with different blue lengths...
BL = .30*FL; DrawFlag( 0, 0,FL,FW,BL,RR,SR)
BL = .35*FL; DrawFlag(25, 0,FL,FW,BL,RR,SR)
BL = .40*FL; DrawFlag(0,16,FL,FW,BL,RR,SR)
BL = .45*FL; DrawFlag(25,16,FL,FW,BL,RR,SR)
```

MATLAB Review

Graphics Functions

User-defined graphics functions are handy whenever there is repetition and/or complexity associated with a particular image that is to be produced. The paradigm is for the graphics function to add something to the current figure window. In our implementations of DrawRect and DrawStar, we assumed that the hold toggle is on and said as much in the specification.

Exercises

M5.3.1 Modify DrawStar so that one of the five points is at 6 o'clock instead of 12 o'clock.

M5.3.2 Modify DrawFlag so that if any of the design constraints given in the problem statement are violated, then it draws an L_1-by-L_1 black flag with lower left corner at (a,b).

M5.3.3 Modify DrawFlag so that it draws 50 stars in the blue area. You are free to lay out the stars as you see fit, but they should more or less be evenly distributed.

M5.3.4 Implement a DrawDisk function analogous to DrawStar:

```
function DrawDisk(xc,yc,r,c)
% Adds a circular disk to the current window.
% Assumes hold is on.
% The disk has radius r, center(xc,yc), and color c where c is either
% an rgb vector or one of 'r', 'g', 'y', 'b', 'w', 'k', 'c', or 'm'.
```

M5.3.5 `fill(x,y,'c')` displays a cyan polygon bounded by a black line. How do you "erase" the black border?

P5.3.6 Write a function `DrawStepPyramid(L,H,c)` to draw a step pyramid and fill it with color c. The base rectangle has length L and height H. Each step has the same height while the length of each step is 2/3 the length of the step below. The top step must have a length no less than H. Use `DrawRect`.

P5.3.7 The specification of a tennis court (in feet) is as follows:

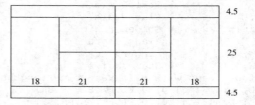

Write a function `DrawTennisCourt(a,b)` that adds a tennis court to the current window with the lower left corner of the court positioned at (a,b). The court should be green and the lines white. Use `DrawRect`. (The lines are very thin rectangles; it is up to you to determine how wide.)

      Write a script that draws a "tennis center" having 12 tennis courts arranged in three rows with four courts per row. There should be 40 feet between each court.

P5.3.8 A phased moon with radius r and center (x_c, y_c) is a partially shaded disk

$$D = \{(x,y): (x - x_c)^2 + (y - y_c)^2 \le r^2\}.$$

The shading depends upon the time T and the period P. If $0 \le T \le P/2$, then a point $(x,y) \in D$ is in the dark region if

$$x \le x_c + \cos(2\pi T/P)\sqrt{r^2 - (y - y_c)^2}.$$

On the other hand, if $P/2 \le T \le P$, then it is in the shaded region if

$$x \ge x_c - \cos(2\pi T/P)\sqrt{r^2 - (y - y_c)^2}.$$

Complete the following function assuming that $P = 28$:

```
function PaintMoon(hc,vc,r,T)
% Draws the moon as it appears T days after the new moon.
% T = 0 or 28 corresponds to the new moon.
% T = 14 corresponds to the full moon.
% The moon is centered at (hc, vc) and has radius r.
```

Use `DrawRect`. Hint: Stack very thin rectangles. Write a script that depicts the moon for $T = 0, 1, \ldots, 27$. Arrange the images in four rows.

P5.3.9 Write a function `DrawOval(xc,yc,a,b,c)` that adds the ellipse

$$\left(\frac{x - x_c}{a}\right)^2 + \left(\frac{y - y_c}{b}\right)^2 = 1,$$

filled in with color c, to the current figure window. Look up the dimensions of the "oval" office in the White House and write a script that displays an ellipse of that shape.

P5.3.10 Look up the specifications of the Swedish flag and write a function that can be used to add it to the current figure window.

P5.3.11 Modify `DrawStar` so that it can put one of the star tips at an arbitrary "clock point." Use your modified function to display the flag of Turkey.

P5.3.12 The 20-star, 35-star, and 48-star U.S. flags have their stars arranged in rows with equal numbers of stars per row. When there were $15, 21, 23, 25, 26, 27, 28, 34, 36, 37, 38, 43, 44, 46$, or 49 states, the star display had different numbers of stars per row, as is the case currently with 50 states. The idea is to distribute the stars evenly across the blue region with a measure of symmetry. Design a 51-star, 52-star, and 54-star flag to handle the cases when (a) Washington, DC becomes a state, (b) Washington, DC and Puerto Rico become states, and (c) Texas is split into five states.

P5.3.13 Define the points $P_1, \ldots, P_n$ and $Q_1, \ldots, Q_n$ by

$$P_k = (r_1 \cos(k\theta), r_1 \sin(k\theta)) \qquad Q_k = (r_2 \cos(k\theta), r_2 \sin(k\theta)) \qquad k = 1{:}n$$

where $0 < r_1 < r_2$, n is an even integer with $n \geq 4$, and $\theta = 2\pi/n$. Here is the picture for $n = 8$:

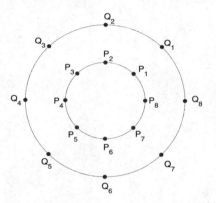

For $k = 1{:}n$, define the kth petal to be the triangle formed by Q_k and P_k's left and right neighbors, e.g., triangles $Q_1 P_2 P_8$, $Q_2 P_3 P_1$, etc. To draw a colored "n-star," (1) draw all the odd-indexed petals with some chosen color, (2) draw all the even-index petals with some chosen color, and (3) draw the disk of radius r_1 with some chosen color. Write a function

```
DrawNstar(r1,r2,n,oddPetalColor,evenPetalColor,diskColor)
```

that adds an n-star to the current figure window centered at (0,0). It is assumed that the `hold` toggle is on. The inner and outer radii are specified by `r1` and `r2`. The number of petals n should be even. The input parameters that specify the colors should be one `'k'`, `'w'`, `'b'`, `'m'`, `'c'`, `'r'`, `'g'`, or `'y'`. Write a script that draws five different n-stars in five different figure windows.

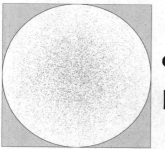

Chapter 6

Randomness

6.1 Safety in Numbers
Monte Carlo Simulation

6.2 Dice and Compass
Random Walks

6.3 Order from Chaos
Polygon Averaging

It is surprising to think that the computer can be used to simulate random processes. After all, computer programs execute with total predictability, which is about as different as you can get from dice rolling, Brownian motion, and chance mutation. But these are deep waters:

> *God does not play dice with the universe.* (Albert Einstein)

> *All chance, direction which thou canst not see.* (Alexander Pope)

> *Chance favors the prepared mind.* (Louis Pasteur)

The message here is that perhaps there are more connections between the random and non-random than meet the (human) eye. This is precisely the case when we use the MATLAB pseudorandom number generators `rand` and `randn`. These functions are capable of generating statistically random sequences of real numbers upon which we can build simulations that require randomness.

We show how to estimate π by simulating a random dart-throwing "game" whose expected score relates to the area of a circular target. This is an instance of *Monte Carlo* simulation. Next, we examine a very special type of simulation called a *random walk*. How long does it take a robot to reach the edge of a giant checkerboard moving randomly one step at a time in any of the north, east, south, or west directions? We conclude our foray into the world of chance by showing how a repeated averaging process can "restore order." A randomly generated polygon having sides that crisscross every which way can be untangled through a succession of midpoint computations. The problem is a metaphor that speaks to the issue of data smoothing.

Programming Preview

Concepts

More complicated iteration involving vectors, more complicated boolean expressions, Monte Carlo, simulation, pseudorandom number generation, random walk, averaging.

Language Features

`rand`: Generates a uniformly random real number in the open interval (0,1).

`randn`: Generates a random number from the standard normal distribution.

`seed`: Determines the sequence of the generated pseudorandom numbers.

`mean`, `std`: Return the mean, standard deviation of an array of numbers.

Out-of-Memory: Memory is limited. A safe upper limit for the number of values in an array is one million.

`bar`: Draws a bar chart.

`hist`: Draws a histogram.

`mod`: Returns the remainder of a division.

`subplot`: Divides the current figure window into multiple sets of axes.

`pause`: Halts program execution for a user-specified number of seconds.

MatTV

Video 17. Debugging

How to use the MATLAB debugging tools in the Editor Window.

6.1   Safety in Numbers

Problem Statement

Consider a target that consists of a 2-by-2 square centered at the origin with a unit disk "bullseye." See Figure 6.1. A dart is thrown at the target and lands randomly inside the square. We say that the dart is a "hit" if it lands inside the circular bullseye. This just means that the landing coordinates (x, y) satisfy

$$x^2 + y^2 \leq 1.$$

If we throw n darts and n is a large number, then the fraction of darts that hit the bullseye should approximate the ratio of the bullseye area to the square area, i.e.,

$$\frac{\text{hits}}{n} \approx \frac{\pi r^2}{(2r)^2}. \tag{6.1}$$

This provides a vehicle for estimating π:

$$\pi \approx 4 \frac{\text{hits}}{n}.$$

Write a script that simulates the throwing of 10,000 darts and displays the resulting π-estimate. The darts should be evenly distributed across the square. What happens if the darts are "aimed" at the origin? How does this affect the resulting estimate of π?

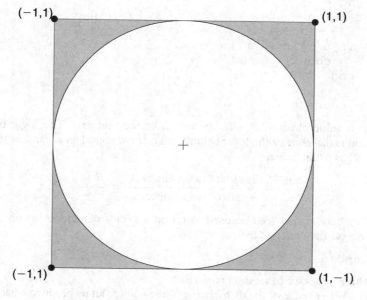

Figure 6.1. *A Target.*

Program Development

The `rand` function can be used to simulate random events. If n is an initialized integer, then the script

```
for k=1:n
    r = rand(1)   % one random number
end
```

displays a sequence of numbers with the properties that (a) each number is in between zero and one and (b) scrutiny of the sequence reveals no discernable pattern, e.g.,

```
0.95012928514718
0.23113851357429
0.60684258354179
0.48598246870930
0.89129896614890
0.76209683302739
0.45646766516834
0.01850364324822
```

This distribution is *uniform* on the interval from 0 to 1 meaning that if L and R satisfy

$$0 < L \le R < 1,$$

then the probability that the value of `r=rand(1)` is in the interval $[L, R]$ is $R - L$. That is, if n is assigned a large integer value, then the script

```
count = 0;
for k=1:n
    r = rand(1);
    if L <= r && r <= R
        count = count + 1;
    end
end
p = count/n;
```

assigns to p a value close to $R - L$, the length of the interval. The logic behind this approximation is the same as the logic behind (6.1). If we regard an r-value in the "target" interval $[L, R]$ as a "hit," then

$$\frac{\text{hits}}{n} \approx \frac{\text{length of target interval}}{\text{length of whole interval}} = \frac{R - L}{1}.$$

The function `rand` can be used to return a vector of random numbers. If n is initialized to a positive integer, then

```
r = rand(n,1)
```

creates a column n-vector of random numbers.

To get a better sense of the *distribution* of the values, let us produce a bar graph that shows the fraction of `rand` values that fall within each decile. That is, how many `rand`-generated values fall between 0 and .1, .1 and .2, etc? The `rand` function allows you to specify the number of random values to produce. Let n be a (large) positive integer and consider the following fragment:[6]

```
r = rand(n,1);    % vector of n random real values between 0 and 1
s = 10*r;         % vector of n random real values between 0 and 10
d = ceil(s);      % vector of n random integers selected from
                  % the set {1,2,...,10}
```

Having established d, all we have to do is count the number in each decile and then "hand over the results" to the built-in function bar, which draws a bar graph:

```
count = zeros(10,1);
for k=1:n
    j = d(k);
    count(j) = count(j) + 1;
end
bar(count,'m')    % bar graph in magenta
```

See Figure 6.2. One can anticipate that the relative discrepancy between the bar heights diminishes as *n* increases.

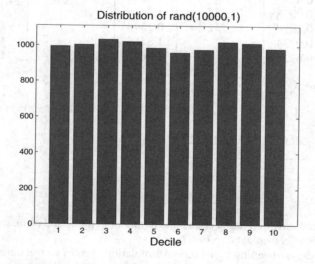

Figure 6.2. *Sampling the Uniform Distribution Using* rand.

We do not intend to go deep into the underlying statistics, but with rand at our disposal we can build up a modest intuition about statistical variation. In this regard, the two most important descriptors of a data set are its *mean* and *standard deviation*. These statistics, respectively, measure the average and the spread of the data and are handily computed using the built-in functions mean and std. For example, the following fragment displays the

[6]Zero is not included in the set of possible integers for d because rand generates a random value in the *open* interval (0,1).

mean and standard deviation of a long vector of values whose entries are sampled from the uniform distribution:[7]

```
n = 1000000;
r = rand(n,1);
mu = mean(r)
sigma = std(r)
```

As n grows, the assigned values to mu and sigma approach $\mu = 0.5000$ and $\sigma = 1/\sqrt{12}$, the true mean and standard deviation of the uniform distribution.

Let us return to the π-via-dart-throwing problem posed at the beginning of the section. We can use rand to generate random values across a specified interval like $[-1, 1]$ by scaling and translating. Similar to how we produced the decile plot in Figure 6.2, we have

```
r = rand(n,1); % vector of n random real values between 0 and 1
s = 2*r;       % vector of n random real values between 0 and 2
t = s-1;       % vector of n random real values between -1 and 1
```

For example,

$$
r = \begin{bmatrix} 0.8147 \\ 0.9058 \\ 0.1270 \\ 0.9134 \\ 0.6324 \end{bmatrix} \Rightarrow s = \begin{bmatrix} 1.6294 \\ 1.8116 \\ 0.2540 \\ 1.8268 \\ 1.2647 \end{bmatrix} \Rightarrow t = \begin{bmatrix} 0.6294 \\ 0.8116 \\ -0.7460 \\ 0.8268 \\ 0.2647 \end{bmatrix}.
$$

Thus, the fragment

```
hits = 0; x = -1+2*rand(n,1); y = -1+2*rand(n,1);
for k=1:n
    if x(k)^2 + y(k)^2 <= 1
        hits = hits + 1;
    end
end
piEstU = 4*(hits/n);
```

simulates the throwing of n darts, counts the number of "hits," and estimates π accordingly. A sample outcome is displayed in Figure 6.3.

The paradigm of setting up a random simulation (game) whose outcome (score) says something about the problem on hand is called *Monte Carlo*. We approached the problem of computing π by simulating a dart game where the score $4(\text{hits}/n)$ sheds light on its value.

What happens if we "aim" the darts at the center of the target? Most likely this will lead to a higher proportion of "hits" and an inflated estimate of π. To investigate this more precisely we build a dart-throwing simulation that is based upon the *normal distribution*. This is the familiar "bell-shaped" distribution displayed in Figure 6.4. The assignment

```
r = randn(n,1);
```

---

[7]Whenever we refer to the "uniform distribution" we mean the uniform distribution across the interval (0,1).

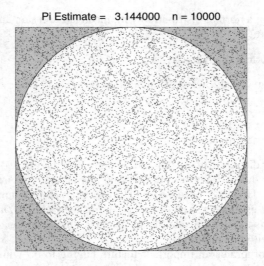

Figure 6.3. *Estimating π via Uniformly Thrown Darts.*

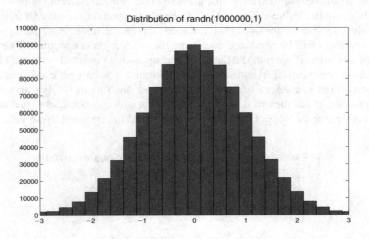

Figure 6.4. *The Normal Distribution.*

produces a vector of values whose entries are sampled from the normal distribution with mean zero and standard deviation one. The histogram in Figure 6.4 is produced using `randn` and `hist`, which is a built-in function for drawing a histogram:

```
r = randn(1000000,1);  % One million samples
x = linspace(-3,3,25); % 25 bins with midpoints across [-3,3]
hist(r,x)              % Display how many samples-per-bin
```

The vast majority (actually over 98%) of r-values are inside the interval $[-3, +3]$. However, with the normal distribution there is always the chance of an abnormally large or small value being generated.

To sample from a normal distribution with mean `mu` and standard deviation `sigma`, simply scale and shift;

```
r = mu + sigma*randn(n,1);
```

Thus, we can simulate the throwing of random darts "aimed" at the bullseye (`mu` is zero) by generating their (x, y)-coordinates as follows:

```
x = sigma*randn(n,1);
y = sigma*randn(n,1);
```

See Figure 6.5 for a display with a standard deviation `sigma` of 0.4. To estimate π, we could proceed as we did with uniform throws and just tabulate the number of throws that land inside the circle. However, because some throws will not even land inside the square, it is more reasonable to estimate π with $(4/n_{square}) \cdot$ hits instead of $(4/n) \cdot$ hits where n_{square} is the number of darts that land inside the square. The final solution script `Eg6_1` shown below estimates π with this quotient.

The script incorporates an important feature having to do with the repeatability of experiments. Without the commands `rand('seed',0)` and `randn('seed',0)`, different results would be obtained each time the script is executed. Random number generation begins with a starting value called the *seed*. Roughly speaking, MATLAB is in charge of this unless the user intervenes by setting the seed. Given the same seed, the same sequence of random numbers will be produced each time the simulation is executed. The simulation confirms the obvious: if we aim the darts we end up with an inflated estimate of π.

We close this section by introducing techniques that can be used to simplify and vectorize structured sequences of boolean operations such as those that arise in `Eg6_1`. The starting point is the idea of a boolean-valued variable. A boolean expression such as `x < y` is either true or false. Ones and zeros are used to represent these values and they

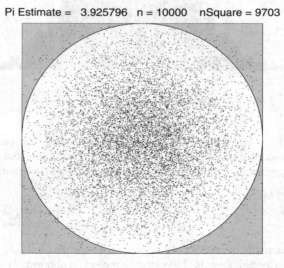

Figure 6.5. *Estimating π via Aimed Darts.*

The Script Eg6_1

```
% Script File: Eg6_1
% Pi computation with uniform and normal distributions

% Initializations
n = 10000; rand('seed',0); randn('seed',0);

% Throw Darts Uniformly...
x = -1+2*rand(n,1);
y = -1+2*rand(n,1);
hits = 0;
for k=1:n
    % Check the kth dart throw...
    if x(k)^2 + y(k)^2 <= 1
        hits = hits + 1;
    end
end
piEstU = 4*(hits/n);

% Throw Darts with Aiming...
sigma = .4;                    ————> standard deviate
x = sigma*randn(n,1);
y = sigma*randn(n,1);
hits = 0;
nSquare = 0;
for k=1:N
    % Check the kth dart throw...
    if abs(x(k))<=1 && abs(y(k))<=1
        nSquare = nSquare + 1;
        if x(k)^2 + y(k)^2 <= 1
            hits = hits + 1;
        end
    end
end
piEstN = 4*(hits/nSquare);

% Display the estimates...
clc
fprintf('n: %1d\n',n)
fprintf('Pi Estimate via Uniform Distribution: %7.5f\n',piEstU)
fprintf('Pi Estimate via N(0,%5.2f)    : %7.5f\n',sigma,piEstN)
```

Sample Output from the Script Eg6_1

```
n: 10000
Pi Estimate via Uniform Distribution: 3.14400
Pi Estimate via N(0, 0.40)           : 3.92580
```

can be stored for "future use." Thus, if x and y are initialized scalar variables with real
values, then

```
B = x < y;
```

assigns to B the value of 1 (true) if the value of x is less than the value of y and the value of
0 (false) if the value of x is not less than the value of y. We refer to B as a *boolean variable*.
In complicated situations, readability is often enhanced through the storage of intermediate
boolean values. Here is a fragment to test if an integer y is a valid leap year:

```
DivBy4       = (mod(y,4)==0);
NotDivBy100 = (mod(y,100)~=0);
DivBy400     = (mod(y,400)==0);
if (DivBy4 && NotDivBy100) || DivBy400
    disp('Leap Year')
else
    disp('Not a Leap Year')
end
```

Notice how the if-else reads just like the natural language specification of the leap year
rule. The mod expressions are enclosed in parentheses for "reader comfort." The assignment

```
DivBy4 = mod(y,4)==0;
```

is perfectly legal but "looks funny."

MATLAB supports boolean operations between vectors that have the same length and
orientation. Thus,

```
x = [10 20 50 40 80];
y = [7 25 60 30 90];
B = (x < y);
```

assigns to B the row vector [0 1 1 0 1] because

$$
\begin{array}{lll}
x(1) & < y(1) & \text{is false} \\
x(2) & < y(2) & \text{is true} \\
x(3) & < y(3) & \text{is true} \\
x(4) & < y(4) & \text{is false} \\
x(5) & < y(5) & \text{is true.}
\end{array}
$$

Notice that the value of sum(B) is 3, the number of true values associated with the vector
comparison.

Using these ideas we can simplify the bookkeeping in the dart-throw simulation
Eg6_1. If n is an initialized integer, then

```
x = -1 + 2*rand(n,1);
y = -1 + 2*rand(n,1);
S = (x.^2 + y.^2 <= ones(n,1));
hits = sum(S);
```

assigns to hits the number of dart throws that landed inside the unit circle. The boolean-
valued vector S is a 0-1 vector with the property that B(i) is 1 if the *i*th dart is a "hit" and
0 if it is a "miss."

Talking Point: Pseudorandom Number Generation

With so much of science and engineering based on computer simulation and with so many simulations mimicking chance events, it is critical to use only random number generation techniques that are statistically sound. While the current state of the art is excellent, it is important to remember some of the past failures if only to appreciate just how high the stakes are.

To see what can go wrong when striving to generate a sequence of random numbers, we consider the method of *middle squaring*. Applied to 4-digit integers, it generates a sequence $\{x_1, x_2, \ldots\}$ according to the recipe

```
x(k+1) = rem(floor(x(k)^2/100),10000).
```

In other words, to get the "next" random integer you square the current random integer and extract from the 8-digit result the middle four digits. A few trials inspire confidence that there are no discernable patterns among the numbers that are so generated. However, a more scientific evaluation of the technique reveals the presence of short cycles, e.g., $2100 \rightarrow 4100 \rightarrow 8100 \rightarrow 6100 \rightarrow 2100$. This totally undermines the idea that the x_k are uncorrelated.

Although middle squaring does not have an important place in the recent history of random number generation, there have been widely used generators that have embarrassingly short cycles such as the above. Fortunately, it is possible to statistically quantify the reliability of modern random number generators such as rand and randn. This is important because, after all, the sequences that these functions generate are deterministic, i.e., completely predictable if you know the underlying algorithm. That is why, technically speaking, rand and randn are *pseudorandom* number generators.

MATLAB Review

rand

If n is initialized to a positive integer, then rand(n,1) is a column *n*-vector whose values are sampled from the uniform distribution in the *open* interval (0,1). To produce a row vector of random values, use rand(1,n). Note that the arguments to rand specify *how many values* to produce, not the interval from which to generate values. The interval is always (0,1).

randn

If n is initialized to a positive integer, then randn(n,1) is a column *n*-vector whose values are sampled from the normal distribution with mean zero and standard deviation one. To produce a row vector of random values, use randn(1,n).

seed

Placing the commands rand('seed',0) and randn('seed',0) at the beginning of a script ensures that the script will produce exactly the same results if it is rerun.

mean and std

If x is an initialized vector, then mean(x) is the average of its values and std(x) is the standard deviation.

sum

If x is a vector, then the value of sum(x) is the sum of its components.

max and min

If x is a vector, then the value of max(x) is the largest component of x. (Note that max(abs(x)) is the largest component of x in absolute value.) A reference of the form [alfa,i] = max(x) assigns to alfa the value of the largest component in x and to i the index of that value. The function min is analogous.

bar

If x is an initialized vector, then bar(x) displays its values in the form of a bar graph. The number of bars is the length of x.

hist

If y and x are vectors, then hist(y,x) displays a histogram of the values in y by distributing them into "bins" centered at x. (The kth bin has the midpoint x(k).)

Out-of-Memory

There is a limit to the size of arrays that MATLAB can work with, depending on the MATLAB version and your computer. A good, safe limit is not to generate arrays that have more than one million entries. Replacing "10000" with "1000000000" in Eg6_1 would result in a "memory exceeded" message.

mod

If x and y are values with the same sign, then mod(x,y) returns the remainder of x/y, exactly like rem(x,y). If x and y have opposite signs, then mod and rem give different results, e.g., mod(-23,7) is 5 while rem(-23,7) is −2.

Boolean Variables

A boolean variable is a term we give to variables that house the value of a boolean expression. In MATLAB, this is either 0 (for false) or 1 (for true). Boolean variables are also called logical variables.

Vectorized Boolean Operations

It is possible to perform boolean operations between vectors as long as the vectors have the same length and orientation. The outcome is a boolean vector, also called logical vector, made up of zeros and ones. The particular value in a component is either 0 (for false) or 1 (for true) according to the outcome of the operation in that component. The non-shortcircuiting "and" and "or" operators (&, |) must be used in vectorized operations. For example,

```
a = [2 0 1]; b = [1 4 3]; c = [2 2 0];
R = (a > b) | (a > c);
S = (a < b) & (b < c);
```

any and all

Applied to a vector, any returns 1 if any component of a vector is nonzero and it returns zero otherwise. Thus, if x and y are vectors, then the value of any(x<y) is 1 if and only if x(k)<y(k) for some subscript k.

Applied to a vector, `all` returns 1 if all components of a vector are nonzero and it returns zero otherwise. Thus, if `x` and `y` are vectors, then the value of `any(x<y)` is 1 if and only if `x(k)<y(k)` for every subscript `k`.

Exercises

M6.1.1 Remove the `rand('seed',0)` and `randn('seed',0)` commands from `Eg6_1` and observe how the π-estimates change from run to run.

M6.1.2 In `Eg6_1`, how is the accuracy of `piEstU` affected by increasing n?

M6.1.3 In `Eg6_1`, how is the accuracy of `piEstN` affected by increasing the standard deviation `sigma`?

M6.1.4 Write functions `MyMean(x)` and `MyStd(x)` that estimate the underlying distribution's mean μ and standard deviation σ from the formulae

$$\mu = \frac{1}{n}\sum_{i=1}^{n}x_i, \qquad \sigma = \sqrt{\frac{1}{n-1}\sum_{i=1}^{n}(x_i-\mu)^2}.$$

M6.1.5 Write a single script that produces plots like those in Figures 6.2 and 6.4.

M6.1.6 Write a single script that produces plots like those in Figures 6.3 and 6.5.

M6.1.7 Write a script that generates 10^6 values from the normal distribution with mean $\mu = 75$ and standard deviation $\sigma = 12$. Show the distribution of the data in a histogram using 17 bins with midpoints across $[-4\sigma, 4\sigma]$. (This is similar to Figure 6.4.)

M6.1.8 Estimate the mean of the uniform distribution by computing the average of one billion `rand`-values. (Hint: Assimilate the data from 1000 calls of the form `rand(1000000,1)`.)

P6.1.9 Write a program that generates a list of 100 integers selected randomly from the set

$$\{-20, -10, 0, 10, 20, 30\}.$$

P6.1.10 Write a program that prints a list of 100 real numbers selected randomly from the set $\{x : 0 < x < 2 \text{ or } 7 < x < 10\}$.

P6.1.11 What is the probability that when three dice are rolled, at least two of the dice have the same value? What is the probability that the value of the third dice roll is strictly between the values of the first two rolls? Use simulation to estimate the probabilities.

P6.1.12 Assume that the coefficients of the quadratic $ax^2 + bx + c$ are selected from the uniform distribution on $(-2, 2)$. What is the probability of complex roots? What if the coefficients are generated with `randn` with mean $\mu = 0$ and standard deviation $\sigma = .4$?

P6.1.13 A dart, thrown at random, hits a square target. Assuming that any two parts of the target of equal area are equally likely to be hit, find the probability that the point hit is nearer to the center than to any edge. Note that the answer does not depend upon the size of the square.

P6.1.14 A coin of diameter 1 inch is thrown onto a surface that is an n-by-n array of square tiles that are each two inches on a side. What is the probability that the coin is entirely within a tile? Assume that the center of the coin lands randomly on the surface.

P6.1.15 Two points on the unit circle are randomly selected. What is the probability that the length of the connecting chord is greater than 1?

P6.1.16 A point (x,y) is randomly selected on the semicircle $S = \{(x,y) : x^2 + y^2 = 1, y \geq 0\}$. What is the expected value of the area of the right triangle formed by (x,y), $(1,0)$, and $(-1,0)$? Note that the random selection of (x,y) is tantamount to selecting a random angle θ from $(0,\pi)$ and setting $x = \cos(\theta)$ and $y = \sin(\theta)$.

P6.1.17 A stick of unit length is broken into two pieces. Assume that the breakpoint is randomly situated. On average, how long is the shorter piece?

P6.1.18 Let N be a positive integer. In a game of "Gap N," a fair coin is repeatedly tossed until the difference between the number of heads and the number of tails is N. The "score" is the number of required tosses. Thus if $N = 3$ and

$$\text{HTTHTHTTHTT}$$

is the sequence of coin tosses, then the score is 11. Notice that

$$|\#\text{tosses} - \#\text{heads}| < 3$$

until the 11th toss. For a given N, what is the expected value (i.e., the average value) of the score? What is the probability that the game is over on or before the $4N$th toss? Give approximate answers to these questions based upon the simulation of a large number of games.

P6.1.19 (a) Write a function $\texttt{p = ProbG(L,R)}$ that assigns to $\texttt{p}$ an estimate of the area under the function

$$f(x) = \frac{1}{\sqrt{2\pi}} e^{-x^2/2} \tag{6.2}$$

from L to R. (Assume $L < R$.) Use Monte Carlo. Hint: Throw darts in the rectangle having vertices $(L,0)$, $(R,0)$, $(R,1)$, and $(L,1)$ and count how many are under the curve.
(b) Write a function $\texttt{p = ProbN(L,R)}$ that estimates the probability that a $\texttt{randn}$ value is between L and R.
(c) Write a script that inputs L and R and displays the values produced by $\texttt{ProbG}$ and $\texttt{ProbN}$.

P6.1.20 The following fragment assigns to $\texttt{deck}$ a length-52 column vector that is a random permutation of the integers 1 through 52:

```
[x,deck] = sort(rand(52,1))
```

(We learn about the MATLAB $\texttt{sort}$ function in §8.2. For now, it is a "black box" method for generating random rearrangements of the first 52 integers.) Let us identify each integer with a playing card:

1	♠ Ace	14	♡ Ace	27	♣ Ace	40	♢ Ace
2	♠ Two	15	♡ Two	28	♣ Two	41	♢ Two
⋮	⋮	⋮	⋮	⋮	⋮	⋮	⋮
13	♠ King	26	♡ King	39	♣ King	52	♢ King

Using boolean variables and vector comparisons we can readily answer "dealt hand" questions. For example, suppose your hand consists of the cards represented by $\texttt{deck(1:13)}$. Here is a statement that assigns to $\texttt{nHearts}$ the number of hearts in your hand:

```
nHearts = sum( 14 <= deck(1:13) & deck(1:13) <= 26 )
```

Here is a statement that computes the number of Jacks in a 5-card hand:

```
nJacks = sum(mod(deck(1:5),13)==11);
```

(a) In poker, a 5-card hand with all the cards in the same suit is called a flush. Write a fragment that assigns to `IsFlush` the value of 1 if `deck(1:5)` is a flush and the value of 0 if it is not a flush. (b) Write a script that estimates the probability that a 5-card hand is a flush. (c) Write a script that estimates the probability that in a 5-card hand no two cards have the same rank. (d) Write a script that estimates the probability that in a 5-card hand at least one suit is missing. (e) Write a script that estimates the probability that in a 5-card hand exactly three of the cards have the same rank.

6.2 Dice and Compass

Problem Statement

Consider a $(2n+1)$-by-$(2n+1)$ square that is centered at the origin and has been covered with 1-by-1 tiles. See Figure 6.6. A robot is placed on the center tile and proceeds to hop from tile to tile according to a set of very simple rules. In particular, if (x_c, y_c) is the current robot location, then

- With probability $P_N = .25$ it moves to its "north" neighbor. Its new location is then $(x_c, y_c + 1)$.

- With probability $P_E = .25$ it moves to its "east" neighbor. Its new location is then $(x_c + 1, y_c)$.

- With probability $P_S = .25$ it moves to its "south" neighbor. Its new location is then $(x_c, y_c - 1)$.

- With probability $P_W = .25$ it moves to its "west" neighbor. Its new location is then $(x_c - 1, y_c)$.

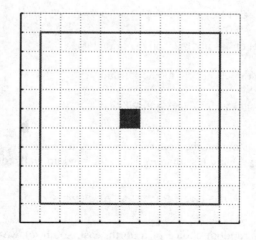

Figure 6.6. *A Tiled Square (n = 5).*

The hopping continues until the robot reaches an edge tile. In the $n = 5$ example, this means that the simulation terminates as soon as $|x_c| = 5$ or $|y_c| = 5$. A simulation of this variety is called a *random walk*.

For a given n, what is the average number of hops required for the robot to reach the boundary?

Program Development

To facilitate our analysis, we begin by implementing a function that simulates a random walk on the grid and returns the "trajectory":

```
function [x y] = RandomWalk2D(n)
% n is a positive integer.
% Simulates a 2D random walk that continues until
% the absolute value of the x-coordinate or y-coordinate
% of the robot is equal to n.
% x and y are row vectors with the property that
% (x(k),y(k)) is the location of the robot after
% k hops, k=1:length(x).
```

Here is a sample trajectory for the $n = 5$ case:

	1	2	3	4	5	6	7	8	9	10	11	12	13	14
x:	0	0	0	1	0	−1	−1	0	−1	−2	−2	−3	−3	−3
y:	−1	0	−1	−1	−1	−1	−2	−2	−2	−2	−3	−3	−4	−5

More generally, if m hops are required, then for $k = 1{:}m$, vector components x(k) and y(k) should house the xy-coordinates of the robot *after* the kth hop. Here is a framework for doing this:

```
% Initialize the hop counter...
k = 0;
% Initialize the current location...
xc = 0; yc = 0;
while   the robot has not reached the boundary

            Choose a direction and update xc and yc
            k = k+1
            Store xc and yc in x(k) and y(k).
end
```

To check if the robot is not on the boundary, we need to make sure that the value of both abs(xc) and abs(yc) are less than n. Thus, the random walk continues as long as the boolean expression

$$\texttt{abs(xc) < n \&\& abs(yc) < n}$$

is true.

To simulate the random choice of a north, east, south, or west hop, we generate a rand value and use its quartile value to select one of the four compass headings:

```
r = rand(1);
if r <= .25
      Hop North
elseif .25 < r && r <= .50
      Hop East
elseif .50 < r && r <= .75
      Hop South
else
      Hop West
end
```

Using the fact that an `if-elseif` construct "acts" on the first true conditional, this is equivalent to

```
r = rand(1);
if r <= .25
      Hop North
elseif r <= .50
      Hop East
elseif r <= .75
      Hop South
else
      Hop West
end
```

Here is how the first four steps in the random walk might play out:

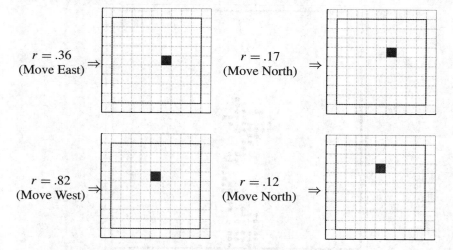

$r = .36$
(Move East) $\Rightarrow$

$r = .17$
(Move North) $\Rightarrow$

$r = .82$
(Move West) $\Rightarrow$

$r = .12$
(Move North) $\Rightarrow$

The finished implementation given below is obtained by noting that hopping north (south) corresponds to increasing (decreasing) the value of `yc` by one and hopping east (west) corresponds to increasing (decreasing) the value of `xc` by one. Displayed in Figure 6.7 is a sample path to the boundary produced by `RandomWalk2D`.

The Function RandomWalk2D

```
function [x y] = RandomWalk2D(n)
% n is a positive integer.
% Simulates a 2D random walk that continues until
% the absolute value of the x-coordinate or y-coordinate of
% the robot is equal to n.
% x and y are row vectors with the property that (x(k),y(k))
% is the location of the robot after k hops, k=1:length(x).

% Initialize the hop counter and current location...
k = 0; xc = 0; yc = 0;
% The random walk...
while abs(xc)<n && abs(yc)< n
    % Robot at (xc,yc), simulate a single hop...
    r = rand(1);
    if r <= .25
        yc = yc+1; % Hop North
    elseif r<=.50
        xc = xc+1; % Hop East
    elseif r < .75
        yc = yc-1; % Hop South
    else
        xc = xc-1; % Hop West
    end
    % Save the new location...
    k = k+1; x(k) = xc; y(k) = yc;
end
```

N = 20 Hops = 136

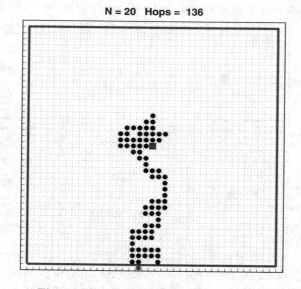

Figure 6.7. *A Sample Trajectory (n = 20).*

The Script Eg6_2

```
% Script Eg6_2
% Estimates the average number of hops required for the robot to
% reach the boundary.

clc
disp('    n      Average to Boundary')
disp('---------------------------')
nTrials = 100;
for n = 5:5:50
    s = 0;
    for k=1:nTrials
        [x,y] = RandomWalk2D(n);
        s = s + length(x);
    end
    ave = s/nTrials;
    fprintf('  %3d          %8.3f\n',n,ave)
end
fprintf('\n\n(Results based on %d trials)\n',nTrials)
```

We can also use this function to solve the problem posed at the start of the section. To estimate the average "length" of a random walk for a chosen value of n, we simply run RandomWalk2D a large number of times and compute the average length of the x (or y) trajectory vector. See script Eg6_2 above.

Sample Output from the Script Eg6_2

```
    n      Average to Boundary
---------------------------
    5          28.569
   10         120.050
   15         263.664
   20         458.544
   25         738.070
   30        1067.283
   35        1437.056
   40        1860.654
   45        2385.057
   50        3056.605

(Results based on 1000 trials)
```

The results suggest that the average length of a random walk grows as the square of the value of n.

Talking Point: Random Web Surfer

Random walks have been used to model diverse phenomena in many fields of study:

Field	Topic
Economics	stock prices
Computer Science	network analysis
Physics	Brownian motion
Population Genetics	genetic drift
Neuroscience	cascade neuron firing
Psychology	decision making
Perception	fixational eye movement

One of the most interesting and important applications is at the heart of PageRank, Google's method for determining the relative importance of a Web page based on the underlying link structure of the Web. Behind the scenes is a random walk. Instead of a robot randomly hopping from tile to tile we have a "random Web surfer" who hops from page to page. When the surfer is on a Web page with k outlinks, she clicks one of the outlinks at random and "goes there." Thus, if there are five outlinks and one of them is to your home page, then with probability 0.2 the surfer's next browsing stop will be there. If there are no outlinks, then the surfer's next browsing stop is determined by randomly selecting one of the 10 billion or so Web pages that currently make up the Web. The PageRank algorithm simulates this process for a large number of random surfers and by tracking their journeys is able to produce a ranking-by-importance of all Web pages. This ranking partly determines the Google browser's response when you enter a query.

MATLAB Review

Functions with More than One Output Parameter

If a function has more than one output parameter, then they must be listed between square brackets:

```
[ Output Parameters List ] = function ( Input Parameters List )
```

Every output parameter in the list must be assigned a value during function execution.

Exercises

M6.2.1 Given that x and y define the robot's trajectory, write a script that prints out the number of times that the robot moved in each of the north, east, south, and west directions.

M6.2.2 Modify function RandomWalk2D so that it does not use an if-statement. Observe that in each iteration the update to the position has the form

$$x_{\text{new}} = x_{\text{old}} + \Delta x$$
$$y_{\text{new}} = y_{\text{old}} + \Delta y.$$

You will need two vectors, deltaX and deltaY, each of length four. Initialize the vectors so that each pair of values deltaX(k) and deltaY(k), where k = 1, 2, 3, or 4, represents a move in one direction.

M6.2.3 Modify function `RandomWalk2D` to simulate a random walk that allows movement in four additional directions: NE, SE, SW, and NW. All eight directions are equally likely to be taken.

P6.2.4 What is the average number of times that the robot revisits the origin? Produce a bar plot that displays these expected values for $N = 5$, 10, 15, 20, and 25.

P6.2.5 We conjecture that the robot is more likely to exit near the middle of an edge than near a corner. Produce a bar plot that sheds light on this conjecture.

P6.2.6 Define the distance d from the current location (x_c, y_c) to the boundary by

$$d = \min\{ |x_c - n|, |x_c + n|, |y_c - n|, |y_c + n| \}.$$

For a given n, produce a bar plot that shows the probability that the robot's distance to the boundary is $1, 2, \ldots, n - 1$ during its trajectory.

P6.2.7 `RandomWalk2D` assumes that each of the directional probabilities p_N, p_E, p_S, and p_W is .25. Generalize `RandomWalk2D` so that it inputs these four numbers in addition to n. Clearly, if one of the directional probabilities is larger than the others, then it is more likely for the token to exit through the corresponding edge. Explore the correlation between the directional probabilities and the exit edges.

P6.2.8 Generalize the two-dimensional random walk discussed in this section to three dimensions. In this regime, the robot can hop north, east, south, west, up, or down. Instead of moving around a planar grid, the token moves around a cubical grid. On average and as a function of n, how many hops are required before the robot reaches a face of the cube?

6.3   Order from Chaos

Problem Statement

If we place four points (x_1, y_1), (x_2, y_2), (x_3, y_3), and (x_4, y_4) in the xy-plane and connect them in order, then we obtain a quadrilateral. See Figure 6.8. We deliberately staged it so that the edges of the quadrilateral "crossed." Interestingly, if we connect the midpoints of this particular quadrilateral, then the "new" quadrilateral is *simple*, meaning that its edges do not cross. See Figure 6.9.

Consider applying the connect-the-midpoint strategy repeatedly to a given random polygon. Will the edges eventually "untangle"? How long does it take as a function of n for the number of sides?

Program Development

The basic operation to encapsulate is that of computing the midpoints of a given polygon. We therefore set out to implement a function

```
[xNew,yNew]  =  Smooth(x,y)
```

where arrays x and y house the x- and y-coordinates of the input polygon, and arrays xNew and yNew house the vertices of the resulting "smoothed" polygon. Recall that if (x_{mid}, y_{mid}) is the midpoint of the line segment that connects (a, b) and (c, d), then

$$x_{mid} = (a + c)/2$$
$$y_{mid} = (b + d)/2.$$

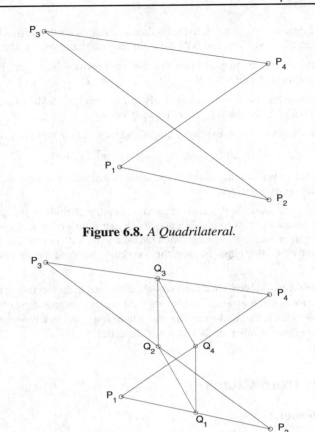

Figure 6.8. *A Quadrilateral.*

Figure 6.9. *A Simple Quadrilateral.*

To compute the edge midpoints of a polygon with vertices $(x_1, y_1), \ldots, (x_n, y_n)$, we must average adjacent x-coordinates and average adjacent y-coordinates. To see what is involved, consider the $n = 5$ case. The statements

```
xNew(1)  =  (x(1)  +  x(2))/2;  yNew(1)  =  (y(1)  +  y(2))/2;
xNew(2)  =  (x(2)  +  x(3))/2;  yNew(2)  =  (y(2)  +  y(3))/2;
xNew(3)  =  (x(3)  +  x(4))/2;  yNew(3)  =  (y(3)  +  y(4))/2;
xNew(4)  =  (x(4)  +  x(5))/2;  yNew(4)  =  (y(4)  +  y(5))/2;
xNew(5)  =  (x(5)  +  x(1))/2;  yNew(5)  =  (y(5)  +  y(1))/2;
```

assign the x- and y-coordinates of the midpoints to the arrays xNew and yNew. For general n we must use a loop. The function smooth given below encapsulates these ideas.

Of course, polygon smoothing can be repeated:

```
for k=1:nRepeat
    [x,y] = Smooth(x,y);
end
```

The Function Smooth

```
function [xNew,yNew] = Smooth(x,y)
% x and y are column n-vectors that define the vertices of
% a polygon P. xNew and yNew are column n-vectors that
% define a polygon Q whose edges are the midpoints of P's edges.

n = length(x); xNew = zeros(n,1); yNew = zeros(n,1);
for i=1:n-1
    % ith new vertex is a midpoint...
    xNew(i) = (x(i) + x(i+1))/2;
    yNew(i) = (y(i) + y(i+1))/2;
end
xNew(n) = (x(n)+x(1))/2;
yNew(n) = (y(n)+y(1))/2;
```

To explore the question of how many iterations are required to obtain a simple polygon, we write a script Eg6_3 that generates a random polygon and then displays the sequence of smoothings. The script has a number of features that are important to discuss. First, to facilitate the comparison of the original polygon and its repeated smoothings, we use subplot

The Script Eg6_3

```
% Script Eg6_3
% Polygon Smoothing

close all
n = input('Enter the number of polygon edges: ');
nSmoothings = input('Enter the number of smoothings: ');

% Generate and display a random polygon
x = rand(n,1);
y = rand(n,1);
figure
set(gcf,'position',[100 100 1000 500])
subplot(1,2,1)
plot([x;x(1)],[y;y(1)],'k',x,y,'or')
axis tight off
title('Original Polygon','FontWeight','bold','FontSize',14)

% Repeatedly smooth and display the polygon...
for k=1:nSmoothings
    subplot(1,2,2)
    [x,y] = Smooth(x,y);
    plot([x ; x(1)],[y ; y(1)],'k',x,y,'or')
    axis tight off
    title(sprintf('After %d Smoothings',k), ...
          'FontWeight','bold','FontSize',14)
    pause(.1)
end
```

to display both polygons in the same figure window. Second, since we are interested only in the *shape*, we hide the axes and use the axis option `tight` to keep the displayed polygons roughly the same size in the figure window. Third, to "animate" the sequence of smoothings we use `pause(.1)` to show each smoothed polygon for a fraction of a second. See Figure 6.10 for some "snapshots" of a 20-gon that is smoothed using `Eg6_3`.

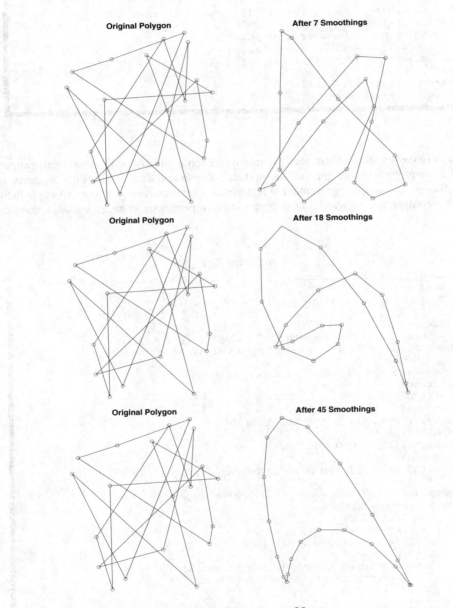

Figure 6.10. *Smoothing a 20-gon.*

Talking Point: Repeated Averaging Is Fundamental

Repeated averaging is one of the very basic ideas in computing. In §5.1 we developed a rectangle averaging process that could be used for computing square roots. Any rectangle can be turned into a square by iterating the idea. In laboratory settings, repeated measurements followed by averaging is a well-known methodology for dealing with noisy data.

The polygon smoothing process described in this section can also be regarded as an averaging process. To illustrate, consider the case $n = 5$. The smoothed pentagon is obtained by the vertex-by-vertex averaging of the given pentagon

$$P: (x_1, y_1), (x_2, y_2), (x_3, y_3), (x_4, y_4), (x_5, y_5)$$

with its "relabelled neighbor"

$$\tilde{P}: (x_2, y_2), (x_3, y_3), (x_4, y_4), (x_5, y_5), (x_1, y_1).$$

Beneath the simplicity of the repeated smoothing process are some deep and very difficult questions. For example, does the iteration always produce a simple polygon? If so, is there a relationship between the number of required smoothings and the number of polygon sides? In §10.3 we develop tools that can be used to automate the termination of the smoothing process once a simple polygon is obtained. For now, we must be content to just "play" with the smoothing sequence via Eg6_3.

MATLAB Review

subplot

This breaks up the figure window into a number of smaller plot windows:

```
subplot( # rows ,    # columns ,    index )
```

The "array" of plot windows has a specified number of rows and a specified number of columns. The plot windows are indexed left to right and top to bottom. The example

```
x = linspace(0,2*pi);
subplot(2,3,2)
plot(x,sin(x))
subplot(2,3,6)
plot(y,cos(x))
```

sets up a figure with six plot windows (2 rows, 3 columns) and displays the sine function in the window 2 (row 1, column 2) and the cosine function in the window 6 (row 2, column 3).

axis tight

This creates an x-range and a y-range that are just big enough to display the plot.

Refined Graphics

See Appendix A for techniques that can be used to improve the display quality of a plot. (Some of these techniques are used in Eg6_3.)

pause(s)

This suspends execution for s seconds. A clock resolution of .01 second may be safely assumed.

Exercises

M6.3.1 Modify the implementation of Smooth so that the loop runs from one to n, obviating the need for the "by hand" computation of the nth midpoint.

M6.3.2 The centroid of a polygon with vertices $(x_1, y_1), \ldots, (x_n, y_n)$ is the point $(\bar{x}, \bar{y})$, where $\bar{x}$ is the average of the x_i and $\bar{y}$ is the average of the y_i. Write a function ShowPolygon(x,y) that plots the polygon defined by the arrays x and y and in the same window displays line segments that connect each vertex to the centroid.

M6.3.3 Write a function [x,y] = GenPoly(n) that returns in x and y the vertices of a polygon that has n vertices randomly placed on the unit circle. Given n, what is the average perimeter of such a polygon?

P6.3.4 Consider "walking" from point (a, b) to point (c, d) along the connecting line segment. If λ satisfies $0 \leq \lambda \leq 1$, then we refer to $(a + \lambda(c - a), b + \lambda(d - b))$ as the λ-point. Note that if $\lambda = 0$, we are at (a, b) while if $\lambda = 1$, then we are at (c, d). The midpoint corresponds to $\lambda = 1/2$. For a given λ that satisfies $0 < \lambda < 1$, how is the smoothing iteration affected by choosing the λ-point of each edge instead of the midpoint?

P6.3.5 Write a function r = DistToReg(x,y) that returns the ratio of the shortest edge length to the longest edge length of the polygon defined by the vectors x and y. How does this ratio change during the smoothing process?

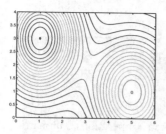

Chapter 7

The Second Dimension

As we have said before, the ability to reason at the array level is very important in computational science. This is challenging enough when the arrays involved are linear, i.e., one-dimensional. Now we consider the two-dimensional array using this chapter to set the stage for more involved applications that make use of this structure. The term "matrix" will be used interchangeably with "two-dimensional array."

To get acquainted with double subscripts and the jargon of rows and columns, we consider a modeling problem in which a matrix interacts with a sequence of vectors. The matrix entries are probabilities that reflect the chance migration of populations from one island to another in an archipelago. The vector entries are island populations. The resulting simulation predicts how the populations vary with time, a type of probabilistic modeling that is ubiquitous in science. We will explore the possibility that the population distribution across the islands settles down to a steady state.

Next we turn to the problem of visualizing a function of two variables. Contour plots and cross sections are key and each requires the systematic sampling of the underlying function. In programming terms, our task is to extend our ability to work with `linspace` and `plot`. MATLAB has tools to support this endeavor.

Lastly we take up the matter of simulation on a two-dimensional grid. This will provide yet another snapshot of the boundary between the continuous and the discrete. We simulate the cooling of a rectangular plate, something that requires discretization in both space and time. There are Δx's, Δy's, and ΔT's.

The lessons learned in this chapter apply even more dramatically when the scene shifts to higher dimensions, e.g., the visualization of a function $f(x, y, z)$ or the cooling of a solid object. The "curse of dimensionality" underlies many of the current challenges in computational science.

Programming Preview

Concepts

Two-dimensional arrays, matrices, rows, columns, matrix operations, submatrices, Markov chains, visualization, contour plots, grid generation, cross sections, shading, functions as parameters, simulation on a grid.

Language Features

Matrix: A two-dimensional array.

`zeros, ones`: Return a matrix of 0's, 1's.

`rand`: Returns a matrix of uniformly random numbers in (0,1).

`randn`: Returns a matrix of random numbers drawn from the standard normal distribution.

`size`: Returns the dimensions of a matrix.

`contour`: Draws a contour plot.

`pcolor`: Draws a color-coded mosaic of tiles to represent values in a matrix.

MatTV

Video 10. Creating Arrays

How to create arrays of numbers.

Video 11. Array Addressing

How to access subarrays.

Video 12. Basic Mathematical Operations on Arrays

How to write simple expressions that perform a mathematical operation on all elements of a vector. *Vectorized code* performs arithmetic (and relational and logical) operations on multiple elements of an array in one statement.

7.1   From Here to There

Problem Statement

Suppose we have four inhabited islands S_1, S_2, S_3, and S_4. (For example, Oahu, Kauai, Maui, and Lanai.) It is observed that each year the inhabitants move from island to island. Data is gathered to reveal more details about the migration pattern, and an array of *transition probabilities* is determined as shown in Figure 7.1. The probability of moving from S_3 to S_4 is .18, the probability of "staying put" if you live in S_2 is .43, etc. Assume that four million people are equally distributed among the four islands in year Y. Estimate the distribution of population in year $Y + 5$.

		From		
	S_1	S_2	S_3	S_4
S_1	.32	.17	.11	.46
S_2	.18	.43	.32	.33
S_3	.27	.22	.39	.14
S_4	.23	.18	.18	.07

To (label at left of the S_1–S_4 rows)

Figure 7.1. *Transition Probabilities.*

Program Development

To get a feel for what is involved in this problem, let us predict the population of island S_1 after one time step. We must account for the contributions from each of the four islands and so

$$
\begin{aligned}
\text{New } S_1 \text{ Pop} \;=\;\; & \text{(Prob Moving from } S_1 \text{ to } S_1)\times(\text{Current } S_1 \text{ Pop}) \\
+\;\; & \text{(Prob Moving from } S_2 \text{ to } S_1)\times(\text{Current } S_2 \text{ Pop}) \\
+\;\; & \text{(Prob Moving from } S_3 \text{ to } S_1)\times(\text{Current } S_3 \text{ Pop}) \\
+\;\; & \text{(Prob Moving from } S_4 \text{ to } S_1)\times(\text{Current } S_4 \text{ Pop}).
\end{aligned}
$$

To make this precise, suppose that x is a 4-by-1 array with the property that the value of $x(i)$ is the number of people living on island S_i at the start of a given time step. Likewise, let y be a 4-by-1 array with the property that the value of $y(i)$ is the number of people living on island S_i at the end of a given time step. We can encode the transition probabilities as follows:

```
P = [.32    .17    .11    .46 ;...
     .18    .43    .32    .33 ;...
     .27    .22    .39    .14 ;...
     .23    .18    .18    .07 ];
```

The variable P is a two-dimensional array, also referred to as a *matrix*. Whereas a single subscript is needed to identify a vector component, a pair of subscripts is required to locate a matrix component. Thus, $P(2,3)$ has the value .32. The first subscript pinpoints the row, while the second is used to specify the column. The matrix P is a 4-by-4 matrix. The square

bracket assembly technique is convenient for the initialization of small matrices. Note that
semicolons are used to separate the values from each row.

In our application, the value of P(i,j) is the probability of moving from S_j to S_i.
Thus,

```
y(1) = P(1,1)*x(1) + P(1,2)*x(2) + P(1,3)*x(3) + P(1,4)*x(4)
```

assigns to y(1) precisely the new S_1 population. The calculations for the other islands are
analogous:

```
y(2) = P(2,1)*x(1) + P(2,2)*x(2) + P(2,3)*x(3) + P(2,4)*x(4)
y(3) = P(3,1)*x(1) + P(3,2)*x(2) + P(3,3)*x(3) + P(3,4)*x(4)
y(4) = P(4,1)*x(1) + P(4,2)*x(2) + P(4,3)*x(3) + P(4,4)*x(4).
```

Using a loop to oversee these four updates we have

```
for i=1:4
    y(i) = P(i,1)*x(1) + P(i,2)*x(2) + P(i,3)*x(3) + P(i,4)*x(4);
end
```

Obviously, we could repeat this update process five times and thereby obtain the population
distribution after five "time steps." However, instead of writing a script that solves this
specific problem, it is more instructive to develop a general framework that can be used to
carry out arbitrarily large "island-hopping" simulations.

To that end, assume that we have islands $S_1, \ldots, S_n$ and that the initial length-n population distribution vector x and the n-by-n transition probability matrix P are set up. The
updating process may proceed as follows:

```
for i = 1:n
    Compute y(i), the new population for S_i.                          (7.1)
end
```

It is clear from our $n = 4$ example that the computation of y(i) is a length-n summation
that involves the transition probabilities from the ith row of P and the values in the current
population vector x. We can use our one-dimensional vector expertise to solve this problem.
We first copy the values from the ith row of P into a vector r:

```
for j=1:n
    r(j) = P(i,j);                                                    (7.2)
end
```

Notice how only the column index varies during the loop—all data come from the ith
row of P.

We next perform the required summation using a familiar one-dimensional summation
strategy, assigning the final sum to y(i):

```
s = 0;
for j=1:n
    s = s + r(j)*x(j);                                               (7.3)
end
y(i) = s;
```

The fragments (7.2) and (7.3) taken in sequence are equivalent to

```
y(i) = 0
for j=1:n
    y(i) = y(i) + P(i,j)*x(j);
end
```

and when this is substituted into (7.1) we obtain

```
for i=1:n
    y(i) = 0
    for j=1:n
        y(i) = y(i) + P(i,j)*x(j);
    end
end
```
(7.4)

This kind of nested-loop computation is typical in applications that involve two-dimensional arrays.

Having worked through the details of computing y from x, we return to the problem posed at the start of the section. In particular, we are to repeat the get-*y*-from-*x* computation five times. This suggests that we encapsulate the transition process with a function:

The Function `Transition`

```
function y = Transition(P,x)
% P is an n-by-n transition matrix.
% x is an n-by-1 vector
% y is an n-by-1 vector obtained by taking a Markov step.

% Initializations...
[n,n] = size(P);
y = zeros(n,1);
for i=1:n
    % Compute the new ith state value...
    for j=1:n
        % Add in the contribution from the current jth state...
        y(i) = y(i) + P(i,j)*x(j);
    end
end
```

In this setting we refer to x and y as *state vectors* because collectively, their components tell us everything about the state of the "system," i.e., how many inhabitants there are on each of the islands. The dimensions of a matrix can be obtained using the built-in function `size`. Notice that we are choosing to represent x and y as column vectors.

With function `Transition` available it is an easy matter to repeat the transition process. The fragment

```
for k=1:N
    x = Transition(P,x);
end
```

overwrites the original state vector with the state vector that describes the system after
N transitions. The script Eg7_1 shows how the population distribution evolves in our
four-island simulation.

The Script Eg7_1

```
% Script Eg7_1
% Illustrates the function Transition.

% Set up the transition probability matrix and initialize
% the state vector....
P = [ .32     .17     .11      .46 ;...
      .18     .43     .32      .33 ;...
      .27     .22     .39      .14 ;...
      .23     .18     .18      .07 ];
x = 1000000*ones(4,1);

% Simulate 5 time steps and display...
clc
disp('      x(1)         x(2)           x(3)          x(4)     ')
disp('--------------------------------------------------------')
disp(sprintf(' %8.0f  ',x))
for t = 1:5
    x = Transition(P,x);
    disp(sprintf(' %8.0f  ',x))
end
```

Sample Output from the Script Eg7_1

x(1)	x(2)	x(3)	x(4)
1000000	1000000	1000000	1000000
1060000	1260000	1020000	660000
969200	1276800	1053600	700400
965280	1291764	1051540	691416
962210	1293869	1051713	692208
961969	1294538	1051525	691968

Talking Point: Markov Chains and Stationary Vectors

The type of discrete modeling illustrated in this section is referred to as a *Markov chain*.
Markov chain modeling is common throughout science and engineering. The state transition
matrix P that underlies the process has several important properties. Most interesting is the
fact that there is (almost always) a vector x such that the value of Transition(P,x)
is x. This means that once the system reaches the state characterized by x, then it "stays
there," i.e., the system has reached a steady state. The vector x is called the *stationary*

vector. For our island-hopping problem, the stationary vector is approximately

$$x = \begin{bmatrix} 961864 \\ 1294673 \\ 1051488 \\ 691975 \end{bmatrix}.$$

We have normalized x so that its entries sum to four million, the total size of the population.[8] Once this distribution is achieved, the island populations remain the same from year to year.

In practice, the steady state is never actually reached, only approximated. That is, if we repeat the computation

```
xNew = Transition(P,x);
x = xNew;
```

then xNew will start to look a lot like x. We begin to see this phenomenon when the script Eg7_1 is run. After five transitions the state vector has begun to "settle down."

MATLAB Review

Rows and Columns

A two-dimensional array has a certain number of rows and a certain number of columns. To say that an array is m-by-n is to say that it has m rows and n columns.

Subscripts

A pair of subscripts are required to pinpoint an entry in a two-dimensional array:

$$\text{Array Name (Row Index , Column Index)}$$

The arithmetic expressions that prescribe the indices must evaluate to an integer that is a valid subscript. If A is a 4-by-5 array, then A(6,1), A(0,1), and A(2.1,3) are illegal references.

Referencing Whole Rows and Columns

A colon all by itself in a subscript position can be used to reference an entire row or column. Thus,

$$\text{Array Name (: , Column Index)}$$

names the column prescribed by the column index while

$$\text{Array Name (Row Index , :)}$$

names the row prescribed by the row index. The fragment

```
c = A(:,2);
A(:,2) = A(:,3);
A(:,3) = c;
```

---

[8]Note that if x is a stationary vector, then so is any scalar multiple of x.

swaps columns two and three in the array A. For this to be legal, A would have to be a matrix with at least three columns.

Small Array Setup

A small two-dimensional array can be set up by specifying its values row by row. The rows are separated by semicolons and the whole thing is enclosed within square brackets, e.g.,

```
A = [1 2 3 4 5; 2 4 6 8 10; 3 6 9 12 15; 4 8 12 16 20]
```

Readability is enhanced by spreading the statement over several lines thereby highlighting the row and column structure:

```
A = [1 2   3   4    5;...
       2 4   6   8   10;...
       3 6   9  12   15;...
       4 8  12  16   20]
```

It is now obvious that this particular 4-by-5 array is a times table.

zeros, ones, rand, randn

If m and n are initialized integers, then A = zeros(m,n) assigns to A the m-by-n matrix of zeros, while A = ones(m,n) assigns to A the m-by-n matrix of ones. Likewise, A = rand(m,n) assigns to A the m-by-n matrix of random numbers using the uniform distribution, while A = randn(m,n) assigns to A the m-by-n matrix of random numbers from the normal distribution.

Classical Matrix Setup

In setting up matrices it is frequently the case that the (i, j) entry is prescribed by a simple function of i and j. A double loop is typically used to carry out the initialization. For example,

```
M = zeros(5,9);
for i=1:5
    for j=1:9
        M(i,j) = i*j;
    end
end
```

In situations like this it is recommended that the array be initialized to the right size using zeros. This enhances readability by making the precise dimensions of the matrix clear. Initializing an array to the right size (also called preallocating an array) decreases execution time by avoiding "growing" the array one component at a time.

size

If A is a matrix, then [m,n] = size(A) assigns the number of rows in A to m and the number of columns in A to n.

Matrix Operations

MATLAB supports matrix-level operations just as it supports vector-level operations. (See §4.1.) To illustrate, suppose variables a and b are initialized as follows:

a:

10	8	−5
4	1	2

b:

2	4	1
1	2	8

These matrices can be

scaled(*)   c = 5*a   ⇒ c:

50	40	−25
20	5	10

scaled(/)   c = a/2   ⇒ c:

5	4	−2.5
2	.5	1

negated   c = -a   ⇒ c:

−10	−8	5
−4	−1	−2

reciprocated   c = 1./a   ⇒ c:

.100	.125	−.200
.25	1	.5

shifted   c = 5+a   ⇒ c:

15	13	0
9	6	7

exponentiated   c = a.^2   ⇒ c:

100	64	25
16	1	4

added   c = a+b   ⇒ c:

12	12	−4
5	3	10

subtracted   c = a-b   ⇒ c:

8	4	−6
3	−1	−6

multiplied   c = a.*b   ⇒ c:

20	32	−5
4	2	16

divided   c = a./b   ⇒ c:

5	2	−5
4	.5	.25

sum

If A is a matrix with n columns, then s = sum(A) is the same as

```
for j=1:n
    s(j) = sum(A(:,j));
end
```

In other words, s is a vector of column sums.

max and min

If A is a matrix with n columns, then m = max(A) is the same as

```
for j=1:n
    m(j) = max(A(:,j));
end
```

In other words, m is the vector of columns max's. The function min is analogous.

Specifying the Print Format for an Array

The elements of an array can be printed using a loop with the usual conversion specifiers, e.g.,

```
A = rand(3,4);
for r = 1:3
    for c= 1:4
        fprintf(' %.2f ', A(r,c))
    end
    fprintf('\n')
end
```

You can also just use one conversion specifier for all the components in a vector (e.g., a row in a matrix):

```
v = rand(1,4);
fprintf(' %.2f ', v)
```

This will print each of the four values in vector v to two decimal places. You have to print separately the new line character \n to advance to the next line. Or you can use disp, which automatically advances to a new line, and sprintf as shown in Eg7_1.

Exercises

M7.1.1 What is the output when the following fragment is executed?

```
A = zeros(3,4)
A(5,2) = 1
```

M7.1.2 What is the output when the following fragment is executed?

```
A = [1 2 3; 4 5 6; 7 8 9];
for i=1:3
    for j=1:3
        A(i,j) = A(j,i);
    end
end
disp(A)
```

M7.1.3 Complete the following function so that it performs as specified:

```
function [p,q] = maxEntry(A)
% A is an m-by-n matrix.
% p and q are indices with the property that |A(p,q)| >= |A(i,j)|
% for all i and j that satisfy 1<=i<=m, 1<=j<=n.
```

Do not use the built-in functions max or min.

M7.1.4 Complete the following function so that it performs as specified:

```
function s = totalSum(A)
% A is an m-by-n matrix.
% s is the sum of all the values in A.
```

Do not use the built-in function `sum` in your implementation.

M7.1.5 Modify `Eg7_1` so that it graphically displays the state vector after each time step.

P7.1.6 Explain why the entries in a column of a transition matrix must sum to 1. Write a function `P = RandomTransMat(n)` that generates a random n-by-n transition matrix. Hint: Use `rand(n,n)` and then divide the values in each column by an appropriate scalar.

P7.1.7 It appears from the output displayed in Figure 7.4 that the state vector tends to a fixed value. Complete the following function so that it performs as specified:

```
function y = stationary(P,x,tol,itMax)
% P is an n-by-n probability matrix.
% x is an n-by-1 state vector.
% tol is a positive real number.
% itMax is a positive integer.
% Let z be the state vector after M Markov steps. If there is an M<=itMax
% such that sum(abs(P*z - z)) <= tol, then y = z. Otherwise, y is the
% state vector after itMax steps.
```

A probability matrix contains only nonnegative real values and each column sums to the value 1.

P7.1.8 Recall that the binomial coefficient

$$\binom{n}{k} = \frac{n!}{k!(n-k)!}$$

can be evaluated using the built-in function `nchoosek(n,k)` $(0 \le k \le n)$. Write a function `P = MakeTrans(n)` that returns the $(n+1)$-by-$(n+1)$ matrix P defined by

$$P(i,j) = \begin{cases} \dfrac{\dbinom{2j-2}{i-1}\dbinom{2n-2j+2}{n-i+1}}{\dbinom{2n}{n}} & 1 \le 2j-i \le n+1 \\ \\ 0 & \text{otherwise.} \end{cases}$$

Write a script that solicits n, generates `P = MakeTrans(n)`, confirms that `P` is a probability matrix, and computes its stationary vector to within three digits of accuracy. A probability matrix contains only nonnegative real values, and each column sums to the value 1.

P7.1.9 Consider a situation where a company has m factories, each of which can produce any of n products. Assume that `Cost` is an m-by-n matrix with the property that `Cost(i,j)` is the cost of producing product j in factory i and that `Inv` is an m-by-n matrix with the property that `Inv(i,j)` is the product j inventory in factory i. (a) Write a function `T = TotalValue(Cost,Inv)` that returns the total value of all the inventory throughout the company (assuming value is the same as cost). (b) Refer to an n-by-1 array `w` as a purchase order array where `w(j)` indicates the quantity of product j that a customer wants to purchase, $j = 1{:}n$. Write a function `[c,i] = Cheapest(Cost,Inv,w)` that returns in `i` the index of the factory that can most cheaply process the purchase order. Return in c the cost to the customer when factory i processes the purchase order. If no factory has enough inventory to fill the order, then set c and i to −1. (c) Write a function NewInv = Update(Inv,i,w) that updates the inventory array assuming that factory i has processed purchase order w. Assume that factory i has enough inventory to process purchase order w.

7.2   Contours and Cross Sections

Problem Statement

A rectangular plate has been warmed by a pair of heat sources, one at (1,3) and the other at (5,1). See Figure 7.2. The temperature drops exponentially away from these points and is modeled by

$$T_{plate}(x,y) = 100e^{-.4((x-1)^2+.7(y-3)^2)} + 80e^{-.2(2(x-5)^2+1.5(y-1)^2)}.$$

Develop an intuition about the variation of T_{plate} across the plate by displaying a contour plot. In addition, display temperature cross sections corresponding to $y = 1, 2,$ and 3.

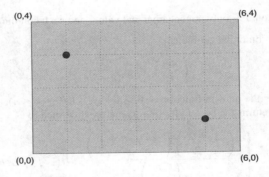

(0,4)   (6,4)

(0,0)   (6,0)

Figure 7.2. *Heat Sources on a Rectangle.*

Program Development

As with the display of a single-variable function $f(x)$ using plot, we must work with a finite set of "snapshots" if we are to visualize a function of the form $T_{plate}(x,y)$. Our plan is to sample T_{plate} over a grid of "mesh points" that are equally spaced across the plate. A sample grid is depicted in Figure 7.3. Observe that the grid is defined by

```
x = linspace(0,6,13)
y = linspace(0,4,9)
```

and consists of the points

$$(p\Delta, q\Delta) \qquad p = 0{:}12, q = 0{:}8,$$

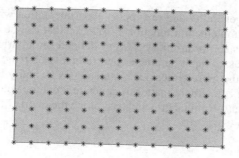

Figure 7.3. *A 9-by-*13 *Grid.*

where $\Delta = 0.5$. More generally, an *m*-by-*n* grid for the rectangle

$$R = \{(x,y): a \leq x \leq b, c \leq y \leq d\}$$

is defined by x = linspace(a,b,n) and y = linspace(c,d,m). Let us assume that these two vectors have been computed and that the following "heat source" function is available.

The Function T_plate

```
function tau = T_plate(x,y)
% tau is temperature at (x,y)
tau = 100*exp(-.4*(  (x-1)^2 + 0.7*(y-3)^2)) + ...
           80*exp(-.2*(2*(x-5)^2 + 1.5*(y-1)^2));
```

In order to produce the required contour plot we must set up a matrix of T_{plate}-evaluations. This boils down to a simple nested loop:

```
TVals = zeros(m,n);
for j=1:n
    for i=1:m
        TVals(i,j) = T_plate(x(j),y(i));
    end
end
```

It may seem more natural to assign T_plate(x(j),y(i)) to TVals(j,i) but this would create an "orientation" problem in the contour plot.[9]

---

[9]Conventional $f(x,y)$ notation for continuous functions uses the first variable position for the variable that varies in the left-to-right direction across the plane, i.e., the *x*-direction. This is in contrast to matrices where the first index position is used to indicate the up-and-down position in the array, i.e., the row. Because of this "inconsistency," *x*-values vary across rows and *y*-values vary up and down columns. Moreover, *y*-values *decrease* and row index increases. All this means that we must pay attention when we map two-dimensional information into a matrix.

For the sake of generality and to support experimentation with alternative temperature distributions, we implement a function fOnGrid that can be used to set up a matrix
of function evaluations for an arbitrary $f(x, y)$ defined on an arbitrary rectangular grid.
fOnGrid therefore has an input parameter that references a *function* (such as T_plate
above), in addition to the more typical array parameters (x and y that specify the "grid").
By using fOnGrid it is a simple matter to generate a contour plot. We simply evaluate
T_plate on a sufficiently refined grid and pass along the matrix of T_plate-evaluations
to the built-in function contour.

The Function fOnGrid

```
function fVals = fOnGrid(x,y,f)
% x is a 1-by-n vector
% y is a 1-by-m vector
% f is a function handle that identifies a function of
% two variables.
% fVals is an m-by-n matrix where fVals(i,j) = f(x(j),y(i)).

n = length(x); m = length(y);
fVals = zeros(m,n);
for j=1:n
   for i = 1:m
       fVals(i,j) = f(x(j),y(i));
   end
end
```

The Script Eg7_2

```
% Script Eg7_2
% Contour plot and cross sections of a function of two variables.

% Generate a matrix of f(x,y) evaluations..
a = 0; b = 6; n = 301; x = linspace(a,b,n);
c = 0; d = 4; m = 201; y = linspace(c,d,m);
TVals = fOnGrid(x,y,@T_plate);
% Display the contour plot
close all
v = linspace(5,100,20);
contour(x,y,TVals,v)

% Display selected cross-sections
figure
TY = fOnGrid(x,[1 2 3],@T_plate);
plot(x,TY(1,:),x,TY(2,:),'--',x,TY(3,:),'-.')
xlabel('x','Fontsize',14)
ylabel('Temperature','Fontsize',14)
legend('y = 1', 'y = 2', 'y = 3')
shg
```

The script `Eg7_2` above displays contours associated with temperature values $5, 10, \ldots, 100$ as shown in Figure 7.4. It also uses `plot` to show the necessary cross sections. The statement `TVals = fOnGrid(x,y,@T_plate)` passes the "handle" of the function `T_plate`, written as `@T_plate`, to `fOnGrid`, which expects a function in its last parameter. `fOnGrid` is called a second time to produce the T_{plate}-evaluations for the cross sections as well. See Figure 7.5. Note that it is necessary to extract rows from the matrix of T_{plate}-evaluations for the cross section plots.

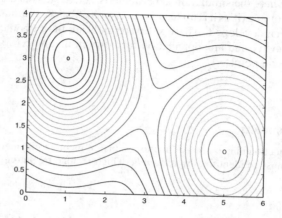

Figure 7.4. *Sample Output from the Script* `Eg7_2`.

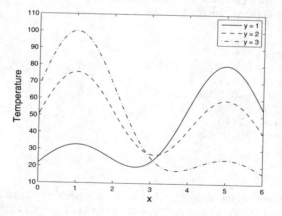

Figure 7.5. *Sample Output from the Script* `Eg7_2`.

Talking Point: Grid Generation

Grid generation refers to the process of distributing a finite number of points throughout a given geometric domain. The most simple example of this is `linspace`, which generates an evenly distributed set of points across an interval. In this section we considered the two-dimensional analogue of this, developing a grid generator for rectangles that basically involves an "x-linspace" and a "y-linspace."

Grid generation is an important tool for bridging the gap between the discrete and the continuous. The simulation of a process over a region can be approximated by tracking what happens at the grid points. See §7.3. In these situations, it is frequently the case that the boundary of the region to be meshed is irregular which adds to the complexity of the grid-generation problem. Moreover, it may be desirable to cluster grid points more densely in critical regions where the simulation is particularly active such as the tip of an airfoil.

Given these complexities it is no surprise that sophisticated, automatic mesh-generation techniques have been developed. These software tools are built upon deep concepts from computational geometry and an appreciation for how simulation errors correlate with the distribution of the grid points.

MATLAB Review

Functions as Parameters

Suppose MyF is a function that expects a function as one of its input parameters. In a call to MyF, the input function must be identified by its *handle* which is done by putting the character "@" in front of its name.

contour and clabel

The simplest way to produce a contour plot of a function $f(x,y)$ is contour(x,y,fVals) where x and y are vectors and fVals(i,j) is the value of f at (x_j, y_i). The length of x and the length of y must equal the column and row dimension of fVals. It is possible to specify the number of contours and the associated "elevations":

```
% 5 contours...
contour(x,y,fVals,5)
% 5 contours with specified elevations...
contour(x,y,fVals,[1 .8 .6 .4 .2])
% 5 contours with mouseclick labelling...
c = contour(x,y,fVals,5);
clabel(c,'manual');
```

Exercises

M7.2.1 How does the output of Eg7_2 change if we modify fOnGrid so that the statement fVals(i,j) = f(x(j),y(i)) is replaced with fVals(i,j) = f(y(i),x(j))?

M7.2.2 Modify Eg7_2 to plot the temperature values at cross sections $y = 2$ and $y = 4$ instead of at the x cross sections.

P7.2.3 Plot the value of the function $T_{plate}(x,y)$ along the line segment that connects (0,0) and (6,4).

P7.2.4 The set of points (x, y) that satisfy

$$Ax^2 + Bxy + Cy^2 + Dx + Ey + F = 0$$

defines an ellipse if $B^2 - 4AC < 0$. Use contour to plot the ellipse defined by

$$2x^2 + 3xy + 6y^2 + 7x - 5y + 10 = 0.$$

P7.2.5 A square playing field with corners at $(1, 1), (1, -1), (-1, -1),$ and $(-1, 1)$ is to be illuminated by four lights positioned at $(x_1, y_1), (x_2, y_2), (x_3, y_3),$ and (x_4, y_4). The total illumination at point (x, y) is given by

$$I(x, y) = \sum_{k=1}^{4} e^{-\sigma((x-x_k)^2 + (y-y_k)^2)}$$

where $\sigma > 0$ is given. Where would you locate the lights if the goal is to maximize the minimum illumination on the field? Proceed experimentally by examining contour plots of the illumination function. How is optimal light placement affected by σ?

7.3 Cool It!

Problem Statement

We continue with the problem presented in the previous section. In particular, let R be a rectangular plate with vertices at $(0,0), (6,0), (6,4),$ and $(0,4)$ and assume that its temperature distribution is given by

$$T_{plate}(x, y) = 100e^{-.4((x-1)^2 + .7(y-3)^2)} + 80e^{-.2(2(x-5)^2 + 1.5(y-1)^2)}.$$

See Figure 7.4. We want to track how the plate cools when, all of a sudden, the boundary temperature is reduced to 0 and held constant. The proper modeling of the cooling process requires some physics and an ability to solve partial differential equations. We shall "jump ahead" in the story and work with a simple discrete model that can be used to simulate how the temperature changes on an m-by-n grid of points that has been superimposed on the region. See Figure 7.6. At the start $(t = 0)$ the temperature at each interior mesh point "+" is prescribed by the function $T_{plate}(x, y)$. The temperature on the boundary mesh

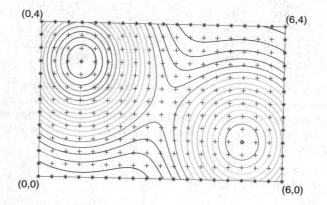

Figure 7.6. *The Temperature at $t = 0$ ($m = 13$, $n = 19$).*

points "*" is set to zero. The simulation proceeds to track the cooling process at times $t = \Delta t,\ 2\Delta t,\ 3\Delta t, \ldots$ according to the following rule:

> The temperature at an interior mesh point at time $(k+1)\Delta t$ is the average of the temperature at its four neighbor mesh points at time $k\Delta t$.

An interior mesh point at (x, y) has a "north" neighbor at $(x, y + \Delta y)$, an "east" neighbor at $(x + \Delta x, y)$, a "south" neighbor at $(x, y - \Delta y)$, and a "west" neighbor at $(x - \Delta x, y)$, where Δx and Δy are the mesh-point spacings in the x and y directions, respectively. Think of Δt as a "time step" but do not be concerned about its actual value.

Choose an appropriate number of mesh points and graphically display the cooling process over a reasonable number of time steps.

Program Development

The first thing to do is to set up a matrix that houses the grid point temperatures at time $t = 0$. This is straightforward using the function fOnGrid developed in the previous section. For the example depicted in Figure 7.6 we have

```
a = 0; b = 6; n = 19; x = linspace(a,b,n);
c = 0; d = 4; n = 13; y = linspace(c,d,m);
TVals = fOnGrid(x,y,@T_plate);
TVals(1,:) = zeros(1,n);    % Temp = zero on bottom boundary
TVals(m,:) = zeros(1,n);    % Temp = zero on top boundary
TVals(:,1) = zeros(m,1);    % Temp = zero on left boundary
TVals(:,n) = zeros(m,1);    % Temp = zero on right boundary
```

It is assumed that the function T_plate is available.

The updating of the interior grid point temperatures is given in the language of "neighbors" and this has to be translated into the language of subscripts. For the (i, j)th grid point we have

Neighbor	Location	Temperature
North	(x(j),y(i+1))	TVals(i+1,j)
East	(x(j+1),y(i))	TVals(i,j+1)
South	(x(j),y(i-1))	TVals(i-1,j)
West	(x(j-1),y(i))	TVals(i,j-1)

Using a nested loop we can visit each interior mesh point and perform the averaging computation. We package the overall cooling step update in the function Average given below. Notice that the loop ranges are abbreviated because the boundary entries are not modified.

The cooling simulation is tantamount to repeatedly overwriting TVals with Average(TVals):

```
for k=1:nSteps
    TVals = Average(TVals);
end
```

The script Eg7_3 carries this out and produces the images that are displayed in Figure 7.7.

The Function Average

```
function B = Average(A)
% A is an m-by-n matrix
% B is an m-by-n matrix
% The first and last row and column of A and B are the same.
% Otherwise, B(i,j) is the average of A(i,j)'s four neighbors,
% A(i+1,j), A(i,j+1), A(i-1,j), and A(i,j-1).

[m,n] = size(A);
B = zeros(m,n);
for i=2:m-1
    for j=2:n-1
        B(i,j) = (A(i+1,j) + A(i,j+1) + A(i,j-1) + A(i-1,j))/4;
    end
end
```

The Script Eg7_3

```
% Script Eg7_3
% Simulates the cooling of a plate whose boundary temperature
% is fixed at zero.

% Establish the Initial Temperature Distribution...
a = 0; b = 6; n = 61; x = linspace(a,b,n);
c = 0; d = 4; m = 41; y = linspace(c,d,m);
TVals = fOnGrid(x,y,@T_plate);
TVals(1,:) = zeros(1,n); TVals(m,:) = zeros(1,n);
TVals(:,1) = zeros(m,1); TVals(:,n) = zeros(m,1);
nSteps = 200;
close all
figure
colormap('hot')
for tau=0:nSteps
    % Display the current temperature distribution...
    pcolor(TVals)
    shading interp
    caxis('manual')
    title(sprintf('tau = %1d',tau),'Fontsize',14)
    axis equal off
    pause(.1)
    shg
    % Update the temperature distribution...
    TVals = Average(TVals);
end
```

To graphically display the temperature distribution that is encoded in TVals, we use the function pcolor. This function essentially displays a matrix by color-coding each entry according to a *color map*. With a color map, a specific color is associated with real numbers in a certain interval. The command caxis('manual') maintains the same number-to-color mapping throughout the simulation which is necessary if we are to observe the cooling process. To produce a smooth display of the temperature variation, we use `shading interp` (interpolation). The built-in color map "`hot`" is used because it does a good job of communicating temperature ranges. For a more detailed discussion of color maps and shading, see §12.1 and §12.2.

tau = 0

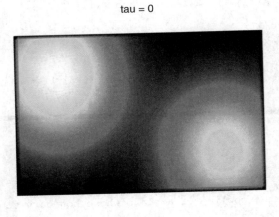

tau = 200

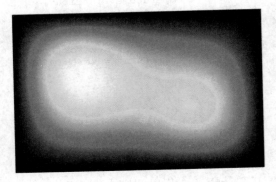

Figure 7.7. *Sample Output from the Script* `Eg7_3`.

Talking Point: Simulation on a Grid

The modeling of a physical phenomenon over a geometric region almost always proceeds by reporting relevant approximations on a grid. Accuracy usually improves as more mesh points are included. If the situation is evolving with time, then another attribute of the discretization is the "time step." Again, accuracy usually improves if shorter time steps are taken.

The penalty for smaller Δx's, Δy's, and Δt's is added work. In our problem, if we halve the grid spacing, then the amount of work associated with a call to `Average` is quadrupled. In actual applications there may be millions of grid points, especially in three-dimensional problems. The bottom line is that it is important to choose the discretization parameters intelligently so that accuracy requirements are met with a minimum of work.

MATLAB Review

Referencing Submatrices

Using the colon notation it is possible to extract and modify subarrays. For example, if

```
A = [1    2    3    4    5;...
     6    7    8    9   10;...
    11   12   13   14   15;...
    16   17   18   19   20];
```

then B = A(2:3,3:5) is the same as

```
B = [8    9   10;...
    13   14   15]
```

If A is as above,

```
C = [100 200 300;...
     400 500 600];
```

and A(2:3,3:5) = C, then

```
A = [1    2    3    4    5;...
     6    7  100  200  300;...
    11   12  400  500  600;...
    16   17   18   19   20];
```

pcolor, colormap, shading, and caxis

If A is a matrix, then pcolor(A) displays A as a color-coded mosaic of tiles. The color-coding is defined by the current *color map* which can be set to a number of predefined possibilities, e.g., colormap('hot'), colormap('cool'), etc. The mapping of numbers into the current color map can be controlled using caxis. For example, if v is a 2-vector, then caxis(v) ensures that numbers across the interval $[v(1), v(2)]$ are mapped uniformly into the range of colors that are specified by the underlying color map. To freeze the current number-to-color mapping, use caxis('manual'). Ordinarily, pcolor will display the matrix with visible tiles. For a "smoother" display of the color variation, execute the command shading interp.

Exercises

M7.3.1 How does the output produced by Eg7_3 change if the command shading interp is deleted? What if colormap('hot') is changed to colormap('cool')? What if the command caxis('manual') is deleted?

M7.3.2 In the function Average, what is the effect of changing the line

```
B(i,j) = (A(i,j+1) + A(i+1,j) + A(i,j-1) + A(i-1,j))/4;
```

to

```
A(i,j) = (A(i,j+1) + A(i+1,j) + A(i,j-1) + A(i-1,j))/4;
```

and adding the assignment B = A after the nested loop?

M7.3.3 Modify function Average so that the temperature at a point is dependent on *eight* neighbors instead of four.

P7.3.4 Suppose x(1:n) is an initialized row vector and that the value of x(1) and x(n) is zero. The fragment

```
y = zeros(1,n);
y(2:n-1) = (x(1:n-2)+x(3:n))/2;
```

is equivalent to

```
y = zeros(1,n);
for i=2:n-1
    y(i) = (x(i-1) + x(i+1))/2;
end
```

Using this vectorization idea, develop an implementation of Average that does not involve any loops. (Hint: B(2:m-1,2:n-1) is the average of four submatrices of A.)

P7.3.5 Modify Eg7_3 so that simulation terminates as soon as the maximum temperature is less that one-tenth the maximum temperature at the start of the simulation. How does the number of iterations depend on the mesh size parameters m and n?

P7.3.6 An interesting two-dimensional Monte Carlo simulation that physicists use to understand pole alignment in a magnetic substance involves the *Ising model*. The components of an Ising model are an n-by-n array A of *cells* that have one of two states ($+1$ and -1), a probability p, and a temperature T. During the simulation, the states of the cells change in a probabilistic fashion. Whether or not a particular cell changes state depends upon the temperature and the states of the four neighbor cells. (a) Complete the following function so that it performs as specified:

```
function  A = InitialIsing(n,p)
% p satisfies 0 < p < 1
% A is an n-by-n array in which A(i,j) is 1 with probability p
% and -1 with probability 1-p.
```

(b) Whether or not a cell changes state depends on its potential. The potential of cell (i, j) is the value of A(i,j)*(N+E+S+W), where N is the state of the north neighbor, E is the state of the east neighbor, S is the state of the south neighbor, and W is the state of the west neighbor. In the Ising setting,

The east neighbor of a cell (i,n) on the east edge is cell $(i,1)$.
The south neighbor of a cell (n, j) on the south edge is cell $(1, j)$.
The west neighbor of a cell $(i, 1)$ on the west edge is cell (i,n).
The north neighbor of a cell $(1, j)$ on the north edge is cell (n, j).

Write a function P = Potential(A,i,j) that returns the potential of cell (i, j). (c) In a *Metropolis sweep* the following is repeated n^2 times:

A cell is chosen at random. Let P be its potential.
If $P < 0$

    The cell's state is flipped.

else

    With probability $e^{-2P/T}$ the cell's state is flipped.

end

Here T is a given temperature. Write a function A = Sweep(A,T) that performs a Metropolis sweep and updates the state array A accordingly. (d) The Ising model captures the idea that subject to random fluctuations, a cell will tend to have the same state as its neighbors, i.e., its magnetic polarity tends to be that of its neighbors. Write a script that explores this behavior.

Chapter 8

Reordering

8.1 Cut and Deal
The Perfect Shuffle

8.2 Size Place
Sorting

Shuffling a deck of n cards, alphabetizing a list of n names so that it is alphabetical, and enumerating all possible itineraries that pass through a set of n cities each involves the notion of *permutation*. Behind every permutation is a reordering. Thus,

B : | 30 | 50 | 10 | 20 | 60 | 40 |

and

C : | 10 | 20 | 30 | 40 | 50 | 60 |

are permutations of

A : | 30 | 10 | 60 | 50 | 20 | 40 |

The array B is obtained from the array A by cutting the latter into a pair of half-length arrays and then alternately selecting values from the top and bottom "half-decks." The array C is obtained from the array A by reordering its values from smallest to largest. There are $6! = 720$ possible reorderings of A. In the language of grand tours, there are 720 possible itineraries should you wish to visit exactly once on a single trip the cities of New York, Chicago, Boston, Seattle, Houston, and Los Angeles.

An ability to compute with permutations and to reason about them is important. Programming permutations is an error-prone task because the underlying subscripting can be intricate. Thus, this chapter can be regarded as an opportunity to strengthen our ability to manipulate arrays. We consider the problem of shuffling a "card deck" and the problem of sorting the values in an array.

What we cover sets the stage for some important topics that are pursued in subsequent chapters. In §14.2 we discuss a recursive sort procedure known as merge sort that is considerably faster than the methods presented in §8.2. The discrete optimization problems considered in §15.1 and §15.2 involve working with permutations.

179

Programming Preview

Concepts

Permutations, bubble sort, insertion sort, perfect shuffle, data motion, worst-case analysis, best-case analysis, average-case analysis, complicated subscripting.

Language Features

`sort`: A built-in function to arrange the components of a real array so that they are ordered (e.g., from small to large).

Colon notation: The colon notation specifies a set of values with a fixed increment, e.g., 1:2:9. When used as array indices, the colon notation allows you to access multiple components of an array.

Subfunction: A function m-file may contain more than one function. The top function is the main function and is accessible by scripts and other functions on the search path; the remaining functions are subfunctions and are accessible only by the top function. Every function in the m-file begins with the keyword `function`.

MatTV

Video 11. Array Addressing

How to access subarrays.

8.1 Cut and Deal

Problem Statement

Suppose we are given a deck of eight cards which we proceed to cut in half:

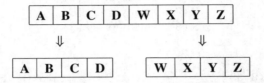

By alternately selecting cards from the two half-decks, we obtain the following *perfect shuffle*:

A	W	B	X	C	Y	D	Z

If we repeat this operation again,

A	C	W	Y	B	D	X	Z

and again,

A	B	C	D	W	X	Y	Z

then we have magically returned to where we began! Is this a coincidence? For larger card decks, will it require a huge number of perfect shuffles to restore the original order? We note that there are $52! \approx 10^{68}$ possible orderings for a common deck of playing cards. Our intuition suggests that a perfect-shuffling card shark would require centuries to pull off the restoration trick.

Write a program to investigate these questions. For decks of size $n = 2:2:100$ display the number of perfect shuffles that are required to restore the original order.

Program Development

We use vectors of real numbers to explore the properties of the perfect shuffle. Assume that $n = 2m$ where m is a positive integer. To be precise, the array $y(1:n)$ is a perfect shuffle of $x(1:n)$ if $x(1:m)$ is copied into $y(1:2:n)$ and $x(m+1:n)$ is copied into $y(2:2:n)$, e.g.,

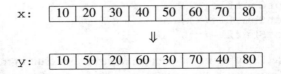

Informally, $x(1:m)$ is the "top half" of the card deck and $x(m+1:n)$ is the "bottom half" of the card deck. The dealing process places top-half cards into odd-indexed positions and bottom-half cards into even-indexed positions. For the $n = 8$ example we see that

$$
\begin{array}{lll}
\texttt{x(1)} & \text{maps to} & \texttt{y(1)} \\
\texttt{x(2)} & \text{maps to} & \texttt{y(3)} \\
\texttt{x(3)} & \text{maps to} & \texttt{y(5)} \\
\texttt{x(4)} & \text{maps to} & \texttt{y(7)} \\
\texttt{x(5)} & \text{maps to} & \texttt{y(2)} \\
\texttt{x(6)} & \text{maps to} & \texttt{y(4)} \\
\texttt{x(7)} & \text{maps to} & \texttt{y(6)} \\
\texttt{x(8)} & \text{maps to} & \texttt{y(8)}
\end{array}
$$

i.e.,

```
y = zeros(8,1);
for k=1:4
   y(2*k-1) = x(k);
   y(2*k)   = x(k+4);
end
```

Extrapolating from this we obtain the following function.

The Function `PerfectShuffle`

```
function y = PerfectShuffle(x)
% x is a column n-vector with n = 2m.
% y is a column n-vector that is the perfect shuffle of x.

% Initializations...
n = length(x);
y = zeros(n,1);
m = n/2;
for k=1:m
   % Save the kth value from the "top half" of the deck...
   y(2*k-1) = x(k);
   % Save the kth value from the "bottom half" of the deck...
   y(2*k) = x(k+m);
end
```

With this function we are set to explore the repetition of the perfect shuffle process. If x0 is a given real array having even length, then

```
x = PerfectShuffle(x0);
x = PerfectShuffle(x);
x = PerfectShuffle(x);
x = PerfectShuffle(x);
```

performs four perfect shuffles of the data and assigns the result to x. We want to keep shuffling until the current x is the same as x0. This is clearly a while-loop situation. Define the *restoration index* r_n to be the number of perfect shuffles required to restore a length-n array having distinct component values. A simple counter is all we need to compute this quantity.

> Initialize x0.

```
x = PerfectShuffle(x0);  r = 1;
while   x is different from x0
    x = PerfectShuffle(x);  r = r+1;
end
```

For the initialization of x0, we need a handy way to generate a column vector with distinct components. The vector of the first n integers is an easy way to do this:

```
x0 = (1:n)'
```

Regarding the termination criteria, observe that the boolean expression

```
sum(abs(x-x0))==0
```

is true if and only if x and x0 are identical. With these choices we obtain the following script.

The Script Eg8_1

```
% Script Eg8_1
% Displays the restoration index for a range of n-values

nVals = 2:2:60;
rVals = [];
for n = nVals
    % Initializations....
    x0 = (1:n)';
    x  = PerfectShuffle(x0);
    k = 1;
    % Keep shuffling until a match with x0...
    while sum(abs(x-x0))>0
        x = PerfectShuffle(x);
        k = k+1;
    end
    rVals = [rVals k];
end
% Display...
bar(nVals,rVals)
axis([0 62 0 60])
xlabel('n','Fontsize',14)
ylabel('Number of Perfect Shuffles ','Fontsize',14)
title('Restoration Via Repeated Perfect Shuffles','Fontsize',14)
grid on
shg
```

The results are displayed in Figure 8.1. We observe that only seven perfect shuffles are required to restore an ordinary deck of playing cards. More generally, it appears that r_n is much less than n, but that every so often, r_n almost equals n.

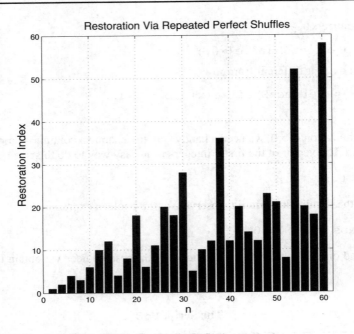

Figure 8.1. *Output from Script* Eg8_1.

Talking Point: Data Motion

In §3.1 we explored the notion of efficiency and used tic and toc to benchmark program fragments. For the examples considered, execution time was highly correlated with the underlying computer's arithmetic capabilities. In applications that involve large data sets, execution time frequently depends much more on the overheads associated with moving data between the computer's memory and its central processing unit where the actual computations are performed.

Here is an analogy that reveals the importance of minimizing "memory traffic." Suppose a human worker is in charge of updating student transcripts at the end of a semester. The worker sits at a table with the current semester grade reports. Across the room are 26 file cabinet drawers housing the student transcripts, one drawer for all the students whose last name begins with a specific letter. Assume that the worker's desk is limited in size and can only accommodate 52 student transcripts at any one time. One processing technique would be to (a) visit each file drawer and select a pair of folders and bring them back to the desk, (b) update the transcripts at the desk, and (c) return the updated transcripts to the filing cabinets. Even if the worker can update the records blazingly fast, overall execution time will not significantly improve unless the overheads associated with (a) and (c) are reduced. One way that this could be accomplished is to change the transcript access patterns. Instead of picking two transcripts from each drawer, it would be much quicker to grab 52 contiguously stored transcripts from a single drawer. The worker would then work his/her way through the file drawers in A-to-Z fashion. The point we are making is that with a little common sense, we can speed up the overall process even though the volume of arithmetic remains the same.

Because they involve minimal floating point computation, reordering algorithms such as the perfect shuffle and (in the next section) sorting are an excellent venue for developing an intuition about how data flows during the course of an algorithm.

MATLAB Review

Generating Integer Vectors

If n is a positive integer, then v = 1:n assigns to v a length-n row vector whose kth component equals k. Other examples include v = 1:2:10 which is equivalent to v = [1 3 5 7 9] and v = 5:-1:2 which is the same as v = [5 4 3 2].

for-Loop Revisited

In a for-loop, the values of the loop index variable can be specified explicitly in a vector. The fragment

```
x = zeros(1,6); a = 1;
for k = [5 3 6]
    x(k) = a; a = a+1;
end
```

assigns [0 0 2 0 1 3] to x.

Permutations and the Colon Notation

Suppose a and b are column n-vectors and idx is a permutation of 1:n. The statement b = a(idx) is equivalent to

```
for k=1:n
    j = idx(k); b(k) = a(j);
end
```

while b(idx) = a is equivalent to

```
for k=1:n
    j = idx(k); b(j) = a(k);
end
```

reshape

If A is an m-by-n array and a = reshape(A,m*n,1), then a is a length-mn vector obtained by stacking the columns of A. For example, if A = [1 2 3; 4 5 6], then

```
a = [1 ; 4 ; 2 ; 5 ; 3 ; 6]
```

Likewise, if B = reshape(a,2,3), then

```
B = [1 2 3; 4 5 6]
```

In general, if A is m-by-n and $m_1 n_1 = mn$, then B = reshape(A,m1,n1) is equivalent to

```
B = reshape(reshape(A,m*n,1),m1,n1)
```

Bar Graphs

If x and y are column n-vectors, then bar(x,y) produces a bar plot. The ith bar is centered around x(i) and its height is y(i). It is possible to stack bars, group bars, and color bars. The width of the bars can also be controlled.

Exercises

M8.1.1 Show how the loop in PerfectShuffle can be replaced by a pair of vector assignments.

M8.1.2 Show that if

```
y = PerfectShuffle(x);
n = length(y);
m = n/2;
y1 = reshape(reshape(x,m,2)',n,1);
```

then y and y1 are the same.

P8.1.3 Suppose we use a vector to represent a deck of n cards. We can "cut" the deck by taking $n/2$ cards from the middle of the deck and putting this half-deck of cards on the top. Complete the following function to perform this "cut":

```
function sd = Cut(d)
% Cut a deck of cards by moving half the cards from the middle to the top.
% d is a vector whose length is a multiple of 4.
% sd is the vector after cutting the deck d.
```

Write a script to find out whether the cards in a deck of 52 would cycle back to the original arrangement after repeated cuts as described above. If so, how many cuts are needed?

P8.1.4 Write a function y = Reverse(x) that reverses the order of values in a vector. Thus,

$$\boxed{2 \mid 1 \mid 5 \mid 8}$$

should be transformed into

$$\boxed{8 \mid 5 \mid 1 \mid 2}$$

P8.1.5 The *left shift* of a given array x(1:n) is obtained by moving each of its values one position "left" with the value in x(1) going to x(n):

(a) Complete the following function so that it performs as specified:

```
function y = LeftShift(x)
% x is a row n-vector and y is a row n-vector that is the left shift of x.
```

(b) Consider the following function:

```
function y = MultipleLeftShift(x,k)
% x is a row n-vector and k is an integer that satisfies 1<=k<n
% y is a row n-vector obtained by left-shifting x k times.
y = x;
for i=1:k
    y = LeftShift(y);
end
```

By thinking about the "final y," develop a noniterative implementation.

P8.1.6 Complete the following function so that it performs as specified:

```
function y = OddEvenStack(x)
% x is a column n-vector and n is even.
% y = [xOdd ; xEven] where xOdd is composed of the odd-index entries
% in x and xEven is composed of the even-indexed entries in x.
```

Thus, [10 ; 20 ; 30 ; 40 ; 50 ; 60] becomes [10 ; 30 ; 50 ; 20 ; 40 ; 60]. If x is a given column vector with even length, then what can you say about the vectors z1 and z2 defined as follows:

```
z1 = OddEvenStack(PerfectShuffle(x))
z2 = PerfectShuffle(OddEvenStack(x))
```

P8.1.7 Suppose we have a length-n vector and that n is a multiple of k. In a *perfect k-shuffle* we reorder the components by "dealing out" the cards to k "players" and then reassemble the deck, putting Player 1's cards first, Player 2's cards second, etc. For example, if $n = 12$, $k = 4$, and

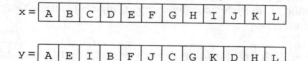

then

$$y = \boxed{A \;\; E \;\; I \;\; B \;\; F \;\; J \;\; C \;\; G \;\; K \;\; D \;\; H \;\; L}$$

is its perfect 4-shuffle.

Notice that in a perfect k-shuffle, Player i receives cards i, $i+k$, $i+2k$, etc. (a) Write a function
y = Perfect_k_Shuffle(x,k) that performs this permutation on x. Do not use reshape. (b)
Explain why

```
n = length(x);
m = n/k;
y = reshape(reshape(x,m,k)',n,1)
```

assigns to y the perfect k-shuffle of x.

P8.1.8 If A is an n-by-n array, then its left-column shift is obtained by shifting each column one position to the left with column 1 becoming column n. Thus,

20	10	30	50
70	30	10	40
80	20	30	90

is transformed into

10	30	50	20
30	10	40	70
20	30	90	80

Write a function B = LeftColShift(A) that carries out this permutation.

P8.1.9 Complete the following function so that it performs as specified:

```
function B = Stagger(A)
% A is an m-by-n array
% B is an m-by-n array with the property that its kth row is
% obtained by left-shifting A's kth row k times.
```

P8.1.10 Complete the following function so that it performs as specified:

```
function idx = MoveTo21(A,p,q)
% A is an n-by-n matrix with A(i,j) == A(j,i) for all i and j.
% Assume that 1 <= q < p <= n
% idx is a permutation of 1:n with the property that if
%     B = A(idx,idx), then B(2,1) = A(p,q).
```

8.2   Size Place

Problem Statement

A real vector a(1:n) is *sorted* if its values satisfy $a_1 \le a_2 \le \cdots \le a_n$. One way to make a vector "more sorted" is to systematically compare adjacent entries, swapping their values if they are out of order, e.g.,

30	50	10	60	**40**	**20**	$\Rightarrow$	30	50	10	60	20	40

30	50	10	**60**	**20**	40	$\Rightarrow$	30	50	10	20	60	40

30	50	**10**	**20**	60	40	$\Rightarrow$	30	50	10	20	60	40

30	**50**	**10**	20	60	40	$\Rightarrow$	30	10	50	20	60	40

30	**10**	50	20	60	40	$\Rightarrow$	10	30	50	20	60	40

Let us refer to this process as the *bubble process* because with the right-to-left scan, the smallest value rises to the top of the array like a bubble. The method of *bubble sort* involves the repeated application of the bubble process:

Apply bubble to a(1:n) $\Rightarrow$ Smallest value now in a(1)
Apply bubble to a(2:n) $\Rightarrow$ Second smallest value now in a(2)
Apply bubble to a(3:n) $\Rightarrow$ Third smallest value now in a(3)
                                    etc.

An alternative sort procedure can be based upon the *insert process*. To illustrate, assume

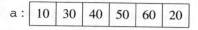

and observe that a(1:5) is sorted. We now proceed to "insert" a(6) into its proper location within the values of a(1:5) through the mechanism of repeated swapping:

| 10 | 30 | 40 | 50 | **60** | **20** | $\Rightarrow$ | 10 | 30 | 40 | 50 | 20 | 60 |

| 10 | 30 | 40 | **50** | **20** | 60 | $\Rightarrow$ | 10 | 30 | 40 | 20 | 50 | 60 |

| 10 | 30 | **40** | **20** | 50 | 60 | $\Rightarrow$ | 10 | 30 | 20 | 40 | 50 | 60 |

| 10 | **30** | **20** | 40 | 50 | 60 | $\Rightarrow$ | 10 | 20 | 30 | 40 | 50 | 60 |

The method of *insertion sort* is based on repeated application of the insert process:

$$\begin{array}{lll}\text{Apply insert to a(1:2)} & \Rightarrow & \text{a(1:2) is sorted}\\ \text{Apply insert to a(1:3)} & \Rightarrow & \text{a(1:3) is sorted}\\ \text{Apply insert to a(1:4)} & \Rightarrow & \text{a(1:4) is sorted}\\ & \text{etc.}\end{array}$$

Implement both bubble sort and insertion sort and, through experimentation and analysis, determine if one method is more efficient than the other.

Program Development

The comparison of two different sorting algorithms can proceed along several lines. Of course, we can get out the stop watch and compare execution times. But since all sorting methods involve comparisons and swapping, it is also interesting to tabulate how many times these operations are performed. Our plan is to implement bubble sort and insertion sort and contrast the number of comparisons and swaps that they require to sort a random input vector. We will also examine execution time using tic and toc.

We start by implementing the bubble process. For a length-*n* vector x, it requires a down-counting loop whose body oversees a compare and swap:

```
for k=n-1:-1:1
    if x(k+1) < x(x)
        t = x(k+1); x(k+1) = x(k); x(k) = t;
    end
end
```

The function Bubble, shown below, performs this task. To facilitate the counting of comparisons and swappings, it includes output parameters C and S that return these efficiency metrics.

The Function `Bubble`

```
function [y,C,S] = Bubble(x)
% x is a column n-vector.
% y is a column n-vector obtained by applying the bubble
%    process to x.
% C is the number of required comparisons.
% S is the number of required swaps.
n = length(x); C = 0; S = 0;
for k=n-1:-1:1
    C = C + 1;
    if x(k+1) < x(k)
        t = x(k+1);
        x(k+1) = x(k);
        x(k) = t;
        S = S + 1;
    end
end
y = x;
```

To derive the method of bubble sort, we note from the preceding discussion that after k applications of the bubble process, the k smallest values of the input array are in their final "resting place." Thus, if $n = 6$, then the fragment

```
[x,C,S]  = Bubble(x)
[x(2:6),C,S] = Bubble(x(2:6))
[x(3:6),C,S] = Bubble(x(3:6))
[x(4:6),C,S] = Bubble(x(4:6))
[x(5:6),C,S] = Bubble(x(5:6))
```

overwrites x with the sorted version of x. In general we have

```
n = length(x);
for k=1:n-1
    [x(k:n),C,S] = Bubble(x(k:n));
end
```

The full implementation is given below in the function `BubbleSort`. We use a `while`-loop instead of a `for`-loop because we want to terminate bubble sort if the array becomes sorted before the $(n-1)$st pass through the loop. How do we know when the array is sorted early? Think about the number of swaps S in `Bubble(x)`. If x is sorted, then the number of swaps performed on x would be zero.

It is important to understand the `while`-loop termination criteria. The iteration comes to a halt if (`k==1 || S>0`) is false or if `k <= n-1` is false. The former happens only if both the boolean expressions `k > 1` and `S == 0` are true. This means that no swapping occurred during the call to `Bubble`, indicating that the array is sorted. Note that when we enter the loop, S is not initialized. However, because of shortcircuiting, the condition `S > 0` is not evaluated when `k == 1` is true. (See §1.2 for discussion of shortcircuiting.)

The Function BubbleSort

```
function [y,TotalC,TotalS] = BubbleSort(x)
% x is a column n-vector.
% y is a column n-vector obtained by permuting the values in x so
%    that they are ordered from smallest to largest.
% TotalC is the total number of required comparisons.
% TotalS is the total number of required swaps.

n = length(x);
TotalC = 0;
TotalS = 0;
k = 1;
while (k==1 || S>0) && k<=n-1
    [x(k:n),C,S] = Bubble(x(k:n));
    k = k+1;
    TotalC = TotalC + C;
    TotalS = TotalS + S;
end
y = x;
```

We next implement the method of *insertion sort*. The central operation involves the insertion of an array value into a sorted subarray. Formalizing the discussion above, if $1 < m \leq n$ and x(1:m) has the property that x(1:m-1) is sorted, then we can sort x(1:m) by moving the value of x(m) a sufficient number of "slots" to the left:

```
k = m-1;
while k>=1 && x(k)>x(k+1)
    t = x(k+1); x(k+1) = x(k); x(k) = t;
    k = k-1;
end
```

The full implementation is shown in function Insert.

The Function Insert

```
function [y,C,S] = Insert(x)
% x is a column m-vector with x(1:m-1) sorted.
% y is a column m-vector obtained by applying the insert
%    process to x.
% C is the number of required comparisons.
% S is the number of required swaps.

m = length(x); S = 0;
k = m-1;
while k>=1 && x(k)>x(k+1)
    t = x(k+1); x(k+1) = x(k); x(k) = t; S = S+1;
    k = k-1;
end
y = x;
C = S+1;
```

As suggested above, the method of insertion sort is basically just a sequence of inserts:

```
for  k=2:n
        Apply Insert to x(1:k).
end
```

The implementation of the function `InsertionSort` is given below.

The Function `InsertionSort`

```
function [y,TotalC,TotalS] = InsertionSort(x)
% x is a column n-vector.
% y is a column n-vector obtained by permuting the values in x so
%    that they are ordered from smallest to largest.
% TotalC is the total number of required comparisons.
% TotalS is the total number of required swaps.

n = length(x); TotalC = 0; TotalS = 0;
for k=2:n
    [x(1:k),C,S] = Insert(x(1:k));
    TotalC = TotalC + C;
    TotalS = TotalS + S;
end
y = x;
```

The script `Eg8_2` given below can be used to build intuition about the performance of bubble sort and insertion sort. It starts by displaying the number of comparisons and swaps for various values of n. The comparison of a pair of real numbers involves very little work— actually just a floating point subtraction and a check of the resulting sign. Why bother to count comparisons if they are so cheap? The reason has to do with the fact that we can apply these algorithms to sort other data objects besides real vectors. For example, in a computer graphics computation we may have to sort physical objects from "front to back" in order to determine what an observer "sees." The underlying geometric computations required for the comparison could be quite costly. Thus, although the number of comparisons is not a serious overhead when sorting real arrays, it can be an important factor in other settings.

The number of required swaps is also an important performance metric for a sorting algorithm since it measures the number of memory accesses. As we discussed in §8.1, the overall efficiency of a method that manipulates very large data sets tends to depend more on the volume of memory traffic than on the volume of arithmetic.

In looking at the sample output of the script `Eg8_2`, we observe two important things. First, if we double n, then work appears to increase by a factor of four. Bubble sort and insertion sort are said to be *quadratic* because work is proportional to the square of n. Second, we note that bubble sort involves about twice the number of comparisons as insertion sort. This is because the latter does not perform any superfluous comparisons by virtue of its `while`-loop structure in the function `insert` and the fact that it does *not* always deal with length-n arrays like bubble sort.

The Script Eg8_2

```
% Script Eg8_2
% Compares bubble sort and insertion sort.

% Tabulate swaps and comparisons for a random x ...
clc
disp('                Bubble Sort                    Insertion Sort  ')
disp('   n     Compares     Swaps        Compares        Swaps')
disp('-----------------------------------------------------------------')
for n = [10 20 40 80 160 320 640 1280]
    x = rand(n,1);
    [yB,TCBubble,TSBubble] = BubbleSort(x);
    [yI,TCInsert,TSInsert] = InsertionSort(x);
    fprintf('%5d    %8d %8d      %8d    %8d   \n', ...
            n, TCBubble,TSBubble,  TCInsert,TSInsert)
end

N = 50000;
x = rand(N,1);
tic
[yB,TCBubble,TSBubble] = BubbleSort(x);
TimeBubble = toc;
tic
[yI,TCInsert,TSINsert] = InsertionSort(x);
TimeInsert = toc;
fprintf('\n\nTimeBubble/TimeInsert = %5.3f   (N = %1d) \n', ...
        TimeBubble/TimeInsert, N)
```

Sample Output from the Script Eg8_2

| | Bubble Sort | | Insertion Sort | |
n	Compares	Swaps	Compares	Swaps
10	45	34	43	34
20	187	68	87	68
40	765	383	422	383
80	3124	1440	1519	1440
160	12444	6923	7082	6923
320	51012	25378	25697	25378
640	204227	101580	102219	101580
1280	818125	407157	408436	407157

```
TimeBubble/TimeInsert = 1.462   (N = 50000)
```

The script Eg8_2 also benchmarks a large ($n = 50000$) example and confirms that insertion sort is indeed the faster of the two methods. It is important to keep in mind that execution time depends on more than just the number of comparisons and swaps. For example, there is an overhead associated with a call to the subfunction bubble or insert. See problem P8.2.6.

Talking Point: Measuring Performance

Our assessment of bubble sort and insertion sort is based on how they perform on random input vectors. The table produced is based on running just one example for each chosen value of n. But even if we ran thousands of random examples for each n we would essentially reach the same conclusion. On average, insertion sort involves half the number of comparisons as bubble sort. This is *average case* analysis.

It is often instructive to examine the performance of an algorithm when it is applied to "special" input vectors. How do our sorting algorithms perform on input vectors that are arranged from big to little, precisely the opposite of what we want? It turns out that in this *worst case* setting, insertion sort requires (approximately) the same number of comparisons and swaps as bubble sort. This is because the while-loop in insert never terminates early—it always runs the loop variable k on down to one instead of (on average) terminating at the halfway point.

At the other extreme, if the input vector is already sorted from little to big, then both sorting methods require approximately n comparisons to discover the fact—a *best-case* scenario.

MATLAB Review

sort

If x is a vector, then y = sort(x) assigns to y the sorted version of x. The values are arranged in ascending order. The output vector y has the same orientation as x. To sort from largest to smallest, use y = sort(x,'descend'). A call of the form [y,idx] = sort(x) assigns to idx a permutation of the integer vector 1:n with the property that y = x(idx).

median and mean

If x is a real array, then m = median(x) assigns to m the median of the component values in x, while a = mean(x) assigns to a the average of the component values.

Benchmarking with tic and toc

To time how long it takes a code fragment to execute, use tic and toc as follows:

```
tic
  Code Fragment
T = toc;
```

This assigns the elapsed time (in seconds) to T. To accommodate clock granularity in situations where the fragment benchmarked is "too fast," use repetition:

```
tic
for i=1:nRepeat
    Code Fragment
end
T = toc/nRepeat;
```

Set the value of nRepeat so that a few seconds elapse from the tic to the toc.

Returning a Subset of Output Values

If a function MyF is designed to return output values $Out\_1, Out\_2, \ldots, Out\_n$, then it is possible to use MyF so that only $Out\_1, Out\_2, \ldots, Out\_k$ are returned where $k < n$. Thus, y = BubbleSort(x) returns the sorted version of x in y. The number of comparisons C and swaps S is not returned.

Exercises

M8.2.1 Implement a function y = sort4(x) that sorts a length-4 vector. Organize your implementation so that it minimizes the maximum number of comparisons.

M8.2.2 Analogous to the MATLAB sort function, add an output parameter idx to the function InsertionSort with the property that if [y,TotalC,TotalS,idx] = InsertionSort(x), then y = x(idx).

M8.2.3 What would happen if the while-statement in BubbleSort is changed to

```
while S>0 && k<=n-1
```

M8.2.4 The script Eg8_2 uses rand to generate the test arrays. Do the results change if randn is used?

M8.2.5 Write a script that produces a bar plot of sort(randn(n,1)).

P8.2.6 Rearrange the implementation of InsertionSort so that it does not make use of the subfunction Insert. (Review §5.2 for a discussion about the efficiencies associated with replacing a function call with in-line code.) Using tic and toc, see if it pays to make Insert in-line.

P8.2.7 Define the *select* process as follows:

```
function y = Select(x)
% x is an n-vector
% y is x with x(1) and x(m) swapped where x(m) is the minimum value in x.
```

The method of *selection sort* is based on the idea that if we sequentially apply Select to x(1:n), x(2:n), x(3:n), etc., then x will be sorted. To faciliate comparison with bubble sort and insertion sort, implement Select with extra output parameters C and S analogous to Insert. Then implement a function [y,TotalC,TotalS] = SelectionSort(x). Modify Eg8_2 so that it compares the selection sort method with BubbleSort and InsertionSort.

P8.2.8 Note that if n is a positive integer and delta is small, then

```
x = sort(randn(n,1)) + delta*randn(n,1)
```

assigns to x a "nearly" sorted vector. Modify Eg8_2 so that it examines the relative behavior of bubble sort and insertion sort for various nearly sorted input vectors.

P8.2.9 Using the MATLAB sort function, implement and benchmark the following function:

```
function m = MyMedian(x)
% x is a column n-vector and m is the median of its values.
```

Compare with the built-in function median.

P8.2.10 Complete the following function so that it performs as specified:

```
function B = DiagSort(A)
% A is an n-by-n matrix.
% B is the n-by-n matrix A(idx,idx) where idx is a permutation of 1:n
%     so that B(1,1) >= B(2,2) >= ... >= B(n,n)
```

Chapter 9

Search

9.1 Patterns in Proteins
Linear Search

9.2 A Roman Numeral Phone Book
Binary Search

9.3 Changing Sign
Bisecting for Roots

Searching through a set of objects (numbers, strings, etc.) for a particular element is one of the most fundamental of all computations. In this chapter we consider two basic methods: linear search and binary search. A continuous version of the latter is also presented.

Consider the case of looking for a value x in a numerical array `a(1:n)`. In linear search we sequentially check `a(1)`, `a(2)`, `a(3)`, etc., stopping as soon as we find x. Of course, we might conclude after scanning `a(1:n)` in its entirety that x does not occur in the array of values. In contrast, binary search is a "divide-and-conquer" strategy that requires the input data to be ordered. It involves a sequence of endpoint–midpoint comparisons of ever-shorter subarrays. The process by which we humans locate a name in a telephone directory is similar to binary search.

Our first two examples involve strings. A protein is a sequence of amino acids of which there are twenty. Each amino acid has several possible 3-letter "names." A string representation for a protein is simply the concatenation of amino acid names. Our goal is to scan the protein string, counting the number of each amino acid. The scanning process is linear. A second example involves searching for a specific string in a list of "alphabetized" strings. In particular, we look for the occurrence of a Roman numeral in a Roman numeral "phone book." We develop a binary search procedure that can be used to determine if the given string represents a valid Roman numeral and if so, its numerical value.

Searching an array is a discrete, finite process. One can also search the continuous real line for a root of a given function f, and the method of bisection is one of many strategies for doing this. It can be regarded as a continuous version of binary search, providing yet another opportunity to contrast the discrete and the continuous.

Programming Preview

Concepts

Search, search space, linear search, binary search, bisection, divide and conquer, roots of functions, approximate roots, strings, substrings, concatenation, string manipulation, efficiency, big-O notation.

Language Features

String: A sequence of characters, including letters, digits, symbols, and blanks, enclosed in quotation marks, e.g., `'search 4 this!'`. A string is a row vector of characters. It may be empty: `' '`

`strcmp`: A function to check whether two strings are identical.

Boolean-Valued Function: A function that returns the *logical* value 0 or 1.

`lower`, `upper`: Functions to convert letters into lower- or uppercase.

`blank`: A function that returns a user-specified number of blanks.

Cell Array: An array whose components can be a combination of things: scalars, matrices, strings, and even other cell arrays.

`length`, `size`: Functions that return the dimensions of a cell array.

Passing a function as an argument to another function.

Special Prerequisites

§9.3 is somewhat mathematical and draws upon the discussion of floating point arithmetic in §4.3.

MatTV

Video 18. Characters & Strings

How to work with strings as arrays of characters. How to "compute" with characters based on their ASCII values.

Video 19. Cell Arrays

How to create and use cell arrays, focusing on their use with strings.

9.1 Patterns in Proteins

Problem Statement

A DNA molecule is a very long chain composed of just four different nucleotides: adenine (A), guanine (G), cytosine (C), and thymine (T). Thus, a DNA fragment can be represented as a string made up of these four letters, e.g.,

$$\text{ATCGTATTGCACATTCTACGGGTAAATGCA} \tag{9.1}$$

A *gene* is a DNA fragment that codes for a particular protein. For this purpose, 3-letter *codons* are used to identify the precise amino acid sequence that defines a protein, e.g.,

$$\text{ATC-GTA-TTG-CAC-ATT-CTA-CGG-GTA-AAT-GCA.}$$

This coding scheme could handle up to $64 = 4 \cdot 4 \cdot 4$ different amino acids. Remarkably, the entire protein world is built up from just twenty different amino acids, and so there is a measure of redundancy as shown in Figure 9.1. The codons used to mark the beginning and end of a protein encoding (TAA, TAG, and TGA) will be ignored in this section.

Index	Amino Acid	Mnemonic	DNA Codons
1	Alanine	Ala	GCT GCC GCA GCG
2	Arginine	Arg	CGT CGC CGA CGG AGA AGG
3	Asparagine	Asn	AAT AAC
4	Aspartic Acid	Asp	GAT GAC
5	Cysteine	Cys	TGT TGC
6	Glutamic Acid	Glu	CAA CAG
7	Glutamine	Gln	GAA GAG
8	Glycine	Gly	GGT GGC GGA GGG
9	Histidine	His	CAT CAC
10	Isoleucine	Ile	ATT ATC ATA
11	Leucine	Leu	CTT CTC CTA CTG TTA TTG
12	Lysine	Lys	AAA AAG
13	Methionine	Met	ATG
14	Phenylalanine	Phe	TTT TTC
15	Proline	Pro	CCT CCC CCA CCG
16	Serine	Ser	TCT TCC TCA TCG AGT AGC
17	Threonine	Thr	ACT ACC ACA ACG
18	Tryptophan	Trp	TGG
19	Tyrosine	Tyr	TAT TAC
20	Valine	Val	GTT GTC GTA GTG
	Stop	Ter	TAA TAG TGA

Figure 9.1. *The Codon Dictionary.*

Using this "dictionary" we see that the sequence of amino acids encoded by the (imaginary) gene (9.1) is

$$\text{Ile-Val-Leu-His-Ile-Leu-Arg-Val-Asn-Ala.} \tag{9.2}$$

Write a script that generates a random protein (string) such as (9.1) and produces a bar plot that displays the frequency of each amino acid.

Program Development

Here is a framework for generating a random protein consisting of *n* amino acids:

```
P = '';
for k=1:n
    Assign to nextAA a random length-3 string          (9.3)
    that corresponds to an amino acid.
    P = [P nextAA];
end
```

This is very similar to how we would organize a numerical summation. P is a string version of the running sum variable. It is initialized as the *empty string*, i.e., the string consisting of no characters. We then repeatedly "add in" the string housed in nextAA using the operation of *concatenation*. To concatenate strings in MATLAB, simply enclose the participant strings with square brackets. Thus, if P houses 'GCCATT' and the value of nextAA is 'TTG', then

```
P = [P nextAA]
```

assigns to P the string 'GCCATTTTG'. When we talk about strings like this, it is understood that the single quotes are not part of the string. They simply serve as *delimiters*.

There are several string computations associated with the refinement of (9.3). First, we set up a single string that is the concatenation of the 61 codon triplets:

```
ListOfAA = ['GCTGCCGCAGCGCGTCGCCGACGGAGAAGGAATAACGATGACTGT'...
            'TGCCAACAGGAAGAGGGTGGCGGAGGGCATCACATTATCATACTT'...
            'CTCCTACTGTTATTGAAAAAGATGTTTTTCCCTCCCCCACCGTCT'...
            'TCCTCATCGAGTAGCACTACCACAACGTGGTATTACGTTGTCGTAGTG'];
```

(Recall that we are ignoring the three "stop" codons.) Next, we compute a random integer between and including 1 and 61,

```
j = ceil(rand(1)*61))
```

and use it to extract a codon substring from ListOfAA. Accessing parts of a string is similar to accessing parts of a vector. This is not surprising since a string can be regarded as a vector of characters. The colon notation is used:

```
k1 = 3*(j-1)+1;
k2 = 3*j;
nextAA = ListOfAA(k1:k2);
```

This assigns to nextAA the string comprised of the characters in positions $3(j-1)+1$, $3(j-1)+2$, and $3(j-1)+3$, i.e., the jth codon in ListOfAA. All of these computations are encapsulated in the function RandomProtein.

The Function `RandomProtein`

```
function P = RandomProtein(n)
% Generates a "random" protein consisting of n amino acids.
% P is a length-3n string that encodes the protein.

% Concatenation of the 61 possible amino acids...
ListOfAA = ['GCTGCCGCAGCGCGTCGCCGACGGAGAAGGAATAACGATGACTGT'...
            'TGCCAACAGGAAGAGGGTGGCGGAGGGCATCACATTATCATACTT'...
            'CTCCTACTGTTATTGAAAAAGATGTTTTTCCCTCCCCCACCGTCT'...
            'TCCTCATCGAGTAGCACTACCACAACGTGGTATTACGTTGTCGTAGTG'];
P = '';
for k=1:n
    % Randomly select the next amino acid...
    j = ceil(61*rand(1));
    nextAA = ListOfAA(3*(j-1)+1:3*j);
    % and incorporate it into P...
    P = [P nextAA];
end
```

Now that we have a method for generating a string P that encodes a protein, our task is to produce an amino acid frequency plot. This requires that we scan P codon by codon and tabulate the number of times each amino acid occurs. A vector of counters does the job:

```
count = zeros(20,1);
for j=1:n
```

Extract the jth codon. (9.4)

Determine the mnemonic of the associated amino acid. (9.5)

Using the mnemonic, assign the index of the associated amino acid to i. (9.6)

```
    count(i) = count(i) + 1;
end
```

Regarding (9.4), the jth codon substring occupies positions $3(j-1)+1$, $3(j-1)+2$, and $3(j-1)+3$ and so this pseudocode fragment refines to

```
s = P(3*(j-1)+1:3*j)
```

The determination of the mnemonic and its index requires accessing the information in the codon dictionary shown in Figure 9.1. We break down this task by writing functions that encapsulate key subcomputations.

We start by building a 61-by-7 *character array* that encodes the codon dictionary. A character array can be regarded as a matrix of characters whose rows are strings. For this to make sense, each row must have exactly the same number of characters. Here is a character array that houses the codon dictionary:

```
C = ['ATT Ile' ;...
     'ATC Ile' ;...
     'ATA Ile' ;...
     'CTT Leu' ;...
     'CTC Leu' ;...

     etc.

     'GTC Val' ;...
     'GTA Val' ;...
     'GTG Val'];
```

Each row of C is a length-7 string. Positions 1, 2, and 3 name a codon and positions 5, 6, and 7 specify the corresponding amino acid mnemonic. Thus, C(5,1:3) and C(5,5:7) tell us that "CTC" codes for the amino acid leucine. The colon notation can be used to "grab" parts of a row in a character array just as it can be used to access part of a row in a two-dimensional numerical array. To support the easy acquisition of the codon dictionary data, we implement the following function.

The Function CodonDictionary

```
function C = CodonDictionary()
% C is a 61-by-7 character array.
% For k=1:61, C(k,1:3) specifies a codon and C(k,5:7) is the
%    corresponding amino acid.

C = [ 'ATT Ile' ; ...
      'ATC Ile' ; ...
      'ATA Ile' ; ...
      'CTT Leu' ; ...

      etc.
```

This is an example of a function that has no input parameters. A statement of the form

```
C = CodonDictionary()
```

simply assigns to C the 61-by-7 character array defined above.

With respect to (9.5), our next task is to implement a function that accepts a codon and returns the mnemonic of the associated amino acid, i.e.,

```
function a = FindMnemonic(s)
% s is a 3-character string that specifies an amino acid.
% a is the amino acid's 3-letter mnemonic.
```

The character array C plays a critical role. Suppose the input codon s is 'CTT'. We look for a match between s and the strings C(1,1:3), C(2,1:3), etc. In this example, success occurs when s is compared with C(4,1:3). The mnemonic for the associated amino acid is specified by C(4,5:7). The search process is clearly a while-loop task:

```
   k = 1
   while   s does not match the kth codon
        k = k+1;
   end
```
(9.7)
```
   Assign to a the mnemonic associated
   with the kth codon.
```

The while condition requires the comparison of two strings, and for that we use the built-in function strcmp:

The value of strcmp(s1,s2) is 1 if and only if the two strings housed in s1 and s2 are identical. Thus, the iteration in pseudocode (9.8) continues as long as the value of strcmp(s, C(k,1:3)) is 0. Here is the full implementation of FindMnemonic.

The Function FindMnemonic

```
function a = FindMnemonic(s)
% s is a 3-character string that specifies an amino acid.
% a is the amino acid's 3-letter mnemonic.

C = CodonDictionary();
k = 1;
while strcmp(s,C(k,1:3))==0
     k = k+1;
end
a = C(k,5:7);
```

It is particularly important to understand the dynamics of the while-loop that oversees the search for the codon match. It is an example of *linear search*. Note that after the loop terminates, the value of k names the row where the amino acid mnemonic can be found. The character array C has 61 rows, and we might be concerned about the possibility of a subscript out-of-range error. However, we know that the value of s must occur among the substrings C(1,1:3), C(2,1:3),...,C(61,1:3), so an out-of-range error cannot occur.

Returning to the top-level pseudocode solution and the fragment (9.6), we see that the last thing to deal with is the determination of the amino acid index given the mnemonic. Similar to FindMnemonic, our solution function FindIndex involves using a character array that encodes information from the codon dictionary.

The derivation of this function is very similar to the derivation of FindMnemonic and is omitted. With both FindMnemonic and FindIndex available, we are able to complete the implementation of a solution script to the section problem.

The Function `FindIndex`

```
function i = FindIndex(s)
% s is a 3-letter mnemonic that names an amino acid.
% i is the index of the amino acid named by s.

% A is a 20-by-3 character array where A(i,:) names
% the ith amino acid..
A = [ 'Ala' ; 'Arg' ; 'Asn' ; 'Asp' ; 'Cys';...
      'Glu' ; 'Gln' ; 'Gly' ; 'His' ; 'Ile';...
      'Leu' ; 'Lys' ; 'Met' ; 'Phe' ; 'Pro';...
      'Ser' ; 'Thr' ; 'Trp' ; 'Tyr' ; 'Val'];
i = 1;
while strcmp(s,A(i,:))==0
    i = i+1;
end
```

The Script `Eg9_1`

```
% Script Eg9_1
% Amino acid frequency counts
n = input('Enter the number of amino acids: ');
P = RandomProtein(n);

count = zeros(20,1);
for j=1:n
    s = P(3*(j-1)+1:3*j);
    a = FindMnemonic(s);
    i = FindIndex(a);
    count(i) = count(i)+1;
end
bar(count(1:20))
title(sprintf('n = %d',n),'Fontsize',14)
```

The size of the random protein is obtained via `input`. The resulting bar plot is shown in Figure 9.2. We mention that this plot, and many of the others in the pages that follow, incorporates various "pretty plotting" features. For example, the tick marks along the x-axis are labelled by the mnemonics. Appendix A discusses how to do this sort of thing. To save space and to avoid being distracted by detail, we will generally omit pretty-plotting commands from displayed scripts and functions.

Talking Point: Linear Search, Linear Time

When applied to a length-n array, linear search is an $O(n)$ algorithm. Roughly speaking, this means that if the length of the array increases by a factor of 10, then the execution time increases by a factor of 10. In other words, the effort of linear search is proportional to the length of the array. This assumes that the values in the array are randomly ordered and that the target value is random.

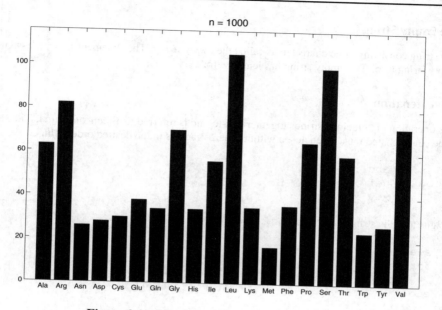

Figure 9.2. *Sample Output from Script* Eg9_1.

If the target value is in the array, then on average, $n/2$ comparisons are required. If possible, it is best to situate the more frequently occurring target values near the beginning of the array—this will prompt an early exit from the while-loop and lead to a more efficient implementation.

MATLAB Review

Strings and Substrings

A string is a sequence of characters enclosed with single quotes. All characters are allowed. Thus, 'abc', '1234', and 'r u 20 or 21?' are all valid strings. If a single quote is to be part of the string, double it: 'She"s one of New York"s finest'. The assignment s = 'abcde' assigns a 5-character string to s. A string is actually a row vector of characters, so s = 'abcde' is the same as s = ['a' 'b' 'c' 'd' 'e']. Individual characters can be referenced in much the same way as components in a real vector. Thus, x = s(2) assigns the length-1 string 'b' to x. Substrings can be specified using the colon notation. The statement y = s(3:5) assigns the string 'cde' to y.

length

The number of characters that make up a string can be determined using the length function. The fragment

```
s = 'abcdef';
n = length(s);
```

results in n having the value of 6.

The Empty String

The string consisting of no characters is called the *empty string*. The statement s = '' assigns the empty string to s. The empty string has length zero.

Concatenation

The operation of "glueing" strings together end-to-end is referred to as *concatenation*. The strings to be concatenated must be enclosed within square brackets in the desired order. Thus,

```
x = 'abc';
y = 'def';
z = [x y x];
```

assigns to z the string 'abcdefabc'. The fragment

```
sleep = 'z';
for k=1:10
    sleep = [sleep sleep];
end
```

assigns to sleep a string composed of 1024 z's.

blanks

The statement s = blanks(n) assigns the string of *n* blanks to s.

lower, upper

If s is a string, lower(s) replaces all uppercase letters in s with their lowercase counterparts. Likewise, upper(s) replaces all lowercase letters with their uppercase counterparts.

String Equality

Suppose S1 and S2 are strings. The expression strcmp(S1,S2) has the boolean value of 1 (true) if S1 and S2 are identical and has the boolean value of 0 (false) if they are not identical. Thus, strcmp('abc','abc') is 1, while strcmp('abc ','a bc') is 0.

find

If x is a real vector, then y = find(x) assigns to y the vector of *subscripts* associated with x's nonzero entries. Thus,

```
x = [2 0 0 3 4 2 0 5];
y = find(x);
```

assigns the vector [1 4 5 6 8] to y. The typical usage is to find the components of a vector that meet certain criteria, e.g., find(abs(x)>10) returns the *positions* at which x is greater than 10 in absolute value. The assignment x(find(abs(x)>10)) = 0 sets to zero all components of x that are greater than 10 in absolute value.

Character Arrays

A character array is an assembly of equal-length strings arranged row by row. The assignment

```
C = ['abcd' ; '12m4' ; '?*;!'];
```

establishes C as a 3-by-4 character array. A character array is a matrix whose entries are single characters. Thus, x = C(2,3) is the character 'm'. The colon notation is handy for accessing particular rows; i.e., s = C(3,:) is the third row of C, which is the string '?*;!'.

Exercises

M9.1.1 Write a script that uses input to solicit a string. If the last character in the string is 'y', then it should be deleted and replaced with 'ies'. The modified string should be displayed. If the input string is 'story', then the output should be 'stories'.

M9.1.2 Write a script that uses input to solicit a string. It should then display the concatenation of the input string with its reverse. Thus, if the input string is 'abcd', then the output should be 'abcddcba'.

M9.1.3 Write a function a = PosAve(x) that takes a real vector x that has at least one positive entry and returns the average of all the positive entries. Your implementation should not have any loops. Make effective use of find.

P9.1.4 Complete the following function so that it performs as specified:

```
function s = Compress(t)
% t is a string
% s is obtained by deleting all the blanks in t.
% Thus, if t = 'ab cd efg', then s should be assigned 'abcdef'
```

P9.1.5 Complete the following function so that it performs as specified:

```
function  n = CountChar(c,A)
% c is a character
% A is a character array
% n is the number of times c occurs in A.
```

P9.1.6 In the DNA double helix, two strands twist together and "face" each other. The two strands are reverse-complementary, i.e., reading one strand in reverse order and exchanging each nucleotide with its complement gives the other strand. Nucleotides A and T are complementary; C and G are complementary. For example, given the DNA sequence

AGTAGCAT

the reverse sequence is

TACGATGA

so the reverse complement is

ATGCTACT

Write a function rComplement(dna) to return the reverse complement of a DNA strand. Assume that dna contains only the letters 'A', 'T', 'C', and 'G'.

P9.1.7 Complete the following function so that it performs as specified:

```
function k = FindSubstring(S1,S2)
% Find the first occurrence of string S1 in string S2.
% If S1 is a substring of S2, then k is the position of the first
%    matching character of the first match in S2.
% If S1 is not a substring of S2, then k is zero.
```

P9.1.8 Write a function countPattern(dna,p) that returns the number of times a pattern p occurs in dna. Note that if p is longer than dna, then p appears in dna zero times.

P9.1.9 Complete the following function so that it performs as specified:

```
function x = CountLetters(s)
% s is a string.
% x is a 26-by-1 vector with the property that x(1) is the number
% of occurrences of 'a' in s, x(2) is the number of occurrences
% of 'b' in s, etc.
```

Using CountLetters, write a script that inputs a string and produces a bar plot that displays the frequency of each letter in the alphabet.

P9.1.10 Modify Eg9_1 so that it displays a 20-by-20 matrix A with the property that A(i,j) is the number of times amino acid j follows amino acid i in the input protein.

9.2   A Roman Numeral Phone Book

Problem Statement

A Roman numeral is a string composed from the characters I, V, X, L, C, D, and M. Each is associated with a particular numerical value:

Numeral	I	V	X	L	C	D	M
Value	1	5	10	50	100	500	1000

Some Roman numeral strings are easy to evaluate because they are straightforward summations, e.g.,

$$MDCCVII = 1000 + 500 + 100 + 100 + 5 + 1 + 1 = 1707.$$

Things are more complicated if a smaller numeral precedes a larger numeral:

$$MCDXLIV = 1000 - 100 + 500 - 10 + 50 - 1 + 5 = 1444.$$

Thus, I, X, and C have a negative value if they precede a larger numeral. Other rules concern order and repetition. For example, D can be preceded only by M and C. C can be preceded only by M, D, C, or X. There can be at most one V, D, or L. There can be no more than three X's in a row, and so forth.

Write a script that determines whether or not an input string is a valid Roman numeral. If it is, the script should display its numerical value.

Program Development

A reasonable solution procedure would be to codify the rules of Roman numeral formation against which the input string could be checked. If the string is valid, then the appropriate signed summation could be computed.

We will pursue a different approach that involves (a) setting up a "phone book" consisting of all valid Roman numeral strings, (b) alphabetizing the phone book by treating the numerals as "names," (c) using the method of *binary search* to look up entries, and (d) using an index array to look up the Roman numeral values. How humans locate names in a phone book has much more in common with binary search than linear search because it is <u>fast</u>.

The construction of the phone book begins with a "place value" observation about the Roman numeral system. If we think of the empty string as a Roman numeral, then a valid Roman numeral is simply the concatenation of four strings, one from each of the following groups:

Thousands		Hundreds		Tens		Ones	
''	0	''	0	''	0	''	0
'M'	1000	'C'	100	'X'	10	'I'	1
'MM'	2000	'CC'	200	'XX'	20	'II'	2
'MMM'	3000	'CCC'	300	'XXX'	30	'III'	3
		'CD'	400	'XL'	40	'IV'	4
		'D'	500	'L'	50	'V'	5
		'DC'	600	'LX'	60	'VI'	6
		'DCC'	700	'LXX'	70	'VII'	7
		'DCCC'	800	'LXXX'	80	'VIII'	8
		'CM'	900	'XC'	90	'IX'	9

Thus, 1907 is the concatenation of 'M', 'CM', '', and 'VII', i.e., 'MCMVII'. Working with this idea, we can build a list of Roman numeral strings by computing all possible concatenations of entries taken from the following "place value" lists of strings:

Ones: { '', 'I', 'II', 'III', ..., 'VIII', 'IX' }
Tens: { '', 'X', 'XX', 'XXX', ..., 'LXXX', 'XC' }
Hundreds: { '', 'C', 'CC', 'CCC', ..., 'DCCC', 'CM' }
Thousands: { '', 'M', 'MM', 'MMM' }

We can use *cell arrays* to store each of these string lists. Each "cell" in the cell array holds one string and the strings have varying lengths. The following statements set up the four cell arrays that we need:

```
C1 = {'', 'I', 'II', 'III', 'IV', 'V', 'VI', 'VII', 'VIII', 'IX'};
C2 = {'', 'X', 'XX', 'XXX', 'XL', 'L', 'LX', 'LXX', 'LXXX', 'XC'};
C3 = {'', 'C', 'CC', 'CCC', 'CD', 'D', 'DC', 'DCC', 'DCCC', 'CM'};
C4 = {'', 'M', 'MM', 'MMM'};
```

Figure 9.3 suggests how to visualize a cell array. "Curly brackets" are used to access a cell in a cell array. For example, the statement s = C4{3} assigns the string 'MM' to variable s.

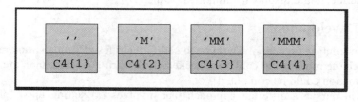

Figure 9.3. *A Cell Array of Strings.*

Since a Roman numeral is a concatenation of four strings, one each from the cell arrays C1, C2, C3, and C4, we can use a 4-deep nested loop to display all possible Roman numerals:

```
k = 0;
for i4=1:4
    % Generate all Roman numerals whose 1000s place is C4{i4}
    for i3=1:10
        % Generate all Roman numerals whose 100s place is C3{i3}
        for i2=1:10
            % Generate all Roman numerals whose 10s place is C2{i2}
            for i1=1:10
                % Generate all Roman numerals whose 1s place is C1{i1}
                s = [C4{i4} C3{i3} C2{i2} C1{i1}];
                fprintf('%4d  %s\n', k, s)
                k = k+1;
            end
        end
    end
end
```

The fragment generates $4000 = 4 \times 10 \times 10 \times 10$ lines of output:

```
   0
   1   I
   2   II
   :   :
3998   MMMCMXCVIII
3999   MMMCMXCIX
```

The order of the loops ensures that the displayed Roman numerals appear in the order of smallest to largest in value.

With a slight modification of this fragment we can produce a nonalphabetized Roman numeral phone book. All we have to do is save the generated Roman numerals in a cell array as they are produced, taking care to "skip over" the empty Roman numeral ' '. Thus, if we replace the `fprintf` statement in the above nested-loop fragment with

```
if k > 0
    RN{k} = s;
end
```

then we emerge with a length-3999 cell array RN that consists of all valid Roman numeral strings. Applying `sort` to RN produces the required alphabetized directory. See the function `RomanPhoneBook` listed below. It returns the index vector that is generated by `sort`, because it is the key to determining Roman numeral value. To see how, assume that we have executed `[RNsort,idx]` = `RomanPhoneBook()`. The following table shows the connection between the components of RNSort and `idx`:

k	RNsort{k}	idx(k)
1	'C'	100
2	'CC'	200
3	'CCC'	300
4	'CCCI'	301
5	'CCCII'	302
:	:	:
3998	'XXXVI	36
3998	'XXXVII	37
3999	'XXXVIII'	38

The reason `idx(k)` specifies the value of RNsort{k} is because (a) `sort` ensures that the value of RNsort{k} is the value of RN{idx(k)} and (b) RN has the property that the index of any component is the numerical value of the Roman numeral that occupies that component.

The advantage of having an alphabetized list of Roman numerals is that it allows us to look up entries using a fast algorithm called *binary search*. This method works by repeatedly halving the "search space" and is generally much faster than linear search. The only requirement is that the search space must be ordered, e.g., alphabetized. To illustrate, let us suppose that A is the following (alphabetized) cell array of strings:

'A'	'B'	'C'	'D'	'E'	'F'	'G'	'H'	'I'	'J'	'K'	'L'	'M'
A{1}	A{2}	A{3}	A{4}	A{5}	A{6}	A{7}	A{8}	A{9}	A{10}	A{11}	A{12}	A{13}

and that we want to check whether or not it contains the string x = 'I'. In binary search, we maintain a pair of indices L and R with the property that if the value of x is in the array, then it is "in between" (or including) A{L} and A{R}. At the start, the search space is the entire array, so L and R "point" to the first and last components. We determine the midpoint index m = `floor((L+R)/2)`,

'A'	'B'	'C'	'D'	'E'	'F'	'G'	'H'	'I'	'J'	'K'	'L'	'M'
A{1}	A{2}	A{3}	A{4}	A{5}	A{6}	A{7}	A{8}	A{9}	A{10}	A{11}	A{12}	A{13}

↑   ↑   ↑
$L=1$ $m=7$ $R=13$

The Function RomanPhoneBook

```
function [RNsort,idx] = RomanPhoneBook()
% RNsort is a 3999-by-1 cell array of alphabetized Roman numerals.
% idx is a 3999-by-1 integer array with the property that idx(k)
%    is the numerical value of the Roman numeral RNsort{k}.

% Cell arrays for the 1's, 10's, 100's, and 1000's place...
C1 = {'', 'I', 'II', 'III', 'IV', 'V', 'VI', 'VII', 'VIII', 'IX'};
C2 = {'', 'X', 'XX', 'XXX', 'XL', 'L', 'LX', 'LXX', 'LXXX', 'XC'};
C3 = {'', 'C', 'CC', 'CCC', 'CD', 'D', 'DC', 'DCC', 'DCCC', 'CM'};
C4 = {'', 'M', 'MM', 'MMM'};

% Generate the unsorted cell array of Roman numeral strings...
RN = cell(3999,1);
k = 0;
for i4=1:4
    Thousands = C4{i4};           % Choose a thousands "digit"
    for i3 = 1:10
        Hundreds = C3{i3};        % Choose a hundreds "digit"
        for i2 = 1:10
            Tens = C2{i2};        % Choose a tens "digit"
            for i1 = 1:10
                Ones = C1{i1};    % Choose a ones "digit"
                if k > 0
                    RN{k} = [Thousands Hundreds Tens Ones];
                end
                k = k+1;
            end
        end
    end
end
% Now alphabetize...
[RNsort,idx] = sort(RN);
```

and ask the question "is the value of x less than or equal to the value of A{7}?" Since the answer is "no," we can safely throw away the first seven "pages" of the phone book and confine our search to what is left. To effect this operation we make the assignment L = m+1 and revise the midpoint value with the assignment m = floor((L+R)/2), giving

'A'	'B'	'C'	'D'	'E'	'F'	'G'	'H'	'I'	'J'	'K'	'L'	'M'
A{1}	A{2}	A{3}	A{4}	A{5}	A{6}	A{7}	A{8}	A{9}	A{10}	A{11}	A{12}	A{13}

$$\uparrow \qquad\qquad \uparrow \qquad\qquad \uparrow$$
$$L=8 \qquad\qquad m=10 \qquad\qquad R=13$$

We again ask the midpoint question "is the value of x less than or equal to the value of A{10}?" This time the answer is "yes" and we safely discard "pages" A{11}, A{12}, and A{13}. To realize this we perform the updates R = m and m = floor((L+R)/2):

'A'	'B'	'C'	'D'	'E'	'F'	'G'	'H'	'I'	'J'	'K'	'L'	'M'
A{1}	A{2}	A{3}	A{4}	A{5}	A{6}	A{7}	A{8}	A{9}	A{10}	A{11}	A{12}	A{13}

$$\uparrow \qquad \uparrow \qquad \uparrow$$
$$L=8 \quad m=9 \quad R=10$$

The pattern should be clear at this point:

```
if   x is less than or equal to A{m}
       % Change the right endpoint...
       R = m; m = floor((L+R)/2);
     else
       % Change the left endpoint...
       L = m+1; m = floor((L+R)/2);
     end
```

In this way, L and R keep getting closer, all the while making sure that the value of x stays in between A{L} and A{R}. In our example, the process plays out in two more steps:

'A'	'B'	'C'	'D'	'E'	'F'	'G'	'H'	'I'	'J'	'K'	'L'	'M'
A{1}	A{2}	A{3}	A{4}	A{5}	A{6}	A{7}	A{8}	A{9}	A{10}	A{11}	A{12}	A{13}

$$\uparrow \qquad \uparrow$$
$$L=8 \quad R=9$$
$$m=8$$

'A'	'B'	'C'	'D'	'E'	'F'	'G'	'H'	'I'	'J'	'K'	'L'	'M'
A{1}	A{2}	A{3}	A{4}	A{5}	A{6}	A{7}	A{8}	A{9}	A{10}	A{11}	A{12}	A{13}

$$\uparrow$$
$$L=9$$
$$m=9$$
$$R=9$$

Because the value of x occurs in the cell array, the final value of L (or R) points to its location. Suppose x = 'INOPE'. The iteration would proceed exactly the same as with x = 'I', but in the end we would not have a match between x and A{L}. From this we conclude that (a) the binary search process terminates with a single-entry, reduced phone book and (b) x is in the original phone book if and only if it is that single entry.

To implement a binary search we need to be able to determine "who comes first" when presented with a pair of strings. MATLAB has no built-in function to carry out such a comparison. However, it is easy to solve this problem since sort can be applied to cell arrays of strings. Refer to the function compare1 listed below. Note that if the value of idx(1) is 1, then C0 is alphabetized, i.e., s1 comes before s2. The input strings are converted into uppercase because we want to treat lowercase numerals the same as uppercase numerals, i.e., 37 is represented by both 'XXXVII' and 'xxxvii'. The output variable a, assigned in the last statement, is a boolean (logical) variable, i.e., its value is 1 (true) or 0 (false).

With the availability of compare1, we are able to implement the method of binary search for looking up values in an alphabetized cell array of strings.

The Function `compare1`

```
function a = compare1(s1,s2)
% If string s1 comes before string s2 or is equal to s2 in ASCII
% dictionary order, then a is 1. Otherwise, a is 0.
% Case is ignored.

C0={upper(s1), upper(s2)};
[C,idx] = sort(C0);
a = (idx(1)==1);
```

The Function `BinSearch`

```
function i = BinSearch(x,S)
% S is an n-by-1 cell array of strings that are in ASCII
%    dictionary order, and x is a string.
% If x occurs in S, then i is the position in S where x is found.
% If x does not occur in S, then i = 0.

n = length(S);
if compare1(S{1},x) &&  compare1(x,S{n})
      % S{1} <= x  <= S{n}
      L = 1; R = n;
      while (L < R)
            % S{L} <= x <= S{R}
            m = floor((L+R)/2);
            if compare1(x,S{m})
                  % S{L} <= x <= S{m}
                  R = m;
            else
                  % S{m} < x <= S{R}
                  L = m+1;
            end
      end
      % L = R
      if strcmp(x,S{L})
            % S{L} = S{R} matches x.
            i = L;
      else
            % S{L} == S{R} does not match x.
            i = 0;
      end
else
      % Either x < S{1} or S{n} < x
      i = 0;
end
```

It is important to appreciate just how rapidly the values of L and R come together. For example, if the original array has length 10^6, then only about 20 iterations are required because of the repeated halving. In general, after k passes through the loop, the value of R−L is about $n/2^k$ where n is the length of the original cell array.

The script `Eg9_2` makes use of `RomanPhoneBook` and `BinSearch` and can be used to check whether or not a given input string represents a valid Roman numeral.

The Script `Eg9_2`

```
% Script Eg9_2
% Checks whether or not a string is a valid Roman Numeral.

clc
% Compute and sort the Roman Numerals...
[RNsort,idx] = RomanPhoneBook();

% Get the input string and see if it occurs in RNsort..
s = input('Enter a Possible Roman Numeral: ');
i = BinSearch(upper(s),RNsort);

% Display the appropriate message...
if i==0
    disp([s ' is not a valid Roman Numeral'])
else
    disp([s sprintf(' is the Roman Numeral for %d',idx(i))])
end
```

Sample Output from the Script `Eg9_2`

```
Enter a Possible Roman Numeral: 'MCDXLIV'
MCDXLIV is the Roman Numeral for 1444

Enter a Possible Roman Numeral: 'VIIII'
VIIII is not a valid Roman Numeral

Enter a Possible Roman Numeral: 'MLD'
MLD is not a valid Roman Numeral
```

Talking Point: Binary Search and Real Telephone Books

Binary search is a prominent member of the family of divide-and-conquer algorithms. The array is "divided" in two and the relevant half is then "conquered." Execution time is proportional to $\log_2(n)$ where n is the length of the input array. You can get an idea of its superiority to linear search, whose execution time is proportional to n, by considering the value of the quotient $n/\log_2(n)$ for large n. For example, if n is a million, then the ratio is about 50,000. Of course, the array must be ordered for binary search to work and this represents a one-time-only overhead. If just a few lookups are required, then it is possible that linear search is preferable because we can then avoid the sorting overhead.

We mentioned earlier that the algorithm we employ when using (say) the Manhattan phone book has a lot in common with binary search. Let us explore this connection by considering how we might find someone whose last name is Smith. We open the directory to its middle page (approximately) and notice that we are "in the L's." For dramatic effect, we tear the book in two, keeping the relevant second half since it contains the S's. We then open this half-sized directory to its approximate middle and discover that we are in the R's. Again we tear the book in half keeping the latter portion since it contains the S's. We continue in this way until we get down to a very short, perhaps single-page directory. At that point it becomes more efficient for us to use linear search, running our finger down the column of names until we get the required match. Apparently, we employ a sophisticated combination of (approximate) linear search and (approximate) binary search when we look for an entry in a phone directory.

MATLAB Review

Cell Arrays

Cell arrays are like numerical arrays, only their entries (called cells) can store anything: numbers, vectors, matrices, strings, other cell arrays, etc. The command B = cell(m,n) creates an m-by-n cell array with empty matrix entries. Likewise, A = cell(m) creates an m-by-m cell array. It usually does not make sense to talk about the orientation of a one-dimensional cell array, so there is little reason to fuss over cell(m,1) versus cell(1,m).

Small cell arrays can be created "by hand" using curly brackets. For example,

```
C = {'abc', rand(3,3), 20}
```

creates a length-3 cell array while

```
C = {'Upper Left', 'Upper Right'; 'Lower Left' , 'Lower Right'}
```

creates a 2-by-2 cell array. Cell array components are identified with exactly the same syntax as real arrays except that curly brackets are used.[10] Thus, C{2,3} names cell (2,3) of a two-dimensional cell array while C{4} names the fourth cell of a linear cell array.

Although we will mostly be using cell arrays to house collections of strings, they can be used to store arbitrary data objects. For example,

```
C = {[1 2; 3 4], 'abc' , 10:10:70}
```

is perfectly legal. Note that in this case, the value of C{1}(2,1) is 3, the value of C{2}(3) is 'c', and the value of C{3}(5) is 50.

The Size and Length of a Cell Array

As with numerical arrays, the functions length and size can be used to determine cell array dimension. If C is a one-dimensional cell array, then m = length(C) assigns the number of cells to m. If C is a two-dimensional cell array, then [m,n] = size(C) assigns its row and column dimensions to m and n, respectively. If you use length on a two-dimensional cell array, then the *larger* dimension is returned.

---

[10] The colon notation can be used to extract portions of a cell array. However, round brackets must be used as with numerical arrays. Thus, if C is a two-dimensional cell array, then C(i,:), C(:,j), and C(i1:i2,j1:j2) are valid (sub)cell arrays assuming that the index ranges are valid. If C is a one-dimensional cell array, then C(i1:i2) is a (sub)cell array made up of components i1 through i2. This is a footnote because the syntax is too quirky to promote with enthusiasm!

ASCII Code

Strings are made up of characters and each character (keystroke) has an *ASCII code*. Here are some examples:

Character	a	b	c	A	B	C	1	2	;	?
ASCII Code	97	98	99	65	66	67	49	50	59	63

If s is a string, then a = real(s) produces a vector with the property that a(k) is the ASCII code for s(k).

The comparison of two length-1 strings (i.e., characters) is a numerical comparison of their respective ASCII codes. Thus, 'c' < ';' is false because 99 < 59 is false. We say that one character comes before another character if its ASCII code is smaller. This defines the *ASCII dictionary order* and amounts to an extension of the familiar, 26-letter notion of alphabetical order.

Sorting a Cell Array of Strings

If C is a one-dimensional cell array with string entries, then [D, idx] = sort(C) produces a cell array D obtained by reordering the components of C so that they are in ASCII dictionary order. The integer vector idx has the property that D{k} = C{idx(k)}.

cellstr

If M is a character array with *m* rows, then C = cellstr(M) is an *m*-by-1 cell array with C{k} = M(k, :).

Exercises

M9.2.1 Write a function C = RandomCell(n,m) that returns a length-*n* cell array of strings with the property that each string is comprised of *m* randomly chosen uppercase letters.

M9.2.2 (a) Write a function C = cell2char(A) that takes a one-dimensional cell array A of equal-length strings and turns it into a character array C with the property that the value of C(k, :) is the value of A{k} for k=1:length(A). (b) Develop a more general version of cell2char that takes a length-*m* cell array of strings and returns an *m*-by-*n* character array where *n* is the length of the longest string in A. The value of C(k, :) should be A{k} padded (if necessary) with trailing blanks.

M9.2.3 Suppose that C is an *m*-by-1 cell array whose cells are vectors. Write a function A = SortByLength(C) that returns in A a permutation of C such that

```
length(A{1}) <= length(A{2}) <= ... <= length(A{m}).
```

P9.2.4 Write a script that produces a 2-column table displaying the ASCII code for all the letters (upper- and lowercase), all the digits, and all the punctuation marks.

P9.2.5 Without using sort, implement the following function so that it performs as specified:

```
function a = compare1(s1,s2)
% s1 and s2 are strings
% If s1 comes before or is equal to s2 in the ASCII dictionary order,
% then a is 1. Otherwise, a is 0. Case is ignored.
```

Here are some helpful implementation tips. (1) Pad the shorter string with blanks, i.e., add trailing blanks to make the two strings the same length. This will not affect the outcome. (2) Find the smallest integer k so that s1(k) is different than s2(k). Use a while-loop. If no such index exists, then the two strings are the same. (3) The value of a is one if and only if s1(k) <= s2(k) is true.

P9.2.6 If s1 and s2 are strings with the same length, then c = s1<=s2 is a 0-1 (boolean) vector. How could you use c to determine whether or not s1 comes before s2 in the ASCII Dictionary order? (Refer to the previous problem.)

P9.2.7 Implement the following function so that it performs as specified:

```
function i = findChar(c,s)
% c is a character and s is a string.
% i is a vector of subscripts associated with all occurrences of c in s.
% Thus, if c = 'a' and s = 'abcaadfea', then i = [1 4 5 9].
% If there are no occurrences, then i is the empty vector.
```

Make effective use of the ASCII code and the built-in function find.

P9.2.8 Recall from §8.2 the method of bubble sort that can be used to sort real vectors. The same idea can be applied to alphabetize a cell array of strings. For example, if

| 40 | 30 | 10 | 20 |

| 'Dogs' | 'Cats' | 'Anteaters' | 'Birds' |

then by stepping through the sequence of pairwise comparisons and swaps we find

| 40 | 30 | **10** | **20** |

⇓

| 40 | **30** | **10** | 20 |

⇓

| **40** | **10** | 30 | 20 |

⇓

| 10 | 40 | **30** | **20** |

⇓

| 10 | **40** | **20** | 30 |

⇓

| 10 | 20 | **40** | **30** |

⇓

| 10 | 20 | 30 | 40 |

| 'Dogs' | 'Cats' | **'Anteaters'** | **'Birds'** |

⇓

| 'Dogs' | **'Cats'** | **'Anteaters'** | 'Birds' |

⇓

| **'Dogs'** | **'Anteaters'** | 'Cats' | 'Birds' |

⇓

| 'Anteaters' | 'Dogs' | **'Cats'** | **'Birds'** |

⇓

| 'Anteaters' | **'Dogs'** | **'Birds'** | 'Cats' |

⇓

| 'Anteaters' | 'Birds' | **'Dogs'** | **'Cats'** |

⇓

| 'Anteaters' | 'Birds' | 'Cats' | 'Dogs' |

Write a function y = StringBubbleSort(x) that takes a cell array of strings x and produces a new cell array y that is an alphabetized permutation of x.

P9.2.9 Implement the following function:

```
function p = IsRoman(s)
% s is a string.
% p is true if and only if the following rules are all satisfied:
%
%     s is comprised of the characters I, V, X, L, C, D, or M.
%     There are at most three I's, X's, C's, and M's.
%     There is at most one V, L, and D.
%     I can only be followed by I.
%     V can only be followed by I.
%     X can only be followed by X, V or I.
%     L can only be followed by X, V, or I.
%     C can only be followed by C, L, X, V, or I.
%     D can only be followed by C, L, X, V, or I.
%     M can only be followed by D, C, L, X, V, or I.
```

Does it follow that this function correctly identifies valid Roman numerals?

9.3 Changing Sign

Problem Statement

Suppose we have a continuous function $f(x)$ with a single zero x_* on an interval $[L_0, R_0]$. The problem of computing that root can be regarded as a search problem because we are, after all, looking for something. However, instead of searching over a finite set of possibilities as we did in the previous two sections, we now must search among the infinity of points between L_0 and R_0. Obviously, we will have to discretize the problem and settle for an approximation to x_*.

To illustrate what we are up against and how we might proceed, suppose $f(x) = x^2 - 2$ and $[L_0, R_0] = [0, 2]$. The zero $x_* = \sqrt{2}$ is not even a floating point number. However, we note that f changes sign across the interval $[\tilde{L}, \tilde{R}]$ where

$$\tilde{L} = 1.414213562373095$$

$$\tilde{R} = 1.414213562373096.$$

If a continuous function changes sign across an interval, then it has at least one zero in the interval. In our example, it follows that

$$\tilde{L} < x_* < \tilde{R}.$$

Given the proximity of $\tilde{L}$ to $\tilde{R}$, it would be most reasonable to accept the midpoint $(\tilde{L} + \tilde{R})/2$ as an approximation to x_*.

The method of bisection is based on these ideas. It works by producing a sequence of ever-shorter intervals that bracket the zero. We say that $[L, R]$ is a *bracketing interval* for a function f if $f(L)f(R) \leq 0$. As noted above, this guarantees that f has a zero in $[L, R]$

assuming that it is continuous. We can compute a half-sized bracketing interval from $[L, R]$ by evaluating f at the midpoint $m = (L + R)/2$ and then checking for a sign change:

> if $f(L)f(m) \le 0$ then
>> $[L, m]$ is a bracketing interval.
>> Replace R with m and continue.
> else
>> $[m, R]$ is a bracketing interval.
>> Replace L with m and continue.
> end

Repetition of this process defines the method of bisection. It culminates in the production of a bracketing interval that is so short we can legitimately declare either endpoint to be an approximate zero.

Implement the method of bisection and use it to compute an approximation to the smallest positive root of the polynomial

$$\tau(x) = 512x^{10} - 1280x^8 + 1120x^6 - 400x^4 + 50x^2 - 1. \tag{9.8}$$

Examine how long it takes to reach the stage where the current bracketing interval is shorter than 10^{-d} for $d = 3{:}20$.

Program Development

We strive for a function of the form

```
[L,R] = Bisection(f,L0,R0,delta)
```

that inputs the name of the function f, the left and right endpoints of the initial bracketing interval $[L_0, R_0]$, and positive error tolerance δ. It should return a bracketing interval $[L, R]$ that satisfies

$$|R - L| \le \delta.$$

The repeated halving of the bracketing interval is clearly an occasion to use a `while`-loop:

```
L = L0;
R = R0;
while R - L > delta
    m = (L+R)/2;
    if f(L)*f(m) <= 0
        R = m;
    else
        L = m;
    end
end
```

The way it stands, there are two f-evaluations per iteration. This overhead can easily be reduced to just a single f-evaluation:

```
L = L0; fL = f(L);
R = R0; fR = f(R);
while R - L > delta
    m = (L+R)/2; fm = f(m);
    if fL*fm <= 0
        R = m; fR = fm;
    else
        L = m; fL = fm;
    end
end
```

This is a particularly important modification because the function f may be very costly to evaluate.

Note that after k passes through the loop, the value of R-L equals (R0-L0)/2^k. Thus, it would seem that the loop will terminate for any positive delta. However, the iteration could reach the stage where L and R are adjacent floating point numbers with a gap between them that is greater than delta. In that case there is a danger that the loop will never terminate. To guard against this we expand Bisection's input parameter list to include a fifth input parameter fEvalsMax that can serve as an iteration maximum. The complete implementation is given below. Notice that the while-loop is guaranteed to terminate because of the upper bound placed upon the number of f-evaluations. The final left and right endpoints L and R are returned together with the total number of required f-evaluations.

The Function Bisection

```
function [L,R,fEvals] = Bisection(f,L0,R0,delta,fEvalsMax)
% f is a handle to a continuous function of a single variable.
% L0 and R0 define an interval [L0,R0] and f(L0)f(R0) <= 0.
% delta is the length of an acceptable final interval.
% fEvalsMax is a positive integer >= 2 that indicates the maximum
%     number of f-evaluations allowed.
%
% Bisection is applied to obtain a new bracketing interval [L,R]
% that usually satisfies R-L <= delta. If this is not possible,
% then R-L is as small as possible given the fEvalsMax
% constraint.

L = L0; fL = f(L);
R = R0; fR = f(R);
fEvals = 2;
while (R-L > delta) && (fEvals < fEvalsMax)
    m = (L+R)/2; fm = f(m);
    fEvals = fEvals+1;
    if fL*fm<=0
        % There is a root in [L,m].
        R = m; fR = fm;
    else
        % There is a root in [m,R].
        L = m; fL = fm;
    end
end
```

One of the input parameters for `Bisection` is a function, a feature that we briefly encountered in §7.2. From one point of view, `f` is just another input. See Figure 9.4. However, recall that there is a special syntax for passing functions as parameters—it is simply to preface the name of the function with the "at" character @. The resulting expression is referred to as a *function handle*. Thus,

```
[L,R,fEvals] = Bisection(@sin,3,4,.000001,30)
```

computes the approximate root, as a bracketing interval of length 10^{-6} (or less), of the sine function within the interval $[3,4]$. The final interval would bracket π.

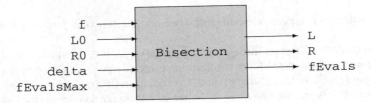

Figure 9.4. *Visualizing the Function* `Bisection`.

Returning to the problem posed at the beginning of the section, the challenge is to compute an approximation to the smallest positive root of the polynomial $\tau(x)$ defined by (9.8) and implemented as follows:

The Function `tau`

```
function y = tau(x)
y = 512*x.^10 - 1280*x.^8 + 1120*x.^6 - 400*x.^4 + 50*x.^2 -1;
```

Let us examine this function graphically so as to determine an initial bracketing interval. From Figure 9.5 we see that if $L_0 = 0$ and $R_0 = 0.3$, then $[L_0, R_0]$ brackets only the smallest positive root.

The script `Eg9_3` applies `Bisection` with the starting interval $[0.0, 0.3]$ for various choices of `delta`. Notice that the function `tau` is passed as an argument to `Bisection` using the function handle syntax `@tau`.

The output highlights a number of important issues. The displayed "root" is the midpoint of the last bracketing interval defined by the output parameters `L` and `R`. If x_* is the true root and δ the value of `delta`, then the absolute error in the computed root is less than or equal to $\delta/2$. Thus, δ quantifies the notion of an approximate zero.

To understand why the function evaluation limit is reached for very small values of `delta`, recall from §4.3 that for IEEE computer arithmetic, the unit roundoff is approximately 10^{-16}. In our problem, the spacing of the floating point numbers near x_* is about $|x_*|10^{-16} \approx 10^{-17}$. Thus, if δ is less than or equal to this quantity, then no matter how many iterations are computed, the length of the current bracketing interval will never go below 10^{-17}. Indeed, the output confirms that the f-evaluation limit is reached if $\delta \leq 10^{-17}$.

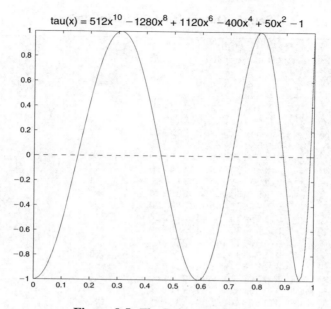

Figure 9.5. *The Polynomial $\tau(x)$.*

The Script `Eg9_3`

```
% Script Eg9_3
% Illustrates the method of bisection applied to finding the
% smallest positive root of
%        tau(x) = 512x^10 - 1280x^8 + 1120x^6 - 400x^4 + 50x^2 -1

% Initializations...
clc
L0 = 0.0;
R0 = 0.3;
fEvalsMax = 100;
fprintf('Initial interval = [%5.2f,%5.2f]\n',L0,R0)
fprintf('f-evaluation maximum = %3d\n\n',fEvalsMax)
disp('   delta              Root             f-Evals')
disp('-----------------------------------------------')
% Apply bisection with increasingly small values for delta...
for delta = logspace(-3,-20,18)
    [L,R,fEvals] = Bisection(@tau,L0,R0,delta,fEvalsMax);
    Root = (L+R)/2;
    fprintf(' %5.1e       %20.18f       %3d\n',delta,Root,fEvals)
end
```

Sample Output from the Script Eg9_3

```
Initial interval = [ 0.00, 0.30]
f-evaluation maximum = 100

     delta              Root                f-Evals
-----------------------------------------------------
  1.0e-003     0.156152343749999980          11
  1.0e-004     0.156408691406249990          14
  1.0e-005     0.156431579589843720          17
  1.0e-006     0.156434726715087900          21
  1.0e-007     0.156434476375579830          24
  1.0e-008     0.156434462964534780          27
  1.0e-009     0.156434464920312160          31
  1.0e-010     0.156434465025085960          34
  1.0e-011     0.156434465038182700          37
  1.0e-012     0.156434465040092620          41
  1.0e-013     0.156434465040263180          44
  1.0e-014     0.156434465040233340          47
  1.0e-015     0.156434465040230950          51
  1.0e-016     0.156434465040230840          54
  1.0e-017     0.156434465040230840         100
  1.0e-018     0.156434465040230840         100
  1.0e-019     0.156434465040230840         100
  1.0e-020     0.156434465040230840         100
```

Talking Point: You Never Know for Sure

Bisection can be regarded as a continuous version of binary search, and our back-to-back treatment of these two methods gives us yet another opportunity to compare the discrete and the continuous. The similarities are obvious. Bisection searches an interval and proceeds by averaging endpoints. Binary search scrutinizes an array and proceeds by averaging endpoint subscripts. Both are examples of the divide-and-conquer process, a solution strategy that we discuss more fully in Chapter 14.

In contrast, the "end game" for bisection is decidedly more complicated because approximation is involved. We must define the notion of an approximate zero. The "front game" which requires the determination of an initial bracketing interval can also be tricky. In situations where f-evaluations are expensive, the production of a revealing exploratory plot may be out of the question. Moreover, the function may have several zeros clustered around the specific one you want. If bisection is applied to a bracketing interval that houses several zeros, then you cannot be sure which is determined. In some applications, it may be required to compute all the zeros of f in some interval. This poses another challenge, How do you know when they have all been found?

The point we are making is that zero-finding can be challenging and is almost always fraught with uncertainty.

MATLAB Review

Functions as Parameters

To pass a function as an argument, preface its name with the character "@". For example, calling function Bisection to find an approximate root of function tau requires that we pass function handle @tau as an argument:

```
[L,R,fEvals] = Bisection(@tau,L0,R0,delta,fEvalsMax)
```

Exercises

M9.3.1 Suppose the line if `fL*fm <= 0` is changed to if `fL*fm < 0` in Bisection. Explain why this can result in an error. Hint: Consider a problem where the midpoint of the initial bracketing interval is a root.

M9.3.2 Modify Eg9_3 so that it computes all five positive roots of $\tau(x)$. Use delta = .000001.

M9.3.3 Modify Bisection so that it includes an additional input parameter delta_f. The loop should terminate if the value of |f(m)| is less than delta_f.

M9.3.4 Although our implementation of bisection is guaranteed to terminate, it is less than ideal from the efficiency point of view. It would make more sense to terminate the iteration as soon as the halving process fails to produce a new interval. Modify Bisection so that it terminates as soon as the new bracketing interval is the same as the current bracketing interval.

P9.3.5 Use Bisection to compute a positive x that satisfies $x = \tan(x)$.

P9.3.6 A zero-finding method of great interest is *Newton's method.* It uses both the value of the function and its derivative at each step. Suppose f and its derivative are defined at x_c. (The "c" is for current.) The tangent line to f at x_c has a zero at $x_+ = x_c - f(x_c)/f'(x_c)$ assuming that $f'(x_c) \neq 0$. See Figure 5.4. Newton's method for finding a zero of the function f is based upon the repeated use of this formula. Complete the following function so that it performs as specified:

```
function [xc,fEvals] = Newton(f,fp,x0,delta,fEvalMax)
% f is a handle to a continuous function  f(x) of a single variable.
% fp is a handle to the derivative of f.
% x0 is an initial guess to a root of f.
% delta is a positive real number.
% fEvalsMax is a positive integer >= 2 that indicates the maximum
%     number of f-evaluations allowed.
%
% Newton's method is repeatedly applied until the current iterate xc
% has the property that |f(xc)| <= delta. If that is not the case
% after fEvalsMax function evaluations, then xc is the current iterate.
%
% fEvals is the number of f-evaluations required to obtain xc.
```

Unlike bisection, the Newton process is not guaranteed to terminate. If $f'(x_c)$ is zero, then the Newton step is not even defined. If $f'(x_c)$ is small, then a Newton step can take us very far away from a root. Experiment with your implementation by trying to find zeros of $f(x) = \sin(x)$ with various values for the initial guess.

P9.3.7 The MATLAB function fzero can be used to compute zeros of real-valued functions. In particular, if the values in L and R define a bracketing interval for a function f that has been implemented, then xStar = fzero(@f,[L,R]) assigns an approximate root to xStar. Write a script to find the roots of $\tau(x)$ as defined in (9.8) on the interval [0,1]. Make effective use of fzero.

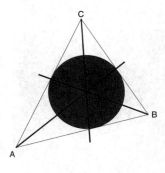

Chapter 10

Points, Polygons, and Circles

10.1 How Far?
Distance Metrics

10.2 Fenced in Twice?
Intersection

10.3 Not Perfect?
Nearness in Shape

Computations that involve points, polygons, and circles obviously give us an opportunity to refine our spatial sense. Equally important, computational geometry is the perfect venue for introducing more complicated data objects and for posing problems with solutions that require an intricate logic.

We start with the problem of computing the diameter of a point set. Given points $P_1, \ldots, P_n$, what is the greatest separation between any pair of points? The calculations are elementary enough, but we learn the value of packaging the two numbers that define a point into a single object. This is a simple example of *data abstraction*—hiding detailed information (the two coordinates) in order to focus on the higher-level object (the point). Data abstraction is the central theme of this chapter.

Next, we consider a problem that involves rectangle intersection. In particular, when is a given rectangle disjoint from a set of other rectangles? Intersection is a "yes-no" property that often calls for rather involved logical manipulations. It is a setting where we can practice our "boolean" skills.

In the last section we solve a pair of optimization problems that can be used to quantify how far a given triangle T is from being an equilateral triangle. The assessment requires the computation of two circles: the largest circle that can fit inside T and the smallest circle that contains T. Both calculations require the manipulation of various bisectors and intersection points.

As we mentioned, the problems in this chapter give us the chance to build an appreciation for data abstraction. Together with procedural abstraction, these "packaging" devices help us manage complexity during the programming process.

Programming Preview

Concepts

Structured variable, distance, intersection, shape, metrics, nearness, more complicated boolean-valued functions, data abstraction.

Language Features

Structured Variable: A "supervariable" that collects values under named fields.

`struct`: A built-in function to create a structured variable. Its arguments are
<fieldname>-<fieldvalue> pairs.

"Dot Notation":   The   syntax   to   access   a   field   in   a   structure   is
<structure>.<fieldname>.

Structure Array: An array whose components are structures of the same type.

Boolean Value: A logical value (0 or 1) resulting from relational and/or logical
operations.

Boolean-Valued Function: A function that returns the *logical* value 0 or 1.

\ (Backslash): A MATLAB operator to solve a system of linear equations.

Special Prerequisites

§10.3 is somewhat mathematical. The problem considered requires solving a
system of linear equations with two unknowns.

MatTV

Video 20. Structure

How to create a *structure*, a kind of "supervariable" to collect values under named
fields.

Video 21. Structure Arrays

How to create and work with structure arrays.

10.1 How Far?

Problem Statement

Suppose we are given n points $P_1, \ldots, P_n$ in the plane. We refer to the set $S = \{P_1, \ldots, P_n\}$ as a *point set*. Assuming that $n \geq 2$, the *diameter* of S is the maximum distance between any pair of points. See Figure 10.1. Write a function DiameterPoints that inputs a point set and returns the two points that define its diameter.

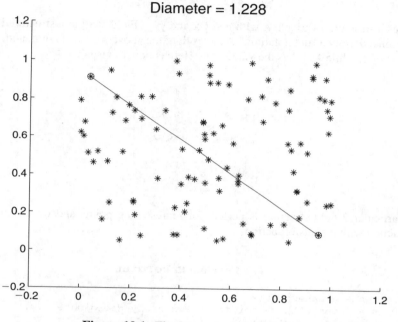

Figure 10.1. *The Diameter of a Point Set.*

Program Development

One approach to the design of DiameterPoints would be to work at the coordinate level, specifying all input and output parameters in terms of the underlying x's and y's, e.g.,

```
function [x1,y1,x2,y2] = DiameterPoints(x,y)
% x and y are column n-vectors that define the point set
% {(x(1),y(1)),...,(x(n),y(n))}.
% (x1,y1) and (x2,y2) are the points that define its diameter.
```

This is less than ideal for several reasons. Imagine developing a complicated, plane-geometry-rich program that involves DiameterPoints and other point set manipulations. Working at the xy coordinate level requires two parameters or variables for every point. It would be handy if we could program at the point level, i.e., it would be convenient for DiameterPoints to accept a point set variable and return a pair of point variables:

```
function [Q1,Q2] = DiameterPoints(P)
% P is a point set and Q1 and Q2 are points that define
% the diameter of P.
```

After all, when we visualize this calculation we visualize points as in Figure 10.1, not their coordinates.

The key to doing this in MATLAB is the notion of a *structure*. The struct command enables us to "package" related quantities. For example, the statement

```
A = struct('x',3,'y',4)
```

produces a structured variable A with *fields* x and y.   Fields within a structured variable are referenced using a "dot notation." As a result of the above struct command, A.x has the value of 3, while A.y has the value of 4. Here is how to visualize A:

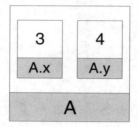

This particular 2-field structure is perfect for representing points and we encapsulate its construction with a "make function."

The Function MakePoint

```
function P = MakePoint(x,y)
% P is a point with x-coordinate P.x and y-coordinate P.y.
P = struct('x',x,'y',y);
```

To illustrate its use, the fragment

```
A = MakePoint(3,4);
B = MakePoint(-1,2);
```

establishes A and B as the points (3,4) and (−1,2), respectively. Recall that the Euclidean distance between (x_1, y_1) and (x_2, y_2) is given by

$$d = \sqrt{(x_1 - x_2)^2 + (y_1 - y_2)^2}.$$

Using this formula, we can compute the distance between A and B as follows:

```
d = sqrt((A.x-B.x)^2 + (A.y-B.y)^2);
```

There are no surprises here, A.x, A.y, B.x, and B.y are the names of simple, real variables. It just so happens that they are fields within the structured variables A and B. We use the dot notation to access field values from a structured variable just as we use subscripts to access component values within an array variable.

Structured variables can serve as input parameters to a function. Here is a function that accepts two points and returns the Euclidean distance between them.

The Function GetDist

```
function d = GetDist(P1,P2)
% P1 and P2 are points.
% d is the Euclidean distance between them.
d = sqrt((P1.x - P2.x)^2 + (P1.y - P2.y)^2);
```

It is also possible to assemble identically structured variables into an array. The fragment

```
P(1) = MakePoint(10,20);
P(2) = MakePoint(30,40);
P(3) = MakePoint(80,90);
```

establishes P as a length-3 array of points. Arrays whose components are structures are called "structure arrays" and our small example shows that a structure array of points is a handy way to represent point sets. The syntax associated with structure array manipulation looks a little strange at first. The statement

```
z = P(2).x
```

assigns to the (simple) variable z the x-coordinate of the second point in array P. Think of P(2).x as an address. Reading left to right, P names the relevant array, P(2) names the relevant component of the relevant array, and P(2).x names the relevant field in the relevant component of the relevant array. The fragment

```
xc = (P(1).x + P(2).x + P(3).x)/3;
yc = (P(1).y + P(2).y + P(3).y)/3;
```

assigns to xc and yc the x- and y-coordinates of the centroid of the points (10,20), (30,40), and (80,90), i.e., (40,50). In fact, the centroid is a point, so it also can be represented using the point structure:

```
PCentroid = MakePoint(xc,yc);
```

It is possible to create the centroid point in one "step" by combining the three previous statements:

```
PCentroid = MakePoint( (P(1).x + P(2).x + P(3).x)/3 , ...
                       (P(1).y + P(2).y + P(3).y)/3 );
```

It is important to recognize that there is usually more than one way to design a structure for the problem at hand. For example, suppose a and b are length-n real vectors that define the Cartesian coordinates of a point set. One design is to package the data as a structure array of points:

```
for i=1:n
    P(i) = MakePoint(a(i),b(i));
end
```

The array P is an array of point structures. Each structure P(i) has two scalar fields as illustrated in Figure 10.2.

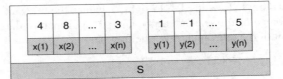

Figure 10.2. *Representing a Point Set with a Structure Array.*

Another design is to have a *single* structure variable representing the entire point set. It would require two fields, one for the x-coordinates and one for the y-coordinates:

```
S = struct('x',a,'y',b);
```

With this design S is a structured variable with two fields, each of which is a numerical array as shown in Figure 10.3.

Figure 10.3. *Representing a Point Set with a Structured Variable.*

To highlight the difference between these two designs, let us assign to z the ith point. In the first design where P is an array of structures,

```
z = P(i)
```

assigns the ith point to z. If we use the second design where S is a structure with two array fields, then the statement

```
z = MakePoint(S.x(i),S.y(i))
```

does the same thing.

The choice of the "right" structure usually involves a mix of readability and efficiency issues. For point sets, we opt for the structure array of points to emphasize the readability value of structures.

We are now in a position to implement `DiameterPoints`. The idea is simply to compute all possible pairwise distances between points in the given point set and "remember" where the maximum occurs.

The Function `DiameterPoints`

```
function [Q1,Q2] = DiameterPoints(P)
% P is a structure array of points.
% Q1 and Q2 are the points in P with maximum Euclidean separation.

n = length(P);
Q1 = P(1); Q2 = P(2); d = GetDist(Q1,Q2);
for i=1:n-1
   for j=i+1:n
      % See if P(i) and P(j) are further apart than Q1 and Q2...
      dij = GetDist(P(i),P(j));
      if dij>d
         % A better choice for Q1 and Q2 has been found...
         d = dij; Q1 = P(i); Q2 = P(j);
      end
   end
end
```

To illustrate further the issues associated with passing structures to functions, here is a function that displays a given point set.

The Function `ShowPointSet`

```
function ShowPointSet(P,s)
% P is a structure array of points.
% s is a string that specifies color, marker type, and line type,
%    e.g., 'k', '*b', 'cx--'
% Displays P in the current figure window according to s.
% Assumes hold is on.

for i=1:length(P)
   plot(P(i).x,P(i).y,s)
end
```

Notice that we can use `length` to determine the dimension of a structure array. Indeed, many MATLAB tools for real arrays can be applied to structure arrays. For example, if P is a length-10 structure array of points, then `R = P(1:2:10)` is a length-5 structure array that represents the odd-indexed points. On the other hand, certain natural-looking operations with structure arrays are illegal. For example, `sum(P)` does not produce the sum of the x- and y-coordinates. A loop is required to assemble all the x-coordinates in structure array P. The fragment

```
for i = 1:length(P)
    xvec(i) = P(i).x;
    yvec(i) = P(i).y;
end
```

assigns to xvec and yvec x-coordinates and y-coordinates of the points represented by the structure array P.

The script Eg10_1 makes effective use of functions DiameterPoints and ShowPointSet. It generates a random point set and then displays both it and its diameter. The plot in Figure 10.1 was produced by this script.

The Script Eg10_1

```
% Script Eg10_1
% Generates and displays a random point set and its diameter

% Set up the figure window...
close all
figure
axis([-.2 1.2 -.2 1.2])
hold on

% Generate a random point set...
n = 100;
x = rand(n,1);
y = rand(n,1);
for i=1:n
    P(i) = MakePoint(x(i),y(i));
end

% Compute the diameter and display...
[Q1,Q2] = DiameterPoints(P);
plot([Q1.x Q2.x],[Q1.y Q2.y],'r')
d = GetDist(Q1,Q2);
ShowPointSet(P,'*k')
ShowPointSet([Q1 Q2],'or')
title(sprintf('Diameter = %5.3f',d),'Fontsize',14)
hold off
```

Talking Point: Data Abstraction

The structure concept is an example of *data abstraction*. Data abstraction is important for the same reason as procedural abstraction: it is a device for hiding cumbersome detail. Our computer problem-solving skills are elevated when the programming languages that we use free us to think and express ourselves as engineers, scientists, and mathematicians.

Overloaded functions are a language feature that multiplies the power of data abstraction. An overloaded version of GetDist(P1,P2) might allow the user to specify the points in either Cartesian or polar coordinates. Or, it might interpret the input points as points on a sphere and return the great circle distance between them. Of course, we could write separate functions to cover each of these situations, e.g., `GetPolarDist`, `GetGreatCircleDist`, etc. But this would burden the user with the headache of keeping track of three separate procedures and their specifications. It is better to have a single overloaded function that frees the programmer to reason about distance without regard to the underlying coordinate system or the "kind" of distance that is required. See P10.1.9.

MATLAB Review

struct

The `struct` command is used to define and initialize a structured variable. It has the form

```
struct( field name , value , field name , value , ...)
```

where the names of the fields are given by strings. Here are some valid examples:

```
A = struct('x',[1 2 3],'y',[4 5 6 7])
B = struct('b1','CER','b2','ALA','b3','VAL')
C = struct('Name','magenta','rgb',[1 0 1])
```

The "dot notation" is used to access field values. Thus, `x = B.b1` assigns to `x` the string `'CER'`.
Another way to create a structured variable is to assign values to the fields of a structure directly. For example, the structured variable A above can be created using this fragment

```
A.x = [1 2 3];
A.y = [4 5 6 7];
```

Make Functions

It is good programming style to use functions to encapsulate the initialization of a structured variable.

Structure Arrays

An array whose components are structured variables is called a structure array. The same structure must be used throughout the array, e.g.,

```
S = [struct('x',1,'y',2) ; struct('x',10,'y',20)]
```

establishes S as a 2-by-1 structure array. The function `length` returns the number of components in a structure array, e.g., `length(S)` returns 2. The square bracket notation can be used to augment a structure array, e.g.,

```
S = [S ; struct('x',30,'y',40)]
```

The assignment `S(3) = struct('x',30,'y',40)` does the same thing.

fieldnames

Applied to a structured variable, the function `fieldnames` returns a cell array of strings that are the names of the variable's fields. Thus,

```
P = struct('x',1,'y',2,'zz',3)
C = fieldnames(P)
```

sets up the length-3 cell array `C = {'x' , 'y', 'zz'}`. This construction is useful in the design of overloaded functions.

Exercises

M10.1.1 Complete the following function by modifying DiameterPoints:

```
function [Q1,Q2] = MinSep(P)
% P is a structure array of points.
% Q1 and Q2 are the points in P with minimum Euclidean separation.
```

M10.1.2 Modify ShowPointSet to compute and plot the centroid of the points.

M10.1.3 How would the implementation of DiameterPoints change if the input parameter P was a structured variable with two array fields that specify the x- and y-coordinates of the point set? Implement this version of DiameterPoints.

P10.1.4 Complete the following function:

```
function d = PolyLength(P)
% P is a structure array of n points.
% d is the length of the polygonal line defined by P(1), P(2),...,P(n).
```

P10.1.5 Implement a function P = RandomPointSet(n,a,b,c,d) that returns a length-n structure array of points selected randomly from the rectangle with vertices (a,c), (b,c), (a,d), and (b,d).

P10.1.6 Complete the following function:

```
function P = LinspaceP(Q1,Q2,n)
% Q1 and Q2 are  points.
% n is an integer >= 2
% P is a length n structure array of points with the property that
%      P(1),...,P(n) are equally spaced along the line segment
%      that connects Q1 and Q2. Note: P(1) = Q1 and P(n) = Q2.
```

P10.1.7 Complete the following function:

```
function Q = ThirdVertex(P1,P2)
% P1 and P2 are distinct points with the same y-coordinate.
% Q is a point such that P1, P2, and Q define an equilateral
% triangle. The y-coordinate of Q should be greater than the
% y-coordinate of P1 and P2.
```

P10.1.8 Write a function Q = SortPoints(P) that sorts a structure array of points in order of increasing distance from the origin. Q is a permutation of P. Hint: Apply sort to a numerical array whose components contain the distances of the corresponding points.

P10.1.9 Write an overloaded version of the function GetDist(P1,P2) so that it returns the distance between points P1 and P2 in three-dimensional space regardless of whether they are specified in Cartesian coordinates, cylindrical coordinates, or spherical coordinates. Use the built-in function fieldnames to determine the representation of the input points.

For a Cartesian representation, assume the use of a structured variable with fields x, y, and z. For a cylindrical representation, assume the use of a structured variable with fields r, theta, and z. For a spherical representation, assume the use of a structured variable with fields rho, theta, and phi.

If necessary, convert into Cartesian coordinates so that the distance formula

$$d = \sqrt{(x_1 - y_1)^2 + (y_1 - y_2)^2 + (z_1 - z_2)^2}$$

can be used. The conversion from cylindrical coordinates to Cartesian xyz-coordinates is given by

$$(r, \theta, z) \quad \rightarrow \quad (r\cos(\theta), r\sin(\theta), z)$$

while

$$(\rho, \theta, \phi) \quad \rightarrow \quad (\rho\cos(\theta)\cos(\phi), \rho\sin(\theta)\cos(\phi), \rho\sin(\phi))$$

specifies the spherical-to-Cartesian conversion.

P10.1.10 Write a function `Pnew = Convert(P,Q)` that converts the point `P` into the coordinate system associated with `Q`. Assume the structures given in the previous problem. Make use of the Cartesian-to-cylindrical conversions

$$r = \sqrt{x^2 + y^2} \qquad \theta = \text{atan2}(y, x)$$

and the Cartesian-to-spherical conversions

$$\rho = \sqrt{x^2 + y^2 + z^2} \qquad \phi = \arccos(z/\rho) \qquad \phi = \text{atan2}(y, x).$$

10.2   Fenced in Twice?

Problem Statement

Suppose we are given a set of rectangles whose sides are parallel to the coordinate axes. See Figure 10.4 where we have shaded the rectangles to reveal the various possibilities of overlap. We say that a rectangle is *isolated* if it does not intersect any other rectangle. How many of the rectangles are isolated? For the example displayed in Figure 10.4 we observe that the answer to this question is twelve.

Program Development

At the heart of this problem is an intersection problem, namely, under what conditions does a pair of rectangles intersect? It is slightly easier to reason about the opposite situation: Under what conditions is a pair of rectangles disjoint? Figure 10.5 sheds light on this question. A rectangle R_1 is disjoint from a rectangle R_2 if and only if one or more of the following situations prevails:

1. R_1's bottom edge is above R_2's top edge.

2. R_1's top edge is below R_2's bottom edge.

3. R_1's left edge is to the right of R_2's right edge.

4. R_1's right edge is to the left of R_2's left edge.

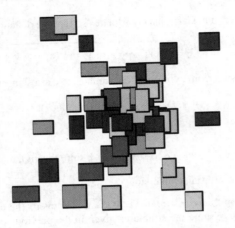

Figure 10.4. *A Set of Rectangles.*

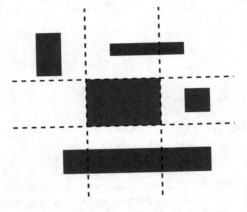

Figure 10.5. *Rectangle Intersection.*

The Function `MakeRect`

```
function R = MakeRect(a,b,c,d)
% a and b are real numbers that satisfy a <= b.
% c and d are real numbers that satisfy c <= d.
% R is a rectangle:  the set of all (x,y) that satisfy
%        R.a <= x <= R.b, R.c <= y <= R.d
R = struct('left',a,'right',b,'bot',c,'top',d);
```

To check out these possibilities it is convenient to represent a rectangle using a 4-field structure. Note that four numbers are required to specify a rectangle whose sides are parallel to the coordinate axes. We could use the length and width together with the xy-coordinates of the center. However, since our problem deals with boundaries, it makes more sense to parameterize based on the left/right x-values and the bottom/top y-values. See the function MakeRect given above.

With this design of the rectangle structure, it is easy to verify if two rectangles R1 and R2 are disjoint. We simply check to see if any of the four criteria listed above are true.

The Function Disjoint

```
function alfa = Disjoint(R1,R2)
% R1 and R2 are rectangles.
% alfa is true if R1 and R2 are disjoint.
% Otherwise alfa is false.

R1_Is_Above = R1.bot > R2.top;
R1_Is_Below = R2.bot > R1.top;
R1_Is_Right = R1.left > R2.right;
R1_Is_Left  = R2.left > R1.right;
alfa = R1_Is_Above || R1_Is_Below || R1_Is_Left || R1_Is_Right;
```

Notice the use of logical variables in the implementation. Each is assigned the result of a boolean expression. It is *not* necessary to use if-statements when setting up a logical variable, e.g.,

```
if R1.bot > R2.top
    R1_Is_Above = 1;
else
    R1_Is_Above = 0;
end
```

This is because an expression such as R1.bot>R2.top has a boolean value (0 or 1) itself and can be assigned directly to R1_Is_Above:

```
R1_Is_Above = R1.bot > R2.top;
```

Now suppose T is a length-n structure array of rectangles and we wish to determine if a given rectangle S is isolated from the rectangles in the array T. This involves a scan through the array T in a manner similar to linear search: we look for the smallest k for which Disjoint(S,T(k)) is false. If no such k can be found, then S is isolated from rectangles T(1),...,T(n). See the function IsIsolated below.

We are now set to write a function that can take a structure array of rectangles R and identify which rectangles are isolated. To motivate the general algorithm we consider the $n = 5$ case. Rectangle

R(1)		R(2), R(3), R(4), R(5)
R(2)		R(1), R(3), R(4), R(5)
R(3)	is isolated if it is disjoint from	R(1), R(2), R(4), R(5)
R(4)		R(1), R(2), R(3), R(5)
R(5)		R(1), R(2), R(3), R(4).

The Function `IsIsolated`

```
function beta = IsIsolated(S,T)
% S is a rectangle and T is a structure array of rectangles.
% beta is true if S is isolated from T.
% Otherwise beta is false.

n = length(T);
k = 1;
while k<=n && Disjoint(S,T(k))
    % S is disjoint from T(1),...,T(k)
    k = k+1;
end
beta = (k==n+1);
```

Thus, to check if R(k) is isolated we simply apply the function IsIsolated(S,T) with S equal to R(k) and T equal to the structure array [R(1:k-1) R(k+1:n)]. See the function ListOfDisjoints.

The Function `ListOfDisjoints`

```
function i = ListOfDisjoints(R)
% R is a structure array of rectangles.
% i is a vector of indices that identify the isolated rectangles.

n = length(R);
i = [];
for k=1:n
    if IsIsolated(R(k),[R(1:k-1) R(k+1:n)])
        % R(i) is disjoint from all other rectangles
        i = [i k];
    end
end
```

Notice that in the if-statement it is enough to write

```
if  IsIsolated(R(k),[R(1:k-1)  R(k+1:n)])
```

Checking whether the returned value is 1 or 0,

```
if  IsIsolated(R(k),[R(1:k-1)  R(k+1:n)]) == 1
```

is redundant since such a check results in 1 or 0, which is precisely the value returned by the function in the first place.

We can now solve the original problem of determining which rectangles in the set are isolated. In order to show the results graphically, we implement the function ShowRect which draws a colored rectangle.

The Function ShowRect

```
function ShowRect(R,s)
% R is a rectangle
% s is one of the characters 'k','w','r','g','b','m','c','y'
% Displays R in the current figure window using the color s
% Assumes hold is on

fill([R.left R.right R.right R.left],...
      [R.bot R.bot R.top R.top],s)
plot([R.left R.right R.right R.left],...
      [R.bot R.bot R.top R.top],'k','Linewidth',2)
```

The script Eg10_2 displays a set of random rectangles and distinguishes between isolated and intersecting rectangles using color. Sample output is shown is Figure 10.6.

The Script Eg10_2

```
% Script Eg10_2
% Displays a random set of rectangles and highlights those
%    rectangles that are isolated from all the others

% Generate n random rectangles...
n = 50;
for i=1:n
    xc = randn(1); yc = randn(1); L = .5+.5*rand(1);
    W = .5+.5*rand(1);
    R(i) = MakeRect(xc-L/3,xc+L/3,yc-W/3,yc+W/3);
end
% Display all the rectangles...
close all
figure
axis equal off
hold on
for i = 1:n
    ShowRect(R(i),'y')
end
% Determine and highlight the isolated rectangles..
i = ListOfDisjoints(R);
for k = 1:length(i)
    j = i(k);
    % Rectangle j is isolated...
    ShowRect(R(j),'r')
end
hold off
title(sprintf('Number of Isolated Rectangles = %1d', ...
       length(i)),'Fontsize',14)
```

Number of Isolated Rectangles = 9

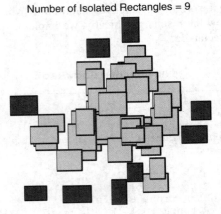

Figure 10.6. Eg10_2 *Sample Output.*

Talking Point: Intersection Problems in Computer Graphics

It is easy to make the rectangle intersection problem that we considered in this section more difficult. For example, if we allowed the rectangles to be tilted, then a more lengthy sequence of tests would be required to check for overlap. Highlighting the intersection would be even more complex.

   If we allow the rectangles to "float" in three-dimensional space, then a new type of problem arises. What would an observer at a specified location "see" when looking into a cloud of randomly oriented rectangles? Problems like this abound in computer graphics. Curved surfaces in three-dimensional space are typically approximated by thousands of small triangles. If we "shoot a ray" from the observer to the curved surface, which triangles does it intersect and in what order? This type of computation arises in "ray tracing," a well-known technique that is used to render images.

   In computer animation, the problem of collision detection requires the fast solution of intersection problems. A flag blowing in the wind can be approximated by huge numbers of connected triangles that are moving about in three-dimensional space. For an accurate rendition, those triangles should never intersect.

MATLAB Review

Logical Variables

Logical variables are sometimes handy for recording the results of true-false tests. We can use the boolean variable InAB to record the result of a test that checks to see if z is in the interval $[a,b]$:

```
InAB = (a <= z) && (z <= b)
```

Just as arithmetic expressions can be rearranged into equivalent forms, so can boolean expressions:

```
InAB = ~((z < a) || (b < z))
```

These two equivalent expressions illustrate *de Morgan's law*, a rule which states that if $b1$ and $b2$ are boolean expressions, then ~(b1 || b2) is equivalent to (~b1) && (~b2).

Boolean-Valued Functions

Boolean-valued functions are essential for the packaging of more complicated logical tests. An ability to encapsulate boolean computations in a boolean function is as important as being able to package numerical computations in a real- or integer-valued function. In a boolean-valued function the returned value is either 0 (false) or 1 (true).

Exercises

M10.2.1 Modify `Disjoint` to implement the following function:

```
function alfa = Overlap(R1,R2)
% R1 and R2 are rectangles.
% alfa is true if R1 and R2 overlap.  Otherwise alfa is false.
```

P10.2.2 Implement the following function:

```
function alfa = IsSquare(R)
% R is a rectangle structure.
% alfa is true if R is a square.  Otherwise alfa is false.
```

P10.2.3 Suppose $L \leq R$. Here is a structure suitable for representing the interval $[L, R]$:

```
I = struct('L',L,'R',R)
```

Complete the following function so that it performs as specified:

```
function alfa = Contain(I1,I2)
% alfa is true if and only if interval I1 is contained in interval I2
%    or vice versa.
```

P10.2.4 Write a function `p = Perimeter(R)` that returns the perimeter of rectangle `R`.

P10.2.5 Write a function `C = Contains(R1,R2)` that is true if either rectangle `R1` is contained in rectangle `R2` or vice versa. The function should return false otherwise.

P10.2.6 Write a function `P = Rotate(R)` that takes a rectangle `R` and produces a rectangle `P` obtained by rotating `R` clockwise 90 degrees about its lower left vertex.

P10.2.7 Any rectangle can be subdivided into a square and a "left over" rectangle. Write a function `[Square,LeftOver] = Split(R)` that does this. The input and output parameters should be rectangle structures.

P10.2.8 By connecting the midpoints of opposite sides, a given rectangle can be subdivided into a set of four equal rectangles. Write a function `LittleRs = Subdivide(R)` that takes a rectangle `R` and produces a length-4 structure array of rectangles that houses the four rectangles obtained by this subdivision process. The order in which the subdivided rectangles appear in the structure array is not important.

P10.2.9 Suppose a and b are radian measures. Here is a structure suitable for representing the chord that connects unit circle points $(\cos(a), \sin(a))$ and $(\cos(b), \sin(b))$:

```
C = struct('a',a,'b',b)
```

Complete the following function so that it performs as specified:

```
function alfa = ChordIntersect(C1,C2)
% alfa is true if and only if chord C1 intersects chord C2.
```

P10.2.10 (a) Write a function A = OverlapArea(R1,R2) that returns the area of the intersection of rectangles R1 and R2. (b) Assuming that R is a length-n structure array of rectangles, write a function [i,j] = MaxOverlap(R) that returns the indices associated with the two rectangles in R that have maximum overlapping area.

P10.2.11 (a) Write a function I = OverlapRect(R1,R2) that returns a rectangle structure representing the intersection of rectangles R1 and R2. Set I to be the empty vector if R1 and R2 do not overlap. (b) By making effective use of ShowRect and OverlapRect, write a script that draws two random rectangles and highlights their intersection. (Use the built-in function isempty to test the value returned by OverlapRect.)

P10.2.12 Write a function P = SortRectangles(R) that returns a permutation of a structure array of rectangles R so that they are in order of increasing area.

P10.2.13 Four numbers are required to specify a rectangle whose sides are parallel to the coordinate axes. The structure we used for rectangle representation involved the left and right x-values (a and b) and the bottom and top y-values (c and d). An alternative choice would be to use the x- and y-coordinates of the rectangle's centroid and its length and width. Define a structure that respresents a rectangle using these four numbers and re-solve problems P10.2.4 to P10.2.6.

10.3   Not Perfect?

Problem Statement

Any triangle T has a unique inscribed circle and a unique circumscribed circle as shown in Figure 10.7. The inscribed circle is the largest circle that fits inside T; its center is at the intersection of the three angle bisectors. Likewise, the circumscribed circle is the smallest circle that encloses T; its center is the common point where the perpendicular bisectors

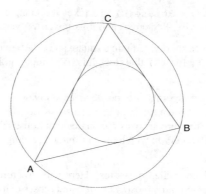

Figure 10.7. *The Inscribed and Circumscribed Circles of a Triangle.*

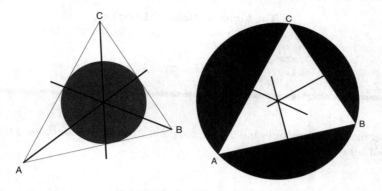

Figure 10.8. *The Construction of the Inscribed and Circumscribed Circles.*

of the three sides meet. See Figure 10.8. If r and R are the radii of the inscribed and circumscribed circles for a given triangle T, then

$$\rho(T) = \sqrt{1 - \left(\frac{2r}{R}\right)}$$

is a metric that measures how far T is from being equilateral. Using elementary trigonometry it is possible to show that $\rho(T) = 0$ if and only if T is equilateral. As the side lengths vary more and more among themselves (as T becomes "more scalene") the value of ρ approaches 1. Write a script that generates and displays a random triangle together with its inscribed circle, circumscribed circle, and ρ-value.

Program Development

This is a problem about circles, lines, and triangles. To facilitate program development we define a number of useful structures through their corresponding make functions.

The Function **MakeCircle**

```
function C = MakeCircle(P,r)
% P is a point and r is a nonnegative number.
% C is a circle with center C.P and radius C.r.
C = struct('P',P,'r',r);
```

The Function **MakeLine**

```
function L = MakeLine(P,del_x,del_y)
% P is a point.
% del_x and del_y are real numbers.
% L is the line through L.P with slope L.del_y/L.del_x.
% (Note that if del_x = 0 then L is vertical.)
L = struct('P',P,'del_x',del_x,'del_y',del_y);
```

The Function `MakeTriangle`

```
function T = MakeTriangle(A,B,C)
% A, B, and C are points.
% T is a triangle with vertices T.A, T.B, and T.C.
T = struct('A',A,'B',B,'C',C);
```

Notice that the above structures build upon the point structure introduced in §10.1 and are reproduced here for convenience.

The Function `MakePoint`

```
function P = MakePoint(x,y)
% P is a point with x-coordinate P.x and y-coordinate P.y.
P = struct('x',x,'y',y);
```

Plane geometry is filled with hierarchies and these examples show that we can have hierarchies of structures. That is, a structure can have a field that is another structure. Thus, the fragment

```
V1 = MakePoint(3,0);
V2 = MakePoint(0,4);
V3 = MakePoint(0,0);
T  = MakeTriangle(V1,V2,V3);
```

assigns to T a 3-4-5 Pythagorean triangle. The command

```
fill([T.A.x T.B.x T.C.x],[T.A.y T.B.y T.C.y],'r')
```

would display the triangle in red. If we have a structure whose fields are also structures, then references involve multiple dots. Thus, T.B.x names the x-coordinate of the B vertex of triangle T. The functions ShowCircle and ShowTriangle are a pair of graphics functions that further illustrate the manipulation of structures that have structure fields.

The Function `ShowCircle`

```
function ShowCircle(C,s)
% C is a circle.
% s is one of the characters 'k','w','r','g','b','m','c','y'.
% Displays C in the current figure window using color s.
% Assumes hold is on.
theta = linspace(0,2*pi);
x = C.P.x + C.r * cos(theta);
y = C.P.y + C.r * sin(theta);
fill(x,y,s)
```

The Function `ShowTriangle`

```
function ShowTriangle(T,s)
% T is a triangle.
% s is one of the characters 'k','w','r','g','b','m','c','y'.
% Displays T in the current figure window using color s.
% Assumes hold is on.
fill([T.A.x T.B.x T.C.x T.A.x],[T.A.y T.B.y T.C.y T.A.y],s)
```

Returning to the problem posed at the beginning of this section, let us write in pseudocode the calculations required for the circumscribed circle. Referring to Figure 10.8, the steps to take are as follows:

1. Compute L_{AB}, the perpendicular bisector for line segment AB.

2. Compute L_{AC}, the perpendicular bisector for line segment AC.

3. Compute the intersection point Q_1 associated with these two line segments.

4. The circumscribed circle has center Q_1 and radius R equal to the distance from Q_1 to vertex A.

We need the formulae for the perpendicular bisector of a line segment. Suppose (A_x, A_y) and (B_x, B_y) are the endpoints of a line segment. The midpoint and slope of the line segment are given by

$$P = \left(\frac{A_x + B_x}{2}, \frac{A_y + B_y}{2} \right)$$

$$s = \frac{B_y - A_y}{B_x - A_x}.$$

The perpendicular bisector passes through P and has slope $-1/s$. We therefore obtain the following function.

The Function `PerpBisector`

```
function L = PerpBisector(A,B)
% A and B are distinct points.
% L is the line that passes through the midpoint of line
%    segment AB and is perpendicular to line segment AB.

% The midpoint
P = MakePoint((A.x+B.x)/2,(A.y+B.y)/2);
% The slope is the negative reciprocal of line segment AB's slope
del_x = B.x-A.x;
del_y = B.y-A.y;
L = MakeLine(P,-del_y,del_x);
```

Before we move on to compute the intersection point of two line segments, let us write the pseudocode for computing the inscribed circle, which is similar to the circumscribed circle computation:

1. Compute L_A, the angle bisector for vertex A.

2. Compute L_B, the angle bisector for vertex B.

3. Compute the intersection point Q_2 associated with these two line segments.

4. The inscribed circle has center Q_2 and radius r equal to the minimum distance from Q_2 to side AB.

For angle bisection, suppose $A = (A_x, A_y)$, $B = (B_x, B_y)$, and $C = (C_x, C_y)$ are distinct points and that we want to construct a line that bisects angle BAC. The slope angles associated with line segments AB and AC are given by

$$\theta_{AB} = \arctan\left(\frac{B_y - A_y}{B_x - A_x}\right) \qquad \theta_{AC} = \arctan\left(\frac{C_y - A_y}{C_x - A_x}\right)$$

and thus the slope angle associated with the angle bisector is $(\theta_{AB} + \theta_{AC})/2$. Using the MATLAB four-quadrant inverse tangent function `atan2` we obtain the following function.

The Function `AngleBisector`

```
function L = AngleBisector(B,A,C)
% B, A, and C are distinct points.
% L is a line through A with the property that it bisects
% angle BAC.

% The slope angles for the rays AB and AC...
thetaAB = atan2(B.y-A.y,B.x-A.x);
thetaAC = atan2(C.y-A.y,C.x-A.x);

% The tangent of the midway angle...
tau = tan((thetaAB+thetaAC)/2);
if tau == inf
    % The bisector is vertical. Slope = 1/0 = inf...
    L = MakeLine(A,0,1);
else
    % The slope of the bisector is finite: tau/1
    L = MakeLine(A,1,tau);
end
```

Both circle computations require the determination of line intersections. The center of the circumscribed circle is at the intersection of any pair of perpendicular bisectors to the sides. The center of the inscribed circle is at the intersection of any pair of vertex bisectors. Recall that our lines are represented in a point-slope format. If a line L_1 passes through point (x_1, y_1) and has slope $\Delta y_1 / \Delta x_1$, then it is defined by the set of points with xy-coordinates

(v_1, w_1) that satisfy the equations

$$v_1(t_1) = x_1 + t_1 \cdot \Delta x_1, \qquad w_1(t_1) = y_1 + t_1 \cdot \Delta y_1, \qquad -\infty < t_1 < \infty. \qquad (10.1)$$

This is the parametric definition of the line L_1. Likewise, if a line L_2 passes through point (x_2, y_2) and has slope $\Delta y_2 / \Delta x_2$, then it is defined by the set of points (v_2, w_2) that satisfy the equations

$$v_2(t_2) = x_2 + t_2 \cdot \Delta x_2, \qquad w_2(t_2) = y_2 + t_2 \cdot \Delta y_2, \qquad -\infty < t_2 < \infty. \qquad (10.2)$$

Assuming that L_1 and L_2 are not parallel, then the intersection is the one and only point that is on both lines. Setting the x-coordinates to be equal, $v_1(t_1) = v_2(t_2)$, and the y-coordinates to be equal, $w_1(t_1) = w_2(t_2)$, we obtain from (10.1) and (10.2)

$$\begin{aligned} x_1 + t_1 \cdot \Delta x_1 &= x_2 + t_2 \cdot \Delta x_2 \\ y_1 + t_1 \cdot \Delta y_1 &= y_2 + t_2 \cdot \Delta y_2. \end{aligned}$$

Rearranging the unknowns t_1 and t_2 to be on the left-hand side gives

$$\begin{aligned} -\Delta x_1 \cdot t_1 + \Delta x_2 \cdot t_2 &= x_1 - x_2 \\ -\Delta y_1 \cdot t_1 + \Delta y_2 \cdot t_2 &= y_1 - y_2. \end{aligned} \qquad (10.3)$$

This is the familiar problem of "two equations in two unknowns." If we call the solution values t_1^* and t_2^*, then the intersection point is given by

$$P = (x_1 + t_1^* \cdot \Delta x_1, y_1 + t_1^* \cdot \Delta y_1) = (x_2 + t_2^* \cdot \Delta x_2, y_2 + t_2^* \cdot \Delta y_2).$$

We could solve (10.3) by substituting one equation into the other, solving for one unknown at a time. Instead, we show below a method that takes advantage of the MATLAB special operator for solving *systems of linear equations*. The simultaneous equation (10.3) can be written as a 2-by-2 system of linear equations:

$$\begin{bmatrix} -\Delta x_1 & \Delta x_2 \\ -\Delta y_1 & \Delta y_2 \end{bmatrix} \begin{bmatrix} t_1^* \\ t_2^* \end{bmatrix} = \begin{bmatrix} x_1 - x_2 \\ y_1 - y_2 \end{bmatrix}.$$

The values in the 2-by-2 matrix on the left are known, as are the values in the length-2 column vector on the right-hand side. The length-2 column vector on the left-hand side is the unknown. Such a linear system in MATLAB can be conveniently solved using the backslash operator "\":

The Function Intersect

```
function P = Intersect(L1,L2)
% P is the single point at which lines L1 and L2 intersect

A = [-L1.del_x L2.del_x; -L1.del_y L2.del_y];
b = [L1.P.x-L2.P.x; L1.P.y-L2.P.y];
tStar = A\b;
P = MakePoint(L1.P.x+tStar(1)*L1.del_x,L1.P.y+tStar(1)*L1.del_y);
```

At this point we have the necessary tools to compute the center Q_1 of the circumscribed circle and the center Q_2 of the inscribed circle. The last order of business is to compute their respective radii. For the circumscribed circle, the radius R is just the distance from Q_1 to any of the three triangle vertices. For the inscribed circle, the radius r is the distance from the center Q_2 to any of sides AB, BC, or CA.

To compute the minimum distance between a point $P_0 = (x_0, y_0)$ and a point on a line that passes through $P_1 = (x_1, y_1)$ and $P_2 = (x_2, y_2)$, we set the derivative of the distance function

$$d(t) = \sqrt{(x(t) - x_0)^2 + (y(t) - y_0)^2}$$

to zero where

$$x(t) = x_1 + t(x_2 - x_1), \qquad y(t) = y_1 + t(y_2 - y_1). \tag{10.4}$$

Again we are using the parametric definition of a line, so $(x(t), y(t))$, where $-\infty < t < \infty$, is the set of points on the line that passes through $P_1 = (x_1, y_1)$ and $P_2 = (x_2, y_2)$. A calculation shows that if

$$t_* = \frac{(x_0 - x_1)(x_2 - x_1) + (y_0 - y_1)(y_2 - y_1)}{(x_2 - x_1)^2 + (y_2 - y_1)^2},$$

then $d'(t_*) = 0$. Thus, $d(t_*)$ is the minimum distance to the *line* through P_1 and P_2 and $(x(t_*), y(t_*))$ is the corresponding closest point.

To compute the nearest point on the *line segment* that connects P_1 and P_2 we have to consider the value of t_*. Note from the parametric description (10.4) that $t = 0$ corresponds to the point P_1, $t = 1$ corresponds to P_2, and t-values in between 0 and 1 correspond to line segment points. Thus, if $t_* \le 0$, then P_1 is the closest point. If $t_* \ge 1$, then P_2 is the closest point. Otherwise, the closest point to the line through P_1 and P_2 is on the connecting line segment. The three cases are depicted in Figure 10.9. The function `Nearest` encapsulates it all.

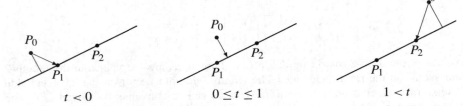

Figure 10.9. *Distance from a Point to a Line Segment.*

With the functions `PerpBisector`, `AngleBisector`, `Intersect`, and `Nearest` we are set to implement our pseudocode procedures for the two circles. See the function `InAndOut`. Notice how the implementation of `InAndOut` "reads" just like the pseudocode because of our judicious use of structures. Here you can see clearly the advantage of both data abstraction and procedural abstraction. Can you imagine solving this problem thinking at the level of xy-coordinates all the way through? Abstracting away the "xy details" allows us to operate at the higher level of points, lines, circles, and triangles. Similarly, breaking down the problem into distinct tasks, as organized in pseudocode,

The Function **Nearest**

```
function P = Nearest(P0,P1,P2)
% P0, P1, and P2 are points with P1 and P2 distinct.
% P is the nearest point to P0 that is on the line segment
%   connecting P1 and P2.

tstar = ((P0.x-P1.x)*(P2.x-P1.x) + (P0.y-P1.y)*(P2.y-P1.y)) ...
          / GetDist(P1,P2)^2;
if tstar <= 0
    P = P1;
elseif tstar >= 1
    P = P2;
else
    P = MakePoint(P1.x + tstar*(P2.x-P1.x), ...
                  P1.y + tstar*(P2.y-P1.y));
end
```

The Function **InAndOut**

```
function [C_In,C_Out] = InAndOut(T)
% T is a triangle.
% C_In  is the associated inscribed circle.
% C_Out is the associated circumscribed circle.

% Extract the vertices...
A = T.A; B = T.B; C = T.C;

% Inscribed circle.
% Construct two angle bisectors, their intersection Q2,
% and the minimum distance from Q2 to side AB.
LA = AngleBisector(B,A,C);
LB = AngleBisector(A,B,C);
Q2  = Intersect(LA,LB);
r   = GetDist(Q2,Nearest(Q2,A,B));
C_In = MakeCircle(Q2,r);

% Circumscribed circle.
% Construct two perpendicular bisectors, their intersection Q1,
% and Q1's distance to vertex A
LAB = PerpBisector(A,B);
LAC = PerpBisector(A,C);
Q1 = Intersect(LAB,LAC);
R = GetDist(A,Q1);
C_Out = MakeCircle(Q1,R);
```

and then packaging each task as a function, allows us to solve this complex problem one subproblem at a time.

Finally, we write a script Eg10_3 to generate a random triangle, draw the inscribed and circumscribed circles, and determine the ρ-value of the triangle that measures its "nearness" to being equilateral. See Figure 10.10 for sample output.

The Script `Eg10_3`

```
% Script Eg10_3
% Displays a random triangle and the associate inscribed
% and circumscribed circles.

% Set up the figure window...
close all
figure
axis equal off
hold on

% Generate a random triangle and its inscribed and circumscribed
% circles...
A = MakePoint(rand(1),rand(1));
B = MakePoint(rand(1),rand(1));
C = MakePoint(rand(1),rand(1));
T = MakeTriangle(A,B,C);
[C_In,C_Out] = InAndOut(T);

% Display...
ShowCircle(C_Out,'y')
ShowTriangle(T,'k');
ShowCircle(C_In,'r')
rho = sqrt(1 - (2*C_In.r/C_Out.r)^2);
title(sprintf('rho(T) = %5.3f',rho),'Fontsize',14)
hold off
shg
```

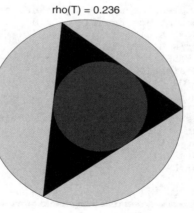

rho(T) = 0.236

Figure 10.10. *Sample Output from the Script* `Eg10_3`.

Talking Point: Nearness Metrics

The radius ratio based on the circumscribed and inscribed circles is an example of a "shape metric." In certain applications where general regions are partitioned into triangles, it is important for the sake of accuracy to have the resulting triangles as near to being equilateral as possible. The function $\rho(T)$ is one way to measure success in this regard.

Nearness metrics are ubiquitous in computational science and engineering. In fitting a curve to experimental data, how do we measure the "goodness" of the approximation? When two DNA sequences are compared, how can their similarity be quantified? Given two sets of fingerprints, how can we assess their proximity in the "space" of fingerprints? These issues are discussed further in Chapter 15.

MATLAB Review

Structures with Fields that Are Structures

It is perfectly legal in the `struct` command for any field value to be a structure. To access a field value that is in a structure that is itself a field of another structure, "chain up" the dot expressions. E.g., the expression `F.G.h` references the value that is in field h of structure G, which is a field of structure F.

atan2

This is the "four-quadrant" arctangent function.

$$\text{If}\begin{cases} x \geq 0,\ y \geq 0 \\ x \leq 0,\ y \geq 0 \\ x \leq 0,\ y \leq 0 \\ x \geq 0,\ y \leq 0 \end{cases}\text{and } z\ =\ \texttt{atan2(y,x)},\ \text{then}\begin{cases} 0 \leq z \leq \pi/2 \\ \pi/2 \leq z \leq \pi \\ -\pi \leq z \leq -\pi/2 \\ -\pi/2 \leq z \leq 0 \end{cases}\text{and } \tan(z) = y/x.$$

Linear Systems of Equations

If A is a nonsingular n-by-n matrix and b is a column n-vector, then x = A\b assigns to x the solution to the linear system defined by A and b. Thus,

```
A = [1 2 ; 3 4];
b = [7 ; 23];
x = A\b;
```

sets x = [9 ; -1] since $x_1 + 2x_2 = 7$ and $3x_1 + 4x_2 = 23$ when $x_1 = 9$ and $x_2 = -1$.

Exercises

M10.3.1 The area of a triangle having side lengths a, b, and c is given by

$$A = \sqrt{s(s-a)(s-b)(s-c)}$$

where $s = (a+b+c)/2$. Write a function A = `TriangleArea(T)` that returns the area of triangle T.

M10.3.2 Write a function alfa = `CircleIntersect(C1,C2)` that returns true if and only if the circles C1 and C2 intersect.

M10.3.3 Write a function Q = `NearTri(P,T)` that returns the point on the boundary of triangle T that is closest to the point P. Make effective use of the functions `Nearest` and `GetDist`.

M10.3.4 By connecting the opposing vertices of a rectangle one obtains four triangles. Write a function SmallTs = Rect2Triangles(R) that returns a structure array of the four triangles that result from connecting the opposing vertices of rectangle R.

P10.3.5 Suppose V is a length-n structure array of points with the property that $V(1),\dots,V(n)$ are arranged clockwise around the unit circle. By connecting these points we obtain a polygon P with n sides. It is possible to show that the centroid of P is inside P. Moreover, we can partition P into n triangles by connecting the centroid to each vertex. Write a function A = PolygonArea(V) that returns the area of P. Make effective use of the TriangleArea function in problem M10.3.1.

P10.3.6 Assume the availability of these two functions:

```
function alfa = DeltaEqual(P1,P2,Q1,Q2,delta)
% P1, P2, Q1, and Q2 are points and delta is a positive real number.
% The line segment from P1 to P2 and the line segment from Q1 to Q2
% are "delta equal" if their length differs by at most delta*D where
% D is the length of the longer of the two line segments.
% alfa is true if and only if these two line segments are delta equal.

function alfa = NearlyParallel(P1,P2,Q1,Q2,delta)
% P1, P2, Q1, and Q2 are points and delta is a positive real number.
% The line through P1 and P2 and the line through Q1 and Q2
% are delta parallel if the sine of their intersection is delta or
% less in absolute value.
% alpha is true if and only if these two lines are delta parallel.
```

A quadrilateral with at least one pair of parallel sides is a *trapezoid*. A quadrilateral with the property that opposite sides are parallel is a *parallelogram*. A parallelogram with four equal sides is a *rhombus*. A rhombus whose diagonals are equal in length is a *square*. Implement the following function by making effective use of NearlyEqual and NearlyParallel:

```
function [T,P,R,S] = SpecialQuads(V1,V2,V3,V4,delta)
% V1,V2,V3,V4 are points that define a quadrilateral Q whose opposite
% sides do not intersect.
% T is true if and only if Q is nearly a trapezoid.
% P is true if and only if Q is nearly a parallelogram.
% R is true if and only if Q is nearly a rhombus.
% S is true if and only if Q is nearly a square.
```

Clearly define the structures that your implementation assumes.

P10.3.7 Write a boolean-valued function LSIntersect that returns the value true if the line segment that connects (x_1,y_1) and (x_2,y_2) intersects the line segment that connects (x_3,y_3) and (x_4,y_4). Show how LSIntersect can be used to terminate the iteration in the script Eg6_3 as soon as the current polygon is simple.

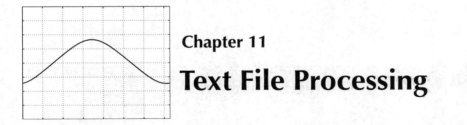

Chapter 11

Text File Processing

11.1 Latitude and Daylight
Data Acquisition and Conversion

11.2 Nearby Millions
Writing and Representation

Sensor technology and storage technology have advanced to the stage where unimaginably large data sets are automatically collected and archived. A radio telescope may acquire 10^{12} bytes of information per week during the course of building a digital star map. Equally large volumes of data may be produced from a flight simulation that is used to design a new airliner. Science and engineering in the 21st century is data-driven science and engineering.

Working with large data sets involves interaction with files. A common pattern is to (a) read data from a file, (b) compute with it, and (c) write the results to another file. Familiarity with this process is critical.

To illustrate these points we consider a pair of file-processing computations. In the first example we use data from the U.S. Naval Observatory to check the accuracy of a simple model that predicts hours of daylight as a function of date and latitude. The daily sunrise/sunset data for a particular city is encoded in a single formatted file. The programming challenge is to convert the information in each file line into numbers that can be subsequently manipulated. Using data to affirm (or undermine) a theory is perhaps the most central activity in all of science.

The second example uses data from the 2000 U.S. census to conveniently explore population density across the country. We build a graphical environment that solicits a U.S. location via the mouse and then displays the number of people who live within a specified distance of that location.

A fringe benefit of our file-processing discussion is that it builds a sensitivity for the overhead associated with memory access. In the three-step paradigm mentioned above, the overall efficiency typically depends much more on the data motion steps (a) and (c) than upon the actual computations in (b). This is a general fact of life about high-performance computing, discussed earlier in Chapter 8.

255

Programming Preview

Concepts

Online data sets, reading a data file, writing to a data file, format, string-numeric conversion, text files, binary files, ReadMe files, benchmarking, megabytes, giga-bytes, terabytes, petabytes.

Language Features

`fopen, fclose`: Commands to open, close a data file.

`feof`: Returns 1 if the end-of-file marker in a data file has been reached.

`fgetl`: Returns as a string the next unread line in a text file.

`fprintf`: Can be used to write data as text to a file.

`str2double, str2num`: Functions to convert strings into double precision values.

`fwrite`: Write binary data to a file.

`fread`: Read binary data from a file.

Special Prerequisites

This chapter involves advanced string manipulation. §9.1 is critical.

MatTV

Video 19. Cell Arrays

How to create and use cell arrays, focusing on their use with strings.

11.1   Latitude and Daylight

Problem Statement

Summer days and winter nights are longer the further away you are from the equator. For example, if you live in Anchorage, Alaska at latitude 61°13′N, then on June 22 (summer solstice) it is about 19 hours and 22 minutes from sunrise to sunset. Likewise, it is about 19 hours and 22 minutes from sunset to sunrise on December 22 (winter solstice). In contrast, the Sun is up (down) for just 13 hours and 55 minutes on June 22 (December 22) for the residents of Miami, Florida at latitude 25°47′N.

Hours of daylight is a surprisingly complicated function of latitude and date. A high-precision estimate would take into account (a) the Earth's variable distance to the Sun, (b) the Earth's variable speed as it orbits the Sun, (c) the diameter of the Sun, (d) the Earth's oblate spheroid shape, and (e) the exact solstice/equinox times.

On the other hand, the computation simplifies a great deal if we assume that (a′) the Earth's orbit is a perfect circle, (b′) the Earth moves at a uniform rate around the Sun once every 365 days, (c′) the Sun is a point source of light infinitely far away, (d′) the Earth is a perfect sphere, and (e′) every Earth location has 12 hours of daylight on March 22 (vernal equinox). Let us pretend that a scientist has developed this simplified model and implemented the following function based upon its assumptions:

```
function  H = Daylight(Lat)
% Lat specifies a latitude in degrees. (-90<=Lat<=90)
% H is a 365-by-1 vector where H(k) is the hours of daylight
% received at latitidude Lat on day k. Days are indexed
% sequentialy from Jan 1 (k=1) to Dec 31 (k=365).
```

The details of the implementation do not concern us. (It involves spherical coordinates, a tangent plane, and trigonometric manipulation.) Our concern is with the *accuracy* of the simplified model.

Using the World Wide Web, get daily sunrise/sunset data for a range of cities at different latitudes from around the world. Treating this data as exact, assess the accuracy of the simplified model as expressed through the function Daylight.

Program Development

The act of acquiring data from the Web and using it in a MATLAB computation is an essential skill. It is a four-step process.

- *Locate*. Find the data source on the Web.

- *Acquire*. Sometimes the file(s) containing the required data can be downloaded with the click of the mouse. For smaller data sets that can be reasonably displayed on the screen, there is the option of "cutting-and-pasting" into a user-created data file.

- *Input*. Read the data from the file line by line (as strings) and place the results in a cell array.

- *Compute*. With the data in a cell array, it is "business as usual." Scripts and functions can access and use the cell array data, perhaps after some decoding.

Depending on how the data file is structured, there are other options for the input step. We have chosen to adopt a file-to-cell-array-of-strings approach because it works well in a wide range of applications and is simple to implement.

We say a few words about data files before we begin. Files have *lines* and *invisible markers* and can be visualized as follows:

Carriage returns mark the end of lines, and the end-of-file (eof) marker signifies the end of the file. The act of reading a file into a cell array C proceeds as follows:

Open the file.   (11.1)

```
i = 0;
```
while The end of the file is not reached   (11.2)
```
    i = i+1;
```
Copy the next line in the file into C{i}.   (11.3)
```
end
```
Close the file.   (11.4)

Special file-processing commands are necessary to implement this fragment. If you want to access a file, then it must first be opened using the fopen command, e.g.,

```
fid = fopen('MyFile.dat','r')
```

This assumes that MyFile.dat is in the current working directory. (Later, we shall deal with the case when the file to be accessed is in a different directory.) Once this "open for business" command is executed, the data in the file MyFile.dat can be read because the read ('r') option was selected. The function fopen returns a *file id*, a number that is uniquely associated with the file and is used by other file-processing commands. File id's are necessary because there may be more than one file that is open during a file-processing program and they need to be distinguishable.

Files are sequentially read one line at a time. The command fgetl(fid) returns (as a string) the next line in the file with identifier fid. For example, if MyFile.dat is the file

```
abcd        ■
10.3        ■
1.123E+08   ■
■■■■■■■
```

then

```
fid = fopen('MyFile.dat','r');
A{1} = fgetl(fid);
A{2} = fgetl(fid);
A{3} = fgetl(fid);
```

is the same as A = {'abcd', '10.3', '1.123E+08'}. Sometimes it is known in advance just how many lines there are in a file, in which case a for-loop can obviously be used to oversee the line-by-line reading. However, for large files it is essential that we be able to terminate the reading based upon the detection of the end-of-file marker. For this purpose the boolean-valued function feof is used. In particular, feof(fid) is true if the eof marker has been reached and is false otherwise. Using these file-processing commands, pseudocode (11.1)–(11.4) transforms into

```
fid = fopen('MyFile.dat','r');
i = 0;
while ~feof(fid)
    i = i+1;
    A{i} = fgetl(fid);
end
fclose(fid);
```

The fclose command closes the file. It is a good programming habit to do this after all the data has been acquired.

Using these basic file-processing tools, we set out to solve the problem posed at the start of the section. We first locate a Web site that can provide the necessary sunrise and sunset data so that we can check the values returned by the given function Daylight. The U.S. Naval Observatory provides a data acquisition tool that is just what we need.[11] The user provides the name of a city and a year and the tool displays a table of daily sunrise and sunset times. It also provides the latitude and longitude of the chosen city. This information can be cut-and-pasted into a separate text file, which we have done for each of the following cities:

Anaheim	Denver	New York	Washington
Baltimore	Johannesburg	Pittsburgh	Atlanta
Boston	Mexico City	Seoul	Bogata
Cleveland	New Delhi	Toronto	Cincinnati
Ithaca	Phoenix	Athens	Houston
Los Angeles	Seattle	Berlin	London
Moscow	Tokyo	Chicago	Minneapolis
Philadelphia	Arlington	Honolulu	Paris
San Francisco	Beijing	Lagos	Rome
Teheran	Cairo	Milwaukee	Tampa
Anchorage	Detroit	Oakland	Wellington
Bangkok	Kansas City	Rio de Janeiro	
Buenos Aires	Miami	Sydney	

We use the city name as the file name. Thus, Boston.dat houses the sunrise and sunset information for Boston. (Text files have a .dat or .txt suffix.) We specify in a "ReadMe" file how the data is laid out.

---

[11]At the time of this writing, http://aa.usno.navy.mil/data/docs/RS_OneYear.php.

```
ReadMe.txt
```
The first line names the city and the second line encodes
its latitude and longitude, e.g.,

Cleveland
W08140N4129

This means that the longitude of Cleveland is 81 degrees
40 minutes west and its latitude is 41 degrees, 29 minutes
north.

Each remaining line has the form

d R1 S1 R2 S2 R3 S3 ....   R12 S12

where d is the day of the month (1-to-31) and the R's and S's
are sunrise and sunset times for each of the 12 months.
(1 = Jan, 2 = Feb, etc.). These times are encoded with a
4-digit integer hhmm where hh specifies the hours and mm the
minutes. Thus, 0447 means 4:47AM. R2 and S2 are blank for
d = 29, 30, and 31 since February has only 28 days. For d = 31,
all R's and S's are blanked out except those that correspond to
January, March, May, July, August, October, and December.

A ReadMe file should be succinct, giving just enough information to support subsequent
manipulation of the data.

Insofar as we will be reading data from these files into cell arrays of strings, we
encapsulate the process in the function `File2Cell`.

The Function `File2Cell`

```
function C = File2Cell(fname)
% fname is a string that gives the complete path to a .dat file.
% C is a cell array with C{i} being the ith line in the file.
fid = fopen(fname,'r');
i = 0;
while ~feof(fid)
    i = i+1;
    C{i} = fgetl(fid);
end
fclose(fid);
```

In order to use this function we need to understand the notion of a complete path to a file. The
complete path to a file is a string that specifies where the file can be found in the directory
hierarchy of the MATLAB environment. If `Boston.dat` is in the working directory, then

```
C = File2Cell('Boston.dat')
```

would assign the Boston data to the cell array C. If `Boston.dat` is not in the current working directory, then we must manufacture its complete path name using the built-in function `pwd` and a convention for housing data files that are used by our textbook scripts and functions. Regarding the latter, we adopt the following strategy:

File-Reading Convention

All the data files used by the textbook programs are assembled in a directory called `InsightData` with subdirectories named after the relevant section, e.g., `\InsightData\11_1`. For programs that access textbook data files, it is necessary for `InsightData` to be a subdirectory of the current working directory.

This enables us to obtain the complete path name for a file using concatenation with the working directory string returned by the built-in function `pwd`. Thus,

```
C = File2Cell([pwd '\InsightData\11_1\Boston.dat']);
```

creates a cell array C that houses the Boston data.

After a file is read into a cell array, we can perform calculations on the data. A little preprocessing is usually required; substrings that encode numerical values need to be converted. Moreover, specialized representations are frequently used for convenience and/or to conserve memory and this requires additional levels of decoding. In our problem special representations are used for longitude, latitude, and time.

From the `ReadMe` file we know that the second line of the file specifies the longitude and latitude of the underlying city. If C is initialized as above and

```
s = C{2}
```

then s is assigned the string `'W07105N4219'` which encodes all the necessary longitude and latitude information for Boston:

Substring	Information	Value
s(1)	Longitude: Hemisphere Portion (E or W)	'W'
s(2:4)	Longitude: Degree Portion	'071'
s(5:6)	Longitude: Minute Portion	'05'
s(7)	Latitude: Hemisphere Portion (N or S)	'N'
s(8:9)	Latitude: Degree Portion	'42'
s(10:11)	Latitude: Minute Portion	'19'

The function `GetLocation` given below can take such an encoding and return numerical values for longitude and latitude. Note the use of the built-in function `str2double` which converts the string representation of a number into the equivalent numerical representation.

The 4-digit sunrise and sunset time encodings in lines 3 through 33 also need to be converted and for that we implement a function `GetTime`.

The Function `GetLocation`

```
function [Long,Lat] = GetLocation(s)
% s is a length-11 string that encodes longitude and latitude,
% e.g., W07536S0322  means  75 degrees 36 minutes West,  and
% 3 degrees 22 minutes South.
% Returns the longitude and latitude as specified by s.

Long = str2double(s(2:4)) + str2double(s(5:6))/60;
if s(1)=='E'
    Long = -Long;
end

Lat = str2double(s(8:9)) + str2double(s(10:11))/60;
if s(7)=='S'
    Lat = -Lat;
end
```

The Function `GetTime`

```
function t = GetTime(tau)
% tau is a vector of nonnegative integers
% Each component has the form hhmm and encodes the time
% "hh hours and mm minutes." Thus, 1427 = 14 hours and
%     27 minutes.
% t has the same dimension and orientation as tau with
%     t(i) equal to the exact time in hours that tau(i)
%     represents.

t = floor(tau/100) + rem(tau,100)/60;
```

Using these two functions together with `File2Cell`, we set out to implement a function

```
[Name,Lat,Long,Hours] = GetRiseSetData(fname)
```

that reads in a sunrise/sunset file specified by `fname` and returns the name of the city, its latitude and longitude, and a 365-by-1 vector of daylight hours. (Convention: January 1 = Day 1,..., December 31 = Day 365.) Having this function will facilitate the graphical display of daylight hours and the comparison with the simplified model.

The name, latitude, and longitude computations are straightforward once we have read the file into a cell array:

```
C = File2Cell(fname);
Name = C{1};
[Long,Lat] = GetLocation(C{2});
```

The setting up of `Hours` is tedious because month length varies. However, it is an instructive exercise because data layout is often inconvenient in practical applications.

From the `ReadMe` file we know that the string `C{d+2}` houses the sunrise/sunset data for day d of each month that has a day d. To appreciate this, here are the January, February, March, and April portions of the strings `C{29}` through `C{33}`:

```
C{29}:    27   0703 1652    0623 1732    0536 1804    0445 1839
C{30}:    28   0702 1653    0621 1733    0534 1806    0444 1840
C{31}:    29   0701 1655                 0532 1807    0443 1842
C{32}:    30   0700 1656                 0531 1808    0441 1843
C{33}:    31   0659 1657                 0529 1809
```

(This happens to be from `Boston.dat`.) Notice that there is no sunrise/sunset data for February on days 29, 30, or 31, nor is there sunrise/sunset data for April on day 31. We use the built-in function `str2num` to convert sunrise/sunset strings into vectors of real values. Noting that

```
z = str2num('10 20 30 40')
```

and

```
z = [10 20 30 40]
```

are equivalent, we see that the fragment

```
x = str2num(C{30});
h28 = GetTime(x(3:2:length(x))) - GetTime(x(2:2:length(x)));
```

assigns to h28 a length-12 vector that specifies the sunrise-to-sunset time for the 28th day of every month. The fragment

```
x = str2num(C{31});
h29 = GetTime(x(3:2:length(x))) - GetTime(x(2:2:length(x)));
x = str2num(C{32});
h30 = GetTime(x(3:2:length(x))) - GetTime(x(2:2:length(x)));
```

assigns to h29 and h30 length-11 vectors that specify the sunrise-to-sunset time for the 29th day and 30th day of every month except February. Finally, the fragment

```
x = str2num(C{33});
h31 = GetTime(x(3:2:length(x))) - GetTime(x(2:2:length(x)));
```

establishes h31 as a length-7 vector that houses the sunrise-to-sunset time for 1/31, 3/31, 5/31, 7/31, 8/31, 10/31, and 12/31.

Using these data extractions we can set up a 31-by-12 array A with the property that $A(i,j)$ houses the daylight for the ith day in the jth month. For example, the assignment

```
A(31,[1 3 5 7 8 10 12]) = h31
```

sets up the day-31 entries. By stacking appropriate subcolumns of A, the required 365-by-1 vector `hours` is obtained. The overall implementation of `GetRiseSetData` is given below.

The Function `GetRiseSetData`

```
function [Name,Lat,Long,Hours] = GetRiseSetData(fname)
% fname is the complete address of a Sunrise/Sunset file.
% Name is a string that names the underlying city.
% Lat is its latitude in degrees.
% Long is its longitude in degrees.
% Hours is a 365-by-1 vector that contains the hours of daylight
%    for day 1 (Jan 1) through day 365 (Dec 31).

% Read the data into cell array C and isolate the Name,
% latitude, and longitude...
  C = File2Cell(fname);
  Name = C{1};
  [Long,Lat] = GetLocation(C{2});

% Set up a 31-by-12 matrix A with the property that A(i,j)
% houses the hours of daylight associated with the ith
% day of the jth month...
  A = zeros(31,12);
  for d=1:31
      x = str2num(C{d+2});
      h = GetTime(x(3:2:length(x))) - GetTime(x(2:2:length(x)));
      if d<=28
          % All months
          A(d,:) = h;
      elseif d<=30
          % All months except February...
          A(d,[1 3 4 5 6 7 8 9 10 11 12]) = h;
      else
          % All months except February, April, June, September,
          % and November...
          A(d,[1 3 5 7 8 10 12]) = h;
      end
  end
% Stack the relevant parts of each A-column...
  Hours = [A(:,1);     A(1:28,2); A(:,3);     A(1:30,4); ...
           A(:,5);     A(1:30,6); A(:,7);     A(:,8);...
           A(1:30,9); A(:,10);    A(1:30,11); A(:,12)];
```

The script `Eg11_1` produces plots and error results for a set of user-designated cities. Of particular interest are the string manipulations that are required to get the complete path to the required `.dat` file. The concatenation of four strings is required:

```
fn = [pwd '\InsightData\11_1\' Cities{k}  '.dat'];
```

Output suggests that the simplified model can predict daylight to within 20 minutes for typical North American latitudes. See Figure 11.1.

The Script Eg11_1

```
% Script Eg11_1
% Examines the accuracy of the simple daylight-predictor model.
% Assumes that InsightData is a subdirectory of the working
% directory.

% Data is available for these cities..
Cities =  {'Anaheim',  'Anchorage', 'Arlington', 'Athens', ...
           'Atlanta',  'Baltimore', 'Bangkok',   'Beijing',...
                               :
           'Tokyo',   'Toronto', 'Washington', 'Wellington'};

% Choose a subset of the city indices 1 through 50 to investigate.
CityChoices = [4 21 25 33 50];
for k = CityChoices
    % The sunrise/sunset data for city k...
    fn = [ pwd '\InsightData\11_1\' Cities{k}  '.dat'];
    % Get the actual and predicted daylight values and display.
    [Name,Lat,Long,Hours] = GetRiseSetData(fn);
    HoursEst = Daylight(Lat);
    err = ceil(max(Hours-HoursEst)*60);
    Days = (1:365)';
    %     Display...
    plot(Days,Hours,'k',Days,HoursEst,'r')
         :
end
```

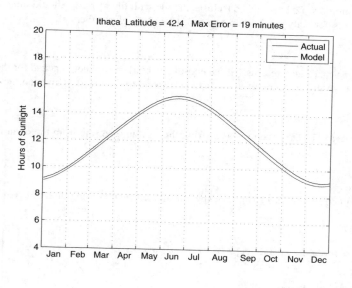

Figure 11.1. *Ithaca Daylight.*

Talking Point: Online Data Sets

With the proliferation of online databases and data acquisition tools, the Internet is having a profound effect on the conduct of science and engineering, where testing models against data is a way of life. File downloading and uploading frequently mark the beginning and end of a computational project. The idea of using experimental data to confirm a mathematical model is as old as the scientific method. What has changed is the volume of experimental data that is typically marshalled as evidence and its ready accessability.

A digitized sky map is a dramatic example of the new world order. These maps are produced using radio telescopes that systematically scan the heavens. The digitized signals are archived and made available on the Web. An astronomer who wants to "check out" a portion of the galaxy no longer has to reserve precious time on an actual telescope. Instead, he or she simply accesses the digital library for the appropriate data.

Another illustration is the RCSB Protein Data Bank. Information concerning the structure of large macromolecules is freely available online. Researchers trying to establish connections between structure and function have tens of thousands of examples to work with. Mechanisms exist that support the addition of new molecules to the library. Precise rules concerning the structure of the data files ensure easy access to the archived information.

MATLAB Review

fopen and fclose

The reference `fid = fopen( file name ,'r')` opens the file with the specified name for reading. The reference `fclose(fid)` closes the file with file id `fid`. Should more than one file be open (which is perfectly legal), then `fclose('all')` closes them all.

feof

The reference `feof(fid)` returns 1 if the end-of-file marker has been reached for the file with id `fid` and 0 otherwise. The value of `fid` must correspond to the file id of an open file.

fgetl

The reference `fgetl(fid)` returns as a string the next unread line from the open file having id `fid`.

pwd

This built-in function returns a string that specifies the current working directory, e.g.,

```
>> s = pwd
s =
C:\Program Files\MATLAB\R2007a\work
```

str2double and str2num

These functions are used to convert strings that specify numbers into the corresponding double precision value. They differ in how they handle the situation when multiple conversions are required:

s	str2double(s)	str2num(s)
'1234'	1234	1234
'1.234'	1.234	1.234
'1.234e-8'	1.2340e-008	1.2340e-008
'1234 567'	NaN	[1234 , 567]
['1234';'5678']	15263748	[1234 ; 5678]
{'1234' , '567'}	[1234 , 567]	Error
{'1234' ; '567'}	[1234 ; 567]	Error

ReadMe Files

A text file that describes the format of a data file. It is useful to include appropriate ReadMe files in a directory that houses data files.

Exercises

M11.1.1 Modify Eg11_1 so that it also displays in the title the index of the day when maximum error occurred.

M11.1.2 Refer to the data files in \InsightData\11_1. Write a script that prints the name of each city and the hours of daylight that it receives on June 22 (day number 173).

M11.1.3 Observe that Daylight(Lat) seems to underestimate consistently the true daylight and that the underestimation increases with latitude. Try fixing this by adding a few minutes to the value returned by Daylight.

P11.1.4 Write a script that graphically displays how much later (in minutes) the Sun rises in New York, Ithaca, Pittsburgh, Cleveland, and Detroit throughout the year compared to Boston. Note that these are all Eastern Time Zone cities.

P11.1.5 Modify Eg11_1 so that it graphically displays the *relative* error associated with Daylight(Lat). The plot should show how the relative error varies during the year and its maximum value.

P11.1.6 Using the method of bisection (see §9.3) and the function Daylight, determine the latitude for which the longest day of the year is exactly 16 hours.

P11.1.7 This problem is about conversion between representations. A "date string" has the form '$m/d/y$' where m is a one- or two-character substring that designates the month, d is a one- or two-character string that designates the day, and y is a four-character string that designates the year. Sample date strings include '1/2/1999', '12/1/1927', '1/12/1947', and '12/12/2012'. Write a function S = FullDate(s) that takes a date string s and produces a string S that is the "full name" representation of the same date, i.e., 'January 2, 1999', 'December 1, 1927', 'January 12, 1947', and 'December 12, 2012'.

P11.1.8 Another way to represent a date is in the mnemonic d/m/y notation:

'4OCT93' ↔ 'October 4, 1993'.

Write a function that converts an m/d/y specified date into its mnemonic d/m/y form, e.g.,

'10/4/93'   →   '4OCT93'.

P11.1.9 Consider the standard "colon" method for representing time, e.g., 7:15, 12:23, 23:59. Write a function Tplus1 = JustAMinute(T) that takes a string T that is a colon encoding of some time *t* and returns a string that is a colon encoding for *t* plus one minute. Thus, '7:15' becomes '7:16', '11:59' becomes '12:00', and '23:59' becomes '0:00'.

P11.1.10 Use the U.S. Naval Observatory sunrise/sunset tool to set up a file for your home town. Place this file in \InsightData\11_1. Modify Eg11_1 so that when it is executed it displays the daylight plot for just your home town.

11.2   Nearby Millions

Problem Statement

Given the latitude and longitude of a point Q in the lower forty-eight states, approximately how many million U.S. residents live within 300 miles of Q? So that the value of this population density factor can be conveniently obtained for many different Q-points, develop a simple graphical environment that displays a map and acquires the latitude and longitude of the Q-points via mouseclicking. When measuring proximity to the Q-point, assume that the Earth is a perfect sphere and use the great circle distance.

Program Development

Obviously, we need distribution-of-population data to solve this problem. To that end we download a data set from the Bureau of the Census Web site that specifies the population, latitude, and longitude of every zipcode area.[12] The file, which we have named Zipcode.dat, has 30,000+ lines, one for each zipcode. Key facts about its structure are as follows:

```
ReadMe.txt
  Columns 1-2: Postal Service State Abbreviation
  Columns 3-7: Name (e.g., 35004)
  Columns 67-75: Total Population (2000 census)
  Columns 76-84: Total Housing Units (2000 census)
  Columns 85-98: Land Area (square meters)
  Columns 99-112: Water Area (square meters)
  Columns 113-124: Land Area (square miles)
  Columns 125-136: Water Area (square miles)
  Columns 137-146: Latitude (decimal degrees)
  First character is blank for North
  First character is "-" for South
  Columns 147-157: Longitude (decimal degrees)
  First character is blank for East
  First character is "-" for West
```

---

[12]http://www.census.gov/geo/www/gazetteer/places2k.html.

Of course, we could acquire the population and location data from this file using the techniques from §11.1, e.g.,

```
C = File2Cell([pwd '\InsightData\11_2\Zipcode.dat']);
n = length(C); P = zeros(1:n), Lat = zeros(1:n); Long = zeros(1:n);
for k=1:length(C)
    P(k)    = str2num(s(67:75));
    Lat(k)  = str2num(s(137:146));
    Long(k) = str2num(s(147:157));
end
```

All we would then have to do is just write a script to input the Q-point and perform the necessary population proximity computations. However, to make things interesting from the file-processing perspective, let us assume that the file Zipcode.dat is *so* big that we cannot actually store the cell array C. This forces upon us the issue of compact data representation; i.e., how can we economically store the population and location data that we need to solve the problem? This is instructive because clever compressions of data are of paramount importance in an age when huge data sets are transmitted across the Internet.

For us, the intelligent packaging of the required population and location values begins with a careful analysis of just how the data are to be used. For a given Q-point we must (a) compute its great circle distance to every zipcode area and (b) sum the populations of those zipcode areas that are deemed to be "nearby." Anticipating that we will be doing this for many different Q-points, let us examine the great circle distance computation. Hopefully, there will be some quantities that can be precomputed and stored before Q-point processing begins.

If (ϕ_0, θ_0) and (ϕ_i, θ_i) are the respective latitude/longitude pairs (in degrees) for the Q-point and the ith zipcode, then their great circle separation is given by

$$d_i = D \arcsin\left(\frac{\sqrt{(x_i - x_0)^2 + (y_i - y_0)^2 + (z_i - z_0)^2}}{2} \right) \tag{11.5}$$

where D is the Earth's diameter (7926 miles) and

$$\begin{aligned}
x_i &= \cos(\pi \phi_i / 180) \cdot \cos(\pi \theta_i / 180) \\
y_i &= \cos(\pi \phi_i / 180) \cdot \sin(\pi \theta_i / 180) \\
z_i &= \sin(\pi \phi_i / 180)
\end{aligned} \tag{11.6}$$

are the normalized Cartesian coordinates. Notice that if n is the number of zipcodes, then the population density factor for every Q-point requires $(x_1, y_1, z_1), \dots, (x_n, y_n, z_n)$. This suggests that we compute and store these xyz values once and for all at the start. For that purpose, it is handy to have the function EarthCartesian given below. Our plan is to use this function to create a file PXYZ.dat that houses just the population and xyz-data for each zipcode. The input data come from the "huge" Zipcode.dat file. To avoid having

The Function EarthCartesian

```
function [x,y,z] = EarthCartesian(Lat,Long)
% Lat and Long specify the latitude and longitude (degrees)
%     of a point on the Earth's surface.
% x, y, and z are scalars that specify the normalized Cartesian
%     coordinates of the point.

kappa = pi/180;
cLat = cos(Lat*kappa);
x = cLat*cos(Long*kappa);
y = cLat*sin(Long*kappa);
z = sin(Lat*kappa);
```

to represent it as a cell array, we adopt a line-by-line processing framework:

Assign to n the number of lines in the "input file" Zipcode.dat.	(11.7)
Create the "output file" PXYZ.dat and write the value of n to the first line.	(11.8)
Repeat for each line in Zipcode.dat	(11.9)
Read in the next line from Zipcode.dat	(11.10)
Apply EarthCartesian to the latitude and longitude values yielding normalized Cartesian values x, y, and z.	(11.11)
Store string representations of the population, x, y, and z in the next line of PXYZ.dat.	(11.12)

To determine n we read Zipcode.dat and count lines. Thus, (11.7) becomes

```
fid  = fopen([pwd '\InsightData\11_2\Zipcode.dat'],'r');
n = 0;
while ~feof(fid)
    s = fgetl(fid);
    n = n+1;
end
fclose(fid);
```

Regarding (11.8), to create a new file in the working directory the fopen command can be used:

```
fid0 = fopen('PXYZ.dat','w');
```

The "w" indicates that it is available for writing. To create a new file in a directory other than the working directory, we must specify its full path. For textbook scripts and functions that do this we adopt the following convention:

File-Writing Convention

All files that are created by textbook programs are stored in MyData, which is assumed to be a subdirectory of the working directory.

As an example of this strategy, the command

```
fid0 = fopen([pwd '\MyData\PXYZ.dat'],'w');
```

would make available for writing the file PXYZ.dat. This file would be situated in MyData.

With respect to (11.9)–(11.12), refer to the function MakePXYZ listed below. Notice that it is possible to have more than one file open at the same time in a program. The program "knows" which file to manipulate in a file-processing command because of the file id. In MakePXYZ, fid identifies Zipcode.dat, while PXYZ.dat is identified through fid0.

An important feature in MakePXYZ concerns the use of fprintf. We are familiar with using this built-in function to write information in the command window. The same rules more or less apply when writing to a file. For example, the command

```
fprintf(fid0,'%6d %12.6f   %12.6f   %12.6f \n',P,x,y,z);
```

takes the four values specified by variables P, x, y, and z and forms a formatted string of characters which is then stored in the next line in the file identified by fid0, i.e., PXYZ.dat. When the process completes, both Zipcode.dat and PXYZ.dat are closed via the command fclose('all').

To affirm the correctness of MakePXYZ, we use a text editor to take a look at the file PXYZ.dat:

```
33103
 6998      0.050809      -0.831308       0.553484
 8985      0.044181      -0.831820       0.553284
 3109      0.040182      -0.833383       0.551234
20157      0.046565      -0.835157       0.548037
21732      0.059638      -0.837467       0.543225
                            :
                            :
```

The first line reveals that the total number of zipcodes is 33,103. The fifth line tells us that the fourth zipcode has population 20,157 and normalized Cartesian coordinates $x = 0.046565$, $y = -0.835157$, $z = 0.548037$, etc.

As when printing to the command window, care should be exercised when choosing the formats in the fprintf command. It is nice to have data files that are easy to read. Formats must also be "long enough" to ensure that no information is "lost in translation."

With the availability of PXYZ.dat we can access the necessary data using the function GetPXYZ listed below. The advantage of storing the number of zipcodes in the first line of PXYZ.dat is that we can then allocate the P, x, y, and z arrays before assigning values to

The Function `MakePXYZ`

```
function MakePXYZ()
% Assumes that InsightData and MyData are subdirectories of the
%    working directory.
% Creates and stores a text file PXYZ.dat in MyData.
% The first line contains the number of zipcodes.
% Subsequent lines specify the population of the zipcode and
%    its normalized Cartesian coordinates.

% Determine the number of lines in the file...
fid  = fopen([pwd '\InsightData\11_2\Zipcode.dat'],'r');
n = 0;
while ~feof(fid)
     s = fgetl(fid);
     n = n+1;
end
fclose(fid);

% Create PXYZ.dat and write the value of n to the first line...
fid0 = fopen([pwd '\MyData\PXYZ.dat'],'w');
fprintf(fid0,'%d \n',n);

% Pass through Zipcode.dat again copying the relevant data
% to PXYZ.dat...
fid  = fopen([pwd '\InsightData\11_2\Zipcode.dat'],'r');
while ~feof(fid)
     % Process the kth line
     s = fgetl(fid);
     P    = str2double(s(67:75));
     Lat  = str2double(s(137:146));
     Long = str2double(s(147:157));
     [x,y,z] = EarthCartesian(Lat,Long);
     fprintf(fid0,'%6d %12.6f   %12.6f   %12.6f \n',P,x,y,z);
end
fclose('all');
```

them. Without this device, these arrays would have to be built up through the much slower process of augmentation, e.g., `P = [P;t(1)]`.

Notice how a single `str2num` command in the function `GetPXYZ` is used to oversee four string-to-numeric conversions. Although these conversions are easy enough to implement, it should be observed that they represent a time-consuming, redundant overhead. Every time a new Q-point is processed we have to repeat the conversion of string data in `PXYZ.dat` to its numerical equivalent.

Fortunately, there is a way to circumvent this problem using *binary files*. Whereas a `.dat` file would store 0.046565 as an 8-character string, one byte of memory per character, a binary file would store 0.046565 in its floating point representation. When the datum is read from the file, it is ready to go in the sense that it can be used in a numerical expression without any conversion. The function `MakePXYZB` given below creates a binary file `PXYZB.bin` that houses exactly the same information as `PXYZ.dat`, only in binary form. The `fwrite` command is required for the conversion.

The Function GetPXYZ

```
function [P,x,y,z] = GetPXYZ()
% Assumes that MyData is a subdirectory of the working directory
%    and that it contains the file PXYZ.dat.
% P, x, y, and z are column vectors that house the population
%    and xyz data encoded in PXYZ.dat

% Open PXYZ.dat, obtain the total number of zipcodes,
%    and initialize the arrays, P, x, y, and z...
fid = fopen([pwd '\MyData\PXYZ.dat'],'r');
n = str2num(fgetl(fid));
P = zeros(n,1); x = zeros(n,1); y = zeros(n,1); z = zeros(n,1);
% Extract the population and xyz data for each zipcode...
for k=1:n
    NextLine = fgetl(fid);
    t = str2num(NextLine);
    P(k) = t(1); x(k) = t(2); y(k) = t(3); z(k) = t(4);
end
fclose(fid);
```

The Function MakePXYZB

```
function MakePXYZB()
% Assumes that MyData is a subdirectory of the working directory
%    and that it contains PXYZ.dat
% Creates a scalar-level, binary version of PXYZ.dat called
%    PXYZB.bin and stores it in MyData.

% Acquire and store n (the total number of zipcodes)...
fid0 = fopen([pwd '\MyData\PXYZ.dat'],'r');
n = str2num(fgetl(fid0));
fid1 = fopen([pwd '\MyData\PXYZB.bin'],'w');
fwrite(fid1,n,'int');

% Process zipcodes 1 through n...
for k=1:n
    NextLineOfData = str2num(fgetl(fid0));
    fwrite(fid1,NextLineOfData(1),'float');    % P
    fwrite(fid1,NextLineOfData(2),'float');    % x
    fwrite(fid1,NextLineOfData(3),'float');    % y
    fwrite(fid1,NextLineOfData(4),'float');    % z
end
fclose('all');
```

Notice that binary files are designated with the .bin suffix. The rules about opening and closing are the same as for .dat files. The fwrite command requires three inputs: (a) the id of the file that is involved, (b) the data which is to be stored, and (c) the data format. In PXYZB.bin, n is stored as an integer while all the P, x, y, and z data is stored using the float format. The float type is a 4-byte floating point representation. The double format is an 8-byte floating point representation. The float format is big enough to house

6 significant digits of information and that is enough for our purposes. Using the double format would double the size of PXYZB.bin.

To appreciate the "data compression" that we have so far realized, here is the amount of storage required by Zipcode.dat, PXYZ.dat, and PXYZB.bin:

File	Size (Kilobytes)
Zipcode.dat	5141
PXYZ.dat	1585
PXYZB.bin	518

Thus, we have reduced by a factor of ten the amount of storage required to house the essential data for our problem.

Reading from a .bin file has much in common with reading from a .dat file. However, there are some critical differences which we discuss relative to the function GetPXYZB listed below. First of all, the fread command is used to get the next datum. Binary files do not have lines per se, and thus fread is used to grab the next "chunk" of data. This is distinct from fgetl which obtains the next line of information in a .dat file. Because it needs to know about the data it is to acquire, an fread command requires the data format and the number of entities that are part of the request. Thus, when the command n = fread(fid1,1,'int') is executed the next datum in the file to be read must have type int. Likewise, as the loop progresses, commands like Pk = fread(fid,1,'float') require the next items of data to be in the float format. It is essential that the reading of a binary file respect the data layout, i.e., the sequence of reads must match in type exactly the sequence of writes used to produce the file.

It is possible to set up a .bin file whose "entries" are vectors, or even matrices, making it possible to acquire more than just a single number with an fread. This is

The Function GetPXYZB

```
function [P,x,y,z] = GetPXYZB()
% Assumes that MyData is a subdirectory of the working directory
%       and that it contains the file PXYZB.bin.
% P, x, y, and z are column vectors that house the population
%       and xyz data encoded in PXYZB.bin

% Acquire n (the total number of zipcodes) and initialize
%       P, x, y, and z...
fid1 = fopen([pwd '\MyData\PXYZB.bin'],'r');
n = fread(fid1,1,'int');
P = zeros(n,1); x = zeros(n,1); y = zeros(n,1); z = zeros(n,1);

% Set up P, x, y, and z...
for k=1:n
    Pk =    fread(fid1,1,'float'); P(k) = Pk;
    xk =    fread(fid1,1,'float'); x(k) = xk;
    yk =    fread(fid1,1,'float'); y(k) = yk;
    zk =    fread(fid1,1,'float'); z(k) = zk;
end
fclose(fid1);
```

important because it takes much longer to get a value from a file than from main memory variables. This overhead is minimized if we do a "big shop" whenever we read from a file. The function `MakePXYZBvec` assembles the data from `PXYZ.dat` as a collection of 4-vectors rather than as a collection of scalars. The function `MakePXYZBmat` aggregates all of the data as just a single matrix in a `.bin` file.

Again, it is important to stress that no matter how we choose to arrange the data in a `.bin` file, it is critical that the reading process respect the chosen layout. Thus,

The Function `MakePXYZBvec`

```
function MakePXYZBvec()
% Assumes that MyData is a subdirectory of the working directory
%     and that it contains PXYZ.dat
% Creates a vector-level, binary version of PXYZ.dat called
%     PXYZBvec.bin and stores it in MyData.

% Acquire and store n (the total number of zipcodes)...
fid0 = fopen([pwd '\MyData\PXYZ.dat'],'r');
n = str2num(fgetl(fid0));
fid2 = fopen([pwd '\MyData\PXYZBvec.bin'],'w');
fwrite(fid2,n,'int');

% Process zipcodes 1 through n...
for k=1:n
    NextLineOfData = str2num(fgetl(fid0));
    fwrite(fid2,NextLineOfData,'float');
end
fclose('all');
```

The Function `MakePXYZBmat`

```
function MakePXYZBmat()
% Assumes that MyData is a subdirectory of the working directory
%     and that it contains PXYZ.dat
% Creates a matrix-level, binary version of PXYZ.dat called
%     PXYZBmat.bin and stores it in MyData.

% Acquire and store n (the total number of zipcodes)...
fid0 = fopen([pwd '\MyData\PXYZ.dat'],'r');
n = str2num(fgetl(fid0));
fid3 = fopen([pwd '\MyData\PXYZBmat.bin'],'w');
fwrite(fid3,n,'int');

% Set up and write the matrix of P, x, y, and z values...
A = zeros(n,4);
for k=1:n
    A(k,:) = str2num(fgetl(fid0));
end
fwrite(fid3,A,'float');
fclose('all')
```

GetPXYZB *cannot* be used to read from the file PXYZBvec. Instead, we must use the function GetPXYZBvec below. Note the form of the fread command. It basically says "get the next four numbers from PXYZBvec.bin stored with the float format and assemble them in the array NextLineOfData." The four values so obtained are then appropriately stored in the arrays P , x, y, and z.

The Function GetPXYZBvec

```
function [P,x,y,z] = GetPXYZBvec()
% Assumes that MyData is a subdirectory of the working directory
%      and that it contains the file PXYZBvec.bin.
% P, x, y, and z are column vectors that house the population
%      and xyz data encoded in PXYZBvec.bin

% Acquire n (the total number of zipcodes) and initialize
%      P, x, y, and z.
fid2 = fopen([pwd '\MyData\PXYZBvec.bin'],'r');
n = fread(fid2,1,'int');
P = zeros(n,1); x = zeros(n,1); y = zeros(n,1); z = zeros(n,1);

% Set up P, x, y, and z...
for k=1:n
    NextLineOfData = fread(fid2,4,'float');
    P(k) = NextLineOfData(1); x(k) = NextLineOfData(2);
    y(k) = NextLineOfData(3); z(k) = NextLineOfData(4);
end
fclose(fid2);
```

Likewise, we can use neither GetPXYZB nor GetPXYZBvec to access the data in PXYZBmat.dat. The sequence of reading formats must match the sequence of writing formats as in the function GetPXYZBmat shown below.

Before we proceed to write the solution script for the problem posed at the beginning of the section, we contrast the time it takes to retrieve the population and xyz data for

The Function GetPXYZBmat

```
function [P,x,y,z] = GetPXYZBmat()
% Assumes that MyData is a subdirectory of the working directory
%      and that it contains the file PXYZBmat.bin.
% P, x, y, and z are column vectors that house the population
%      and xyz data encoded in PXYZBmat.bin

% Acquire n (the total number of zipcodes)...
fid3 = fopen([pwd '\MyData\PXYZBmat.bin'],'r');
n = fread(fid3,1,'int');

% Acquire and take apart the matrix of P, x, y, and z values...
A = fread(fid3,[n,4],'float');
P = A(:,1); x = A(:,2); y = A(:,3); z = A(:,4);
fclose(fid3);
```

each of the four file-storing strategies outlined above. The script `FileSetUp` listed below benchmarks the several possibilities.

The Script `FileSetUp`

```
% Script FileSetUp
% Contrast four different ways to store the population and
% location data in a file.

  MakePXYZ();          % PXYZ.dat
  MakePXYZB();         % PXYZB.bin
  MakePXYZBvec();      % PXYZBvec.bin
  MakePXYZBmat();      % PXYZBmat.bin

% Benchmark how long it takes to extract and convert
% P, x, y, z...
  tic; [P,x,y,z] = GetPXYZ();        T    = toc;
  tic; [P,x,y,z] = GetPXYZB();       T_bin = T/toc;
  tic; [P,x,y,z] = GetPXYZBvec();  T_binVec = T/toc;
  tic; [P,x,y,z] = GetPXYZBmat();  T_binMat = T/toc;
```

The results confirm that it is much more efficient to grab big chunks of data when reading from a `.bin` file:

```
    T_bin   =      1.68
    T_binVec =     4.95
    T_binMat =   548.68
```

In particular, `GetPXYZBmat` with just a single `fread` outperforms `GetPXYZBvec` which involves over 33,000 `fread`'s. Likewise, `GetPXYZBvec` is more efficient than `GetPXYZB` because the latter involves over 130,000 `fread`'s.

We are finally ready to develop a script that solicits a mouseclick, converts it into a latitude and longitude, and evaluates the nearby population. To acquire the coordinates of the Q-point we implement a function `USAClick`. We suppress the details because they include some MATLAB image-processing commands that are covered in the next chapter. The script `Eg11_2` uses `USAClick`. After the Q-point is determined and its xyz values are computed, the great circle distances are computed. This computation is easily vectorized

The Function `USAClick`

```
function [Lat,Long] = USAClick()
% Displays a map of the continental United States and
% solicits a mouseclick.
% The latitude and longitude (in degrees) corresponding
% to the click point are returned in Lat and Long.
% The click point is displayed on the map.
```

The Script Eg11_2

```
% Script Eg11_2
% Environment for examining the population density factor

% Acquire the data...
MakePXYZ();
MakePXYZBMat();
[P,x,y,z] = GetPXYZBmat();

close all
% The distance that defines "nearby"...
Rho = 300;

% The number of trials...
nTries = 5;
for k=1:nTries
    figure

    % Enter the Q-point and compute its xyz values...
    [Lat0,Long0] = USAClick();
    [x0,y0,z0] = EarthCartesian(Lat0,Long0);

    % Compute the vector of great circle distances
    % to the zipcode areas...
    d = 7926*asin(sqrt((x-x0).^2 + (y-y0).^2 + (z-z0).^2)/2);

    % Determine the indices associated with the
    % ``nearby'' zipcodes...
    i_Rho = find(d<=Rho);

    % Sum the associated populations and display...
    NearbyPop = sum(P(i_Rho))/10^6;
            :
    pause(1)
end
```

and the results are stored in the vector d with the convention that the great circle distance between the kth zipcode and the Q-point is stored in d(k). Note how the use of find and sum vectorize the following calculation of nearby population:

```
NearbyPop = 0;
for k=1:length(P)
    if d(k) <= Rho
        NearbyPop = NearbyPop + P(k);
    end
end
NearbyPop = NearbyPop/10^6;
```

For sample output, see Figure 11.2.

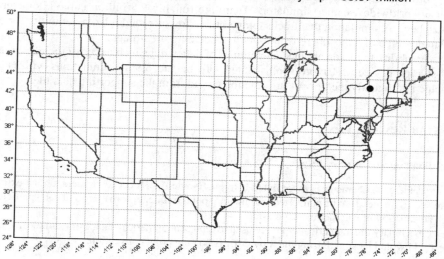

Lat = 41.98 Long = −76.09 Rho = 300 NearbyPop = 65.97 million

Figure 11.2. *Sample Output from the Script* Eg11_2.

Talking Point: Megabytes, Gigabytes, Terabytes, and Petabytes

Most of us have a "media" appreciation for large data sets. A rock song requires a couple of megabytes of storage as does a photograph with reasonable resolution. DVDs involve about 8 gigabytes, etc. It is important to have an intuition about data sets that are this large and larger:

Terminology	Size	How to Think about It
Megabyte	10^6	One minute of MP3 music. A 500-page novel.
Gigabyte	10^9	The human genome. A 20-minute DVD.
Terabyte	10^{12}	A typical university library. Daily photo record of all USA airline passengers.
Petabyte	10^{15}	The amount of text on the Web. 50 Million trees turned into printed matter.

Large-scale simulations in engineering and science may require terabytes or petabytes of storage just to house the variables of interest. For example, a simulation that explains surface salinity of the seas may require a temperature estimate for every 100 m-by-100 m patch of of ocean. That is a terabyte of data.

Storage requirements are particularly dramatic in three-dimensional settings. Consider a worldwide weather simulator. There are roughly 2.5 billion cubic kilometers of atmosphere. A simulation that tracks temperature, pressure, and relative humidity for each 100 meter cube of atmosphere would involve petabytes of storage.

An ability to reason about such volumes of data will be increasingly crucial as models and storage devices get more sophisticated. To be successful, simulations will have to manage intelligently the flow of information to and from the supporting data files.

MATLAB Review

Text Files versus Binary Files

In a text file each character is represented using its 1-byte ASCII code. Numerical data extracted from such a file needs to be converted into floating point or integer form before it can "participate" in the evaluation of a numerical expression.

In a binary file, numerical types are used to represent numerical data. For example, a number like 1.234 would be stored using the 8-byte IEEE floating point convention.

Creating a File For Writing

The reference `fid = fopen( file name ,'w')` creates the file with the specified name and makes it available for writing. A file id is returned.

fwrite and fread

An `fwrite` command has the form

$$\text{fwrite}(\boxed{\text{File id}}, \boxed{\text{Matrix}}, \boxed{\text{Precision}})$$

The file id must name an open `.bin` file. Allowable precisions include

`'int'`	integer, 8 bits
`'uint8'`	unsigned integer, 8 bits
`'single'`	floating point, 32 bits
`'double'`	floating point, 64 bits.

Thus,

```
s = 3; v = [9 7]; M = [4 5 6; 7 8 9];
fid = fopen('MyFile.bin','w');
fwrite(fid,s,'int');
fwrite(fid,v,'double');
fwrite(fid,M,'double');
fclose(fid);
```

sets up a three-item binary file called `MyFile`.

An `fread` command has the form

$$\boxed{\text{Matrix}} = \text{fread}(\boxed{\text{File id}}, \boxed{\text{Size}}, \boxed{\text{Precision}})$$

The file id must name an open .bin file. The second input parameter must specify the size of the object to be written. The precision indicates the type of the object to be read. Thus,

```
fid = fopen('MyFile.bin','r');
s1 = fread(fid,1,'int');
v1 = fread(fid,[1,2],'double');
M1 = fread(fid,[2,3],'double');
fclose(fid);
```

successfully reads the file MyFile.bin.

ginput

This function stores the xy coordinates of user mouseclicks on a figure window. A call [x,y] = ginput(n) returns column n-vectors x and y where x(k) and y(k) are the coordinates of the kth mouseclick. [x,y] = ginput() accepts mouseclicks until the "Enter" key is pressed.

Exercises

M11.2.1 Modify Eg11_2 so that it solicits and displays two U.S. points together with their great circle separation.

M11.2.2 Write a script that prints the 5-digit zipcode associated with the zipcode area that has the largest population.

M11.2.3 Modify Eg11_2 so that it displays the population that is at least Rho1 miles from the Q-point but no more than Rho2 miles from the Q-point.

P11.2.4 Write a script that prints a table that displays the population of each state.

P11.2.5 Modify Eg11_2 so that it also displays the centroid of the U.S. population.

P11.2.6 Compare GetPXYZBvec with an implementation that sets up P, x, y, and z using repeated augmentation:

```
P = []; x = []; y = []; z = [];
while ~feof(fid2)
    NextLineOfData = fread(fid2,4,'float');
    P = [P ; NextLineOfData(1)];
    x = [x ; NextLineOfData(2)];
    y = [y ; NextLineOfData(3)];
    z = [z ; NextLineOfData(4)];
end
fclose(fid2);
```

P11.2.7 Write a script that sets up a binary file that houses the great circle distance from each zipcode to the zipcode 'NY14853'.

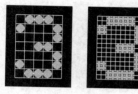

Chapter 12

The Matrix: Part II

This chapter is about the representation and manipulation of visual data. Of course, everything boils down to numbers which in turn have to be converted into the zeros and ones that the computer likes. Matrices arise simply because discretized pictures *are* matrices. Preferences for high-definition TV and glossy brochures reflect concerns about the granularity of the image matrix.

The first section is concerned with color and how it can be used to communicate numerical values. It builds on §4.2 where we showed how linear interpolation could be applied to generate "in between colors."

The same ideas extend naturally to two dimensions and can be used to solve the problem of shading. Linear interpolation can be applied in both the x and y directions, enabling us to shade correctly a square given prescribed color values at its corners.

Dot matrix displays are rapidly becoming obsolete, but the idea behind them—using on/off switches and a grid of light bulbs to depict letters and numbers—is simple, instructive, and lasting. We use the 7-by-5 representation to introduce the principle of image discretization and to motivate the notion of mesh refinement.

The last section is concerned with the manipulation of image files and the data that they contain. We consider the problem of removing dirt specks and identifying edges. Many image-processing applications require the automatic identification of objects, e.g., a missile silo in a satellite picture, a tumor in an X-ray, a face in a newspaper photo, etc. Often these computations begin with the filtering of noise and the search for edges.

Programming Preview

Concepts

Color maps, shading, interpolation, bilinear interpolation, grid refinement, sub-matrices, dot matrix displays, jpeg, RGB, grayscale, image processing, median filtering, noise removal, edge detection, data types.

Language Features

Row Operations, Column Operations: Vectorized code can be used to operate on whole rows and columns in a matrix.

`max`, `min`, `sum`: These functions can take a matrix as argument. The operation is performed columnwise so a row vector is returned.

`axis ij`: An axis option consistent with the ij system of matrix subscripts.

Cell Array of Matrices: Use curly brackets to enclose cell array subscripts, parentheses to enclose matrix subscripts, e.g., `D{k}(i,j)`.

`imread`: Convert compressed image data, e.g., jpeg format, into a three-dimensional array of pixel values of type `uint8`. The three layers house the red, green, and blue values.

`uint8`: Unsigned, 8-bit, integer type. Possible values are from 0 to 255.

`imshow`: Display the image encoded by an array of pixel values.

`imwrite`: Create an image file, e.g., jpeg, from a three-dimensional array of pixel values.

`rgb2gray`: Return a matrix of grayscale values that correspond to a three-dimensional array of pixel values.

Special Prerequisites

Image computations are matrix computations, so thorough familiarity with Chapter 7 is essential. The interpolation ideas discussed in §4.2 are built upon in §12.1 and §12.2. For §12.4, you should be familiar with the File-Reading Convention and the File-Writing Convention presented in §11.1 and §11.2, respectively.

MatTV

Video 22. Vectorized Logical Operations

How to create and use logical arrays.

12.1 Saving Private Rainbows

Problem Statement

Recall from §4.2 the rgb method for encoding color. In that scheme a particular color is encoded by a length-3 vector whose components specify the red, green, and blue intensities on a zero-to-one scale. A p-by-3 array whose rows specify colors is referred to as a *color map*, e.g.,

```
C = [0.00 1.00 1.00 ; ...
     0.25 0.75 1.00 ; ...
     0.50 0.50 1.00 ; ...
     0.75 0.25 1.00 ; ...
     1.00 0.00 1.00];
```

In this example, the first and last rows encode cyan and magenta, respectively, and the three "in between" colors are obtained by linear interpolation. See Figure 12.1 in which the kth tile (counting from the left) has color C (k, :). Simple, interpolation-based color maps such as this can be combined to produce more complex color maps that "step though" a specified sequence of endpoint colors. For example, here is a cyan-to-magenta-to-yellow-to-blue color map:

```
A = [0.00 1.00 1.00 ; ...    % A(1:5,:)   = cyan-to-magenta
     0.25 0.75 1.00 ; ...
     0.50 0.50 1.00 ; ...
     0.75 0.25 1.00 ; ...
     1.00 0.00 1.00 ; ...
     1.00 0.50 0.50 ; ...    % A(5:7,:)   = magenta-to-yellow
     1.00 1.00 0.00 ; ...    % A(7:10,:) = yellow-to-blue
     0.67 0.67 0.33 ; ...
     0.33 0.33 0.67 ; ...
     0.00 0.00 1.00];
```

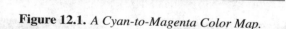

Figure 12.1. *A Cyan-to-Magenta Color Map.*

There are three colors between cyan and magenta, one color between magenta and yellow, and two colors between yellow and blue.

Write a function A = MakeColorMap (B, q) that constructs a color map A given a set of endpoint colors defined by a color map B and an integer vector q that specifies the number of in-between colors. As an example,

```
A = MakeColorMap([ 0 1 1; 1 0 1; 1 1 0; 0 0 1],[ 3 1 2])
```

should produce the above color map.

Program Development

MATLAB has a number of built-in color maps that are designed with the MakeColorMap strategy. See Figure 12.2. The first order of business is to write a function that generates a color map based on a pair of endpoint colors and a predetermined number of in-between colors. This linear interpolation calculation is discussed in §4.2. Our job is simply to assemble the colors in a matrix row by row. To clarify the process, suppose c1 = [0 1 1] and c2 = [1 0 1] are rgb vectors that define the endpoint colors and that we want three equally spaced in-between colors. Here is how we can generate the required color map:

```
s = (c2-c1)/4;   % s = [.25 -.25  0.0] = "the step"
d = c1;          % d = [0 1 1];
C = d;           % C = [0 1 1];
d = d + s;       % d = [.25 .75 1];
C = [C;d];       % C = [0 1 1; .25 .75 1]
d = d + s;       % d = [.50 .50 1]
C = [C;d];       % C = [0 1 1; .25 .75 1; .50 .50 1]
d = d + s;       % d = [.75 .25 1]
C = [C;d];       % C = [0 1 1; .25 .75 1; .50 .50 1; .75 .25 1]
d = d + s;       % d = [1 0 1]
C = [C; d];      % C = [0 1 1; .25 .75 1; .50 .50 1; .75 .25 1; 1 0 1]
```

More generally, the repeated updating of C and d can be handled by a for-loop. See the function InterpColors below. The vector s represents the color "step length." It is the difference between the red, green, and blue components divided by $m+1$, the number of steps needed to go from c1 to c2.

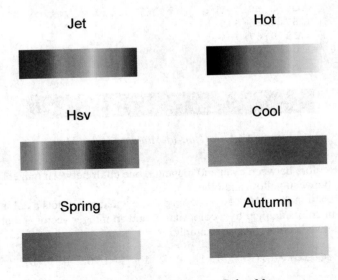

Figure 12.2. *Some* MATLAB *Color Maps.*

The Function `InterpColors`

```
function C = InterpColors(c1,c2,m)
% c1 and c2 are rgb vectors
% m is a nonnegative integer
% C is an (m+2)-by-3 color map whose first and last
%      rows are c1 and c2, respectively.
% Rows 2 through m+1 are obtained via linear interpolation.

n = m+2;
s = (c2 - c1)/(n-1);
d = c1;
C = d;
for k=2:n
    % Append the kth color...
    d = d + s;
    C = [C;d];
end
% Make sure all the entries are in the interval [0,1]...
C = max(zeros(n,3),min(C,ones(n,3)));
```

We next develop a function that builds complex color maps by splicing together simple color maps as produced by `InterpColors`. To illustrate the process, we return to the cyan-magenta-yellow-blue example from above. Once we have set up

```
B = [0 1 1 ;...     % cyan
     1 0 1 ;...     % magenta
     1 1 0 ;...     % yellow
     0 0 1];        % blue
q = [3 1 2];        % in-between color counts
```

then the synthesis of the overall color map A can proceeds as follows:

```
A = [];
D = InterpColors(B(1,:),B(2,:),q(1));
A = [A ; D];
D = InterpColors(B(2,:),B(3,:),q(2));
A = [A ; D(2:size(D,1),:)];
D = InterpColors(B(3,:),B(4,:),q(3));
A = [A ; D(2:size(D,1),:)];
```

The idea is to stack the interpolation-based color maps on top of each other, taking steps to ensure that there is no repetition of colors at the "boundaries." B is a color map whose rows specify the endpoint colors for `InterpColors`. The number of interpolated colors to generate in between each pair of endpoint colors is specified by the integer vector q. The array A starts out as the empty matrix. We then proceed to compute the interpolation-based color maps

D

0.00	1.00	1.00
0.25	0.75	1.00
0.50	0.50	1.00
0.75	0.25	1.00
1.00	0.00	1.00

D

1.00	0.00	1.00
1.00	0.50	0.50
1.00	1.00	0.00

D

1.00	1.00	0.00
0.67	0.67	0.33
0.33	0.33	0.67
0.00	0.00	1.00

augmenting A as we go along:

A

0.00	1.00	1.00
0.25	0.75	1.00
0.50	0.50	1.00
0.75	0.25	1.00
1.00	0.00	1.00

A

0.00	1.00	1.00
0.25	0.75	1.00
0.50	0.50	1.00
0.75	0.25	1.00
1.00	0.00	1.00
1.00	0.50	0.50
1.00	1.00	0.00

A

0.00	1.00	1.00
0.25	0.75	1.00
0.50	0.50	1.00
0.75	0.25	1.00
1.00	0.00	1.00
1.00	0.50	0.50
1.00	1.00	0.00
0.67	0.67	0.33
0.33	0.33	0.67
0.00	0.00	1.00

The general procedure is encapsulated in the function `MakeColorMap`. It can handle an arbitrary number of endpoint colors and an arbitrary number of in-between colors.

The Function `MakeColorMap`

```
function A = MakeColorMap(B,q)
% B is a p-by-3 color map
% q is a length-p - 1 vector of nonnegative integers
% A is a color map obtained by stacking the color maps
%       InterpColors(B(k,:),B(k+1,:),q(k)) for k=1:p-1
p = size(B,1);
A = [];
for k=1:p-1
   D = InterpColors(B(k,:),B(k+1,:),q(k));
   if k==1
       A = [A ; D];
   else
       A = [A; D(2:size(D,1),:)];
   end
end
```

As an application, `Eg12_1` is a short script that produces a color map that steps through the familiar ROY G BIV[13] spectrum. See Figure 12.3. It makes use of the following color map display function `ShowColorMap`.

---

[13]Red, Orange, Yellow, Green, Blue, Indigo, Violet.

The Function `ShowColorMap`

```
function ShowColorMap(C)
% Displays the p-by-3 color map C

p = size(C,1);
W = p/4;
hold on
for k=1:p
    c = C(k,:);
    fill([k-1 k k k-1],[0 0 W W],c,'EdgeColor',c)
end
hold off
axis off equal
```

The Script `Eg12_1`

```
% Script Eg12_1
% Illustrates MakeColorMap
close all
figure
% The endpoint colors...
B = [0 0 0; 1 0 0; 1 1 0; 0 1 0; 0 1 1; 0 0 1; 1 0 1;...
                                    1 0 0; 0 0 0];
% The in-between color counts...
q = [1 9 7 8 12 8 9 1];
% Generate and display the color map...
C = MakeColorMap(B,q);
ShowColorMap(C)
```

Figure 12.3. *Sample Output from the Script* `Eg12_1`.

Talking Point: Color Maps

Color maps are important for several reasons. First, they can be used to "color code" numerical results in a way that makes it easier to assimilate large volumes of numerical output. (More on this in the next section.) Second, they make it possible to store color images more compactly. Instead of storing the three numbers that encode a color we simply store the color's index in the color map. Third, graphical applications often run faster when the underlying colors are precomputed and stored in special-purpose memory.

The design of effective color maps is far from trivial. Colors that are "equally spaced" in the rgb sense may not be equally spaced from the standpoint of human perception. Special interpolation techniques must sometimes be used to ensure that there is not too much discontinuity within the color map. Moreover, color maps that "work" for one application may not be suitable for another. All in all, the subject of color maps is a fascinating topic within the field of color science which embodies aspects of both physics and human perception.

MATLAB Review

Number of Rows and Columns

If A is a matrix, then `size(A,1)` is the number of its rows, while `size(A,2)` is the number of its columns.

Building Matrices Row by Row

A standard way to set up an m-by-n matrix is with a for-loop:

```
A = zeros(m,n);
for k=1:m
      Fragment that assigns to row a 1-by-n array.
    A(k,:)   = row;
end
```

It is sometimes handier to proceed through repeated augmentation:

```
A = [ ];
for k=1:m
      Fragment that assigns to row a 1-by-n array.
    A = [A ; row];
end
```

Building Matrices Column by Column

A standard way to set up an m-by-n matrix is with a for-loop:

```
A = zeros(m,n);
for k=1:n
      Fragment that assigns to col an m-by-1 array.
    A(:,k)  = col;
end
```

It is sometimes handier to proceed through repeated augmentation:

```
A = [ ];
for k=1:n
      Fragment that assigns to col an m-by-1 array.
    A = [A col];
end
```

Aggregating Matrices

If A and B are matrices with the same number of columns, then C = [A ; B] produces a matrix in which A is stacked on top of B. For example, C = [zeros(2,3) ; ones(3,3)] is the same as

```
C = [0 0 0; 0 0 0; 1 1 1; 1 1 1; 1 1 1]
```

Similarly, if A and B are matrices with the same number of rows, then C = [A B] produces a matrix in which A is to the left of B. For example, C = [zeros(3,2) ones(3,3)] is the same as

```
C = [0 0 1 1 1; 0 0 1 1 1; 0 0 1 1 1]
```

max, min, sum

If A is an m-by-n matrix, then v = max(A) is a 1-by-n vector with the property that v(j) is assigned the largest value in A(:,j). If [v,idx] = max(A), then v and idx are 1-by-n vectors with the property that v(j) is assigned the largest value in A(:,j) and idx(j) is the row index of the largest value in A(:,j). If A and B are matrices that have the same number of rows and columns, then C = max(A,B) assigns to C the matrix whose (i, j) entry is the larger of A(i,j) and B(i,j). The min function is analogous.

If A is an m-by-n matrix, then v = sum(A) is a 1-by-n vector with the property that v(j) is the sum of the values in A(:,j).

Built-in Color Maps and `colormap`

MATLAB has a number of built-in color maps and they can be retrieved by using the colormap function, e.g.,

```
C = colormap('Jet')
```

Other color maps include 'Hsv', 'Hot', 'Cool', 'Spring', 'Summer', 'Autumn', 'Winter', 'Gray', 'Bone', 'Copper', and 'Pink'.

Exercises

M12.1.1 As a function of size(B,1) and the values in q, how many colors make up the color map MakeColorMap(B,q)?

M12.1.2 What is the effect of replacing the line

```
fill([k-1 k k k-1],[0 0 W W],c,'EdgeColor',c)
```

with

```
fill([k-1 k k k-1],[0 0 W W],c)
```

in the function ShowColorMap?

M12.1.3 Write a script that reproduces Figure 12.1.

M12.1.4 Write a function c = AveColor(C) that returns the average color in the color map C defined by taking the average of the red, green, and blue values of each color in C.

M12.1.5 Write a function A = WhiteWash(C) that produces a new color map A from a color map C by averaging each color in C with white [1 1 1].

P12.1.6 The command C = colormap('Jet') assigns the built-in color map Jet to C. Examine its values. Determine a color map B of endpoint colors and a vector of in-between color counts q so that MakeColorMap produces the Jet color map. Repeat for color maps Hsv, Hot, Cool, Spring, Copper, Gray, and Pink.

P12.1.7 Implement a function ShowColorWheel(C) that displays the color map C in color wheel format. That is, if C encodes p colors, then ShowColorWheel should draw a regular polygon with p sides and color its p sectors (pizza slices) with the colors in C.

P12.1.8 Implement a function A = Rotate(C) that creates a new color map A from color map C with the property that the red, green, and blue values in C become, respectively, the green, blue, and red values in A.

P12.1.9 Implement a function A = Refine(C) that creates a new color map A from color map C by inserting a color in between every pair of colors in C. Each inserted color should be the average of its two neighbors. Thus, if

    C = [1 0 0 ; 1 1 0 ; 1 1 1]

then

    A = [1 0 0 ; 1 0.5 0 ; 1 1 0 ; 1 1 0.5 ; 1 1 1].

P12.1.10 Implement a function A = DeleteReds(C) that returns a color map A obtained by deleting from the color map C all colors whose red intensity level is higher than 0.5.

12.2   Known on the Corner

Problem Statement

The value of a function F is known at the four corners of a square in the xy-plane. Interpolate its value at a finite number of equally spaced points inside the square and display the results in the form of a color-coded "checkerboard." This is essentially the problem of shading a square as shown in Figure 12.4.

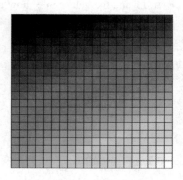

Figure 12.4. *Shading a Square.*

The size of the checkerboard and the mapping of numerical values to color are parameters to play with.

Program Development

There are two distinct subproblems that we must deal with. First, there is the problem of taking the four corner values and producing an n-by-n matrix of interpolated values for a given n, e.g.,

$$\begin{bmatrix} 57 & 120 \\ 3 & 30 \end{bmatrix} \longrightarrow \begin{bmatrix} 57 & ? & ? & 120 \\ ? & ? & ? & ? \\ ? & ? & ? & ? \\ 3 & ? & ? & 30 \end{bmatrix} \longrightarrow \begin{bmatrix} 57 & 78 & 99 & 120 \\ 39 & 56 & 73 & 90 \\ 21 & 34 & 47 & 60 \\ 3 & 12 & 21 & 30 \end{bmatrix}. \qquad (12.1)$$

Second, there is the problem of taking a matrix and a color map and producing a color-coded mosaic whose tile colors correspond to the values in the matrix:

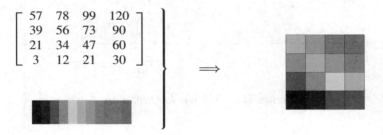

$$\left. \begin{bmatrix} 57 & 78 & 99 & 120 \\ 39 & 56 & 73 & 90 \\ 21 & 34 & 47 & 60 \\ 3 & 12 & 21 & 30 \end{bmatrix} \right\} \implies$$

The central concept behind the solution to the first problem is *bilinear interpolation*. Bilinear interpolation is the two-dimensional analogue of linear interpolation which we used in both §4.2 and §12.1 to solve one-dimensional "color generation" problems. The act of taking a one-dimensional computational idea and extending it to higher dimensions is an important research paradigm.

To set the stage, we formalize the problem of linearly interpolating a function f on an interval $[a,b]$. If $a \leq p \leq b$ and we know $f_a = f(a)$ and $f_b = f(b)$, then we estimate the value of f at p with

$$f_p = f_a + \gamma(f_b - f_a) = (1 - \gamma)f_a + \gamma f_b,$$

where

$$\gamma = \frac{p - a}{b - a}.$$

Think of γ as a "journey fraction." If we are that far along in the journey from a to b, then we should be that far along in the change from $f(a)$ to $f(b)$.

Bilinear interpolation is based on a twofold application of this idea. Suppose F_{11}, F_{12}, F_{21}, and F_{22} are the values of the function F at the corners of a square and that we want to use this information to interpolate F at the interior point P. See Figure 12.5 where

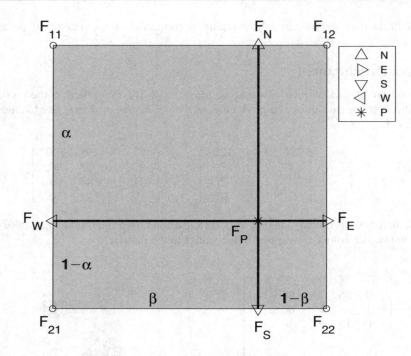

Figure 12.5. *Bilinear Interpolation.*

α and β are the associated journey fractions as measured from the upper left corner in the vertical and horizontal directions, respectively. Using linear interpolation along the top and bottom edges, we have the following interpolations of F at the points N and S:

$$F_N = (1-\beta)F_{11} + \beta F_{12}$$
$$F_S = (1-\beta)F_{21} + \beta F_{22}.$$

Since P is on the line segment connecting N and S, we can apply linear interpolation again using the values F_N and F_S:

$$F_P = (1-\alpha)F_N + \alpha F_S \tag{12.2}$$
$$= (1-\alpha)((1-\beta)F_{11} + \beta F_{12}) + \alpha((1-\beta)F_{21} + \beta F_{22})$$
$$= (1-\alpha)(1-\beta)F_{11} + (1-\alpha)\beta F_{12} + \alpha(1-\beta)F_{21} + \alpha\beta F_{22}.$$

Thus, the interpolation of F at P is a linear combination of the corner values F_{11}, F_{12}, F_{21}, and F_{22}. The same value is produced if we work with interpolated values on the left and right edges. Indeed, if

$$F_W = (1-\alpha)F_{11} + \alpha F_{21}$$
$$F_E = (1-\alpha)F_{12} + \alpha F_{22},$$

then it is easy to verify that

$$F_P = (1 - \beta)F_W + \beta F_E$$

$$= (1 - \beta)((1 - \alpha)F_{11} + \alpha F_{21}) + \beta((1 - \alpha)F_{12} + \alpha F_{22})$$

$$= (1 - \beta)(1 - \alpha)F_{11} + (1 - \beta)\alpha F_{21} + \beta(1 - \alpha)F_{12} + \beta \alpha F_{22}.$$

Returning to the shading problem, let us use bilinear interpolation to set up an n-by-n matrix A consisting of interpolated estimates of F across the square. We start by assigning the "corner" values:

```
A(1,1) = F(1,1); A(1,n) = F(1,2);
A(n,1) = F(2,1); A(n,n) = F(2,2);
```

For a given i and j,

```
beta = (j-1)/(n-1);
alfa = (i-1)/(n-1);
```

are the horizontal and vertical journey fractions associated with matrix entry (i, j). Following (12.2), we therefore compute

```
FN = (1-beta)*F(1,1) + beta*F(1,2);
FS = (1-beta)*F(2,1) + beta*F(2,2);
A(i,j) = (1-alfa)*FN + alfa*FS;
```

Encapsulating this we obtain the following function.

The Function BilinearInterp

```
function A = BilinearInterp(F,n)
% F is a 2-by-2 matrix and n>1 is an integer.
% A is an n-by-n matrix with A(1,1)=F(1,1), A(1,n)=F(1,2),
% A(n,1)=F(2,1), A(n,n)=F(2,2), and the rest of the A(i,j)
% are obtained via bilinear interpolation.

A = zeros(n,n);
for j=1:n
   beta = (j-1)/(n-1);
   FN = (1-beta)*F(1,1) + beta*F(1,2);
   FS = (1-beta)*F(2,1) + beta*F(2,2);
   for i=1:n
      alfa = (i-1)/(n-1);
      A(i,j) = (1-alfa)*FN + alfa*FS;
   end
end
```

Note that the "north point" value FN is assigned to A(1,j) while the "south point" value FS is assigned to A(n,j).

Next, we consider the display of a mosaic whose tile colorings reflect the values in a given m-by-n matrix A. Scale is not important so we may assume without loss of generality that the tiles are 1-by-1. This yields the following solution framework assuming that C is a color map:

```
figure
axis ij off equal
for i =1:m
    for j=1:n
        Based on A(i,j), assign to c a color from C.
        fill([j j+1 j+1 j],[i i i+1 i+1],c)
    end
end
```

The `axis ij` command is handy for displaying matrix values the "right way." Notice that for a matrix A, the first subscript (the row index) measures distance from the top of the matrix while the second subscript (the column index) measures distance from the left edge of the matrix. In other words, the origin is in the upper left corner. This is a different orientation than what we use for a function $f(x, y)$, where the x-value measures distance in the horizontal direction and the y-value measures distance in the vertical direction.

Our plan for coloring tiles is to partition the interval $[A_{min}, A_{max}]$ into p equal subintervals where A_{min} is the smallest value in A, A_{max} is the largest value in A, and p is the

The Function ShowMatrix

```
function ShowMatrix(A,C)
% A is an m-by-n matrix whose values are not all the same.
% C is a p-by-3 color map matrix.
% Displays the matrix A as an m-by-n array of colored tiles.

[m,n] = size(A);
p = size(C,1);
A_min = min(min(A));
A_max = max(max(A));
h = (A_max - A_min)/p;

figure
axis ij off equal
hold on

for i =1:m
    for j=1:n
        % Display A(i,j)
        k = max(ceil((A(i,j)-A_min)/h ),1);
        c = C(k,:);
        fill([j j+1 j+1 j],[i i i+1 i+1],c)
    end
end
hold off
```

number of rows (colors) in C. If the value of A(i,j) is in the kth subinterval, then tile (i, j) is displayed with color C(k,:). The index k is a simple computation that involves ceil and the subinterval length $h = (A_{max} - A_{min})/p$. The function ShowMatrix(A,C) shown above packages these ideas and displays the matrix A according to the color map C.

The test script Eg12_2 generates random corner values and then computes and displays a 20-by-20 shading matrix. See Figure 12.4 for sample output.

The Script Eg12_2

```
% Script Eg12_2
% Interpolate F(x,y) given 4 random corner values.
n = 20;
C = colormap('hot');
close all
F = randn(2,2); % Assume the 4 values are different
A = BilinearInterp(F,n);
ShowMatrix(A,C)
shg
```

Talking Point: Rendering Is Complicated

Shading is central to the act of rendering an image in computer graphics, but it typically involves much more than interpolation. One factor is the type of light source. It may be a point source or an area source. It may be highly directional or diffuse. The inverse square law is also an issue, but if the source is very far away from the illuminated object, then there will be little falloff because the distance to the source is essentially uniform. All that changes if the source is nearby or "in the picture."

As we have mentioned several times already, curved surfaces are often approximated by millions of "little polygons." The accurate rendering of each polygon may require a calculation that involves the polygon's orientation in space and the angle that it makes with an incoming light ray. The physics of reflection is also an issue. It is overly simplistic to assume that reflection is a surface phenomenon. In practice, light rays "bounce around" inside a material before exiting in different directions with different properties.

It is easy to see why accurate rendering in computer graphics is computationally intensive—all the more reason to develop sophisticated interpolation schemes that effectively reduce the amount of work.

MATLAB Review

axis ij

With this orientation, the figure window coordinate system is consistent with the "ij" system of matrices. The i-axis is vertical and is numbered from top to bottom. The j-axis is horizontal and is numbered from left to right.

Exercises

M12.2.1 Explain why replacing the statement

```
k = max(ceil((A(i,j)-A_min)/h),1);
```

with

```
k = ceil((A(i,j)-A_min)/h);
```

would lead to an execution error in Eg7_3.

M12.2.2 Extend BilinearInterp(F,n) to BilinearInterp(F,n,m) so that it generates an m-by-n matrix of interpolated values.

M12.2.3 Write a script that uses ShowMatrix to display n-by-n matrices generated by randn. Design a color map that makes it easy to distinguish between the positive and negative entries.

M12.2.4 Write a function ShowMagic(n) that displays the n-by-n magic square produced by magic(n). Use ShowMatrix and a color map consisting of n^2 equally spaced colors that range from black to white.

P12.2.5 Write a function B = Refine(A) that takes an m-by-n matrix A and produces a $(2m-1)$-by-$(2n-1)$ matrix B with the properties that B(1:2:2*m-1,1:2:2*n-1) is the same as A and all other entries are obtained using bilinear interpolation.

P12.2.6 Implement a function ShowMatrixLog(A,C) suitable for displaying matrices with entries that range over several orders of magnitude.

P12.2.7 The script

```
close all, n = input('Enter n:'); C = [1 1 0 ; 1 0 1 ];
for i=1:n
    for j=1:n
        if i>j
            A(i,j) = 0;
        else
            A(i,j) = 1;
        end
    end
end
ShowMatrix(A,C)
```

produces the following image:

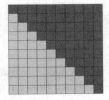

for the input value $n = 10$. Develop comparable scripts for each of the following mosaics:

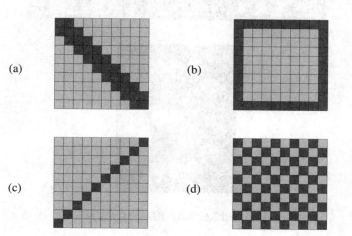

12.3   Seven-by-Five

Problem Statement

The large-scale display of alphanumeric data frequently makes use of the *dot matrix* idea. Figure 12.6 shows how each of the 10 digits might be represented using a 7-by-5 dot matrix. Think of the display as an array of "light bulbs," each of which is either off or on according to whether the corresponding matrix entry is zero or one. If D_k is the dot matrix associated with the digit k, then for the digit 3 illustrated in Figure 12.6 we have

$$D_3 = \begin{bmatrix} 0 & 1 & 1 & 1 & 0 \\ 1 & 0 & 0 & 0 & 1 \\ 0 & 0 & 0 & 0 & 1 \\ 0 & 0 & 1 & 1 & 0 \\ 0 & 0 & 0 & 0 & 1 \\ 1 & 0 & 0 & 0 & 1 \\ 0 & 1 & 1 & 1 & 0 \end{bmatrix}.$$

Noting that the 7-by-5 representation is pretty crude up close, how would the appearance improve if we "halved the mesh size," i.e., if we used 14-by-10 displays? Build a simple point-and-click environment that supports the design of 14-by-10 dot matrices for each digit.

Program Development

There are three main programming issues to work out. First, we must decide how to represent a collection of dot matrices. In our problem we have ten dot matrices, one for

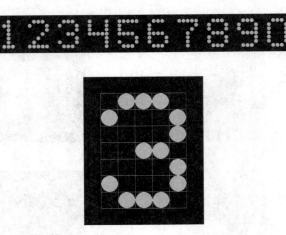

Figure 12.6. *7-by-5 Dot Matrices.*

each digit. Second, it will be handy to have a function that displays the digit given its dot matrix representation. The format of the display of the digit 3 in Figure 12.6 is what we have in mind. Third, we need to develop a "ginput" framework for turning lights on and off as we design the 14-by-10 dot matrices. Our plan is to change the on/off "state" of a light by clicking on it.

The starting point is to choose a handy data structure for storing the ten dot matrices. A length-10 cell array works well. The idea is simply to let D{1},...,D{10} be the dot matrix representations for 1,...,9, and 0. The function TheDigits, shown below in abbreviated form, assigns to D the dot matrices for the 7-by-5 representations depicted in Figure 12.6.

When you have a cell array of matrices like this, a reference to a matrix entry requires a mix of curly brackets and round brackets. Assuming that D = TheDigits(), here is how we could "turn on the corner light bulbs" associated with the display of the digit zero:

```
D{10}(1,1) = 1;  D{10}(1,5) = 1;  D{10}(7,1) = 1;  D{10}(7,5) = 1;
```

It would not be very convenient to design a dot matrix "by hand" with assignment statements like this!

We next develop a function DrawDigit(a,b,width,M,...) that adds a dot matrix digit to the figure window. Refer to Figure 12.7. The digit's location will be specified by a and b, the *xy*-coordinates of the background rectangle's lower left-hand corner. The input parameter width will specify the width of the rectangle and M will identify the underlying dot matrix. Observe from Figure 12.7 that the 7-by-5 "grid" is pulled in from the edge of the bounding rectangle so that the side-by-side display of digits (e.g., 1234567890) looks okay. In our problem we will want to display 7-by-5's and 14-by-10's so DrawDigit needs to accommodate different dot matrix dimensions.

As it involves routine graphics, we show only the specifications of DrawDigit without the implementation details below. However, for ginput processing it is going to be important that we know the precise location of the *mn* tiles that make up the digit grid. See Figure 12.7 which depicts the case $m = 14$, $n = 10$. Note that the point (x, y) is in the dot matrix tile (i, j) if

The Function TheDigits

```
function D = TheDigits()
% D is a 10-by-1 cell array.
% D{k} is a 7-by-5 matrix that encodes the digit k, k=1:9
% D{10} encodes 0.

  D = cell(10,1);
  D{1}  = [0 0 1 0 0;...
           0 1 1 0 0;...
           0 0 1 0 0;...
           0 0 1 0 0;...
           0 0 1 0 0;...
           0 0 1 0 0;...
           0 1 1 1 0];
          :
  D{10} = [0 1 1 1 0;...
           1 0 0 0 1;...
           1 0 0 0 1;...
           1 0 0 0 1;...
           1 0 0 0 1;...
           1 0 0 0 1;...
           0 1 1 1 0];
```

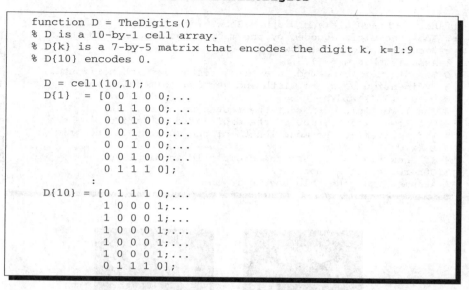

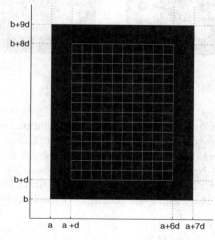

Figure 12.7. *A Dot Matrix Grid.*

$$a + d + (j-1)\cdot e \ \leq\ x \ \leq\ a + d + j\cdot e$$

and

$$b + 9d - i\cdot e \ \leq\ y \ \leq\ b + 9d - (i-1)\cdot e,$$

where $e = 5d/n$.

The Function DrawDigit

```
function DrawDigit(a,b,width,M,ShowGrid)
% Adds the digit encoded by the m-by-n dot matrix M to the
%   current figure window.
% Assumes that m = (7/5)n.
% The digit is centered in a black rectangle with horizontal
%   dimension equal to width and vertical dimension equal
%   to (9/7)*width;
% The lower left corner of the rectangle is at (a,b).
% The lower left corner of the digit grid is (a+d,b+d) where
%   d = width/7. The edge length of the squares in the grid is
%   (width - 2*d)/n.
% If ShowGrid == 1, then the digit grid is displayed.
% Otherwise, it is not.
% Assumes that the hold toggle is on.
```

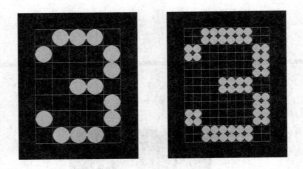

Figure 12.8. *Embedding.*

We now turn our attention to the heart of the problem which involves turning a given 7-by-5 representation into an "improved" 14-by-10 representation. So as not to start the design of the 14-by-10 digit from scratch, we can obtain a "rough draft" through an embedding process that is displayed in Figure 12.8. Each "1" in the 7-by-5 dot matrix becomes a 2-by-2 submatrix of 1's in the 14-by-10 dot matrix. Likewise, each "0" in the 7-by-5 dot matrix becomes a 2-by-2 submatrix of 0's in the 14-by-10 dot matrix. The function Embed below carries out this doubling. The assignment statement in the loop body is equivalent to

```
NewM(2*i-1,2*j-1)  = M(i,j);
NewM(2*i-1,2*j)    = M(i,j);
NewM(2*i,2*j-1)    = M(i,j);
NewM(2*i,2*j)      = M(i,j);
```

As an application of Embed, here is how to convert the cell array D=TheDigits() of 7-by-5 dot matrices into a cell array of 14-by-10 dot matrices:

```
for k=1:10
    D{k} = Embed(D{k});
end
```

The Function **Embed**

```
function NewM = Embed(M)
% M is an m-by-n matrix of zeros and ones.
% NewM is a (2m)-by-(2n) matrix of zeros and ones obtained by
%    "replacing" the (i,j) entry in M with ones(2,2) if M(i,j)
%    is 1 and zeros(2,2) if M(i,j) is zero.

[m,n] = size(M); NewM = zeros(2*m,2*n);
for i=1:m
   for j=1:n
      NewM(2*i-1:2*i,2*j-1:2*j)=M(i,j);
   end
end
```

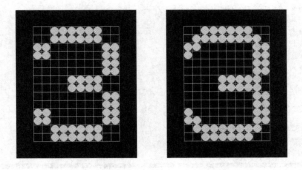

Figure 12.9. *An Improved "3".*

To improve a 14-by-10 dot matrix representation we need to "smooth" the corners.
See Figure 12.9 which displays Embed(D{3}) on the left and an improvement on the right.
The binary, on/off situation in each tile makes it ideal for ginput-driven modifications.
We start by displaying the digit so that the lower left corner of the digit grid is at (0,0) and
the tile squares are 1-by-1. See Figure 12.10. Locating and sizing the display of the digit
in this way makes it easy to process the ginput mouseclicks. In the function Refine
listed below, the mouseclicks are assimilated until the click falls outside the digit grid. Note
that mouseclick processing is very easy since the grid area is $2m$-by-$2n$ and cornered at the
origin. A possible concern is what to do if the mouseclick falls on the edge of a tile, e.g.,
$(x, y) = (2.5, 1)$. This is highly unlikely, but it does deserve some attention. See problem
M12.3.2.
    The function Refine given below is more general than is required to solve our
problem since we shall only be concerned with the improvement of a 7-by-5 display. But
recognize that the refinement process can be repeated. For example, if M is an initialized
7-by-5 dot matrix representation, then the sequence

```
M = Refine(M);   % 14-by-10
M = Refine(M);   % 28-by-20
M = Refine(M);   % 56-by-40
```

The Function `Refine`

```
function NewM = Refine(M)
% M is an m-by-n dot matrix representing a digit.
% NewM is a 2m-by-2n dot matrix that represents the same digit
% but "looks better."

% Compute and display the embedded digit...
[m,n] = size(M);
NewM = Embed(M);
d = 2*n/5;
base = 7*d;
DrawDigit(-d,-d,base,NewM,1)

% Turn lights on and off until the design is satisfactory.
% The process is terminated by clicking outside the digit grid...
[x,y] = ginput(1);
while x>0 && x<=2*n && y>=0 && y<=2*m
    i = 2*m-floor(y);
    j = ceil(x);
    if NewM(i,j)==1
        % Turn this light off...
        NewM(i,j) = 0;
    else
        % Turn this light on...
        NewM(i,j) = 1;
    end
    DrawDigit(-d,-d,base,NewM,1)
    [x,y] = ginput(1);
end
```

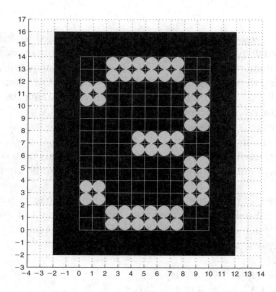

Figure 12.10. *The* `Refine` *Environment.*

would result in the production of a 56-by-40 dot matrix. From the graphical point of view, the tile squares would be getting too small for our simple `ginput` environment to be effective.

The script `Eg12_3` uses `Refine` to produce 14-by-10 improvements of each digit as shown in Figure 12.11.

The Script `Eg12_3`

```
% Script Eg12_3
% Environment for designing 14-by-10 dot matrix
% representations of the ten digits.

close all
% Get the 7-by-5 representations...
SevenByFive = TheDigits();

% Improve the 14-by-10's...
FourteenByTen = cell(10,1);
for k=1:10
    figure
    set(gcf,'position',[20,20,800,600])
    axis equal off
    hold on
    % Design and  save the kth digit...
    FourteenByTen{k} = Refine(SevenByFive{k});
    close
end

% Display the 7-by-5's and 14-by-10's side-by-side...
figure
axis([1 11 -1.3 1.3])
set(gcf,'position',[20,20,800,600])
axis equal off
hold on
for k=1:10
    DrawDigit(k,1,1,SevenByFive{k},0)
    DrawDigit(k,-1.3,1,FourteenByTen{k},0)
end
hold off
```

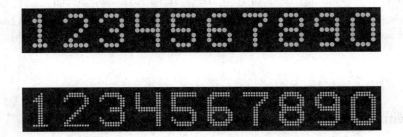

Figure 12.11. *Sample Output from the Script* Eg12_3.

Talking Point: Font Design

With the advent of plasma screens and LCD displays there have evolved much more sophisticated encodings for displaying alphanumeric data. Nevertheless, our 7-by-5 example provides insight into the issues that surround the discretization of images, a topic that we take up in the next section.

It also points to the fascinating subject of font design. This field has been revolutionized by the computer. In our example, we set out to design a set of 14-by-10 digits. This is a very limited font-design problem. Our goal (presumably) was to make the refined digit displays more pleasing to the eye than what could be achieved in the 7-by-5 framework. It is not hard to see that there would be many more design options if the target layout was 140 by 100. Font designers are driven by a mix of aesthetic and practical concerns. Highly mathematical models are developed to determine the spacing between letters. Research papers have been written on the design of the letter "S," which turns out to be among the most challenging of the twenty-six letters. Font design is a good example of how small, take-for-granted details are transformed into large, up-for-grabs design issues because of the computer.

MATLAB Review

Cell Arrays of Matrices

In problems that involve sets of matrices, it is handy to collect them all in a cell array. In this setting, it is important to be clear about the use of curly brackets and parentheses. If D is a cell array of matrices, then D{k}(i,j) correctly refers to the (i, j) entry of matrix D{k}. A reference of the form D(i,j){k} is illegal.

Exercises

M12.3.1 Write a script that displays the ten digits upside down.

M12.3.2 Is there a danger of getting a subscript out of bounds in Refine if the mouseclick "lands" on the edge of the digit grid? If so, how could this be corrected?

M12.3.3 Write a script that displays a 14-by-10 rendition of the letter "A."

P12.3.4 There are 35 "lightbulbs" associated with the 7-by-5 representation. Which one goes on and off the most if we display a sequence of 1000 random digits?

P12.3.5 Write a function NewM = Embed97(M) that takes a 7-by-5 dot matrix representation of a digit and produces a "rough draft" of a 9-by-7 representation of the same digit.

P12.3.6 Write a function mu = sep(M1,M2) that computes the "distance" between two 7-by-5 dot matrices M1 and M2. It is up to you to determine the underlying metric.

12.4   Picture This

Problem Statement

A black-and-white photograph can be approximated by an array of dots, each displayed with the appropriate amount of "grayness." The dots are called *pixels*, a mnemonic for "picture elements." The image in Figure 12.12 is a 3390-by-4200 array of pixels. It is represented as a 3390-by-4200 matrix in the computer where the value of matrix element (i, j) quantifies the grayness associated with pixel (i, j).

Figure 12.12. *A Black-and-White Picture Is a Matrix.*

For black-and-white images it is customary to use the integers 0 through 255 to represent level of grayness with 0 corresponding to black and 255 corresponding to white. The choice of 255 means that a single byte of storage can be used for the encoding.

Referring to its matrix representation as A, here are the pixel values for a 9-by-8 patch from the clock tower picture:

$$A(2000{:}2008, 2856{:}2863) = \begin{bmatrix} 214 & 210 & 207 & 207 & 152 & 106 & 74 & 62 \\ 174 & 174 & 173 & 164 & 77 & 50 & 40 & 39 \\ 178 & 179 & 171 & 147 & 62 & 46 & 40 & 36 \\ 173 & 177 & 157 & 120 & 47 & 46 & 46 & 42 \\ 176 & 163 & 132 & 97 & 48 & 52 & 51 & 48 \\ 136 & 106 & 72 & 54 & 38 & 45 & 44 & 48 \\ 113 & 76 & 49 & 45 & 45 & 44 & 38 & 44 \\ 75 & 53 & 40 & 41 & 44 & 42 & 38 & 46 \\ 51 & 45 & 43 & 43 & 43 & 43 & 41 & 49 \end{bmatrix}.$$

The `uint8` data type is used to store pixel values. This is a 1-byte, unsigned integer format that is more economical than the 8-byte `double` format which supports floating point arithmetic. Thus, when we say that "a picture is a matrix" we really mean that "a picture is a `uint8` matrix."

A color picture can be represented with three matrices, one for each of the colors red, green, and blue. See Figure 12.13. Again, one typically uses a 0-to-255 scale to represent color intensity. Thus, if A_{red}, A_{green}, and A_{blue} are the matrix encodings for the red, green, and blue components of the picture, then pixel (i, j) is displayed with the rgb color triplet $\left(A_{red}(i, j), A_{green}(i, j), A_{blue}(i, j)\right)$.

Figure 12.13. *A Color Picture Is Three Matrices.*

Because a picture is a matrix, image processing involves numerical computing with the underlying pixel values. For example, if a black-and-white picture is contaminated with specks of dirt, then it will have random pixels with grayness values that are very much less than its neighbors. We should be able to scan the picture (matrix) for instances of this and "repair the damage" by replacing the errant pixel value with a number that is more consistent with its pixel neighbors.

Another example where local pixel changes are informative concerns the problem of edge detection. Pixel values change rapidly in the vicinity of an edge. For example, along the "bright side" of a boundary we might find rgb triplets such as (220,240,198), while on the "dark side" we would find colors with lower intensities, e.g., (52,29,38). Thus, it should be possible to locate edges by computing differences between nearby pixels.

Write a function RemoveDirtSpecks that can be used to clean up a "dirty" image and a function Edges that can be used to identify its edges. Exploit the fact that speck-of-dirt detection and edge detection involve looking at local pixel variation.

Program Development

We assume that the input to the problem comes in the form of an image file. There are many different types of image file formats, each identified with a unique suffix. For simplicity, we shall confine ourselves to the widely used "jpeg" format. The `imread` command can be used to acquire the pixel data from a jpeg file. Once that data is in the MATLAB workspace, it can be displayed using `imshow`:

```
fname = [pwd '\InsightData\12_4\Cornell_Clock.jpg']
A = imread(fname,'jpg');
imshow(A)
```

The complete path to the file `Cornell_Clock.jpg` is assigned to `fname`. (Recall the file-reading convention from §11.1.) This fragment produces the color image displayed in Figure 12.13 (without the axes).

As we mentioned, it takes three matrices to represent a color image. For this purpose three-dimensional arrays are used and in the above fragment, `A` has this form. Three subscripts are used to identify components, e.g., `A(20,400,3)`. Applied to a color image that is m pixels high and n pixels wide, the built-in function `imread` returns an m-by-n-by-3 array A with the property that $A(i,j,1)$, $A(i,j,2)$, and $A(i,j,3)$ are the red, green, and blue intensity values for pixel (i,j). As a way of illustrating the manipulation of a three-dimensional array, here is a fragment that displays the red component of the image in Figure 12.13:

```
ARed = A;              % Copy.
ARed(:,:,2) = 0;       % Set the green pixel values to zero.
ARed(:,:,3) = 0;       % Set the blue pixel values to zero.
imshow(ARed)           % Display what is left.
```

The convenience of the colon notation is appreciated when compared to the following equivalent code fragment:

```
[m,n,p] = size(A);
Ared = unit8(zeros(m,n,p));
for i=1:m
   for j=1:n
       Ared(i,j,1) = A(i,j,1);
       Ared(i,j,2) = 0;
       Ared(i,j,3) = 0;
   end
end
imshow(Ared)
```

For simplicity, we will develop procedures for dirt detection and edge detection in the context of black-and-white images. Using the built-in function `rgb2gray`, we can convert a three-dimensional array that represents a color image into a matrix representation of the same picture in black and white. Here is a fragment that computes and saves in the subdirectory `MyData` a black-and-white image of the clock tower, assuming that `A` has been initialized as above:

```
B = rgb2gray(A);
imshow(B)
fname = [pwd '\MyData\Cornell_Clock_Gray.jpg'];
imwrite(B,fname,'jpg')
```

The black-and-white image in Figure 12.12 was produced in this way. The uint8 matrix B is a matrix of gray values; its entries are integers between (and including) 0 and 255. The function imwrite is used for creating image files. It has three input parameters: (a) the matrix (or three-dimensional array) that represents the picture, (b) the full name of the file that is to store the pixel values, and (c) the format of the file.

It is easy to display and work on a "cropped" version of a black-and-white image. For example, if B is initialized as above, then the fragment

```
C = B(850:1150,2350:2650);
for k=1:200
    i = floor(1+rand(1)*300); j = floor(1+rand(1)*300);
    C(i:i+1,j:j+1) = floor(10*rand(2,2));
end
imshow(C)
```

pulls out a 301-by-301 section of the clock tower picture in Figure 12.12, randomly adds two-hundred 2-by-2 "specks of dirt," and displays the result. See Figure 12.14. How might we "filter out" the specks? In terms of pixel values, our model of a dirt speck is a 2-by-2 submatrix whose values are typically much less than the surrounding pixel values. For example, here is a contaminated 6-by-6 patch of sky from the contaminated image in Figure 12.14:

$$X = \begin{bmatrix} 155 & 160 & 157 & 154 & 160 & 160 \\ 155 & 161 & 155 & 152 & 161 & 158 \\ 154 & 160 & 6 & 7 & 161 & 155 \\ 150 & 157 & 5 & 3 & 163 & 156 \\ 160 & 159 & 157 & 157 & 159 & 159 \\ 161 & 155 & 156 & 158 & 156 & 159 \end{bmatrix}.$$

We would like to replace the "dirty" pixel values with values that are more typical in its surrounding neighborhood. To automate this idea we need to quantify the notions of "neighborhood" and "typical." We say that pixel (i_1, j_1) and pixel (i_2, j_2) are neighbors if $|i_1 - i_2| \le 1$ and $|j_1 - j_2| \le 1$. It follows that an "interior" pixel has nine neighbors (including itself) while edge pixels have either four or six neighbors. Our dirt speck filtering plan is to visit each pixel in the image and replace its value by the median value of its neighbors. If

Figure 12.14. *Dirt Speck Removal (Before and After).*

we apply this strategy to the contaminated 6-by-6 patch above, then here is how $X(2:5, 2:5)$ changes:

$$\begin{bmatrix} 161 & 155 & 152 & 161 \\ 160 & 6 & 7 & 161 \\ 157 & 5 & 3 & 163 \\ 159 & 157 & 157 & 159 \end{bmatrix} \rightarrow \begin{bmatrix} 155 & 155 & 155 & 158 \\ 155 & 152 & 152 & 156 \\ 157 & 157 & 157 & 157 \\ 157 & 157 & 157 & 158 \end{bmatrix}.$$

This is called *median filtering*. The technique is very successful in our example because the pixel values in the sky are extremely uniform and the dirt specks are small and sharply defined. Median filtering (more or less) works to the extent that it leaves alone pixels that look like their neighbors and it will adjust those that do not. It should be noted that it is much better to base this kind of filtering on the median rather than on the mean. Here is what happens to $X(2:5, 2:5)$ when we apply *mean filtering*, i.e., when we replace its entries with the average neighborhood value:

$$\begin{bmatrix} 161 & 155 & 152 & 161 \\ 160 & 6 & 7 & 161 \\ 157 & 5 & 3 & 163 \\ 159 & 157 & 157 & 159 \end{bmatrix} \rightarrow \begin{bmatrix} 140 & 124 & 124 & 141 \\ 123 & 90 & 90 & 124 \\ 123 & 90 & 91 & 124 \\ 140 & 123 & 124 & 141 \end{bmatrix}.$$

Notice how the dirt speck "pulls down" the surrounding pixel values and that none of the revised pixel values are what you would call "typical."

The implementation of `MedianFilter` below requires a double loop to oversee the complete scan of the image and some careful subscripting to avoid out-of-bound references near the picture edges. When applied to a vector, the built-in function `median` returns the median value. The 3-by-3 matrix `Neighbors` is reshaped into a 9-by-1 vector via `Neighbors(:)`.

The edge detection problem is similar to the dirt-speck detection problem in that both involve abrupt changes in pixel values in the grayness-level matrix A. However, the ultimate goal in edge detection is to use the discontinuities rather than to clean them up. Working

The Function `MedianFilter`

```
function B = MedianFilter(A)
% A is an m-by-n uint8 array.
% B is an m-by-n uint8 array obtained from A by
% median filtering

[m,n] = size(A);
B = uint8(zeros(m,n));
for i=1:m
   for j=1:n
      % The 3-by-3 matrix of neighbors...
      iMin = max(1,i-1); iMax = min(m,i+1);
      jMin = max(1,j-1); jMax = min(n,j+1);
      Neighbors = A(iMin:iMax,jMin:jMax);
      % The median value...
      B(i,j) = median(Neighbors(:));
   end
end
```

again with 3-by-3 patches, at pixel (i, j) define the rate of change ρ_{ij} to be the maximum discrepancy between $A(i,j)$ and its neighbors $A(i-1,j-1), A(i-1,j), A(i-1,j+1),$ $A(i,j-1), A(i,j+1), A(i+1,j-1), A(i+1,j),$ and $A(i+1,j+1)$. (This assumes that pixel (i, j) is not on the edge of the image, for otherwise we would get a subscript-out-of-range error.) As an example of a rate-of-change computation, if

$$A(8:10,20:22) = \begin{array}{|c|c|c|} \hline 240 & 26 & 18 \\ \hline 237 & 242 & 31 \\ \hline 236 & 241 & 241 \\ \hline \end{array}$$

then $\rho_{9,21} = |242 - 18| = 224$.

Our plan is to have a threshold value τ and to define pixel (i, j) as a "pixel of interest" if $\rho_{ij} \geq \tau$. Of course, a dirt-speck pixel most likely has a high rate of change and so it would (mistakingly) be identified as a pixel of interest. However, edges have structure so if we highlight all the pixels of interest in an image, then we would hopefully expect to see curves/lines in the vicinity of true edges. Here is a patch of pixel values taken from the clock tower in Figure 12.12:

$$X = \begin{bmatrix} 168 & 153 & 134 & 145 & 121 & 60 & 47 & 51 & 58 \\ 178 & 152 & 124 & 134 & 109 & 53 & 49 & 56 & 53 \\ 176 & 157 & 126 & 122 & 110 & 64 & 55 & 52 & 52 \\ 158 & 138 & 108 & 120 & 136 & 68 & 53 & 51 & 56 \end{bmatrix}.$$

The patch brackets the strong vertical edge readily seen in the clock tower. Even though this is perhaps the sharpest edge in the image, we see that the transition from bright to dark does not happen instantly, a clue that edge detection is a complicated calculation. Nevertheless, let us proceed to construct an image with the property that pixel (i, j) is black (0) if $\rho_{ij} < \tau$ and white (255) if $\rho_{ij} \geq \tau$. The function Edges given below produces a jpeg representation of this "edge" image. As anticipated, the rate-of-change computation picks up more than just edges. See Figure 12.15. The script Eg12_4 that produces this image and others throughout this section is given below.

In conclusion, we have introduced a pair of elementary 3-by-3 frameworks that just begin to address the extremely difficult problems of speck-of-dirt filtering and edge detection.

Figure 12.15. *Edges (and More).*

The Function Edges

```
function Edges(jpegIn,jpegOut,tau)
% jpegIn is a string that specifies the address of a jpeg file
%     that encodes an image I.
% tau is a threshold value between 0 and 255.
% Builds an image of I's edges and stores it as a jpeg file
%     whose address is specified by the string jpegOut.

% Convert the jpegIn into a grayscale matrix...
A = rgb2gray(imread(jpegIn));
% Visit each pixel and see if the rate of change is above the
% threshold...
[m,n] = size(A);
Rho = uint8(zeros(m,n));
for i=1:m
   for j = 1:n
      % The 3-by-3 matrix of neighbors...
      Neighbors = A(max(1,i-1):min(i+1,m),...
                    max(1,j-1):min(j+1,n));
      % Color white those pixels above the threshold...
      if max( max( abs(double(Neighbors)-double(A(i,j))))) > tau
         Rho(i,j) = 255;
      end
   end
end
imwrite(Rho,jpegOut,'jpg')
```

What makes image processing so interesting as a research area is that problems like these are so trivial for the human visual system.

Talking Point: Jpeg, Gif, and All That

The familiar adage that "a picture is worth a thousand words" is actually a gross under-estimate in terms of the storage that is required to represent an image. The clock tower photo that we use throughout this section is 3390-by-4200, over 14 million pixels. Thus, the explicit storage of the rgb values would require over 42 megabytes. How can it be that the jpeg file that houses this picture requires only about 9 megabytes of storage? The answer has to do with an important technique known as *image compression*.

There is a lot of redundancy in the clock tower picture; entire regions such as the sky have the property that the pixel values hardly change. Moreover, there are correlations between the red, green, and blue values at each pixel location. An image compression scheme is able to exploit these redundancies.

Different types of images call for different types of compression. For ordinary pictures where pixel values typically vary slowly, jpeg is ideal. This explains its widespread use in digital photography. For line drawings and related graphical designs, the gif format is preferable. Sometimes it is critical for the decompressed image to be exactly the same as the original. The tiff format has that property. Many different compression schemes are available. Each addresses some corner of the market and each addresses the fact that a picture is worth millions of bytes.

The Script Eg12_4

```
% Script Eg12_4
% Illustrates median filtering and edge detection.
close all
% Acquire and show the original color image...
A = imread([pwd '\InsightData\12_4\Cornell_Clock.jpg'],'jpg');
imshow(A)

% Turn into black-and-white, display, and save...
B = rgb2gray(A);
figure; imshow(B)
imwrite(B,[pwd '\MyData\Cornell_Clock_Gray.jpg'],'jpg')

% Extract a portion of the black-and-white image, add some noise,
% and observe the effect of median filtering...
figure
C = B(850:1150,2350:2650);
for k=1:200
    i = floor(1+rand(1)*300); j = floor(1+rand(1)*300);
    C(i:i+1,j:j+1) = floor(10*rand(1)(2,2));
end
imshow(C)

figure
D = MedianFilter(C);
imshow(D)

% Find and display the edges in the black-and-white image...
figure
jpegIn  = [pwd '\InsightData\12_4\Cornell_Clock.jpg'];
jpegOut = [pwd '\MyData\Cornell_Clock_Edges.jpg'];
for tau = 30:10:50
    Edges(jpegIn,jpegOut,tau);
    imshow(imread(jpegOut))
    title(sprintf('Tau = %2d',tau),'Fontsize',14)
    pause
end
```

MATLAB Review

The uint8 Data Type

This way of representing numbers is perfect in situations where a pixel value is an integer between (and including) 0 and 255. The matrix uint8(zeros(m,n)) requires mn bytes of storage, whereas zeros(m,n) requires eight times that amount.

Care has to be exercised when computing with uint8 variables. If x has type uinit8, then x = 1000 assigns 255, the largest possible uint8 value, to x.

Three-Dimensional Arrays

Three-dimensional arrays have rows, columns, and "layers." Three subscripts are required to name its entries. Thus, A(2,6,3) refers to the (2,6) entry of the third layer. The command A = zeros(m,n,p) establishes A as an m-by-n-by-p array. The statement M = A(:,:,k) assigns the kth layer (a matrix) to M.

Turning Matrices into Column Vectors

If A is a matrix with m rows and n columns, then v = A(:) assigns to v a length-mn column vector obtained by stacking its columns, i.e.,

```
v = [];
for k=1:n
   v = [v; A(:,k)];
end
```

imread

The function imread is used to get the pixel values of an image into the MATLAB workspace.

    A = imread(Full Path to File ,   File Format)

Typical formats include jpeg, gif, and png. The array A has type uint8 and is a matrix of grayscale values if the image is black and white and is a three-dimensional array if the image is color. In the latter case, A(:,:,1), A(:,:,2), and A(:,:,3) house the red, green, and blue pixel values.

imshow

The function imshow is used to display an image in the current figure window.

    imshow(Array housing the pixel values)

imwrite

This function takes an array of pixel values and creates an image file.

    imwrite(Array of Pixel Values ,   Full Path to File ,   Format)

rgb2gray

If A is an m-by-n-by-3 array housing the pixel values that represent a color image I, then A_gray = rgb2gray(A) assigns to A_gray a matrix of grayscale values that correspond to a black-and-white version of I.

Exercises

M12.4.1 Write a function ShowNeg(P) that converts into black and white the picture encoded in the jpeg file P and displays its negative, e.g.,

M12.4.2 Write a function `DisplayMosaic(P,q,r)` that displays a q-by-r mosaic of the color picture encoded in the jpeg file P, e.g.,

P12.4.3 Write a function `Rotate90(P)` that displays, with a clockwise 90-degree rotation, the color picture encoded in the jpeg file P, e.g.,

P12.4.4 Without using the built-in function `median`, complete the following function so that it performs as specified:

```
function mu = ArrayMedian(A)
% A is an m-by-n matrix.
% mu is the median of its mn values.
```

P12.4.5 Assume that P is a string that specifies the address of a jpeg file. Write a function `HistoPixel(P)` that displays a histogram of pixel values for the black-and-white version of the image that P encodes. The histogram should indicate the number of pixels that are in the ranges $0–15, 16–31, \ldots, 240–255$.

P12.4.6 Write a function `Crop(P,Q)` that reads in a jpeg file P and stores a cropped version of the image in Q. For example, the lower left and upper right corners of the cropped image can be obtained using `ginput`.

P12.4.7 Write a function `Border(P,Q)` that reads in a jpeg file P and stores a bordered version of the image in Q. The border should be black and have a suitable width.

P12.4.8 Write a function Oval(P,Q) that reads in a jpeg file P and stores an oval version of the image in Q. In particular, determine the largest ellipse that fits inside the input image and then blacken all the pixels outside the ellipse.

P12.4.9 Write a function ShowSlideShow(C,deltaT) that inputs a cell array of strings whose cells name jpeg files and produces a slide show that displays each image deltaT seconds. The slide show should keep repeating.

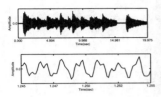

Chapter 13

Acoustic File Processing

13.1 The Clock Strikes
Acquisition and Playback

13.2 Dial N for Noise
Frequency and Sampling

When an image is discretized, a two-dimensional array of numbers is obtained. When sound is discretized, a one-dimensional array of numbers is obtained. Sound is a wave form and if it is rapidly sampled over a relatively long period of time, then a very long vector results. These vectors can be modified, searched, and combined.

There are several different formats for representing acoustic data just as there are several formats for visual data. This is well known to all music downloaders. We shall work with the popular `.wav` format. The acquisition of a `.wav` file and its conversion into a real vector is typically how a sound-related computation begins.

The first example in the chapter entails working with a recording of a clock tower that signals the time of day through a short chime sequence followed by a series of "gongs." We take apart the given sound file and use its parts to build a specific "sound track" that signals any particular hourly strike.

The second example uses the touch-tone dialing system to introduce some of the ideas that support the field of acoustic signal processing. The concepts of frequency, noise, and phase shifts are presented. The special role of the sine function in signal processing is highlighted as we develop an elementary system that can (almost always) identify a touch-tone signal that is contaminated with noise.

Both examples point to deep and complicated problems associated with the processing of sound, notably, the problem of segmentation. As human data processors, it is not too hard for us to look at the clock tower wave form and spot where one gong ends and the next begins. However, the automation of that process is far from trivial, especially when the signal is corrupted by noise. It is a problem area where artificial intelligence ideas from computer science are combined with powerful sine-cosine ideas from the field of real-time signal processing. Life as we know it would be very different without this combination of technologies. Being able to process data as fast as it arrives is the province of real-time signal processing, a field that is dominated by some of the most powerful algorithms of our time.

Programming Preview

Concepts

Frequency, sampling rate, representation, compression, segmentation, synthesis, signals, and noise.

Language Features

`wavread`: Reads a `.wav` file and returns the sound signal vector, sampling rate, and bit length of each sample.

`sound`: Plays the sound corresponding to the sound signal vector at a specified sampling rate.

`wavwrite`: Creates a `.wav` file from the sound signal vector given the sampling rate and bit length of each sample.

Inner Product: For column vectors `x` and `y` of the same length, the inner product `x'y` is equivalent to `sum(x.*y)`.

13.1 The Clock Strikes

Problem Statement

Here is Big Ben:

And here is Big Ben telling us that it is 1 o'clock:

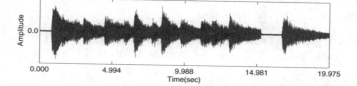

In reality, sound is a continuous wave form. Notice the quiet period between the end of the chimes ($T \approx 15.3$) and the beginning of the single, 1 o'clock "gong" ($T \approx 17$). If we look at Big Ben's message up close, then sinusoidal patterns emerge:

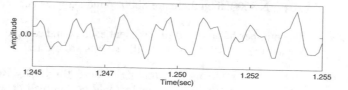

Just as (a continuous) image can be digitized through regular sampling (the pixels) and numerical representation (the rgb values), so can we digitize a sound wave:

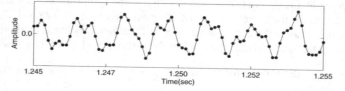

Obviously, the sampling must be fast enough to capture the underlying sinusoid. For the Big Ben sound byte, if we sample 8000 times per second we could represent a digitized version in a vector `BigBenVec` having length $19.95 \times 8000 \approx 160,000$. Here is a portion of this long vector

```
BigBenVec(20004:20008) =
    -0.0547
    -0.0156
     0.0547
     0.0391
    -0.0391
```

Once a "sound" vector is in the MATLAB workspace it can be manipulated, "played," or stored in a file for later use.

   Assume the availability of a sound file `BigBen1` that encodes the 1 o'clock "message." Write a script that acquires the data in `BigBen1` and proceeds to create sound files `BigBen2,BigBen3,...,BigBen12`, each of which encodes the appropriate recording for 2 o'clock, 3 o'clock, etc.

Program Development

The first order of business is to acquire the digitized Big Ben sound track. There are many different sound file formats just as there are many image file formats. We shall work with the `.wav` format. Assume that the file `BigBen.wav` is in the subdirectory `\InsightData\13_1`. The command

```
fname = [pwd '\InsightData\13_1\BigBen.wav'];
[OneOclock,rate,nBits] = wavread(fname);
```

opens this file and sets up three variables:

OneOclock   A column vector that houses the values of the sampled sound track.

rate   The rate at which the sound track was sampled. If the value of
            rate is 8000, then there are 8000 sound samples per second.

nBits   The number of bits used to represent each sound sample. If the
            value of nBits is 8 (typical), then 8 bits are used.

The term "hertz" is used when referring to sampling. The 8000 Hz Big Ben sound bite is actually pretty crude. The rate at which a signal should be sampled depends upon the application, e.g., speech over the telephone (8000 Hz), MP3 files (44,100 Hz), high definition audio tracks (192,400 Hz).

   In a `.wav` file, the numbers associated with a sound sampling are stored as integers using 8 bits. This permits the representation of 256 possible values: $-128, -127, \ldots, 126, 127$. When `wavread` extracts the data from a `.wav` file, it converts these integers into floating point and adjusts the scale so that they fall in the interval $[-1, 1]$.[14] Because we will only

---

[14] Thus, if `OneOclock(20000)` has the value of -0.0547, then in `BigBen1.wav` it is stored as the integer $-7 = -.0547 * 128$.

be dealing with .wav files, we can remain blissfully unaware of these details. The nBits output parameter can be ignored when using wavread.

To clarify all of these notions, here is a script that reads BigBen1.wav and displays the associated wave form as a function of time:

```
fname = [pwd '\InsightData\BigBen.wav'];
[OneOclock,rate] = wavread(fname);
% Number of sampled values...
n = length(OneOclock);
% Duration of the sound track (in seconds)...
T = (n-1)/rate;
% Sampling times...
tVals = linspace(0,T,n);
% Display...
plot(tVals,OneOclock)
```

Of course, we would also like to play the sound track and for that we invoke the function sound:

```
sound(OneOclock,rate)
```

This function has two input parameters. The first is the vector that represents the digitized sound and the second is the playback rate. Almost always the playback rate is the same as the rate that is obtained via wavread. However, it is perfectly legal to use a modified rate during playback. Thus, sound(OneOclock,2*rate) would play the 1 o'clock sound bite at twice the recording rate. It would also sound higher.

Let us turn our attention to the problem of creating and storing Big Ben sound tracks for clock strikes 2 through 12. The first task is to extract the "chimes portion" and "gong portion" from OneOclock and assign them to vectors chimes and gong, respectively. Assuming that we have successfully done this, we can create and play the 2 o'clock sound track as follows:

```
TwoOclock = [chimes; gong; gong];
sound(TwoOclock,rate)
```

Having done this,

```
ThreeOclock = [TwoOclock; gong];
sound(ThreeOclock,rate)
```

creates and plays the 3 o'clock sound track, etc.

We can save these sound tracks in files using the function wavwrite. This built-in function requires the vector of sound samples, the sample rate, the number of bits for the representation (always 8), and the name of the target file. Thus,

```
fname = [pwd '\MyData\BigBen2.wav'];
wavwrite(TwoOclock,8000,8,fname)
```

creates a file called BigBen2 that encodes the 2 o'clock sound track.

The script Eg13_1 solves the problem posed at the beginning of this section. It uses ginput to determine just where in the sound wave the gong begins.

The Script `Eg13_1`

```
% Script Eg13_1
% Creates sound files for each of the twelve clock strikes
% using the data in BigBen.wav.

close all
% Read in the 1 o'clock sound file...
fname = [pwd '\InsightData\13_1\BigBen.wav'];
[OneOclock,rate] = wavread(fname);
n = length(OneOclock);

% Display the wave form and click in between the chimes
% portion and the gong portion...
plot(OneOclock)
title('Click at the beginning of the gong.')
[m,y] = ginput(1);
m = round(m);
Chimes = OneOclock(1:m);
Gong = OneOclock(m+1:n);

% For each hourly strike, create a .wav file.
% Name them BigBen1, BigBen2,...,BigBen12.
F = Chimes;
for k=1:12
    F = [F; Gong];
    fname = [pwd '\MyData\BigBen' num2str(k) '.wav'];
    wavwrite(F,rate,8,fname)
end

% Play back a chosen subset of the sound tracks...
PlayList = [2 3];
for k = PlayList
    fname = [pwd '\MyData\BigBen' num2str(k) '.wav'];
    [Oclock,rate] = wavread(fname);
    sound(Oclock)
end
```

Note how string concatenation is used to build up the file name together with its complete directory location.

Talking Point: The Problem of Segmentation

By clicking on the Big Ben sound wave to separate the chimes part from the gong part, we solved a *segmentation problem*. Segmentation problems abound in signal processing and they tend to be very hard. For example, a speech recognition system might begin by partitioning the input signal into parts that correspond to words. When does one word end and the next begin?

Even the Big Ben wave form poses challenging segmentation problems. The chimes part consists of 16 bell strikes arranged in four groups. Although we definitely can spot some of the strikes, the time scale is too compressed for us to see 16 well-formed "gongs." It is easy enough to "magnify" the time scale by displaying subvectors of `OneOclock`. We can then proceed to isolate the individual bell strikes. However, the real challenge is how to automate the process. An interesting subproblem immediately surfaces: How might we identify a period of quiet in a sound track? It is tempting to say that if `max(abs(OneOclock(L:R)))` `<= tol` is true for some small tolerance `tol`, then the sound track is quiet from sample point L to sample point R. The trouble with this test is that it will fail should there be a burst of noise, even if it lasts for just a millisecond. Thus, some kind of filtering is required before we can reach any kind of conclusion about a sound bite segment.

MATLAB Review

wavread

This is used to acquire data in a `.wav` file:

[Sound Vector , Sampling Rate , Precision] = wavread(File Name)

Thus, `[SoundVec,rate,nBits] = wavread('MySoundFile.wav')` assigns the sampled sound values to the column vector `SoundVec`, the sampling rate (in Hertz) to `rate`, and the length of the bit encoding used to store the sample values (usually 8) to `nBits`. A call of the form `[SoundVec,rate] = wavread('MySoundFile.wav')` is an allowable shortcut.

sound

This is used to play the sound encoded in a sound vector.

sound(sound vector , Sampling Rate)

Thus, if `MySoundVec` is a vector with values in between -1 and $+1$ and `MyRate` houses a sampling rate value, then `sound(MySoundVec,MyRate)` plays the encoded sound at the specified rate.

wavwrite

This is used to construct a `.wav` file.

wavwrite(Sound Vector , Sample Rate , Precision , File Name)

Thus, `Wavwrite(MySoundVec,8000,8,'MySoundFile.wav')` sets up a `.wav` file called `MySoundFile` that encodes the acoustic data in `MySoundVec`.

Exercises

M13.1.1 Vary the playback rate in `Eg13_1` and observe the effect.

M13.1.2 Modify `Eg13_1` so that the chimes are played in reverse.

P13.1.3 Segment the data in `Chimes` so that the sixteen notes are split into four groups A, B, C, and D, each having four notes. Write a script that inputs a time of the form `'hh:mm'` where hh designates the hour and mm is either `'00'`, `'15'`, `'30'`, or `'45'`. The script should then sound out as follows:

Time	Play
Quarter Past the Hour	A
Half Past the Hour	A and B
Three-Quarters Past the Hour	A and B and C
On the Hour	A and B and C and D and Gongs

13.2   Dial N for Noise

Problem Statement

How rapidly the function $y(t) = \sin(2\pi\omega t)$ varies with time depends upon the frequency ω:

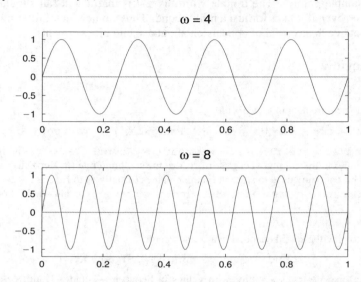

Elementary sinusoids such as these can be scaled and combined to produce more complicated signals:

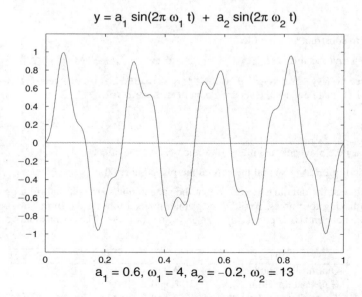

This principle is at work when you use a touch-tone telephone. Each button-push generates a signal that is the sum of two elementary sinusoids. See Figure 13.1. Corresponding to rows 1

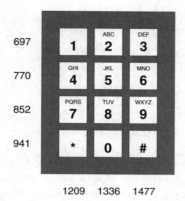

697

770

852

941

1209 1336 1477

Figure 13.1. *Buttons and Frequencies.*

through 4 of the touch-tone pad are frequencies 697, 770, 852, and 941, while frequencies 1209, 1336, and 1477 are associated with columns 1 through 3. When a button is depressed, a signal is formed by averaging the two sinusoids whose frequencies are identified by the button's row/column location. Thus, when "6" is pushed the signal

$$y = \frac{1}{2}\sin(2\pi\omega_{row}t) + \frac{1}{2}\sin(2\pi\omega_{col}t) \tag{13.1}$$

is generated, where $\omega_{row} = 770$ and $\omega_{col} = 1477$. With this scheme each button has its own "fingerprint." See Figure 13.2. Although the waveforms for different buttons are visually similar, they are actually very different mathematically and this enables the receiver to

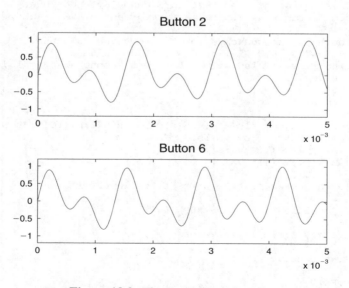

Figure 13.2. *The Touch-Tone Signals.*

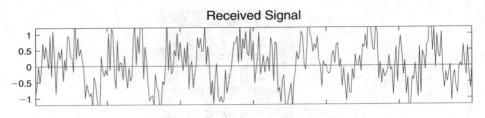

Figure 13.3. *Signal Plus Noise.*

decipher accurately the incoming signal, even in the presence of noise. Figure 13.3 displays either touch-tone 2 plus noise or touch-tone 6 plus noise. Which is it?

Program Development

We start by building an appreciation for the fact that a touch-tone signal is a digitized signal. A good way to do this is to experiment with the function MakeShowPlay that plays and displays a one-quarter second "sound bite" for a particular button-push.

The Function MakeShowPlay

```
function [tVals,y] = MakeShowPlay(i,j)
% i (1<=i<=4) and j (1<=j<=3) are integers that identify
% the row i and column j button in the touch-tone pad.
% Displays the associated wave form and plays the tone.
% The sample times and signal are returned in tVals and y.

% The touch-pad frequencies for the rows and columns...
fR = [ 697   770   852   941]; fC = [ 1209   1336   1477];
% Sampling rate. (This many numbers per second are sampled from
%    the signal.)
Fs = 32768;
% Duration of the tone is .25 sec.
tVals = (0:(1/Fs):.25)';
% Sample the signal sin(2*pi*fR(i)*t) + sin(2*pi*fC(j)*t)
% at times specified by tVals...
yR  = sin(2*pi*fR(i)*tVals);
yC  = sin(2*pi*fC(j)*tVals);
y   = (yR + yC)/2;
% Display a representative part of the wave form...
figure
set(gcf,'position',[100 550 800 160])
m = 300;
plot((1:m)',y(1:m),(1:m)',zeros(m,1),'-r')
            :
% Play the tone...
pause(1)
sound(y,Fs)
```

A key point brought out by this function is that a digitized signal is a vector and that to play the vector we need to specify a rate. The sampling rate is $2^{15} = 32768$ meaning that the signal is to be sampled that many times per second. We want to play the tone for one-quarter second, so the sample times are set up by the fragment

```
fs = 32768;
tVals = (0:(1/Fs):.25)';
```

The fragment

```
yR  = sin(2*pi*fR(i)*tVals);
yC  = sin(2*pi*fC(j)*tVals);
y   = (yR + yC)/2;
```

averages the "row signal" and the "column signal." Note that combining digitized signals amounts to combining vectors. Vectors that represent signals are typically very long, so to visualize the wave form it is best to display just a relatively short subvector. In MakeShowPlay we display y(1:300). Finally, to play the signal we use the function sound which requires the vector housing the digitized signal and the rate at which it is to be played.

We now turn our attention to the receiver of the touch-tone signal and the issue of noise. Noise can be simulated by using the randn function. In the function SendNoisy we add to each digitized signal value a random number selected from a scaled normal distribution.

The Function SendNoisy

```
function yNoisy = SendNoisy(tVals,y)
% Adds noise to the signal y.
% Displays and plays the resulting signal yNoisy.

n = length(y);
% Add noise...
A = .5;
yNoisy = y + A*randn(n,1);
% Display a representative part of the sinusoid...
    :
m = 300;
plot((1:m)',yNoisy(1:m),(1:m)',zeros(m,1),'-r')
    :
% Play the noisy tone...
Fs = 32768;
pause(1)
sound(yNoisy,Fs)
```

Now imagine receiving a vector that encodes the sound for a particular touch tone. The challenge is to decipher the digitized signal and identify the button that was pushed. To that end, let us assemble in two matrices trueR and trueC the "perfect signals," associated with the row frequencies and the column frequencies:

```
Fs = 32768;
tVals = 0:(1/Fs):.25;
tau = 2*pi*tVals';
fR = [697 770 852 941];
trueR = [sin(tau*fR(1)) sin(tau*fR(2)) sin(tau*fR(3)) sin(tau*fR(4))];
fC = [1209 1336 1477];
trueC = [sin(tau*fC(1)) sin(tau*fC(2)) sin(tau*fC(3))];
```

A key feature of the perfect signal vectors is that they are very different from one another. Equivalently, there is very little correlation between the perfect signal vectors. One way to measure the correlation between two column n-vectors x and y is to compute the cosine of the angle between them from the formula

$$\cos_{xy} = \frac{\left| \sum_{i=1}^{n} x_i y_i \right|}{\sqrt{\sum_{i=1}^{n} x_i^2} \sqrt{\sum_{i=1}^{n} y_i^2}}.$$

There is an easy way to compute this quantity in MATLAB.

The Function cos_xy

```
function c = cos_xy(x,y)
% x and y are column n-vectors
% c is the cosine of the angle between them

c = abs(sum(x.*y))/(sqrt(sum(x.*x))*sqrt(sum(y.*y)));
```

To appreciate the fact that this mysterious quotient is indeed a cosine, suppose

$$x = \begin{bmatrix} \cos(\theta_1) \\ \sin(\theta_1) \end{bmatrix} \quad \text{and} \quad y = \begin{bmatrix} \cos(\theta_2) \\ \sin(\theta_2) \end{bmatrix}$$

where θ_1 and θ_2 are given. It is easy to show that

$$\cos_{xy} = |\cos(\theta_1)\cos(\theta_2) + \sin(\theta_1)\sin(\theta_2)| = |\cos(\theta_1 - \theta_2)|.$$

Thus, if $\theta_1 = 45°$ and $\theta_2 = 60°$, then x and y make an angle of $15°$.

To further enhance our intuition, if $\cos_{xy}$ is close to 1, then x and y identify very similar directions and are highly correlated:

$$x = \begin{bmatrix} 3.1 \\ 4.9 \end{bmatrix}$$
$$\Rightarrow \quad \cos_{xy} = 0.9988.$$
$$y = \begin{bmatrix} 2.9 \\ 5.1 \end{bmatrix}$$

On the other hand, if $\cos_{xy}$ is close to 0, then x and y identify very different directions and are hardly correlated:

$$x = \begin{bmatrix} 3.1 \\ 4.9 \end{bmatrix}$$

$$y = \begin{bmatrix} 5.1 \\ -2.9 \end{bmatrix}$$

$$\Rightarrow \qquad \cos_{xy} = 0.0470.$$

Let us examine the correlations among the perfect signal vectors. Assuming that the matrices `trueR` and `trueC` are initialized as above, then the script

```
A = [trueR trueC];
CosVals = zeros(7,7);
for i=1:7
    for j=1:7
        CosVals(i,j) = cos_xy(A(:,i),A(:,j));
    end
end
```

yields

```
CosVals =

  1.0000    0.0092    0.0045    0.0001    0.0001    0.0013    0.0001
  0.0092    1.0000    0.0000    0.0034    0.0011    0.0000    0.0006
  0.0045    0.0000    1.0000    0.0068    0.0015    0.0000    0.0007
  0.0001    0.0034    0.0068    1.0000    0.0001    0.0019    0.0001
  0.0001    0.0011    0.0015    0.0001    1.0000    0.0053    0.0001
  0.0013    0.0000    0.0000    0.0019    0.0053    1.0000    0.0043
  0.0001    0.0006    0.0007    0.0001    0.0001    0.0043    1.0000
```

Each off-diagonal entry reflects the correlation between two different perfect signals. The results confirm that these seven signals are "very different" from one another.

We propose to decipher the noisy touch-tone signal based upon its correlation with the seven perfect signals. Our intuition suggests that if the button pushed is in row i and column j of the touch-tone pad, then

1. among the four perfect signals housed in `trueR`, the input signal should have its strongest correlation with `trueR(:,i)`;

2. among the three perfect signals housed in `trueC`, the input signal should have its strongest correlation with `trueC(:,j)`.

The function `ShowCosines` explores these conjectures using bar plots. The script `Eg13_2` applies `ShowCosines` to ten different random "button-pushes." The plots reveal that our cosine method does a good job of predicting the right perfect signals. See Figure 13.4. The mystery signal in Figure 13.3 was in fact button 6 plus noise!

The Function ShowCosines

```
function ShowCosines(y)
% Shows the cosine that signal y makes with each of the
% four perfect row signals and each of the three perfect
% column signals.

% Set up the perfect signal matrices...
Fs = 32768;
tVals = 0:(1/Fs):.25;
tau = 2*pi*tVals';
fR = [697 770 852 941];
trueR = [sin(tau*fR(1)) sin(tau*fR(2)) ...
         sin(tau*fR(3)) sin(tau*fR(4))];
fC = [1209 1336 1477];
trueC = [sin(tau*fC(1)) sin(tau*fC(2)) sin(tau*fC(3))];
% Compute the row and column cosines...
for i=1:4
    rowCosine(i) = cos_xy(y,trueR(:,i));
end
for j=1:3
    colCosine(j) = cos_xy(y,trueC(:,j));
end
% Display...
   :
subplot(1,2,1)
bar(rowCosine)
subplot(1,2,2)
bar(colCosine)
   :
```

The Script Eg13_2

```
% Script Eg13_2
% Examines the touch-tone system in the presence of noise.
for Trial = 1:10
    close all
    % Choose a button at random...
    i = ceil(rand(1)*4);
    j = ceil(rand(1)*3);
    % Generate the tone...
    [tVals,y] = MakeShowPlay(i,j);
    % "Send" a noisy version...
    y = SendNoisy(tVals,y);
    % "Receive" and decipher...
    ShowCosines(y)
    pause(2)
end
```

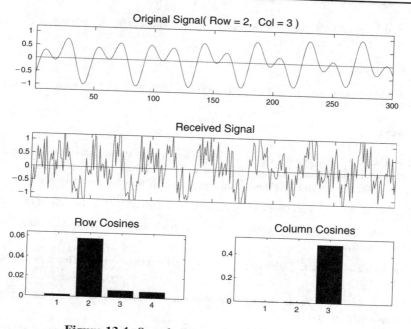

Figure 13.4. *Sample Output from Script* `Eg13_2`.

Talking Point: Signals and Noise

A great deal of acoustic signal processing builds on the remarkable properties of the sine and cosine functions. The correlation properties alluded to in this section are central but it goes well beyond that. The regular structure of matrices like `trueR` and `trueC` makes it possible to formulate a collection of superfast signal processing algorithms. The most famous of these is called the *fast Fourier transform*. It is not an exaggeration to say that this algorithm has revolutionized science and engineering.

Our simple-minded technique for fingerprinting a noisy touch-tone signal addresses just one of several challenges. Obviously, a phone number is a sequence of touch-tone signals. The overall signal has to be segmented into parts, each of which encodes one of the digits that make up the number. As we mentioned in §13.1, segmentation is a hard problem.

MATLAB Review

Inner Products and Norms

If x and y are column vectors of the same dimension, then `s = x'*y` is equivalent to `s = sum(x.*y)`, i.e.,

```
s = 0;
for i=1:length(x)
    s = s + x(i)*y(i);
end
```

We refer to this operation as the *inner product* between x and y. The `norm` function can be used to evaluate s = sqrt (sum(x.*x)):

```
    s = norm(x)
```

Notice that the implementation of `cos_xy` involves an inner product and two `norm` calculations.

Exercises

M13.2.1 The row and column frequencies in the touch-tone system are chosen to facilitate the deciphering process. Change the row frequencies to 200, 400, 600, and 800 and the column frequencies to 900, 1100, and 1300 and rerun `Eg13_2`. Explain what you discover.

M13.2.2 Rerun `Eg13_2` with tones that last one half of a second. Does this affect the output?

M13.2.3 Write a script that plays each of the twelve touch tones and at the same time displays the associated wave form.

M13.2.4 Increase the noise factor in `SendNoisy` and examine how it affects the quality of the deciphering.

P13.2.5 Write a script that generates 1000 random button-pushes and reports the number of failures of our deciphering method.

P13.2.6 Write a function `PlayNumber(s)` that "dials" the telephone number encoded by the string s, e.g., `'16072551234'`. Write a function `AutoDialer(C)` that dials every number encoded in a cell array C of such strings.

P13.2.7 Complete the following function so that it performs as specified:

```
function F = OmegaTable()
% F is a 12-by-6 matrix whose (i,j) entry is given by
%     55*omega^(i-1)*2^(j-1) where omega = 2^(1/12)
```

Treating each F(i,j) as a frequency, write a single script that plays the sound associated with each matrix entry.

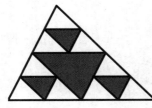

Chapter 14

Divide and Conquer

Divide-and-conquer is a well-known strategy in both politics and war. It is equally prominent in computing. Indeed, many of the most important algorithms in use today have this attribute. The idea is to (a) partition the given problem into two or more independent subproblems of the same variety and then (b) obtain the overall solution by synthesizing the subproblem solutions. For example, suppose your boss asks you to alphabetize a deck of 128 cards, each having the name of a customer. You split the deck in half and ask coworker A to alphabetize cards 1–64 and coworker B to alphabetize cards 65–128. After you receive the two alphabetized half-decks, it is an easy matter to merge the two piles into the single, required alphabetized deck. The interesting thing about this approach is that coworkers A and B can apply the same problem-solving strategy. For example, A can delegate to coworkers A_1 and A_2 the task of alphabetizing cards 1–32 and 33–64, respectively. B can do the same with quarter-decks 65–96 and 97–128. The quarter-deck problems could also be subdivided, etc.

The example illustrates the process of recursion, and in this chapter we learn how to program divide-and-conquer strategies using this technique. We start with a recursive tiling problem in which triangles are repeatedly subdivided into smaller triangles. By using graphics we are able to track visually the "dividing" and the "conquering." Next, we develop a sorting procedure along the lines of the motivating example above. The method is called *merge sort* and it turns out to be dramatically more efficient than the methods of §8.2. Our final example involves the production of plots where the underlying function f is sampled nonuniformly across a given interval. The idea is to cluster f-evaluations in regions where f is highly nonlinear. The "discovery" of the nonlinearity zones is done through an interval subdivision process that is determined by estimating the quality of a linear approximation.

Programming Preview

Concepts

Recursion, recursion versus iteration, infinite recursion, base case, induction, merge sort, efficiency, adaptive interpolation, heuristics.

Language Feature

Recursive Function: A function can call itself in the function body. Care must be taken to avoid infinite recursion.

14.1 Patterns within Patterns

Problem Statement

Suppose we are given a triangle T as in Figure 14.1 and are instructed to carry out a subdivision process that we will refer to as "Operation S":

Operation S

Connect the midpoints of T's three sides thereby forming
   three "corner" triangles and one inner triangle.
Shade the inner triangle.

The resulting "level-1" partitioning is displayed in Figure 14.2. If we apply Operation S to each of the three unshaded, corner triangles, then we obtain a level-2 partitioning. See Figure 14.3. In general, we can obtain the level-$(k + 1)$ partitioning by applying Operation S to each of the unshaded triangles in the level-k partitioning. See Figure 14.4.

Write a function MeshTriangle(x,y,L) that displays a level-L subdivision of the triangle whose vertices (x_1, y_1), (x_2, y_2), and (x_3, y_3) are prescribed by the column 3-vectors x and y.

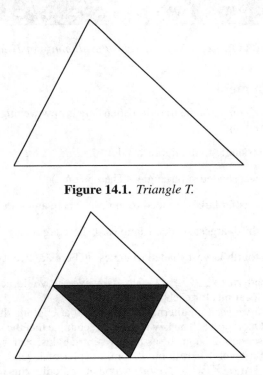

Figure 14.1. *Triangle T.*

Figure 14.2. *A Level-1 Partitioning of Triangle T.*

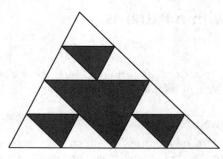

Figure 14.3. *A Level-2 Partitioning of Triangle T.*

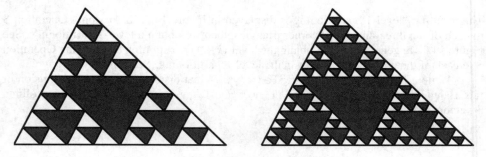

Figure 14.4. *Level-3 and Level-4 Partitionings of Triangle T.*

Program Development

If we think in terms of conventional iteration, then here is how we might proceed to produce (say) a level-4 partitioning:

- Add the given triangle to the figure window, i.e., fill(x,y,'w').

- Add in the largest shaded subtriangle. (There is one.)

- Add in all the second largest shaded triangles. (There are three.)

- Add in all the third largest shaded triangles. (There are nine.)

- Add in all the fourth largest shaded triangles. (There are twenty-seven.)

There is a definite pattern: 3^0, 3^1, 3^2, 3^3, etc. However, it would be extremely painful to work out the vertex locations for each triangle.

For that reason we seek an alternative strategy that exploits the notion of level and makes direct use of Operation S. The key idea is to recognize that the subdivision of a given triangle requires lesser subdivisions of its corner subtriangles. Refer to Figure 14.5 which shows how to build a level-4 partitioning from a triplet of level-3 partitionings. Let us implement MeshTriangle(x,y,L) in a way that embodies this hierarchical synthesis.

Note that if the value of L is zero, then there is nothing to do except to draw the triangle, i.e., fill(x,y,'w'). Otherwise, we need to initiate the subdivision process

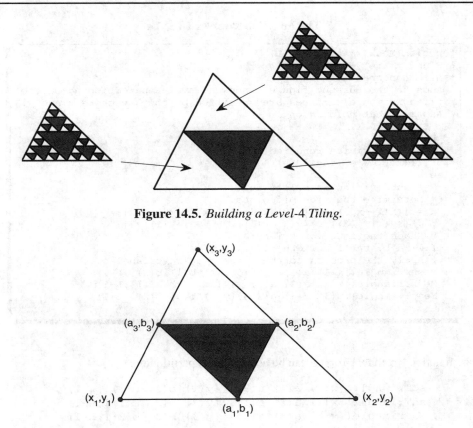

Figure 14.5. *Building a Level-4 Tiling.*

Figure 14.6. *Midpoints and Vertices.*

by computing the xy-coordinates of the side midpoints and shading the inner triangle as depicted in Figure 14.6. This is a routine `fill` computation.

```
a = [(x(1)+x(2))/2 (x(2)+x(3))/2 (x(3)+x(1))/2];
b = [(y(1)+y(2))/2 (y(2)+y(3))/2 (y(3)+y(1))/2];
fill(a,b,[.3 .3 .3])      % Shade the inner triangle gray
```

The remaining challenge is to partition the corner triangles. In particular, we must

1. obtain a level-$(L-1)$ partitioning of the triangle with vertices (x_1, y_1), (a_1, b_1), and (a_3, b_3);

2. obtain a level-$(L-1)$ partitioning of the triangle with vertices (x_2, y_2), (a_2, b_2), and (a_1, b_1);

3. obtain a level-$(L-1)$ partitioning of the triangle with vertices (x_3, y_3), (a_3, b_3), and (a_2, b_2).

The Function `MeshTriangle`

```
function MeshTriangle(x,y,L)
% x and y are 3-vectors.
% L is a nonnegative integer.
% Adds to the current figure window a level-L partitioning of the
% triangle whose vertices are specified by the 3-vectors x and y.
% Assumes that hold is on.

if L==0
    % No subdivision required...
    fill(x,y,'w','linewidth',1.5)
else
    % A subdivision is called for...
    % Determine the side midpoints...
    a = [(x(1)+x(2))/2 (x(2)+x(3))/2 (x(3)+x(1))/2];
    b = [(y(1)+y(2))/2 (y(2)+y(3))/2 (y(3)+y(1))/2];
    % Shade the interior triangle...
    fill(a,b,'r','linewidth',1.5)
    % Apply the process to the three "outer" triangles...
    MeshTriangle([x(1) a(1) a(3)],[y(1) b(1) b(3)],L-1)
    MeshTriangle([x(2) a(2) a(1)],[y(2) b(2) b(1)],L-1)
    MeshTriangle([x(3) a(3) a(2)],[y(3) b(3) b(2)],L-1)
end
```

The function `MeshTriangle` can be used for each partitioning:

```
MeshTriangle([x(1) a(1) a(3)],[y(1) b(1) b(3)],L-1)
MeshTriangle([x(2) a(2) a(1)],[y(2) b(2) b(1)],L-1)
MeshTriangle([x(3) a(3) a(2)],[y(3) b(3) b(2)],L-1)
```

This is a dramatic turn of events. Using `MeshTriangle` to produce a level-L partitioning requires that it calls itself three times to acquire the level-$(L-1)$ partitionings of the corner triangles. Functions that call themselves in this way are said to be *recursive*.

The three calls to `MeshTriangle` are *recursive* function calls. Note that if the incoming value of L is zero, then there are no recursive function calls. In that case,

The Script `Eg14_1`

```
% Script Eg14_1
% Illustrates the function MeshTriangle

close all
x = [0  3  1];
y = [0  0  2];
for L = 0:4
    figure
    axis equal off
    hold on
    MeshTriangle(x,y,L)
end
```

`MeshTriangle` simply draws the input triangle. The script `Eg14_1` produces the partitionings displayed in Figures 14.1–14.4.

To understand the flow of control when a recursive function is called, it is helpful to use
a *tree*. See Figure 14.7. Each dot in the schematic corresponds to a call to `MeshTriangle`.
Note that there are $40 = 1 + 3 + 9 + 27$ dots. Associated with each big dot is a shaded triangle
while each unshaded triangle in the final level-4 partitioning is associated with a tiny dot.

Tree structures are very important in computer science. What we called "dots" are
technically referred to as *nodes*. Nodes have *children* and in our example, each big dot node
has three children. The top node is the *root node* while the 27 nodes across the bottom are
leaf nodes.

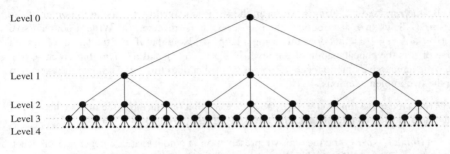

Figure 14.7. *A Tree Depiction of* `MeshTriangle`.

Talking Point: Recursive Mesh Generation

Mesh generation refers to the process of distributing a finite number of points throughout a
given geometric domain. The most simple example of this is `linspace`, which generates
an evenly distributed set of points across an interval. In this section we basically developed
a two-dimensional mesh generator for triangles.

Mesh generation is an important tool for bridging the gap between the discrete and the
continuous. The simulation of a process over a continuous region can be approximated by
tracking what happens at the intersection points in the mesh. See §7.3. Challenging aspects
of mesh generation include (a) dealing with complicated boundaries and (b) the automatic
packing of mesh points in regions that are critical to the simulation, e.g., the tip of an airfoil.

With these complexities it is no surprise that sophisticated, automatic mesh-generation
techniques have been developed. These software tools are built upon deep concepts from
computational geometry and an appreciation for how simulation errors correlate with the
distribution of the mesh points.

MATLAB Review

Reaching the Base Case

Just as it is possible for a loop not to terminate, so it is possible for a recursive function to keep
calling itself without end. To avoid "infinite recursion," carefully identify and implement the "base
case(s)." The base case is the condition under which no further call to the function itself is necessary.
Step through the logic that guarantees the ultimate reaching of the base case.

Exercises

M14.1.1 Insert a `pause(.2)` statement after each `fill` command in the recursive function `MeshTriangle`. Rerun `Eg14_1` and describe the order in which the subtriangles are displayed.

P14.1.2 Recall that if n is a positive integer, then $n! = 1 \cdot 2 \cdots n$, i.e,

$$n! = n \cdot (n-1)!.$$

Write a recursive function `m = FactorialR(n)` that returns the factorial of n. (Recall that by convention, $0! = 1$.)

P14.1.3 By the *reverse* of a string s we mean the string obtained by reversing the order of the characters in s. Thus, if s = 'abcde', then 'edcba' is its reverse. (a) Write a nonrecursive function `t = Reverse(s)` that does this using a loop. (b) Note that if n is the length of s, then the reverse of s is the concatenation of the reverse of `s(1:n-1)` and `s(1)` in that order. Using this idea, write a recursive function `t = ReverseR(s)` that does this. (c) Compare the execution times for the two implementations.

P14.1.4 Write a recursive function `y = MyPower(x,m)` that returns the value of x^m where x is a real number and m is a positive integer. Hint: If `p = floor(m/2)`, then $x^m = x^p x^{n-p}$.

P14.1.5 Let $(b_t b_{t-1} \cdots b_2 b_1)_2$ be the binary representation of a nonnegative integer n. Here, each b_i is a zero or one. Thus, $(1101)_2 = 13$. It is not hard to show $(b_t b_{t-1} \cdots b_2 b_1)_2 = 2(b_t b_{t-1} \cdots b_2)_2 + (b_1)_2$. For example, $(1101)_2 = 2(110)_2 + (1)_2$, i.e., $13 = 2 \cdot 6 + 1$. Using these observations, write a recursive implementation of the following function:

```
function  n = BinToInt(s)
% s is a string of 0's and 1's that represents  a number  in base-2 notation
% n is the value of the number.
```

P14.1.6 Any rectangle can be subdivided into a square and another rectangle, e.g.,

The process can be repeated on the subrectangle. Write a recursive function

```
    function PartitionRect(a,b,base,height,L)
```

that applies this subdivision L times on the rectangle whose lower left-hand corner is at (a,b) and whose base and height are prescribed by `base` and `height`. Randomly color the squares that are produced and color white the smallest "left over" rectangle.

P14.1.7 Write a recursive function `RandomMondrian(a,b,L,W,Lev)` that produces Mondrian-like designs of the form

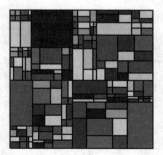

The overall shape is an L-by-W rectangle having lower left corner (a,b). The basic idea is to repeatedly subdivide a rectangle into four subrectangles, e.g.,

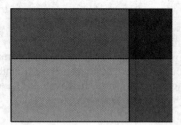

The subdivision point is to be randomly selected from the "inner rectangle" whose vertices are $(a+L/4, b+W/4)$, $(a+3L/4, b+W/4)$, $(a+L/4, b+3W/4)$, and $(a+3L/4, b+3W/4)$. The input parameter Lev prescribes the number of subdivisions to be performed.

If the value of Lev is zero, then the rectangle should be randomly colored and added to the figure window. It is up to you to specify the possible colors. (You can use an array whose rows specify rgb values and then randomly select a row any time you "need" a color.) So as to produce subrectangles of varying size, incorporate a feature that randomly terminates the recursion if Lev has the value of 1 or 2.

P14.1.8 Consider the problem of finding the largest equilateral triangle that fits inside a given triangle:

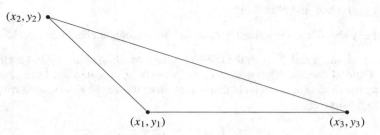

Assume that the side between (x_1, y_1) and (x_2, y_2) is the shortest side and that the side between (x_2, y_2) and (x_3, y_3) is the longest side. Define the quantities

$$\alpha = ((x_3 - x_1)(x_2 - x_1) + (y_3 - y_1)(y_2 - y_1)) / ((x_3 - x_1)^2 + (y_3 - y_1)^2)$$

$$\beta = |(y_1 - y_3)(x_2 - x_1) + (x_3 - x_1)(y_2 - y_1)| / ((x_3 - x_1)^2 + (y_3 - y_1)^2)$$

$$\mu = 1/(1 + \beta/\sqrt{3} - \alpha) \qquad \lambda = 2\mu(1 - \alpha) - 1$$

It can be shown that if

$$
\begin{aligned}
u_1 &= (1-\lambda)x_3 + \lambda x_1 & u_2 &= (1-\mu)x_3 + \mu x_2 \\
v_1 &= (1-\lambda)y_3 + \lambda y_1 & v_2 &= (1-\mu)y_3 + \mu y_2
\end{aligned}
$$

then the sought-after equilateral triangle has vertices (x_1, y_1), (u_1, v_1), and (u_2, v_2):

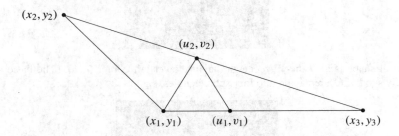

(a) Write a function $[A, B, C]$ = Split(T) that performs this partition. Here, the input and output parameters are structures of your own design that represent triangles. Assign to A the equilateral triangle. (b) Write a recursive graphics function DrawTriangleMesh(T) that partitions triangle T into equilateral triangles and very small "left over" triangles.

14.2   N and Half N

Problem Statement

Suppose you have a "deck" of 16 cards and on each card is written a name. Your job is to alphabetize the deck, and with the help of two friends A and B, you adopt the following "DWM" strategy:

(a) Delegate to A and B the task of alphabetizing a half-deck.

(b) Wait for both A and B to finish.

(c) Merge A and B's alphabetized half-decks into a single alphabetized deck.

Not to be outdone, A and B apply the DWM strategy, handing off a length-4 sorting problem to their A and B friends. The process can obviously be repeated until the given task is to sort a length-1 deck. Here is a table that summarizes the activity associated with each level of the subdivision:

Level	Problem Size	Number of Problems
0	16	1
1	8	2
2	4	4
3	2	8
4	1	16

The *binary tree* shown in Figure 14.8 displays the same information but in a way that helps us anticipate how we might program the DWM process. (Compare to Figure 14.7.) In our alphabetizing problem, the level-k subdivision involves halving an array of length $16/2^k$.

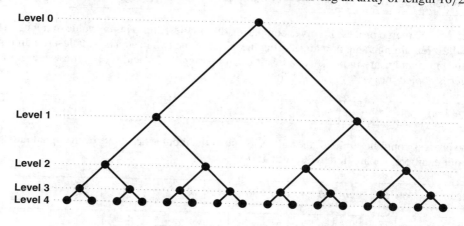

Level 0

Level 1

Level 2

Level 3
Level 4

Figure 14.8. *A Binary Tree.*

The same tree can be used to reason about the hierarchy of merges that take place. For $k = 3, 2, 1$, and 0, each level-k node receives alphabetized subdecks from its two level-$(k + 1)$ children. The assembly of the final alphabetized deck takes place at the single, level-0 root node.

This method of sorting is called *merge sort* and we have talked our way through the $N = 16$ case. If N is any power of 2, then the subdivisions are always equal in size and that size is a power of 2, e.g., $2^{10} = 1024 \rightarrow 512 \rightarrow 256 \rightarrow \cdots \rightarrow 2 \rightarrow 1$. If the incoming dimension N is not a power of 2, then the problem can be split into a length-m subproblem and a length-$(m + 1)$ subproblem where $m = \texttt{floor(N/2)}$.

The above "story" is about alphabetizing names. Obviously, the same framework can be used to order the values in a numerical vector. Write a function $z = \texttt{MergeSortR(x)}$ that sorts a column N-vector of real numbers using the algorithm of merge sort.

Program Development

We start by deriving a function $w = \texttt{Merge(u,v)}$ that takes a pair of sorted vectors u and v and merges them into a single, sorted vector w. Throughout this section we assume that "sorted" means sorted from small to large. We step through the situation with

$$u = \boxed{20 \quad 30 \quad 50 \quad 65}$$

and

$$v = \boxed{10 \quad 30 \quad 45 \quad 75 \quad 80}$$

Our goal is to *merge* these two arrays into a combined sorted array w made up of their values:

$$w = \boxed{10 \quad 20 \quad 30 \quad 30 \quad 45 \quad 50 \quad 65 \quad 75 \quad 80}$$

At the start of the merge we have the arrays u, v, and an uninitialized w:

| **20** | 30 | 50 | 65 | | **10** | 30 | 45 | 75 | 80 | | | | | | | | | | | |

A step in the merge process involves comparing the smallest "remaining" value in u with the smallest remaining value in v and storing the lesser of the two in w. The smallest remaining values in u and v are in bold. As a result of comparing u(1) and v(1), the value of the latter is copied into w(1):

| **20** | 30 | 50 | 65 | | **10** | 30 | 45 | 75 | 80 | | 10 | | | | | | | | | |

The process continues until all the values in one of the input arrays have been copied into w. In our example, we are done with u first:

20	**30**	50	65		10	**30**	45	75	80		10	20						
20	**30**	50	65		10	**30**	45	75	80		10	20	30					
20	**30**	50	65		10	30	**45**	75	80		10	20	30	30				
20	30	**50**	65		10	30	**45**	75	80		10	20	30	30	45			
20	30	**50**	65		10	30	45	**75**	80		10	20	30	30	45	50		
20	30	50	**65**		10	30	45	**75**	80		10	20	30	30	45	50	65	

The remaining two values in v are then copied into w:

| 20 | 30 | 50 | 65 | | 10 | 30 | 45 | **75** | 80 | | 10 | 20 | 30 | 30 | 45 | 50 | 65 | 75 | |
| 20 | 30 | 50 | 65 | | 10 | 30 | 45 | 75 | **80** | | 10 | 20 | 30 | 30 | 45 | 50 | 65 | 75 | 80 |

The function Merge given below encapsulates these ideas.

Note how the "pointer" variables i, j, and k reference "where we are" in the arrays u, v, and w, respectively. In particular, u(i) is the next value to be selected from u, v(j) is the next value to be selected from v, and w(k) is the target for the next value to be stored in w. The first while-loop handles the case when both u and v have more values to merge. After that loop terminates, then we have incorporated into w either all of u or all of v. The second and third while-loops ensure that any remaining values in u or v are copied into w.

With the function Merge now available, let us revisit the $N = 16$ divide-and-conquer process depicted in Figure 14.8. Suppose we have a function y = Sort8(x) that returns in y the sorted version of a length-8 vector x. Using Sort8 we can implement a function for sorting length-16 vectors:

```
function y = Sort16(x)
y1 = Sort8(x(1:8)); y2 = Sort8(x(9:16)); y = Merge(y1,y2);
```

The Function `Merge`

```
function w = Merge(u,v)
% u and v are column vectors and w is their merge.

n = length(u); m = length(v); w = zeros(n+m,1);
i = 1;   % The index of the next u-value to select.
j = 1;   % The index of the next v-value to select.
k = 1;   % The index of the next w-component to fill.
while i<=n && j<=m
    %     u and v have not been exhausted...
    if u(i) <= v(j)
        w(k) = u(i); i = i+1; k = k+1;
    else
        w(k) = v(j); j = j+1; k = k+1;
    end
end
% If any elements in u remain, then copy them into w...
while i<=n
    w(k) = u(i); i = i+1; k = k+1;
end
% If any elements in v remain, then copy them into w...
while j<=m
    w(k) = v(j); j = j+1; k = k+1;
end
```

Sort8 could be implemented if we had a function Sort4 capable of sorting length-4 vectors:

```
function y = Sort8(x)
y1 = Sort4(x(1:4)); y2 = Sort4(x(5:8)); y = Merge(y1,y2);
```

Likewise, we could implement Sort4 if we had a Sort2:

```
function y = Sort4(x)
y1 = Sort2(x(1:2)); y2 = Sort2(x(3:4)); y = Merge(y1,y2);
```

A Sort2 implementation involves just a compare and (possibly) a swap:

```
function y = Sort2(x)
y1 = x(i);
y2 = x(2);
y  = Merge(y1,y2);
```

For any N that is a power of 2, we can apply this tedious implementation game and develop a sort procedure that would work for any vector of that length. However, noting the similarity between Sort16, Sort8, and Sort4, it is far more sensible to implement a single recursive function MergeSortR to handle all the cases. Assuming that the length of x is a power of 2, we obtain the following preliminary implementation:

```
function y = MergeSortR(x)
N   = length(x);
if N==1
    y = x;
else
    y1 = MergeSortR(x(1:N/2));
    y2 = MergeSortR(x(N/2+1:N));
    y  = Merge(y1,y2);
end
```

Observe that if the input vector has length greater than one, then it is split in two with the individual halves sorted by `MergeSortR`. The results are then merged to form a single sorted array y. We are guaranteed to reach the `N==1` base case because the input vector length is halved with each new level of the recursion.

Let us trace the execution of our recursive merge sort implementation when it is applied to a length-16 vector. Each node in Figure 14.8 corresponds to a `MergeSortR` call. The level-0 call splits the original unsorted length-16 vector into a pair of length-8 vectors:

Black dots are used to indicate that the values in the array are not yet sorted. The merge associated with this call to `MergeSortR` cannot proceed until the two 8-vectors are sorted. As a step in that direction, we apply `MergeSortR` to the first of these:

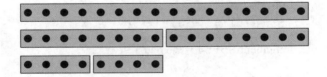

Again, the merge associated with this recursive call cannot take place until the two length-4 subvectors are sorted. So let us again apply `MergeSortR`, this time to the first of the two length-4 subvectors:

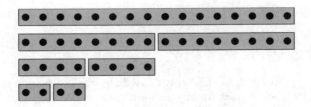

When `MergeSortR` is applied to the first length-2 subvector, we arrive at the base case because the length-1 splittings are automatically sorted:

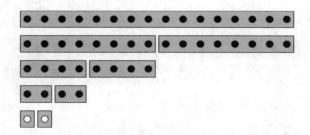

At this stage there are four `MergeSortR` calls in progress, corresponding to the nodes along the left edge of the tree in Figure 14.8. Since the last of these takes us to the base case, we can merge the two length-1 subvectors:

With this operation, control passes back to the level-3 call where the task is to sort the second length-2 subvector. A level-4 call to `MergeSortR` takes care of that:

Then a level-3 merge takes place, after which we arrive back at level-2 ready to sort the second length-4 vector:

After that is accomplished, it is merged to complete the first level-1 call:

We are now back at level-1, ready to sort the second length-8 vector:

After that is accomplished, we perform the final merge:

The sorting of the original vector is now complete.

It is a simple matter to extend this process so that vectors of arbitrary length can be handled. For example, if the original vector has length 17, then it is split into a length-8 subproblem and a length-9 subproblem, e.g.,

```
y1 = MergeSortR(x(1:8));
y2 = MergeSortR(x(9:17));
y  = Merge(y1,y2);
```

More generally, if N = length(x), then x(1:m) and x(m+1:N) are sorted and merged where m = floor(N/2). Overall we obtain the following function.

The Function **MergeSortR**

```
function y = MergeSortR(x)
% x is a column N-vector.
% y is a column N-vector consisting of the values in x sorted
% from smallest to largest.

N = length(x);
if N==1
   y = x;
else
   m  = floor(N/2);
   % Sort the first half...
   y1 = MergeSortR(x(1:m));
   % Sort the second half...
   y2 = MergeSortR(x(m+1:N));
   % Merge...
   y  = Merge(y1,y2);
end
```

It is important to appreciate the simplicity of this recursive implementation; it mimics exactly the DWM strategy that we used to pose the problem. Moreover, it does this with a minimum of subscripting. On the other hand, it is not hard to see that there are a large number of recursive function calls associated with the execution of MergeSortR, an overhead that is sometimes significant.

For these reasons it is instructive to develop a nonrecursive, iterative implementation of `MergeSortR` that we will call `MergeSortI`. Exactly the same merges arise, but they are carried out in a different order. To illustrate, we return to the $N = 16$ example. The first step is to sort the subvectors x(1:2), x(3:4),...,x(15:16) using `Merge`:

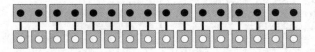

We then pair up the results from this step to produce sorted length-4 subvectors:

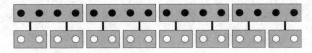

A quartet of merges is required:

```
x(1:4)    = Merge(x(1:2),x(3:4));
x(5:8)    = Merge(x(5:6),x(7:8));
x(9:12)   = Merge(x(9:10),x(11:12));
x(13:16)  = Merge(x(13:14),x(15:16));
```

Again, these newly sorted length-4 subarrays can be pairwise merged:

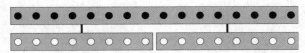

This time, only two merges are involved:

```
x(1:8)   = Merge(x(1:4),x(5:8));
x(9:16)  = Merge(x(9:12),x(13:16));
```

The last synthesis,

requires just a single merge: `x(1:16)` = `Merge(x(1:8),x(9:16))`. For an arbitrary vector with length 2^d we obtain the function `MergeSortI` given below.

Recall from §8.2 that counting the number of required comparisons is a good way to anticipate the efficiency of a sort procedure. Techniques like insertion sort require $O(N^2)$ comparisons, where N is the length of the input vector. Let us look at this statistic for merge sort, assuming that $N = 2^d$ for simplicity. We first observe that `Merge(u,v)` requires at most 2^{e+1} comparisons if the u and v vectors have length 2^e. A given pass through the outer loop in `MergeSortI` involves p merges, each with input vectors having length $N/(2p)$. Thus, there are at most N comparisons per pass and so the total number is at most $dN = N \cdot \log_2(N)$. For even small values of N, this suggests that merge sort should be remarkably faster than (say) insertion sort because $N \cdot \log_2(N) \ll N^2$. The script Eg14_2 bears this out. Indeed, insertion sort takes so long for large N that we do not even try to benchmark its performance.

The Function `MergeSortI`

```
function y = MergeSortI(x)
% x is a column N-vector with N a power of 2.
% y is a column N-vector consisting of the values in x sorted
% from smallest to largest.
N = length(x);
d = round(log2(N));
for Level = d-1:-1:0
    % Number of merges to perform at this level...
    p = 2^Level;
    % Length of the output vector for each call to Merge...
    q = N/p;
    % Length of the input vectors for each call to Merge....
    r = q/2;
    % Starting index for the next Merge...
    i = 1;
    for k=1:p
        % Perform the kth merge at the current Level...
        x(i:i+q-1) = Merge(x(i:i+r-1),x(i+r:i+q-1));
        i = i+q;
    end
end
y = x;
```

The Script `Eg14_2`

```
% Script Eg14_2
% Benchmarks MergeSortI
clc
disp('       N           tMerge    tInsert')
disp('-----------------------------------')
dRange = 14:20;
for d = dRange
    N = 2^d; x = randn(N,1);
    if d<=15
        tic;
        y = InsertionSort(x);
        tInsert = toc;
        tic;
        y = MergeSortI(x);
        tMerge = toc;
        fprintf('%10d  %6.3f %6.3f\n',N,tMerge,tInsert)
    else
        tic
        y = MergeSortI(x);
        tMerge = toc;
        fprintf('%10d   %6.3f\n',N,tMerge)
    end
end
```

Sample Output from the Script `Eg14_2`

N	tMerge	tInsert
16384	0.448	12.719
32768	0.999	55.182
65536	1.817	
131072	3.568	
262144	7.183	
524288	14.450	
1048576	29.022	

Talking Point: Tiny, Tiny Log N

For large N, the execution time difference between merge sort and insertion sort is *huge* and the ratio $N/\log_2(N)$ explains it all. When N is about a million, the quotient is about 50,000. Speedups of this magnitude are revolutionary.

One of the most famous and important $N \log(N)$ algorithms is associated with the computation of the discrete Fourier transform (DFT). The DFT is used throughout digital signal processing, e.g., the decoding of touch-tone signals. See §13.2. When a signal is sampled N times and processed by the DFT, computer time is proportional to N^2. In 1965, an alternative approach called the fast Fourier transform (FFT) was discovered that could produce the same output in time proportional to $N \log(N)$. Life as we know it today would be very different without the FFT. It created brand-new applications because it made it possible to process signals as fast as they were generated, something not possible with the DFT.

The FFT and other "fast" procedures have truly revolutionized science and engineering, a tribute to divide-and-conquer problem solving.

MATLAB Review

Recursion Overheads

It is important to appreciate that there are two hidden overheads associated with recursive implementations. First, there is the cost of a function call. This can be significant if the amount of computation per level is spare. A second concern has to do with memory. During the execution of a recursive function, multiple copies of the function are active and the local variables associated with each active copy must be saved. This may cause a problem in certain applications.

Exercises

M14.2.1 How many times is the function `Merge` called when `MergeSortR` is applied to a length-17 vector?

M14.2.2 Through benchmarking, determine if the MATLAB function `sort` runs in a time proportional to $N \cdot \log(N)$.

M14.2.3 Refer to Figure 14.8. In what order are the subvectors sorted when MergeSortR is applied? Now reverse the order of the two recursive calls in MergeSortR. In what order are the subvectors sorted?

M14.2.4 Modify MergeSortR so that if $N \leq 128$, then it sorts the input vector using the function InsertionSort.

P14.2.5 Develop a 3-way merge function y = Merge3(u,v,w) that takes three sorted vectors u, v, and w and returns in y the sorted vector of their values.

P14.2.6 Compare the efficiency of MergeSortR and MergeSortI through benchmarking.

P14.2.7 Generalize MergeSortI so that it can handle input vectors with arbitrary length.

14.3   Looking for Trouble

Problem Statement

If the value of a variable N is a positive integer, then the fragment

```
x = linspace(0,2*pi,N+1);
y = sin(x);
plot(x,y)
```

displays a *piecewise linear interpolant* of the sine function. This is a more precise way of describing the nature of the approximation than "connect the dots," which was the terminology used in §4.1. From the graphical point of view, the quality of a piecewise linear interpolant depends upon its departure from the underlying function. For a smooth function like $\sin(x)$, setting N equal to a couple of hundred is normally good enough for producing a nice plot.

Now suppose the function f that we want to display across a given interval $[L, R]$ has two properties.

Property 1. There are places in $[L, R]$ where the function f is nearly linear and other places where it is very nonlinear. In other words, the second derivative of f varies greatly across the interval.

Property 2. An f-evaluation is very expensive, say $1000.

Figure 14.9 displays a function Rough(x) that satisfies Property 1 and (we will pretend) Property 2. It is highly nonlinear in the vicinity of $x = 1.3$, $x = 1.6$, and $x = 1.9$ and we had to set $N = 500$ in order for the plot to appear smooth near these points. Thus, Figure 14.9 cost a half-million dollars to produce! However, it is clear that we have wasted a lot of money; the function is very linear across much of the interval and in these regions the function evaluations could have been spaced more widely apart without sacrificing the overall quality of the plot. Instead of using linspace with a large N, we need a method for determining the evaluation points that is based on estimates of local nonlinearity.

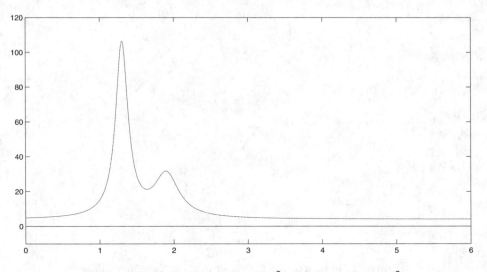

Figure 14.9. Rough$(x) = 4 + 1/((x-1.3)^2 + .01) + 1/((x-1.9)^2 + .04)$.

Write a function of the form $[x,y]$ = pwLAdapt(f,L,R,tol) that takes a function f, an interval $[L, R]$, an error tolerance tol, and returns "short-as-possible" vectors x and y so that plot(x,y) is suitably smooth relative to the value of tol.

Program Development

The idea is to cluster the f-evaluations in regions where f appears to be highly nonlinear and to space out the evaluations when this is not the case. Before we begin it is important to understand the rules of the game. We are *not* allowed to plot the function and then, based on the plot, select the evaluation points. The idea is to automate the selection process.

We start by looking at the "atomic" operation which is to interpolate f across an interval $[L, R]$ with a single line segment and to estimate the quality of the fit. One idea is to compute the distance between $(m, f(m))$ and the connecting line segment where $m = (L+R)/2$ is the interval midpoint. See Figure 14.10. Let us tentatively adopt the convention that if this discrepancy measure is small compared to a tolerance tol, then we accept the linear interpolant. Otherwise, we split the problem in half and examine the quality of the left-hand interpolant on $[L,m]$ and the right-hand interpolant on $[m, R]$. If necessary, these subproblems can in turn be halved.

This subdivision process can be used to "discover" just where f is highly nonlinear because more subdivisions will typically be needed in these regions. By following the divide-and-conquer paradigm, we can build a piecewise linear interpolant with the property that on each subinterval the quality of the approximation is acceptable. Figure 14.11 shows how the interval subdivision process might play out. The linear interpolant over the original interval $[0, 16]$ is too crude so we seek acceptable piecewise linear interpolants over $[0,8]$ and $[8,16]$. Once they are found we can "glue" them together. (More on this later.) It turns out that linear interpolation is still not good enough across the half-length interval $[0,8]$, so that subproblem is itself subdivided. Linear interpolation across the quarter-length subintervals $[0,4]$ and $[4,8]$ reveals that the $[0,4]$ interpolant is fine but that we must refine

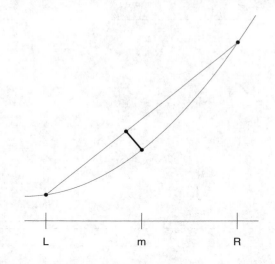

Figure 14.10. *Measuring the Quality of a Linear Interpolant.*

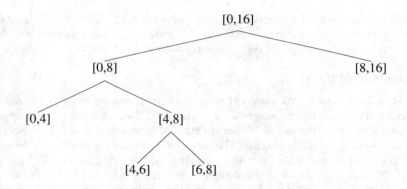

Figure 14.11. *Interval Subdivision.*

the [4,8] interpolant. Subdivision of this subproblem leads to adequate interpolations on [4,6] and [6,8]. It follows that

```
plot([4 6 8],[f(4) f(6) f(8)])
```

would produce a suitable rendition of f across [4, 8]. Earlier in the process it was discovered that the [0,4] interpolant was acceptable and so

```
plot([0 4 6 8],[f(0) f(4) f(6) f(8)])
```

is a satisfactory piecewise linear plot across [0,8]. Backtracking to the first subdivision, we now must consider interpolation across [8,16]. In our example, a single linear interpolant works across this interval and so

```
plot([0 4 6 8 16],[f(0) f(4) f(6) f(8) f(16)])
```

is the final plot. Notice the variable spacing of the evaluation points and how easy it is to "glue" together the left and right interpolants. Here is a rough draft of a recursive function that carries out this process:

```
function [x,y] = pwLAdapt(f,L,R,tol)
m = (L+R)/2;
fm = f(m);
if   the linear interpolant of f across [L,R] is acceptable
    x = [L;R];
    y = [f(L);f(R)];
else
    % Subdivide obtaining the left subproblem...
    [xL,yL] = pwLAdapt(f,L,m,tol);
    % and the right subproblem...
    [xR,yR] = pwLAdapt(f,m,R,tol);
    % Synthesis...
    x = [xL;xR(2:length(xR))];
    y = [yL;yR(2:length(yR))];
end
```
(14.1)

To complete the implementation we need to quantify the acceptability criteria. Referring to Figure 14.10, we need a recipe for the minimum distance between a point and a line segment. This problem is discussed in §10.3 and the solution involves elementary calculus. We encapsulate the computation as follows.

The Function Pt2LineSeg

```
function d_min = Pt2LineSeg(a,b,x1,y1,x2,y2)
% d_min is the minimum distance between (a,b) and a
% point that is on the line segment that connects
% the points (x1,y1) and (x2,y2).

t_min = ((x2-x1)*(a-x1) + (y2-y1)*(b-y1))/...
                 ((x1-x2)^2 + (y1-y2)^2);
if 0<=t_min && t_min<=1
    tStar = t_min;
elseif t_min<0
    tStar = 0;
else
    tStar = 1;
end
xStar = x1 + tStar*(x2-x1);
yStar = y1 + tStar*(y2-y1);
d_min = sqrt((a-xStar)^2+(b-yStar)^2);
```

Returning to our preliminary implementation (14.1), our plan is to accept the linear interpolant on $[L, R]$ if the boolean expression

```
Pt2LineSeg(m,fm,L,f(L),R,f(R)) <= tol
```

is true. Unfortunately, for highly oscillatory functions this runs the risk that we may subdivide far too many times. To ensure that this does not happen, we declare a subinterval to be acceptable if

```
Pt2LineSeg(m,fm,L,f(L),R,f(R)) <= tol  ||  R-L <= tol
```

is true. In other words, the subdivision process is guaranteed to halt once the subintervals get sufficiently short. This leads to the following refinement of (14.1):

```
function [x,y] = pwLAdapt(f,L,R,tol)
if R-L <= tol
    % Subinterval acceptable by virtue of being short...
    x = [L;R];
    y = [f(L);f(R)];
else
    % Check discrepancy at the midpoint...
    m = (L+R)/2;
    fm = f(m);
    if Pt2LineSeg(m,fm,L,f(L),R,f(R)) <= tol
        % Subinterval acceptable...
        x = [L;R];
        y = [f(L);f(R)];                                          (14.2)
    else
        % Subdivide and synthesize...
        [xL,yL] = pwLAdapt(f,L,m,tol);
        [xR,yR] = pwLAdapt(f,m,R,tol);
        x = [xL;xR(2:length(xR))];
        y = [yL;yR(2:length(yR))];
    end
end
```

Notice that the function evaluation at the midpoint is skipped if the length of the subinterval is less than the tolerance. The nested if-else organization is consistent with the assumption that we must minimize the number of f-evaluations.

We can further improve the efficiency of (14.2) by observing that there are redundant f-evaluations associated with the recursive calls. In particular, the left subinterval calculation pwLAdapt(f,L,m,tol) starts out by evaluating f at both $x = L$ and $x = m$ even though those evaluations have already been performed. Likewise, the function call pwLAdapt(f,m,R,tol) unnecessarily computes $f(m)$ and $f(R)$.

A way out of this predicament is to extend the input parameter list to include the evaluations of f at the endpoints. This leads to our finished implementation shown below. Note also that if the midpoint acceptability test is satisfied, then [L;m;R] and [fL;fm;fR] are returned instead of just [L;R] and [fL;fR] as in (14.2). The rationale for doing this is simply not to waste the base-case midpoint f-evaluation. The script Eg14_3 applies pwLAdapt to the function Rough(x). Observe the unequal spacing of the f-evaluations in Figure 14.12.

The Function pwLAdapt

```
function [x,y] = pwLAdapt(f,L,fL,R,fR,tol)
% Produces column n-vectors x and y so that plot(x,y) is a good
% rendition of the function f across the interval [L,R].
% fL is the value of f at L and fR is the value of f at R.
% tol > 0 determines how close the piecewise linear interpolant
% is to f. The x and y vectors may be as long as 2(R-L)/tol so
% tol should not be too small.

if (R-L) <= tol
    % The subinterval is acceptable...
    x = [L;R];  y = [fL;fR];
else
    m   = (L+R)/2; fm = f(m);
    d_min = Pt2LineSeg(m,fm,L,fL,R,fR);
    if d_min <= tol
        % The linear interpolant is acceptable...
        x = [L;m;R];   y = [fL;fm;fR];
    else
        % Produce left and right piecewise linear interpolants...
        [xL,yL] = pwLAdapt(f,L,fL,m,fm,tol);
        [xR,yR] = pwLAdapt(f,m,fm,R,fR,tol);
        % and synthesize...
        x = [ xL;xR(2:length(xR))];
        y = [ yL;yR(2:length(yR))];
    end
end
```

The Script Eg14_3

```
% Script Eg14_3
% Illustrates pwLAdapt with the function Rough on [0,6].
close all
% Produce a nice "linspace" plot...
N = 1000;
figure
set(gcf,'position',[50 50 1000 500])
L = 0.0;    R = 6.0;
x = linspace(L,R,N); y = Rough(x);
plot(x,y,'r',[L R],[0 0],'k')
axis([L R -10 120])
% Now show a more efficient distribution of f-evals...
tol = (R-L)/(N-1); fL = Rough(L); fR = Rough(R);
hold on
[x,y] = pwLAdapt(@Rough,L,fL,R,fR,tol);
plot(x,y,'.k','Markersize',5)
title(sprintf('Number of f-Evaluations = %d',length(x)))
% And connect...
plot(x,y,'k')
```

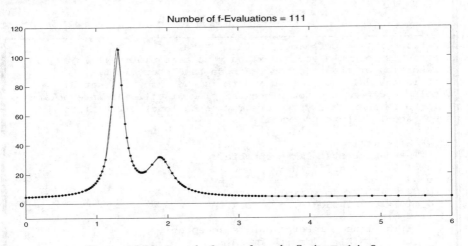

Figure 14.12. *Sample Output from the Script* `Eg14_3`.

Talking Point: Heuristics

The midpoint discrepancy scheme for "discovering" regions of strong nonlinearity is a good example of a *heuristic*. A heuristic is a rule of thumb, usually cheap and usually with loopholes, that nudges a computation in the right direction. Our goal was to subdivide an interval if the function was "too nonlinear," and our rule-of-thumb does just that if the midpoint discrepancy is sufficiently large. However, this test for nonlinearity can be fooled. If $a = 0$, $b = 2\pi$, and $f = \sin$, then the linear interpolant just happens to be perfect at the midpoint. The function `pwLAdapt` would conclude that a line segment connecting (0,0) and $(2\pi, 0)$ is an excellent approximation to the sine function across $[0, 2\pi]$.

Of course, steps can be taken to close the loopholes in a given heuristic. In our problem, we could base our acceptance of the linear interpolant upon the discrepancy at two selected points in $[a, b]$, say at $x = (2a + b)/3$ and $x = (a + 2b)/3$. This would reduce the chance of mistaken acceptance but would increase the number of required f-evaluations, a typical efficiency versus reliability trade-off.

Heuristics abound in computational science and engineering because, most of the time, there are no cheap, airtight solution procedures for hard problems.

Matlab Review

Functions as Parameters

Suppose `MyF` is a function that expects a function as one of its input parameters. In a call to `MyF`, the input function must be identified by its *handle* which is done by putting the character "@" in front of its name.

Exercises

M14.3.1 Modify `pwLAdapt` so that the linear interpolant is accepted if

```
R-L<=tol  ||  abs(fm - (fL+fR)/2)<=tol
```

is true. Is this a better criterion?

M14.3.2 Explain why the maximum length of the output vectors for `pwLAdapt` is roughly $2(R-L)/tol$.

P14.3.3 Suppose we have an m-vector z with the property that $L < z_1 < z_2 < \cdots < z_m < R$. How would you compute an adaptive piecewise linear interpolant of a function f across the interval $[L, R]$ with the property that the evaluation points include $z_1, \ldots, z_m$?

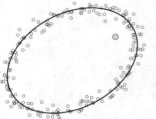

Chapter 15

Optimization

15.1 Shortest Route
The Combinatoric Explosion

15.2 Best Bike
Constraints and Objective Functions

15.3 Most Likely Orbit
Model Building

Optimization problems involve finding the "best" of something. The search for the optimum ranges over a set called the *search space* and the notion of best is quantified through an *objective function*. We already have some experience with these concepts. In §10.3 we considered the problem of finding the nearest point on a line L to a given point P. Thus, L is the search space and Euclidean distance is the objective function. Using calculus, a formula can be given that explicitly specifies the optimal point. However, in practice 1-line formulae give way to complicated algorithms and exact solutions give way to approximations. Suboptimal solutions are happily accepted if they are cheap to compute and "good enough."

For the first example we consider the traveling salesperson problem where the aim is to find the shortest round trip path that visits each of n given points exactly once. The search space is huge, consisting of $(n - 1)!$ possible itineraries. A brute force search plan that considers every possibility is out of the question except for very small values of n. But with a simple approximation idea, we show how to compute cheaply a low-mileage itinerary.

Next, we use an engineering design problem to discuss the important role that constraints play in optimization. The task is to build a 10-sprocket bicycle with a desirable range of gear ratios. The constraints reduce the size of the search space but make it trickier to organize the search for the "best bike."

In the last problem we consider how to approximate a given set of noisy orbit points with an ellipse. In contrast to the traveling salesperson and best-bike problems, this is a continuous optimization problem with a genuinely infinite search space. Instead of harnessing the power of advanced calculus to solve this problem, we set up a graphical environment that can be used to obtain a "very good," orbit-fitting ellipse.

Programming Preview

Concepts

Objective functions, constraints, the combinatoric explosion, the design process, search space, data fitting, model building and design.

Language Features

`inf`: A built-in constant that represents positive infinity. For any valid floating point value x, `x<inf` gives 1 (true). `inf` is the result of division by zero. `inf` also can be used in arithmetic operations, e.g., `1/inf` gives 0.

Section Prerequisites

Chapters 7 and 11 are essential. The examples in §15.1 and §15.2 involve complex array manipulation. A hierarchical structure is utilized in §15.2.

15.1 Shortest Route

Problem Statement

What is the shortest possible round trip that passes through the capitals of the "lower" forty-eight states? This is an example of the justly famous traveling salesperson problem (TSP). In our situation there are $47! \approx 10^{60}$ different itineraries, so the search for the optimum path cannot proceed by evaluating the mileage of every possible route. The TSP is a member of a challenging family of problems that are *NP hard*, a term that is used whenever all known, exact-answer methods require an exponential amount of work. As a function of n, the time required to solve a TSP with n cities $C_1, \ldots, C_n$ grows like $(n-1)!$. In everyday terms this means that the exact solution is unaffordable for all but modest values of n. What we need is a technique that can be used to find cheaply a "very good" solution.

Let us consider the $n = 5$ situation depicted in Figure 15.1 together with the 5-by-5 "distance matrix" that houses all the city-to-city distances. The distance from city C_i to city C_j is given by d_{ij}. Assume that we have two travelers who determine their itineraries using Heuristic H defined by

> **Heuristic H:** *Go to the Nearest Unvisited City*

As we discussed in §14.3, a heuristic is a sensible rule-of-thumb that tends to move a computation in a favorable direction. (No pun intended!) Heuristic **H** is certainly a rational way to proceed. Assuming that Traveler 1 starts at C_4 and Traveler 2 starts at C_1, we see that they produce distinct paths:

$$\text{Traveler 1:} \quad C_4 \;\rightarrow\; C_2 \;\rightarrow\; C_3 \;\rightarrow\; C_1 \;\rightarrow\; C_5 \;\rightarrow\; C_4$$
$$d_{42} + d_{23} + d_{31} + d_{15} + d_{54} = 410$$

$$\text{Traveler 2:} \quad C_1 \;\rightarrow\; C_3 \;\rightarrow\; C_5 \;\rightarrow\; C_2 \;\rightarrow\; C_4 \;\rightarrow\; C_1$$
$$d_{13} + d_{35} + d_{52} + d_{24} + d_{41} = 390$$

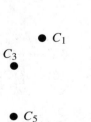

$$D = \begin{array}{|c|c|c|c|c|}
\hline
0 & 100 & 30 & 120 & 70 \\
\hline
100 & 0 & 70 & 100 & 90 \\
\hline
30 & 70 & 0 & 120 & 50 \\
\hline
120 & 100 & 120 & 0 & 140 \\
\hline
70 & 90 & 50 & 140 & 0 \\
\hline
\end{array}$$

Figure 15.1. *Input for a Traveling Salesperson Problem ($n = 5$).*

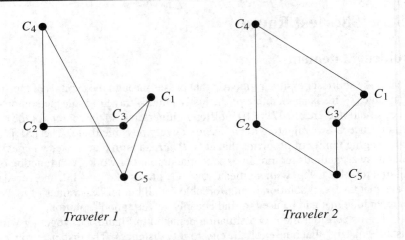

Traveler 1   *Traveler 2*

Figure 15.2. *Paths.*

Their routes are displayed in Figure 15.2. We see by inspection that Traveler 2 follows a path that is the shortest possible. Traveler 1's path is reasonable, but longer. The heuristic is ill-advised when that traveler is at C_2, because the wiser move would have been to visit C_5 instead of C_3.

How good is Heuristic **H**? Does it produce the shortest round trip if we just start at the right city? Compared to checking every itinerary, how fast is this method for determining a path? Experiment with the state capital data.

Program Development

Before we address the algorithmic issues associated with the TSP, we implement three utility functions. The first encapsulates the state capital location data.

The Function `Capitals`

```
function City = Capitals()
% Creates a length-48 structure array where each component
% has three fields:
%     Name    length-24 string with state and capital name
%     Lat     latitude in degress
%     Long    longitude in degrees
A = [...
        'AL   Montgomery             32.38       86.37';...
        'AZ   Phoenix                33.43      112.22';...
                        :
        'WY   Cheyenne               41.15      104.80'];
for k=1:48
   Lat  = str2num(A(k,25:29));
   Long = str2num(A(k,34:39));
   City(k) = struct('Name',A(k,1:24),'Lat',Lat,'Long',Long);
end
```

The second function computes the great circle distance between two cities given their respective latitude and longitude.

The Function GCDist

```
function d = GCDist(C1,C2)
% Great circle distance between city C1 and city C2.
theta1 = C1.Lat*pi/180;
phi1   = C1.Long*pi/180;
theta2 = C2.Lat*pi/180;
phi2   = C2.Long*pi/180;
xDiff  = cos(theta1)*cos(phi1) - cos(theta2)*cos(phi2);
yDiff  = cos(theta1)*sin(phi1) - cos(theta2)*sin(phi2);
zDiff  = sin(theta1) - sin(theta2);
d = 7926*asin(sqrt(xDiff^2 + yDiff^2 + zDiff^2)/2);
```

The third function sets up the distance matrix given a set of input cities and their locations.

The Function CityDistTable

```
function D = CityDistTable(City)
% City is a length-n structure array where the name, latitude,
% and longitude of the kth city is housed in City(k).name,
% City(k).lat, and City(k).long.
% D is an n-by-n matrix with D(i,j) being the great circle
% distance from City(i) to City(j).

% Set up the city-to-city distance matrix...
n = length(City);
D = zeros(n,n);
for i=1:n
    for j=i+1:n
        D(i,j) = GCDist(City(i),City(j));
        D(j,i) = D(i,j);
    end
end
```

We proceed to implement a function [S,Odom] = Route(StartCity,D) that takes an n-by-n distance matrix D, the starting city index StartCity, and uses Heuristic **H** to produce an itinerary encoded by a pair of column vectors S and Odom. In particular, for k=1:n+1, S(k) should contain the index of the kth stop in the itinerary and Odom(k) should be the accumulated mileage at that point of the journey. Thus, the value of S(1) and S(n+1) should be the value of StartCity. For the $n = 5$ example above, Traveler 1 executes Route(4,D) giving

S:	4	2	3	1	5	4

Odom:	0	100	170	200	270	410

while Traveler 2 heeds the advice of Route (1, D):

S:

1	3	5	2	4	1

Odom:

0	30	80	170	270	390

The key to implementing the function Route is how to use the data in the distance matrix. For example, if we start the journey in C_1, then the values in D (1, :) are relevant as these are the distances from C_1 to all other cities. But we cannot simply look for the minimum of these values because among them is 0, the distance from C_1 to itself.

This suggests a simple strategy of assigning inf to entries in D as they become irrelevant to the find-the-next stop computation. We step through an example. Let Here be the index of the current stop. If the journey begins at C_3, then we start the process with the assignments

```
Here = 3; S(1) = Here; Odom(1) = 0;
```

Since we are at C_3, it makes sense to reset D with the assignment D (:, Here) = inf:

D:

0	100	inf	120	70
100	0	inf	100	90
30	70	inf	120	50
120	100	inf	0	140
70	90	inf	140	0

Now the smallest value in D (3, :) identifies the next stop:

```
[Leg,Next] = min(D(Here,:));
Odom(2) = Odom(1) + Leg;
Here = Next;
S(2) = Here;
```

This assigns 30 to Leg and 1 to Next. The variables Odom, S, and Here are updated to reflect the fact that we are now at C_1. The D array is modified via D (:, Here) = inf to show that C_1 is a visited city:

D:

inf	100	inf	120	70
inf	0	inf	100	90
inf	70	inf	120	50
inf	100	inf	0	140
inf	90	inf	140	0

The smallest value in row 1 (i.e., the smallest value in D (Here, :)) is 70 and it occurs in column 5. This means that the next stop is C_5:

```
[Leg,Next] = min(D(Here,:));
Odom(3) = Odom(2) + Leg;
Here = Next;
S(3) = Here;
D(:,Here) = inf;
```

This assigns 70 to `Leg` and 5 to `Next`. `Odom`, `S`, and `Here` are updated to reflect the fact that we are now at C_5. The `D` array is modified to show that C_5 is a city that has been visited:

`D:`

inf	100	inf	120	inf
inf	0	inf	100	inf
inf	70	inf	120	inf
inf	100	inf	0	inf
inf	90	inf	140	inf

The general process should be clear. We next visit C_2 yielding

`D:`

inf	inf	inf	120	inf
inf	inf	inf	100	inf
inf	inf	inf	120	inf
inf	inf	inf	0	inf
inf	inf	inf	140	inf

and then C_4. After that update the remaining task is to "return home" to the starting city C_3. Motivated by this example, we arrive at the function `Route` displayed below. Because the values in `D` are overwritten, we must make a copy of `D(StartCity,:)` so that when the time comes, we are able to carry out the "back home" step.

The Function `Route`

```
function [S,Odom] = Route(StartCity,D)
% D is an n-by-n matrix whose (i,j) entry is the distance
%     between city i and city j.
% StartCity is an index with 1 <= StartCity <= n
% S and Odom are column vectors of length n+1.
% S(k) is the index of the kth stop and Odom(k) is the
% accumulated mileage at that point. Note that S(1) = StartCity,
% Odom(1) = 0, S(n+1) = StartCity, and S(n+1) is the total
% distance of the journey.

[n,n] = size(D);
% Get set at the starting city...
S     = zeros(n+1,1); Odom  = zeros(n+1,1);
Here  = StartCity; S(1) = Here;
% Remember the distance to the starting city...
dStart = D(StartCity,:);
for j=1:n-1
    % Figure out where to go next, i.e., stop j+1...
    D(:,Here) = inf; [Leg,Next] = min(D(Here,:));
    % Update the odometer and move on...
    Odom(j+1) = Odom(j) + Leg; S(j+1) = Next; Here = Next;
end
% Return to the starting city...
S(n+1) = StartCity; Odom(n+1) = Odom(n) + dStart(Here);
```

The script `Eg15_1` applies `Route` forty-eight times, once for each possible starting city. It determines that the best we can do using Heuristic **H** is to start in Baton Rouge, Louisiana.

The Script `Eg15_1`

```
% Script Eg15_1
% Heuristic solution of the traveling salesperson problem.

% Get the data and set up the distance matrix...
City = Capitals();
D = CityDistTable(City);

Shortest = inf;
% Examine the route obtained for each possible starting city...
for StartCity = 1:48
    [S,Odom] = Route(StartCity,D);
    if Odom(49) < Shortest
        % A new best route discovered. Display...
        Shortest = Odom(49);
        clc
        disp('       Stop              Odometer')
        disp('--------------------------------')
        for k=1:49
            disp([City(S(k)).Name  sprintf(' %6.0f',Odom(k)) ])
        end
        pause
    end
end
```

Sample Output from the Script `Eg15_1`

```
        Stop              Odometer
--------------------------------
   LA  Baton Rouge            0
   MS  Jackson              125
   AR  Little Rock          309
   MO  Jefferson City       574
   IL  Springfield          735
   IN  Indianapolis         915
   KY  Frankfurt           1045
   OH  Columbus            1209
   WV  Charleston          1341
            :
   TX  Austin             11079
   LA  Baton Rouge        11470
```

Is this the absolutely shortest round trip through the forty-eight capitals? A crude display of the circuit reveals that it is not. See Figure 15.3. There is a better way to handle the route where there are "crossovers." If we adjust the route in these areas (around Maine and in the southwest), then we obtain what looks like the optimal solution. See Figure 15.4. Unfortunately, "proof by picture" is not always acceptable!

Odometer = 11470

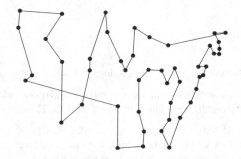

Figure 15.3. *Starting in Baton Rouge with Heuristic H.*

Odometer = 10738

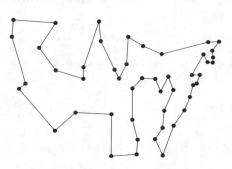

Figure 15.4. *Optimal?*

Talking Point: Theory and Practice

Many important look-for-the-best problems have exponentially huge search spaces like the TSP. Research focuses on the search for affordable heuristics and what you can "say" about them. For example, can we prove that the Heuristic **H** solution is within 10 percent of the optimal solution? Is there an input city distribution for which the heuristic solution does particularly well (or poorly)? It is clear that this kind of theoretical analysis has huge practical ramifications. Time is money and your boss will be very happy if you can produce a more effective path generator. Mathematically proven results about its performance will help make the case for a new idea.

The example brings up an important issue that is all too often phrased as "theory versus practice." There is a popular misconception that theory is the opposite of practice— the purview of abstract researchers who are blissfully unaware of "real world" problems.

The fact is, it is impossible to disentangle *sensible* theoretical research from practice. Consider a computer program that controls a silo with a nuclear-tipped missile. The act of proving that program is correct is a theoretical exercise much in the spirit of mathematically proving the Pythagorean theorem. Yet, the production of the missile-silo correctness proof could not be a more practical endeavor. So much for the "versus" in "theory versus practice."

Exercises

M15.1.1 How many different round trips are produced by `Eg15_1`?

M15.1.2 Instead of round trips through all the capitals, consider one-way trips that simply do not return home after the forty-eighth stop. Does the best Heuristic-**H** route start from Baton Rouge?

M15.1.3 The latitude and longitude for Juneau, Alaska are 58.30° and 134.44°, respectively. Likewise, the latitude and longitude for Honolulu, Hawaii are 21.32° and 157.83°. Building on `Eg15_1`, use Heuristic **H** to approximate the shortest round trip through all 50 state capitals.

P15.1.4 Write a script that produces Figures 15.3 and 15.4. If possible, obtain a U.S. map and superimpose the path on top of it.

P15.1.5 In this problem you write a TSP solver that checks out all possible itineraries. Start by understanding the following recursive procedure that can be used to print all possible permutations of a given string:

```
function PrintAll(t,s)
% t and s are strings
% Prints all strings of the form [s p] where p is a
% permutation of the string t.
n = length(t);
if n==1
   disp([s t])
else
   for k=1:n
       PrintAll([t(1:k-1) t(k+1:n)],[s t(k)])
   end
end
```

For example, `PrintAll('abc','')` prints abc, acb, bac, bca, cab, and cba. Using the structure of `PrintAll` as a guide, write a function i = `Trip(x,y)` that returns in the $(n+1)$-vector i the itinerary of the shortest round-trip route through the points specified by the n-vectors x and y. In particular, i(k) should be the index of the point that is the kth stop along the journey. Note: $7! = 5040$ so n probably should not be too much bigger than 7.

15.2   Best Bike

Problem Statement

A bicycle has 3 pedal sprockets and 7 wheel sprockets. If the chain goes over a pedal sprocket with p teeth and a wheel sprocket with w teeth, then the gear ratio for that pair of sprockets is given by the quotient p/w. With three possible numerators and seven possible denominators, we see that there are 21 possible quotients. (The higher the ratio, the harder it is to pedal.) As an example, if pedal sprockets p_1, p_2, p_3 and wheel sprockets $w_1, \ldots, w_7$ are given by

$$[p_1 \ p_2 \ p_3 \ / \ w_1 \ w_2 \ w_3 \ w_4 \ w_5 \ w_6 \ w_7] = [48 \ 40 \ 32 \ / \ 32 \ 29 \ 26 \ 23 \ 20 \ 17 \ 14],$$

then the gear ratios are as follows:

	$w_1 = 32$	$w_2 = 29$	$w_3 = 26$	$w_4 = 23$	$w_5 = 20$	$w_6 = 17$	$w_7 = 14$
$p_1 = 48$	1.50	1.66	1.85	2.09	2.40	2.83	3.43
$p_2 = 40$	1.25	1.38	1.54	1.74	2.00	2.35	2.86
$p_3 = 32$	1.00	1.10	1.23	1.39	1.60	1.88	2.29

Our goal is to choose the 10 sprockets so that the actual gear ratios $r_1 \leq \cdots \leq r_{21}$ are as equally spaced as possible across the interval $[1, 4]$. Ideally, we would have $r_k = 1.00 + .15(k-1) = \tilde{r}_k$. This is not quite the case for the above bicycle:

k	p	w	r_k	$\tilde{r}_k$
1	32	32	1.00	1.00
2	32	29	1.10	1.15
3	32	26	1.23	1.30
4	40	32	1.25	1.45
5	40	29	1.38	1.60
6	32	23	1.39	1.75
7	48	32	1.50	1.90
8	40	26	1.54	2.05
9	32	20	1.60	2.20
10	48	29	1.66	2.35
11	40	23	1.74	2.50
12	48	26	1.85	2.65
13	32	17	1.88	2.80
14	40	20	2.00	2.95
15	48	23	2.09	3.10
16	32	14	2.29	3.25
17	40	17	2.35	3.40
18	48	20	2.40	3.55
19	48	17	2.83	3.70
20	40	14	2.86	3.85
21	48	14	3.43	4.00

Indeed, it is unlikely that we will be able to build the ideal bicycle simply because there are 21 conditions to satisfy but only 10 parameters to "play" with. Thus, we need to (a) formulate an *objective function* ϕ that measures deviation from the ideal bicycle and (b) choose the 10 sprockets so that ϕ is minimized. To that end we define

$$\phi(p_1, p_2, p_3, w_1, w_2, w_3, w_4, w_5, w_6, w_7) = \sum_{k=1}^{21} |r_k - \tilde{r}_k| \qquad (15.1)$$

i.e., the sum of the discrepancies between the kth smallest actual ratio r_k and the kth smallest ideal ratio $\tilde{r}_k$. Note that if r is the vector of actual gear ratios ordered from smallest to largest, then

```
phiVal = sum(abs(r-linspace(1,4,21)))
```

assigns to `phiVal` the value of the summation in (15.1). For the above bicycle, the value of `phiVal` is 13.14.

To make our optimization problem realistic, we impose constraints on the range of possible sprocket sizes. Assume that the "sprocket supplier" offers a limited selection of pedal sprockets and wheel sprockets leading to constraints C_1 and C_2:

$$C_1: \quad 32 \leq p_i \leq 52 \quad i = 1{:}3$$

$$C_2: \quad 12 \leq w_i \leq 42 \quad i = 1{:}7.$$

This sets up a *constrained* optimization problem:

> Subject to the constraints C_1 and C_2, choose pedal sprockets p_1, p_2, and p_3 and wheel sprockets $w_1, \ldots, w_7$ so that the objective function ϕ in (15.1) is minimized.   (15.2)

Not to be outdone, the "marketing department" insists that the smallest gear ratio should equal 1 and the largest gear ratio should equal 4:

$$C_3: \quad r_1 = 1$$

$$C_4: \quad r_{21} = 4.$$

This leads to a second constrained optimization problem:

> Subject to the constraints C_1, C_2, C_3, and C_4, choose pedal sprockets p_1, p_2, and p_3 and wheel sprockets $w_1, \ldots, w_7$ so that the objective function ϕ in (15.1) is minimized.   (15.3)

Write a script that solves (15.3). Since there are 21 possible pedal sprockets and 31 possible wheel sprockets, we see that there are upwards of

$$N_1 = 21^3 31^7 \approx 2.54 \cdot 10^{14}$$

different bikes to check. In view of this large number, we will settle for an approximate solution.

Program Development

The act of finding the best bicycle B_{opt} appears to require the evaluation of ϕ over the set of all "legal" bicycles, i.e., the set of all bicycles whose sprockets satisfy the constraints C_1 through C_4. We start with some observations about redundant checking. If B_1 is the bike

$$[p_1 \; p_2 \; p_3 \, / \, w_1 \; w_2 \; w_3 \; w_4 \; w_5 \; w_6 \; w_7 \,] = [40 \; 48 \; 32 \, / \, 23 \; 29 \; 26 \; 32 \; 17 \; 14 \; 20 \,]$$

and B_2 is the bike

$$[p_1 \; p_2 \; p_3 \; / \; w_1 \; w_2 \; w_3 \; w_4 \; w_5 \; w_6 \; w_7 \,] = [48 \; 40 \; 32 \; / \; 32 \; 29 \; 26 \; 23 \; 20 \; 17 \; 14\,],$$

then each has exactly the same set of gear ratios. Thus, the objective function has the same value for each of these bikes.

In general, if B is a bicycle and we permute its pedal sprockets and permute its wheel sprockets, then the new bicycle renders exactly the same ϕ-value. With this observation we adjust constraints C_1 and C_2 to rule out redundancy:

$$\tilde{C}_1: \quad 32 \leq p_3 < p_2 < p_1 \leq 52$$

$$\tilde{C}_2: \quad 12 \leq w_7 < w_6 < w_5 < w_4 < w_3 < w_2 < w_1 \leq 42.$$

Minimizing ϕ subject to constraints $\tilde{C}_1$ and $\tilde{C}_2$ produces the same minimum value of the objective function.

Simplifications also result by thinking carefully about C_3 and C_4. Observe that if $r_1 = 1$, then we must have $w_1 = p_3$. Thus, once we select the smallest pedal sprocket p_3, then the largest wheel sprocket w_1 is automatically determined. This leads to a refinement of the constraint C_3:

$$\tilde{C}_3: \quad w_1 = p_3 \quad \text{and} \quad p_3 \leq 42.$$

Similarly, by insisting that the largest gear ratio satisfies $r_{21} = p_1/w_7 = 4$, we see that p_1 must be divisible by 4. So once its value is selected, then $w_7 = p_1/4$. The constraint that $12 \leq w_7$ means that p_1 must be either 52 or 48. Thus, we may replace the constraint C_4 with

$$\tilde{C}_4: \quad p_1 = 48 \text{ or } 52 \quad \text{and} \quad w_7 = p_1/4.$$

Given $\tilde{C}_1$, $\tilde{C}_2$, $\tilde{C}_3$, and $\tilde{C}_4$, the following nested-loop structure can be used to search for the optimal bicycle:

```
for p₁ = [48 52]
    w₇ = p₁/4
    for p₂ = 32:p₁ − 1
        for p₃ = 32:min(p₂ − 1, 42)
            w₁ = p₃
```

$$\boxed{\begin{array}{l} \text{Given } p_1, p_2, p_3, w_1, \text{ and } w_7, \text{ check all bicycles} \\ [p_1, p_2, p_3 \; / \; w_1, w_2, w_3, w_4, w_5, w_6, w_7] \\ \text{that satisfy } w_7 < w_6 < w_5 < w_4 < w_3 < w_2 < w_1 \end{array}} \qquad (15.4)$$

The upper limit in the p_3-loop follows from the constraint $\tilde{C}_3$. The refinement of (15.4) requires the selection of wheel sprockets $w_2, \ldots, w_6$. A five-deep loop does the job:

```
for w₂ = w₇ + 5:w₁ − 1
    for w₃ = w₇ + 4:w₂ − 1
        for w₄ = w₇ + 3:w₃ − 1
            for w₅ = w₇ + 2:w₄ − 1
                for w₆ = w₇ + 1:w₅ − 1
```

$$(15.5)$$

$$\boxed{\text{Check } [p_1, p_2, p_3 \; / \; w_1, w_2, w_3, w_4, w_5, w_6, w_7]}$$

The loop ranges require an explanation. Since $w_6 > w_7$, it follows that w_6 must be at least $w_7 + 1$. Since $w_5 > w_6$, it follows that w_5 must be at least $w_7 + 2$, etc. Thus, the loop in charge of w_i begins at $w_7 + 7 - i$.

The size of the search space has been drastically reduced as a result of our observations about redundant checking. Now there are "just"

$$N_2 \approx 10^7 \tag{15.6}$$

bicycles to check. A computer able to evaluate 10,000 bikes per second would require about 20 minutes to find the optimum bicycle. This is certainly feasible for our 10-parameter design problem. However, let us pretend that it takes one second to evaluate ϕ. Now the search computation takes a couple of months and we are driven to consider an alternative strategy.

One idea is to confine the search for $w_2, \ldots, w_6$ to a set of short intervals. For example, suppose our intuition about gear ratio design tells us that

$$\tilde{w}_2 = 28 \qquad \tilde{w}_3 = 25 \qquad \tilde{w}_4 = 22 \qquad \tilde{w}_5 = 19 \qquad \tilde{w}_6 = 16 \tag{15.7}$$

are good estimates for the optimal $w_2, \ldots, w_6$. We could then proceed to just check out "nearby" choices. For example, we could insist that w_i equal $\tilde{w}_i - 1$, $\tilde{w}_i$, or $\tilde{w}_i + 1$. With these restrictions (15.5) transforms into

$$
\begin{array}{l}
\text{for } w_2 = \tilde{w}_2 - 1 : \tilde{w}_2 + 1 \\
\quad \text{for } w_3 = \tilde{w}_3 - 1 : \tilde{w}_3 + 1 \\
\qquad \text{for } w_4 = \tilde{w}_4 - 1 : \tilde{w}_4 + 1 \\
\qquad\quad \text{for } w_5 = \tilde{w}_5 - 1 : \tilde{w}_5 + 1 \\
\qquad\qquad \text{for } w_6 = \tilde{w}_6 - 1 : \tilde{w}_6 + 1 \\
\qquad\qquad\qquad \boxed{\text{Check } [p_1, p_2, p_3 \;/\; w_1, w_2, w_3, w_4, w_5, w_6, w_7]}
\end{array}
\tag{15.8}
$$

This reduces the number of bicycles to check to about

$$N_3 \approx 64000. \tag{15.9}$$

However, the ensuing reduction in execution time involves a hidden danger. If our intuition is wrong, then the optimal bicycle might not be discovered by the above process. For example, if the optimal bicycle has $w_2 = 30$, then it will not be among the bicycles that are evaluated by (15.7)–(15.8). Nevertheless, let us proceed to see how well our restricted search idea plays out. We start by defining a useful structure for representing a bicycle. Refer to the function `MakeBike` given below. We have chosen to use a 4-field structure that packages the vector of pedal sprockets in `B.p`, the vector of the wheel sprockets in `B.w`, the sorted gear ratios in `B.G`, and the value of the objective function in `B.phiVal`. Notice that we are using a structure array to represent the 21 gear ratios, as it is necessary to represent the ratios $r_1, \ldots, r_{21}$ *and* the p and w values that produce them.

We are now set to implement a function that returns the best bike subject to constraints $\tilde{C}_1$, $\tilde{C}_2$, $\tilde{C}_3$, and $\tilde{C}_4$, with the added proviso that we only check bikes that have wheel sprockets $w_2, \ldots, w_6$ that are near $\tilde{w}_2, \ldots, \tilde{w}_6$. In the function `BestBike` that follows, the lower and upper loop bounds for w_i ensure that we only check bicycles that satisfy $w_{i+1} < w_i < w_{i-1}$ *and* $|w_i - \tilde{w}_i| \leq 1$.

We return to the point made earlier that our restricted search strategy may fail to compute the best bicycle because of a flawed choice for $\tilde{\omega}_2, \ldots, \tilde{\omega}_6$. A hint that this may be

The Function `MakeBike`

```
function B = MakeBike(p,w)
% p is a length-3 vector of pedal sprocket values
% w is a length-7 vector of wheel sprocket values.
% B is a structure with 4 fields:
%     p is the vector of pedal sprocket values
%     w is the vector of wheel sprocket values
%     G is a length-21 structure array with three fields...
%       G(k).r  is the kth gear ratio
%       G(k).i  is the index of the associated pedal sprocket
%       G(k).j  is the index of the associated wheel sprocket
%     phiVal is the value of the phi for B

% Compute the gear ratios...
k = 0;
for i=1:3
   for j=1:7
      k = k+1;
      r(k) = p(i)/w(j);
      G(k) = struct('i',i,'j',j,'r',r(k));
   end
end

% Sort and evaluate the objective function...
[r,idx] = sort(r);
G = G(idx);
phiVal = 0;
for k=1:21
   phiVal = phiVal + abs(r(k) - (1+.15*(k-1)));
end

% Create B...
B = struct('p',p,'w',w,'G',G,'phiVal',phiVal);
```

the case can be deduced from the output to a `BestBike` call. For example, if

$$\texttt{wTilde(2:6)} \quad = \quad 23 \quad 17 \quad 16 \quad 14 \quad 13$$

then `BestBike` returns a bicycle with optimum wheel sprockets 2 through 6 given by

$$\texttt{w(2:6)} \quad = \quad 24 \quad 18 \quad 16 \quad 14 \quad 13.$$

It would seem that the search process was "blocked" at the upper bound constraints for the second and third wheel sprockets. Thus, it makes sense to redo the search with a revised constraints on w_2 and w_3. Instead of

$$22 \leq w_2 \leq 24$$

we should try

$$24 \leq w_2 \leq 26.$$

Likewise, instead of $16 \leq w_3 \leq 18$ we should try $18 \leq w_3 \leq 20$. When we make these changes, the bicycle returned by `BestBike` renders a smaller ϕ-evaluation.

The Function `BestBike`

```
function B = BestBike(wTilde)
% The entries in wTilde(2:6) are initial guesses for B.w(i),
% for i=2:6.
% B is the best bike subject to constraints  C1, C2, C3(tilde),
% and C4(tilde) with the added stipulation that for i=2:6 we have
%           wTilde(i)-1 <= B.w(i) <= wTilde(i)+1

phiValBest = inf;
for p1 = [48 52]
   for p2 = 33:p1-1
      for p3 = 32:min(42,p2-1)
         w1 = p3;
         w7 = p1/4;

         min2 = max(w7+5,wTilde(2)-1);
         max2 = min(wTilde(2)+1,w1-1);
         for w2 = min2:max2

            min3 = max(w7+4,wTilde(3)-1);
            max3 = min(wTilde(3)+1,w2-1);
            for w3 = min3:max3

               min4 = max(w7+3,wTilde(4)-1);
               max4 = min(wTilde(4)+1,w3-1);
               for w4 = min4:max4

                  min5 = max(w7+2,wTilde(5)-1);
                  max5 = min(wTilde(5)+1,w4-1);
                  for w5 = min5:max5

                     min6 = max(w7+1,wTilde(6)-1);
                     max6 = min(wTilde(6)+1,w5-1);
                     for w6 = min6:max6

                        % Construct the bike defined by p and w
                        p = [p1 p2 p3];
                        w = [w1 w2 w3 w4 w5 w6 w7];

                        % See if it is the best bike found so far
                        B = MakeBike(p,w);
                        if B.phiVal<phiValBest
                           B_best = B;
                           phiValBest = B.phiVal;
                        end

                     end
                   :
                :
           :
end
B = B_best;
```

The script `Eg15_2` automates this "movable boundary" revision process. The iteration is terminated as soon as the new `wTilde(2:6)` is the same as the current

The Script `Eg15_2`

```
% Script Eg15_2
% Find the best bike.

% Initial guess for w(2:6)...
wTilde(2:6) = [ 22 16 15 14 13];
B = BestBike(wTilde);
its = 1;
while its==1 || (diff>0 && its<=10)
   % Display the current best bike...
      :
   % Revise the search space and try again...
   wTildeNew(2:6) = [B.w(2) B.w(3) B.w(4) B.w(5) B.w(6)];
   diff = max(abs(wTildeNew(2:6) - wTilde(2:6)));
   wTilde = wTildeNew; B = BestBike(wTilde); its = its + 1;
end
```

Sample Output from the Script `Eg15_2`

```
Pedal Sprockets = [ 48   46   34 ]
Wheel Sprockets = [ 34   26   21   16   14   13   12 ]
wTilde(2:6)     =        26   21   16   14   13

   pedal   wheel      ratio
   ----------------------------
      3       1        1.000
      3       2        1.308
      2       1        1.353
      1       1        1.412
      3       3        1.619
      2       2        1.769
      1       2        1.846
      3       4        2.125
      2       3        2.190
      1       3        2.286
      3       5        2.429
      3       6        2.615
      3       7        2.833
      2       4        2.875
      1       4        3.000
      2       5        3.286
      1       5        3.429
      2       6        3.538
      1       6        3.692
      2       7        3.833
      1       7        4.000

phi =   0.904
```

`wTilde(2:6)`. Note that even with these changes we cannot guarantee that `Eg15_2` returns the absolutely best bike. To inspire more confidence in the solution, we could widen the range of the restricted searches, e.g., $\tilde{w}_2 - 2 \leq w_2 \leq \tilde{w}_2 + 2$. However, such modifications would increase the size of the search space and the running time of the script.

Talking Point: The Design Process

In this section we solved a 10-parameter discrete design problem. This is a *tiny* problem considering that in many applications there may be tens of thousands of design parameters, e.g., the design of an automobile engine. Thus, tools are needed to navigate the combinatoric explosion of possibilities.

For example, having a nice graphical user interface (GUI) that makes it easy for a human being to assess the status of an optimal design search is important. More powerful are GUIs that permit the designer to "nudge" the algorithmic search in a profitable direction. This is the philosophy behind the development of computer aided design (CAD) tools. Modern engineering would be inconceivable without CAD tools to handle complexity.

For continuous optimization problems, search techniques usually rely upon the tools provided by advanced calculus. Such methods are able to steer one towards the critical points of a multivariable objective function by making intelligent use of derivatives. The truly Fundamental Theorem of Calculus is that rate-of-change information is priceless!

Analogous tools exist for discrete objective functions despite the absence of formal derivatives. The movable boundary idea implemented in `BestBike` illustrates this point. It is the discrete version of how we might look for the minimum value of a function f whose derivative f' is either positive or negative across an interval $[L, R]$. If f' is positive, look to the left of L. If f' is negative, look to the right of R.

Exercises

M15.2.1 Modify the objective function ϕ so that gear ratios 5 through 15 are as close as possible to $2.0, 2.1, \ldots, 3.0$. Disregard gear ratios 1 through 4 and 16 through 21.

M15.2.2 Justify the approximations (15.6) and (15.9).

P15.2.3 Gears determined by the largest pedal sprocket and the largest wheel sprocket (p_1/w_1), and the smallest pedal sprocket and the smallest wheel sprocket (p_3/w_7), tend to be unstable because the chain is highly skewed for these combinations. Change the objective function so that the 19 "good gears" have ratios that are as close as possible to $1 + (k-1)(3/18)$, $k = 1, \ldots, 19$.

P15.2.4 A gear ratio r is low if $1 \leq r < 2$, medium if $2 \leq r \leq 3$, and high if $3 < r \leq 4$. Develop an objective function that expresses a preference for bikes that have 10 uniformly spaced low gear ratios, 7 uniformly spaced medium gear ratios, and 4 uniformly spaced high gear ratios. In addition, the function should also "reward" bikes that have ratios 2 and 3.

P15.2.5 Assume that the cost of a sprocket is proportional to the number of teeth. If $\lambda \geq 0$, then

$$\tilde{\phi}(p_1, p_2, p_3, w_1, w_2, w_3, w_4, w_5, w_6, w_7) = \sum_{k=1}^{21} |r_k - \tilde{r}_k| + \lambda \left(\sum_{i=1}^{3} p_i + \sum_{i=1}^{7} w_i \right)$$

is an objective function that takes into consideration both the distribution of the gear ratios *and* the cost associated with the sprocket choice. How does the value of λ affect the design of the optimum bike?

P15.2.6 Repeat the design problem in this section under the assumption that there are to be just two pedal sprockets and five wheel sprockets.

15.3 Most Likely Orbit

Problem Statement

A well-known data-fitting problem involves finding a line $y = a + bx$ that best approximates a given set of points $(x_1, y_1), \ldots, (x_n, y_n)$. See Figure 15.5. A commonly used goodness-of-fit measure is the sum of the squares of the discrepancies between the points and the line, i.e.,

$$\phi(a,b) = \sqrt{\sum_{k=1}^{n} |(a + bx_i) - y_i|^2} \, .$$

This is an example of *least squares fitting*, and in this case there are simple formulae for the solution. Suppose

$$\bar{x} = \frac{1}{n} \sum_{k=1}^{n} x_k \qquad \sigma_{xx} = \frac{1}{n} \sum_{k=1}^{n} (x_i - \bar{x})^2$$

$$\bar{y} = \frac{1}{n} \sum_{k=1}^{n} y_k \qquad \sigma_{xy} = \frac{1}{n} \sum_{k=1}^{n} (x_i - \bar{x})(y_i - \bar{y})$$

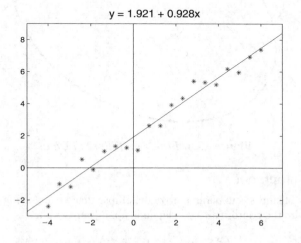

y = 1.921 + 0.928x

Figure 15.5. *Fitting a Line to Data.*

It can be shown using calculus that if

$$b_{opt} = \sigma_{xy}/\sigma_{xx} \qquad a_{opt} = \bar{y} - b_{opt}\bar{x},$$

then $\phi(a_{opt}, b_{opt})$ is minimum.

Least squares fitting plays a prominent role in science, serving as a bridge between experimental data and the design of a model that explains the data. For example, a plant scientist might conjecture that the height H attained by a particular species of plant is a function of the form $a + bS$, where S is the hours of sunlight that it receives during the summer. The coefficients a and b are *model parameters* and are to be determined. To that end, n experiments are performed. In experiment i, a single plant is exposed to S_i hours of sunlight and the resulting height H_i is measured. The least squares fitting formulae given above can be used to determine the line $H = a_{opt} + b_{opt}S$ that best fits the data (S_i, H_i), $i = 1:n$. If the fit is good, then the linear model is affirmed. If not, then it may be necessary to rethink the model or the set of experiments. This kind of interplay between computation, experimentation, and model building is at the heart of modern science.

Of course, rarely are situations so simple that they boil down to the fitting of a line to data. To build an appreciation for the complexities of nonlinear data fitting and the challenge of choosing the right quality-of-fit metric, we consider the problem of fitting an ellipse to experimentally determined orbital data. See Figure 15.6. Assume that $(x_1, y_1), \ldots, (x_n, y_n)$ are approximate locations of a comet that is orbiting the Sun, which we position at $(0,0)$. According to Kepler, the comet follows an elliptical orbit with one of its two foci at $(0,0)$. What is the best fitting ellipse to the data?

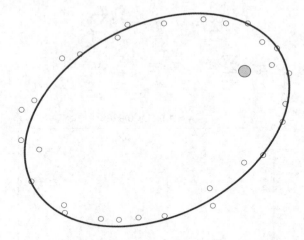

Figure 15.6. *Fitting an Ellipse to Data.*

Program Development

The first order of business is to parameterize the ellipse that we are trying to find. An ellipse that is aligned with the coordinate axes depends upon four parameters:

$$\left(\frac{x - x_c}{a}\right)^2 + \left(\frac{y - y_c}{b}\right)^2 = 1.$$

Here, (x_c, y_c) is the center and a and b are the semiaxes. An equivalent parametric description is

$$x(t) = x_c + a\cos(t)$$
$$y(t) = y_c + b\sin(t)$$

where $0 \le t \le 2\pi$. A fifth parameter θ is required if we allow the ellipse to be tilted:

$$x(t) = x_c + a\cos(t)\cos(\theta) - b\sin(t)\sin(\theta)$$
$$y(t) = y_c + a\cos(t)\sin(\theta) + b\sin(t)\cos(\theta).$$

The parameter θ is the counterclockwise rotation angle.

Our data fitting problem requires the ellipse to have one of its two foci positioned at the origin. For a general ellipse, with center (x_c, y_c), major semiaxis a, minor semiaxis b, and tilt θ, the two foci are given by

$$F_1 = (x_c + c\cos(\theta), \, y_c + c\sin(\theta))$$
$$F_2 = (x_c - c\cos(\theta), \, y_c - c\sin(\theta))$$

where

$$c = \sqrt{a^2 - b^2}.$$

It follows that we are looking at a 5-parameter constrained optimization problem:

> Determine the parameters x_c, y_c, a, b, and θ subject to the constraint $F_1 = (0,0)$ so that the resulting ellipse "best fits" the given data $(x_1, y_1), \ldots, (x_n, y_n)$.

From the computational point of view, it is much handier to work with an alternative orbit representation that is tailored to our problem:

$$x(t) = \left[\frac{P - A}{2} + \frac{P + A}{2}\cos(t)\right]\cos(\theta) - \left[\sqrt{AP}\sin(t)\right]\sin(\theta) \tag{15.10}$$

$$y(t) = \left[\frac{P - A}{2} + \frac{P + A}{2}\cos(t)\right]\sin(\theta) + \left[\sqrt{AP}\sin(t)\right]\cos(\theta). \tag{15.11}$$

This is a 3-parameter characterization of an ellipse that has one of its foci at $(0,0)$. P is the minimum distance from a point on the ellipse to the origin, while A is the maximum distance. These are, respectively, the *perihelion* and *aphelion* attributes of the orbit. Refer to Figure 15.7 in which the displayed ellipse has tilt $\theta = \pi/6$.

Let $\mathcal{E}(P, A, \theta)$ denote the ellipse defined by (15.10)–(15.11). An advantage of this representation is that it transforms the 5-parameter constrained optimization problem into a 3-parameter unconstrained optimization problem:

> Determine the parameters P, A, and θ so that the resulting ellipse "best fits" the given data $(x_1, y_1), \ldots, (x_n, y_n)$.

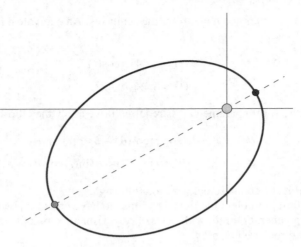

Figure 15.7. *An Ellipse with* $F_1 = (0,0)$.

It often pays to reduce the dimension of the search space. We are now just looking for three things without restriction instead of five things with restriction.

So far we have been vague about the meaning of "best fits." One possibility is to choose the three parameters so that

$$\phi(P, A, \theta) \;=\; \sum_{i=1}^{n} d_i^2$$

is minimized, where d_i is the Euclidean distance from (x_i, y_i) to the $\mathcal{E}(P, A, \theta)$. This is an example of nonlinear least squares fitting.

We will use a different goodness-of-fit metric that is simpler and enables us to develop an interactive point-and-click framework that can be used to carry out an approximate optimization. It is based on the idea that if (x, y) is on $\mathcal{E}(P, A, \theta)$, then the sum of its distance to foci $F_1 = (0,0)$ and its distance to foci

$$F_2 \;=\; ((P - A)\cos(\theta),\, (P - A)\sin(\theta))$$

is a constant s where

$$s = A + P.$$

This mathematical fact can be turned into a practical method for drawing an ellipse given two pins and a length-s piece of string that connects them. Locate the pins at the desired foci. By "pushing out" with a pencil against the string, an ellipse will be traced. See Figure 15.8. If we know $F_2 = (\alpha, \beta)$ and s, then it can be shown that

$$\theta = \arctan(\beta/\alpha) \tag{15.12}$$

$$P = \left(s - \sqrt{\alpha^2 + \beta^2}\,\right)/2 \tag{15.13}$$

$$A = \left(s + \sqrt{\alpha^2 + \beta^2}\,\right)/2. \tag{15.14}$$

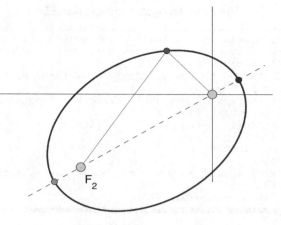

Figure 15.8. $\mathcal{E}(P, A, \theta)$ *via s and* F_2.

The point of working with the $\mathcal{E}(\alpha, \beta, s)$ representation instead of the $\mathcal{E}(P, A, \theta)$ representation is that we can enter $F_2 = (\alpha, \beta)$ via the mouse and then generate an intelligent estimate of the "string length" s. Indeed, given the data $(x_1, y_1), \ldots, (x_n, y_n)$, we define for $i = 1{:}n$ the string-length estimates

$$s_i = \sqrt{x_i^2 + y_i^2} + \sqrt{(x_i - \alpha)^2 + (y_i - \beta)^2}$$

and their average

$$\bar{s} = \frac{1}{n} \sum_{i=1}^{n} s_i.$$

If the data is exactly on the ellipse with second focus F_2, then we would have $s_i = \bar{s}$ for $i = 1{:}n$. If not, then

$$\phi(\alpha, \beta, \bar{s}) = \sqrt{\sum_{i=1}^{n} |s_i - \bar{s}|^2}$$

can be regarded as a least squares measure of how well $\mathcal{E}(\alpha, \beta, \bar{s})$ fits the data.

We write two functions to support the point-and-click minimization of ϕ. The function GetFocusAndString solicits the second focus F_2 and computes the average of the string-length estimates and the goodness-of-fit. The function ShowEllipse graphically displays an ellipse with specified second focus and string length. The implementation of these functions is given below.

The script Eg15_3 uses these functions to manage an improvement framework whereby the user tries to fit some noisy orbital data. The data is obtained by using randn to contaminate points that are exactly on an ellipse. After entering an initial approximation, nine chances are given to improve upon the fit. A sample approximating ellipse is displayed in Figure 15.9.

The Function `GetFocusAndString`

```
function [alpha,beta,sbar,phiVal] = GetFocusAndString(x,y)
% x and y are column n-vectors that represent approximate
%      orbital points.
% alpha and beta are the xy-coordinates of focus F2, obtained
%      via ginput.
% sbar is the average of the string-length estimates s(i).
% phiVal is the square root of
%      |s(i)-stilde|^2 + ... + |s(n)-stilde|^2.

[alpha,beta] = ginput(1);
n = length(x);
sVec = sqrt(x.^2 + y.^2) + sqrt((x-alpha).^2 + (y-beta).^2);
sbar = sum(sVec)/n;
phiVal = sqrt(sum((sVec-sbar).^2)/n);
```

The Function `ShowEllipse`

```
function ShowEllipse(alpha,beta,s,phiVal)
% Adds the ellipse with focus F2 = (alpha,beta) and string
% length s to the current figure window. Displays F2 in the
% figure window and the input parameters in the title.

% Obtain perihelion, aphelion, and tilt...
A = (s+sqrt(alpha^2+beta^2))/2;
P = (s-sqrt(alpha^2+beta^2))/2;
theta = atan(beta/alpha);

% Plot...
    :
```

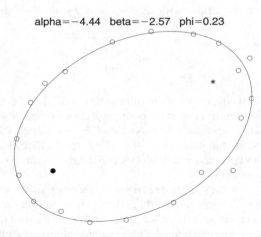

alpha=−4.44 beta=−2.57 phi=0.23

Figure 15.9. *Sample Output from the Script* `Eg15_3`.

The Script Eg15_3

```
% Script Eg15_3
% Fitting an ellipse to data

% Generate noisy orbit data...
NoiseFactor = .2;
P = 1; A = 6; theta = pi/6;
n = 20; t = linspace(0,2*pi,n);
x1 = (P-A)/2 + ((P+A)/2)*cos(t); y1 = sqrt(A*P)*sin(t);
x = cos(theta)*x1-sin(theta)*y1; y = sin(theta)*x1+cos(theta)*y1;
x = x + NoiseFactor*randn(1,n);  y = y + NoiseFactor*randn(1,n);

% Solicit and display the first approximation...
close all; axis equal off; hold on
plot(x,y,'or',0,0,'*k')
[alpha,beta,sbar,phiValBest] = GetFocusAndString(x,y);
ShowEllipse(alpha,beta,sbar,phiValBest)

% Try to improve the fit...
nTries = 10;
for Try = 2:nTries
    [alpha,beta,sbar,phiVal] = GetFocusAndString(x,y);
    if phiVal < phiValBest
        % Redisplay if an improvement...
        phiValBest = phiVal;
        close all; axis equal off; hold on
        plot(x,y,'or',0,0,'*k')
        ShowEllipse(alpha,beta,sbar,phiValBest)
    end
end
```

Talking Point: Science and Engineering with the Computer

Design is typically the province of engineering while model building is usually associated with science. Nevertheless, the two activities have much in common. Indeed, when computation is involved, there is really only a single, four-step research methodology.

Step 1. Identify What Is Important

Engineer: Determine the key attributes of the object to be built. These are the design parameters.

Scientist: Determine the key factors that characterize the phenomena to be explained. These are the model parameters.

Step 2. Choose a Metric to Measure Success

Engineer: Determine a function of the design parameters that is good to optimize. This is the objective function.

Scientist: Determine a function of the model parameters that quantifies how close the model comes to predicting the phenomena. This is the goodness-of-fit function.

Step 3. Compute, Compute, Compute

Engineer: Optimize the objective function subject to constraints on the
design parameters.

Scientist: Optimize the goodness-of-fit function subject to constraints on
the model parameters.

Step 4. Analyze and Refine

Engineer: Contemplate the revision of the design space based on the optimized
value of the objective function.

Scientist: Contemplate the revision of the underlying model based on how
well the computed model captures reality.

Appreciate the role of the computer in each step. In particular, it supports complexity in
Steps 1 and 2 and stimulates creativity in Step 4.

The parallels between engineering and science are bound to become more striking as
the role of computation increases. The aeronautical engineer who is designing an airfoil has
much in common with the mathematical ornithologist who is modeling bird flight. Welcome
to the world of computational science and engineering.

Exercises

M15.3.1 Modify Eg15_3 so that the initial F_2 is $(2\bar{x}, 2\bar{y})$, where $(\bar{x}, \bar{y})$ is the centroid of the
orbital data. Why does this make sense?

P15.3.2 For a given set of data points, produce an $\alpha\beta$ contour plot of the objective function
$\phi(\alpha, \beta, \bar{s})$. (Note that $\bar{s}$ is a function of α and β.)

P15.3.3 Consider the problem of fitting the line

$$y = a + bx$$

to the data points $(x_1, y_1), \ldots, (x_n, y_n)$. Develop an interactive environment that facilitates the minimization of

$$\psi(a, b) = \sum_{k=1}^{n} |(a + bx_i) - y_i|.$$

This kind of fitting handles *outliers* better than least squares. An outlier is a data point that "bucks
the trend" defined by its neighbors. Confirm this experimentally.

P15.3.4 Write a function [a,b] = WeightedLS(x,y,w) that minimizes

$$\phi(a, b) = \sum_{k=1}^{n} w_i |(a + bx_i) - y_i|^2$$

where the w_i are positive "weights." Note that if we increase a particular weight relative to the
others, then the fitting line will tend to go through that point. Confirm this through experimentation.

Appendix A

Refined Graphics

The following are techniques that can be used to produce nice-looking graphics. It is also possible to realize these refinements by using the MATLAB Figure Editor. See MatTV-16.

A.1   Scaling Axes

By using `axis equal` and `axis square` you can control axis scaling.

The Script `ShowAxisStyles`

```
% Script: ShowAxisStyles
% How to scale the axes.

theta = linspace(0,2*pi);
x = cos(theta);
y = sin(theta);
close all

figure
plot(x,y)
title('Autoscaling','Fontsize',14)

figure
plot(x,y)
axis equal
title('axis equal','Fontsize',14)

figure
plot(x,y)
axis equal square
title('axis equal square','Fontsize',14)

figure
plot(x,y)
axis([-1.2 1.2 -1.2 1.2])
title('axis([-1.2 1.2 -1.2 1.2])','Fontsize',14)

figure
plot(x,y)
axis([-1.2 1.2 -1.2 1.2])
axis equal
title('axis([-1.2 1.2 -1.2 1.2]); axis equal','Fontsize',14)

figure
plot(x,y)
axis([-1.2 1.2 -1.2 1.2])
axis equal square
title('axis([-1.2 1.2 -1.2 1.2]); axis square','Fontsize',14)
```

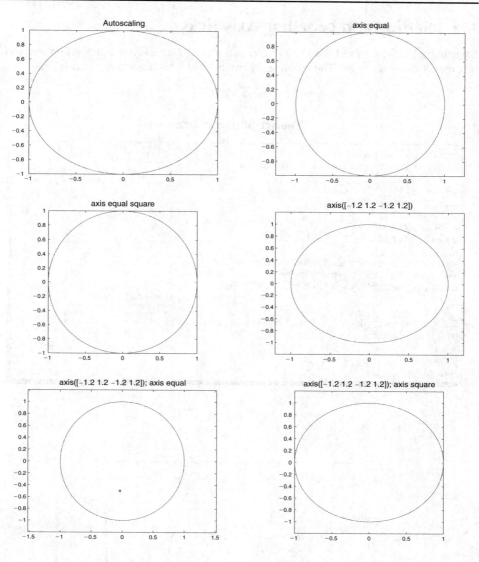

A.2   Setting and Labelling Axis Ticks

By using xTick, xTickLabel, yTick, and yTickLabel you can position and label
tick marks along the axes. These define where the grid lines are when grid is on.

The Script ShowTicks

```
% Script: ShowTicks
% How to set and label axis ticks.

close all
x = linspace(0,4*pi);
y = sin(x);
plot(x,y)
axis([0 4*pi -1.2 1.2])

% Define x-ticks and their labels..
set(gca,'xTick',0:pi/2:4*pi)
set(gca,'xTickLabel',{'0', ' ', 'pi', ' ', '2pi',...
                         ' ', '3pi', ' ', '4pi'})

% Define y-ticks and let them be auto-labelled...
set(gca,'yTick',-1:.5:1)

grid on
shg
```

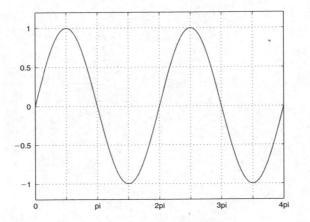

A.3   Fancy Labelling

It is possible to display subscripted variables using `text`, `xlabel`, `ylabel`, and `title`.

The Script ShowFancyLabelling

```
% Script: ShowFancyLabelling
% How to label points with subscripted variable names.

close all
r = 1; t = pi/6 + linspace(0,2*pi,7);
x = r*cos(t); y = r*sin(t); plot(x,y);
axis equal off
HA = 'HorizontalAlignment'; VA = 'VerticalAlignment';
text(x(1),y(1),'\leftarrow {\itP}_{1}',...
                    HA,'left','FontSize',14)
text(x(2),y(2),'\downarrow',...
                    HA,'center',VA,'baseline','FontSize',14)
text(x(2),y(2),'{\itP}_{2}',   ...
                    HA,'left',VA,'bottom','FontSize',14)
text(x(3),y(3),'{\itP}_{3} \rightarrow',...
                    HA,'right','FontSize',14)
text(x(4),y(4),'{\itP}_{4} \rightarrow', ...
                    HA,'right','FontSize',14)
text(x(5),y(5),'\uparrow',...
                    HA,'center',VA,'top','FontSize',14)
text(x(5),y(5),'{\itP}_{5}   ', ...
                    HA,'right',VA,'top','FontSize',14)
text(x(6),y(6),'\leftarrow {\itP}_{6}',...
                    HA,'left','FontSize',14)
text(0,.4*r,'A Labelled Hexagon^{1}',...
                    HA,'center','FontSize',14)
text(0,-.4*r,'^{1} A hexagon has six sides.',...
                    HA,'center','FontSize',10)
```

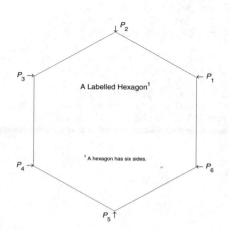

A.4   Aligning Text

text(x,y,s) displays the string s at coordinate (x,y). It is possible to control whether the string is above, below, to the right of, or to the left of (x,y).

The Script ShowTextAlignment

```
% Script: ShowTextAlignment
% How to place text relative to a coordinate point.
close all
HA = 'HorizontalAlignment'; HV = 'VerticalAlignment';

figure, plot(0,0,'*'), axis([-1 1 -1 1]), axis equal square
set(gca,'xTick',[-1 0 1],'yTick',[-1 0 1])
grid on
text(0,0,'  (0,0)  ',HA,'left',...
                     'color','r','Fontweight','bold')
title('Left edge of text aligned.')

figure, plot(0,0,'*'), axis([-1 1 -1 1]), axis equal square
set(gca,'xTick',[-1 0 1],'yTick',[-1 0 1])
grid on
text(0,0,'  (0,0)  ',HA,'right',...
                     'color','r','Fontweight','bold')
title('Right edge of text aligned.')

figure, plot(0,0,'*'), axis([-1 1 -1 1]), axis equal square
set(gca,'xTick',[-1 0 1],'yTick',[-1 0 1])
grid on
text(0,0,'  (0,0)  ',HA,'center',...
                     'color','r','Fontweight','bold')
title('Center of text aligned.')

figure, plot(0,0,'*'), axis([-1 1 -1 1]), axis equal square
set(gca,'xTick',[-1 0 1],'yTick',[-1 0 1])
grid on
text(0,0,'  (0,0)  ',HA,'left',HV,'top',...
                     'color','r','Fontweight','bold')
title('Left top edge of text aligned.')

figure, plot(0,0,'*'), axis([-1 1 -1 1]), axis equal square
set(gca,'xTick',[-1 0 1],'yTick',[-1 0 1])
grid on
text(0,0,'  (0,0)  ',HA,'right',HV,'bottom',...
                     'color','r','Fontweight','bold')
title('Right bottom edge of text aligned.')
```

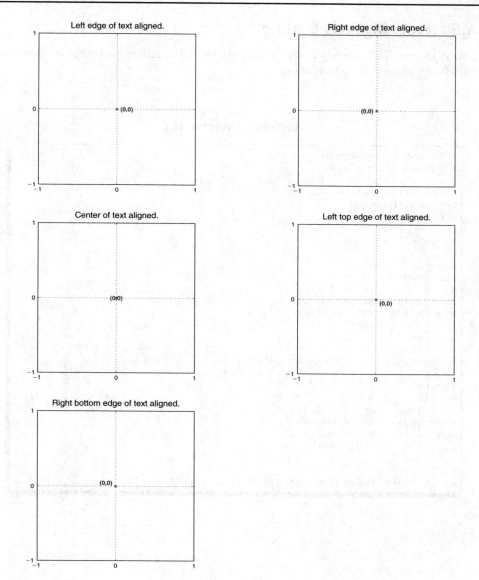

A.5   Freezing Axis Scaling

Use `axis manual` when you want to keep the same axis scaling and range as additional objects are added to the plot window.

The Script ShowManual

```
% Script: ShowManual
% How to freeze axes.

theta = linspace(0,2*pi);
c = cos(theta);
s = sin(theta);

close all

figure
plot(c,s)
axis([-1.2 1.2 -1.2 1.2])
axis equal square
x = -2 + 4*rand(500,1);
y = -2 + 4*rand(500,1);
hold on
plot(x,y,'.')
title('axes not frozen at [-1.2 1.2 -1.2 1.2]')

figure
plot(c,s)
axis([-1.2 1.2 -1.2 1.2])
axis equal square manual
x = -2 + 4*rand(500,1);
y = -2 + 4*rand(500,1);
hold on
plot(x,y,'.')
title('axes frozen at [-1.2 1.2 -1.2 1.2]')
```

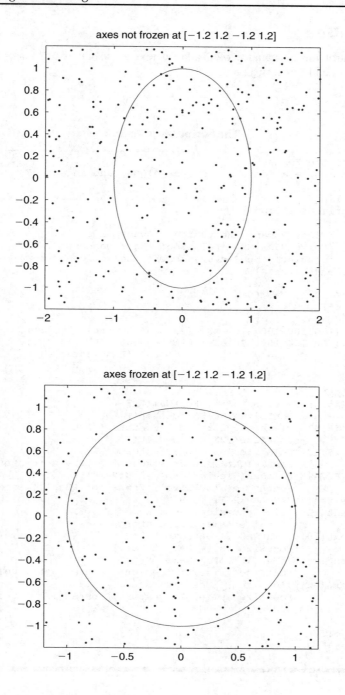

A.6   Fonts

You can control the appearance of displayed text by using FontName, Fontsize, Fontweight, and FontAngle.

The Script ShowFonts

```
% Script: ShowFonts
% How to choose a font, a size, a weight, and an angle.

close all
HA = 'HorizontalAlign';

fonts = {'Times-Roman' 'Helvetica' 'AvantGarde' ...
         'Comic Sans MS' 'Palatino' 'ZapfChancery' ...
         'Courier' 'NewCenturySchlbk' 'Helvetica-Narrow'};
for k=1:length(fonts)
   figure
   axis([-20 100 -5 60])
   axis off
   hold on
   fill([-20 100 100 -20 -20],[-5  -5  60  60  -5],'w')
   plot([-20 100 100 -20 -20],[-5  -5  60  60  -5],'k',...
                                   'Linewidth',3)


   v=38;
   F = fonts{k};
   text(45,55,F,'color','r','FontName',F,...
           'FontSize',24,HA,'center')
   text(10,47,'Plain','color','b','FontName',F,...
           'FontSize',22,HA,'center')
   text(45,47,'Bold','color','b','FontName',F,...
           'Fontweight','bold', 'FontSize',22,HA,'center')
   text(82,47,'Oblique','color','b','FontName',F,...
           'FontAngle','oblique','FontSize',22,HA,'center')
   for size=[22 18 14 12 11 10 9]
       text(-12,v,int2str(size),'FontName',F,...
             'FontSize',size,HA,'center')
       text(10,v,'Matlab','FontName',F,...
             'FontSize',size,HA,'center')
       text(45,v,'Matlab','FontName',F,...
             'FontSize',size,HA,'center','FontWeight','bold')
       text(82,v,'Matlab','FontName',F,...
             'FontSize',size,HA,'center','FontAngle','oblique')
       v = v-6;
   end
   hold off
   pause(1)
end
```

Helvetica–Narrow			
	Plain	**Bold**	*Oblique*
22	Matlab	**Matlab**	*Matlab*
18	Matlab	**Matlab**	*Matlab*
14	Matlab	**Matlab**	*Matlab*
12	Matlab	**Matlab**	*Matlab*
11	Matlab	**Matlab**	*Matlab*
10	Matlab	**Matlab**	*Matlab*
9	Matlab	**Matlab**	*Matlab*

A.7   Greek Symbols

It is possible to use Greek letters displayed by text, xlabel, ylabel, and title.

The Script ShowGreek

```
% Script: ShowGreek
% How to produce Greek letters.

close all
figure
axis off
hold on
fill([-1 12 12 -1 -1],[-1 -1 12 12 -1],'w')
plot([-1 12 12 -1 -1],[-1 -1 12 12 -1],'k','Linewidth',3)

text(3,10,'Greek Symbols','color','r','FontSize',18)
x = 0; x1 = x+.7;
y = 4; y1 = y+.7;
z = 8; z1 = z+.7;


text(x,8,'\alpha :');     text(x1,8,'\\alpha')
text(x,7,'\beta :');      text(x1,7,'\\beta')
text(x,6,'\gamma :');     text(x1,6,'\\gamma')
text(x,5,'\delta :');     text(x1,5,'\\delta')
text(x,4,'\epsilon :');   text(x1,4,'\\epsilon')
text(x,3,'\kappa :');     text(x1,3,'\\kappa')
text(x,2,'\lambda :');    text(x1,2,'\\lambda')
text(x,1,'\mu :');        text(x1,1,'\\mu')
text(x,0,'\nu :');        text(x1,0,'\\nu')

text(y,8,'\omega :');     text(y1,8,'\\omega')
text(y,7,'\phi :');       text(y1,7,'\\phi')
text(y,6,'\pi :');        text(y1,6,'\\pi')
text(y,5,'\chi :');       text(y1,5,'\\chi')
text(y,4,'\psi :');       text(y1,4,'\\psi')
text(y,3,'\rho :');       text(y1,3,'\\rho')
text(y,2,'\sigma :');     text(y1,2,'\\sigma')
text(y,1,'\tau :');       text(y1,1,'\\tau')
text(y,0,'\upsilon :');   text(y1,0,'\\upsilon')


text(z,8,'\Sigma :');     text(z1,8,'\\Sigma')
text(z,7,'\Pi :');        text(z1,7,'\\Pi')
text(z,6,'\Lambda :');    text(z1,6,'\\Lambda')
text(z,5,'\Omega :');     text(z1,5,'\\Omega')
text(z,4,'\Gamma :');     text(z1,4,'\\Gamma')
```

Greek Symbols

α : \alpha	ω : \omega	Σ : \Sigma
β : \beta	ϕ : \phi	Π : \Pi
γ : \gamma	π : \pi	Λ : \Lambda
δ : \delta	χ : \chi	Ω : \Omega
ε : \epsilon	ψ : \psi	Γ : \Gamma
κ : \kappa	ρ : \rho	
λ : \lambda	σ : \sigma	
μ : \mu	τ : \tau	
ν : \nu	υ : \upsilon	

A.8   Mathematical Symbols

Various mathematical symbols can be displayed using text, xlabel, ylabel, and title.

The Script ShowMathSymbols

```
% Script: ShowMathSymbols
% How to produce math symbols.

close all
figure
axis off
hold on
fill([0 12 12 0 0],[0 0 12 12 0],'w')
plot([0 12 12 0 0],[0 0 12 12 0],'k','Linewidth',3)
hold off
text(6,10.5,'Math Symbols','color','r',...
               'FontSize',18,'HorizontalAlign','center')
x = 1; x1 = x+.7;
y = 4.6; y1 = y+.7;
z = 9; z1 = z+.7;
n = 12;

text(y,9,'\leftarrow :');          text(y1,9,'\\leftarrow')
text(y,8,'\rightarrow :');         text(y1,8,'\\rightarrow')
text(y,7,'\uparrow :');            text(y1,7,'\\uparrow')
text(y,6,'\downarrow :');          text(y1,6,'\\downarrow')
text(y,5,'\Leftarrow :');          text(y1,5,'\\Leftarrow')
text(y,4,'\Rightarrow :');         text(y1,4,'\\Rightarrow')
text(y,3,'\Leftrightarrow :');     text(y1,3,'\\Leftrightarrow')
text(y,2,'\partial :');            text(y1,2,'\\partial')

text(x,9,'\neq :');                text(x1,9,'\\neq')
text(x,8,'\geq :');                text(x1,8,'\\geq')
text(x,7,'\approx : ');            text(x1,7,'\\approx')
text(x,6,'\equiv :');              text(x1,6,'\\equiv')
text(x,5,'\cong :');               text(x1,5,'\\cong')
text(x,4,'\pm :');                 text(x1,4,'\\pm')
text(x,3,'\nabla :');              text(x1,3,'\\nabla')
text(x,2,'\angle :');              text(x1,2,'\\angle')

text(z,9,'\in :');                 text(z1,9,'\\in')
text(z,8,'\subset :');             text(z1,8,'\\subset')
text(z,7,'\cup :');                text(z1,7,'\\cup')
text(z,6,'\cap :');                text(z1,6,'\\cap')
text(z,5,'\perp :');               text(z1,5,'\\perp')
text(z,4,'\infty :');              text(z1,4,'\\infty')
text(z,3,'\int :');                text(z1,3,'\\int')
text(z,2,'\times :');              text(z1,2,'\\times')
```

Math Symbols

$\neq$: \neq	$\leftarrow$: \leftarrow	$\in$: \in
$\geq$: \geq	$\rightarrow$: \rightarrow	$\subset$: \subset
$\approx$: \approx	$\uparrow$: \uparrow	$\cup$: \cup
$\equiv$: \equiv	$\downarrow$: \downarrow	$\cap$: \cap
$\cong$: \cong	$\Leftarrow$: \Leftarrow	$\perp$: \perp
$\pm$: \pm	$\Rightarrow$: \Rightarrow	∞ : \infty
∇ : \nabla	$\Leftrightarrow$: \Leftrightarrow	$\int$: \int
$\angle$: \angle	∂ : \partial	$\times$: \times

A.9   Legends

Legends are useful for labelling complicated plots and their location can be controlled.

The Script `ShowLegend`

```
% Script: ShowLegend
% How to position a legend.

loc = { 'North' ,        'South' ,           'East' , 'West' ,...
        'NorthEast' , 'NorthWest' ,         'SouthEast' ,...
        'SouthWest' , 'NorthOutside' , 'SouthOutside' ,...
        'EastOutside','WestOutside' ,    'NorthEastOutside',...
        'NorthWestOutside' , 'SouthEastOutside' ,...
        'SouthWestOutside' , 'Best' , 'BestOutside'  };

close all
t = linspace(0,2);
axis([0 2 -1.5 1.5])
y1 = sin(t*pi);
y2 = cos(t*pi);
plot(t,y1,t,y2,'--',[0 .5 1 1.5 2],[0 0 0 0 0],'o')
set(gca,'XTick',[])
set(gca,'YTick',[0])
grid on
for k=1:length(loc)
   legend('sin(\pi t)','cos(\pi t)','roots','location',loc{k})
   title('                                ')
   title(loc{k},'FontSize',14)
   pause
end
```

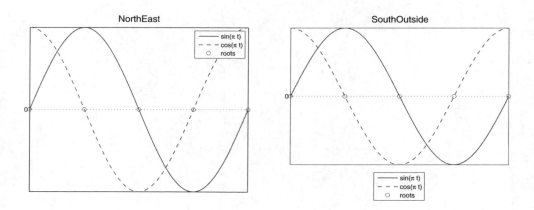

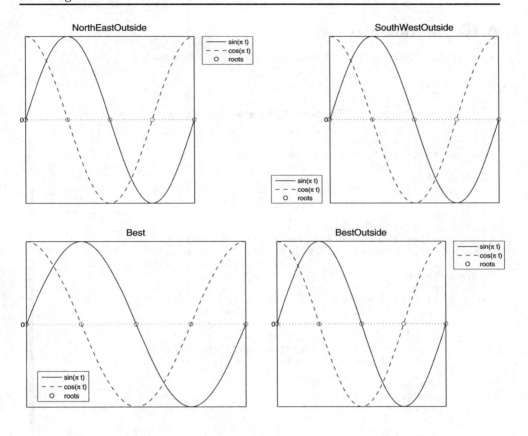

A.10 Marker Size

By using `Markersize` you can control the size of plot markers.

The Script **ShowMarkerSize**

```
% Script: ShowMarkerSize
% How to draw markers with specified size.

close all
figure
axis off
hold on
fill([0 14 14 0 0],[0 0 14 14 0],'w')
plot([0 14 14 0 0],[0 0 14 14 0],'k','Linewidth',3)
text(7,13,'Markersize','color','r','FontSize',18,...
                       'HorizontalAlign','center')
for mSize=0:10
   if mSize>0
      plot(4,11-mSize,'.k','Markersize',mSize);
      plot(5,11-mSize,'*k','Markersize',mSize);
      plot(6,11-mSize,'ok','Markersize',mSize);
      plot(7,11-mSize,'xk','Markersize',mSize);
      plot(8,11-mSize,'hk','Markersize',mSize);
      text(1,11-mSize,sprintf('%3d',mSize),'FontSize',14)
   else
      plot(4,11,'.k');
      plot(5,11,'*k');
      plot(6,11,'ok');
      plot(7,11,'xk');
      plot(8,11,'hk');
      text(1,11,'default')
   end
end
hold off
```

Markersize

default	·	*	○	×	✩
1		·	·	·	·
2		·	○	·	·
3		·	○	×	✩
4	·	*	○	×	✩
5	·	*	○	×	✩
6	·	*	○	×	✩
7	·	*	○	×	✩
8	·	*	○	×	✩
9	·	*	○	×	✩
10	·	*	○	×	✩
11	·	*	○	×	✩
12	·	*	○	×	✩
13	·	*	○	×	✩
14	·	*	○	×	✩
15	·	*	○	×	✩

A.11   Line Width

By using `LineWidth` you can control the width of plotted lines.

The Script `ShowLineWidth`

```
% Script: ShowLineWidth
% How to draw lines with specified width.
close all
figure
axis off
hold on
fill([0 14 14 0 0],[0 0 14 14 0],'w')
plot([0 14 14 0 0],[0 0 14 14 0],'k','Linewidth',3)
text(7,13,'LineWidth','color','r','FontSize',18,...
               'HorizontalAlign','center')
for width=0:10
   if width>0
      plot([3 12],[11-width 11-width],'k','Linewidth',width);
      text(1,11-width,sprintf('%3d',width),'FontSize',14)
   else
      plot([3 12],[11-width 11-width],'k');
      text(1,11-width,'default','FontSize',14)
   end
end
hold off
```

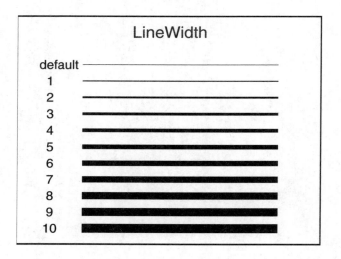

A.12   Window Colors

The plot window and the figure window can be colored.

The Script `ShowWindowColor`

```
% Script: ShowWindowColor
% How to color the plot and figure windows.
close all
figure
% Plot the sine function...
hold on
x = linspace(0,1);
plot(x,sin(2*pi*x),'k','linewidth',2)
hold on
plot([0  1],[0 0],'k')
axis([0 1,-1.2 1.2])
grid on
% Set the plot window color to be magenta...
set(gca,'color',[1 0 1])
% Set the figure color to be black...
set(gcf,'color',[0 0 0])
% Draw the axis labellings in white...
set(gca,'xcolor',[1 1 1], 'ycolor',[1 1 1],'fontsize',14)
```

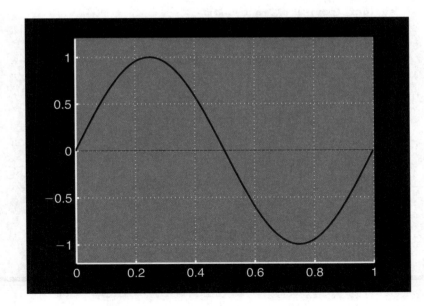

A.13   Positioning the Figure Window

It is possible to control the location and size of the figure window. The command

$$\texttt{set(gcf,'position',[a b L W])}$$

places the lower left corner of an *L*-by-*W* figure window at (a, b).

The Script ShowPosition

```
% Script: ShowPosition
% How to position the current figure window.
%
% Syntax:   set(gcf,'position',[a b L W])
%
%         (a,b) = is the lower left corner
%            L  = the horizontal length of the window
%            W  = the vertical width of the window
%
% Different screens have different dimensions.
% A window that fits on one screen may not fit on another.

% Vary the lower left corner...
close, figure, shg
L = 600; W = 400;
for a = 50:100:350
   for b = 50:50:200
      set(gcf,'position',[a b L W])
      title(sprintf(...
         '[ a , b , L , W ]  =  [%1d , %1d , %1d , %1d]',...
         a,b,L,W),'Fontsize',14)
      text(.3,.5,'Vary Lower Left Corner (a,b)','Fontsize',14)
      pause
   end
end

% Vary the length and width of the figure...
close, figure, shg
a = 100; b = 100;
for L = 500:100:900
   for W = 100:100:500
      set(gcf,'position',[a b L W])
      title(sprintf(...
         '[ a , b , L , W ]  =  [%1d , %1d , %1d , %1d]',...
         a,b,L,W),'Fontsize',14)
      text(.3,.5,'Vary Length and Width','Fontsize',14)
      pause
   end
end
```

Appendix B

Mathematical Facts

The level of "mathematical maturity" assumed by this text can be anticipated by browsing through the following summary of math facts. Judge yourself by the number of these facts that you would be comfortable *using*, not by the number of these facts that you are able to memorize or derive.

Numbers

A real number is an *integer* if it has no fraction part.

If there is a zero remainder when an integer a is divided by an integer b, then b is a *divisor* of a.

A positive integer is *prime* if its only divisors are one and itself.

The *greatest common divisor* of two positive integers a and b is the largest integer that is a divisor of both a and b.

A real number is *rational* if it is the quotient of two integers.

Complex numbers have the form $a + bi$ where a and b are real and $i = \sqrt{-1}$.

Important Functions

Exponential. The function $f(x) = e^x$ where $e = 2.718\ldots$ is called the *exponential*.

Logarithm. The base-b logarithm of a positive number y is the solution to $b^x = y$. $\ln(x)$ denotes the natural, base-e logarithm.

Sine and Cosine. The ray from $(0,0)$ to $(\cos(\theta), \sin(\theta))$ makes a counterclockwise angle θ with the positive x-axis. These functions have period 2π, meaning that $\cos(x + 2\pi) = \cos(x)$ and $\sin(x + 2\pi) = \sin(x)$ for all real numbers x.

Tangent. The tangent of an angle θ is given by $\tan(\theta) = \sin(\theta)/\cos(\theta)$ with the understanding that the tangent is infinite if $\cos(\theta) = 0$.

Arctangent. The arctangent of a real number y is the solution x to $\tan(x) = y$ that satisfies $-\pi/2 < x < \pi/2$.

Arcsine. The arcsine of a real number y that satisfies $-1 \le y \le 1$ is the solution x to $\sin(x) = y$ that satisfies $-\pi/2 \le x \le \pi/2$.

Arccosine. The arccosine of a real number y that satisfies $-1 \le y \le 1$ is the solution x to $\cos(x) = y$ that satisfies $0 \le x \le \pi$.

Polynomials. A polynomial of degree d has the form $a_0 + a_1 x + \cdots + a_d x^d$ where $a_d \ne 0$. It has exactly d roots.

Rational Functions. A rational function is the quotient of two polynomials.

Angles

Angle Measures. Angles can be measured in radians or degrees-minutes-seconds. 2π radians equals 360 degrees. One degree equals 60 minutes. One minute equals 60 seconds.

Quadrants. We say that

$$(x, y) \text{ is in the} \left\{ \begin{array}{l} \text{First} \\ \text{Second} \\ \text{Third} \\ \text{Fourth} \end{array} \right\} \text{ quadrant if } \left\{ \begin{array}{l} x \ge 0,\ y \ge 0 \\ x \le 0,\ y \ge 0 \\ x \le 0,\ y \le 0 \\ x \ge 0,\ y \le 0 \end{array} \right\}.$$

Notation

Dot-Dot-Dot. $a_1, \ldots, a_n$ means a sequence of n numbers a_1, a_2 "on up to" a_n.

Summation. $\displaystyle\sum_{k=1}^{n} a_k = a_1 + \cdots + a_n$.

Product. $\displaystyle\prod_{k=1}^{n} a_k = a_1 a_2 \cdots a_n$.

Base-2. If $d_0, \ldots, d_k$ are bits (either 0 or 1), then $(d_k \cdots d_1 d_0)_2$ has the value $d_0 + 2d_1 + \cdots + 2^k d_k$.

Absolute Value. If $x \ge 0$, then $|x| = x$. If $x < 0$, then $|x| = -x$.

Polygons

Polygons are known by the number of their sides. The *triangle* (3), *quadrilateral* (4), *pentagon* (5), *hexagon* (6), and *octagon* (8) are important special cases.

A triangle with two equal sides is an *isosceles* triangle. A triangle with three equal sides is an *equilateral* triangle.

A quadrilateral with one pair of parallel sides is a *trapezoid*. A quadrilateral with two pairs of parallel sides is a *parallelogram*. A quadrilateral with four equal sides is a *rhombus*. A quadrilateral with four equal angles is a *rectangle*. A rhombus that is a rectangle is a *square*.

A polygon with equal interior angles and equal side lengths is a *regular* polygon.

If every line segment that connects two points in a polygon is entirely inside the polygon, then the polygon is said to be *convex*.

Distance, Area, Volume

The Euclidean distance between (x_1, y_1) and (x_2, y_2) is

$$d = \sqrt{(x_1 - x_2)^2 + (y_1 - y_2)^2}.$$

The area of a triangle with side lengths a, b, and c is

$$A = \sqrt{s(s-a)(s-b)(s-c)}$$

where $s = (a+b+c)/2$.

The area of a triangle with side lengths a and b and in-between vertex having angle θ is

$$A = \frac{ab}{2}\sin(\theta).$$

The area of a polygon having n equally spaced vertices around a circle of radius r is

$$A = \frac{nr^2}{2}\sin\left(\frac{2\pi}{n}\right).$$

The surface area of a sphere with radius r is

$$A = 4\pi r^2.$$

The volume of a sphere with radius r is

$$V = \frac{4}{3}\pi r^3.$$

Parametric Equations

A line through distinct points (x_1, y_1) and (x_2, y_2):

$$\begin{aligned}
x(t) &= x_1 + t(x_2 - x_1) \\
y(t) &= y_1 + t(y_2 - y_1)
\end{aligned} \qquad -\infty < t < \infty.$$

An ellipse with center (x_c, y_c) and semiaxes a and b:

$$\begin{aligned}
x(t) &= x_c + a\cos(t) \\
y(t) &= y_c + b\sin(t)
\end{aligned} \qquad 0 \le t < 2\pi.$$

Combinations

The number of ways that n objects can be arranged is given by n factorial:

$$n! = 1 \cdot 2 \cdot 3 \cdots n.$$

The number of ways that k objects can be selected from n objects is given by the binomial coefficient n-choose-k:

$$\binom{n}{k} = \frac{n!}{k!(n-k)!} = \frac{n(n-1)\cdots(n-k+1)}{1\cdot 2\cdots k}.$$

Trigonometric Identities

$$\cos(\theta/2) = \sqrt{\frac{1+\cos(\theta)}{2}} \qquad 0 \leq \theta \leq \pi/2$$

$$\sin(\theta/2) = \sqrt{\frac{1-\cos(\theta)}{2}} \qquad 0 \leq \theta \leq \pi/2$$

$$\cos(-\theta) = \cos(\theta)$$

$$\sin(-\theta) = -\sin(\theta)$$

$$\cos(\theta+\phi) = \cos(\theta)\cos(\phi) - \sin(\theta)\sin(\phi)$$

$$\sin(\theta+\phi) = \cos(\theta)\sin(\phi) + \sin(\theta)\cos(\phi).$$

Sets

If A is a set, then $x \in A$ means that x belongs to A.

$\mathbb{R}$ denotes the set of real numbers.

Types of Intervals:
$$\begin{aligned}
[a,b] &= \{x \in \mathbb{R} : a \leq x \leq b\} \\
[a,b) &= \{x \in \mathbb{R} : a \leq x < b\} \\
(a,b] &= \{x \in \mathbb{R} : a < x \leq b\} \\
(a,b) &= \{x \in \mathbb{R} : a < x < b\}.
\end{aligned}$$

The *union* of two sets A and B: $A \cup B = \{x : x \in A \text{ or } x \in B\}$.

The *intersection* of two sets A and B: $A \cap B = \{x : x \in A \text{ and } x \in B\}$.

Differentiation

If f is differentiable at x_0, then $f'(x_0)$ is the slope of f at x_0 and is a limit:

$$f'(x_0) = \lim_{h \to 0} \frac{f(x_0+h) - f(x_0)}{h}.$$

The zeros of f' are referred to as *critical points*. The second derivative $(f')' = f''$ determines the nature of the critical point:

$$f'(x_*) = 0, \ f''(x_*) > 0 \ \Rightarrow \ x_* \text{ is a local minimum}$$

$$f'(x_*) = 0, \ f''(x_*) < 0 \ \Rightarrow \ x_* \text{ is a local maximum}$$

$$f'(x_*) = 0, \ f''(x_*) = 0 \ \Rightarrow \ x_* \text{ is a saddle point.}$$

Some well-known derivatives:

$f(x)$	$f'(x)$
$\sin(x)$	$\cos(x)$
$\cos(x)$	$-\sin(x)$
e^x	e^x
$a_0 + a_1 x + \cdots + a_d x^d$	$a_1 + 2a_2 x + \cdots + d a_d x^{d-1}$
$g(x)h(x)$	$g(x)h'(x) + g'(x)h(x)$
$\dfrac{g(x)}{h(x)}$	$\dfrac{h(x)g'(x) - h'(x)g(x)}{g(x)^2}$

Appendix C

MATLAB, Java, and C

Given the ubiquity and importance of computation tools, students do not commonly ask why they should study programming; the more common question is how to go about it. There are two equally valid answers to this question—on one hand, they should choose a language applicable to their field, but on the other, most languages can be applied to any field. Regardless, both answers are good reasons to consider using MATLAB.

The spectrum of typical introductory languages can be roughly divided into three camps. The first of these comprises imperative languages—particularly C—which closely correspond to the underlying machine and encourage the programmer to manage every low-level detail of the program. The second consists of object-oriented languages such as Java, which provide rich idioms for expressing programming concepts and hide many frustrating differences between various hardware and operating systems. Finally, scientific languages such as MATLAB offer powerful data analysis tools and comprehensive mathematical libraries particularly suited to engineering and science applications. Despite their differences, each of these languages can be an appropriate starting point for a beginning programmer. It is worth considering the advantages and disadvantages of each when trying to choose a first programming language (keeping in mind that many students will ultimately learn several different programming languages).

The C programming language is one of the oldest, yet it still sees regular service. It was developed in 1972 by Dennis Richie and remains one of the most widely used programming languages. Among its most popular relatives are C++ and Objective-C.

Advantages: The language is small and its libraries are concise, so the language features are easy to learn (though difficult to master). Its design and capabilities closely mirror assembly languages that computer processors understand directly, so learning C confers valuable insights into computer hardware architecture. Because of its brevity and low-level design, there is no "magic" in the way C works. While other, higher-level languages may hide complicated programming techniques behind simple interfaces or language features, C has no such artifice; students can genuinely understand how their programs work at every level. The performance of C is excellent; by virtue of its austerity, it can evade many of the overheads incurred by more complicated languages. Finally, C is quite universal—just about every computer and operating system offers a C compiler.

Disadvantages: Low-level languages may aid in understanding programs, but they complicate their design. There is a reason higher-level languages offer abstractions and rich libraries—it makes programming much easier. Memory management is a prime example— even simple programs written in C require careful memory management. This is a challenge, even for experienced programmers, and can present an insurmountable obstacle to students writing their first program. Furthermore, the language does little to protect the programmer from making errors, creating a trial-by-fire environment for students who choose to learn C as their first language.

Java is a relatively modern language, released in 1995 by Sun Microsystems. Its syntax is based on C, but it provides extensive libraries, comprehensive tools that run on a wide variety of platforms, and some very useful features to prevent errors. Java, like its close relative C++, is an object-oriented language. Its program constituents are not functions (as in MATLAB and C) but are "objects," which are programming structures that contain *both* data and a set of functions that operate on the data.

Advantages: The biggest advantage of Java is its safety; Java does not run directly on a processor, but rather on a "virtual machine"—a kind of private sandbox that protects against all sorts of errors, especially those commonly made by beginning programmers. Many classes of errors common in C do not even exist in Java. There are implementations for a large variety of platforms, and few (if any) changes are required to move from one to another. It has thorough libraries for diverse applications, allowing programmers to write complex, fully featured programs quickly. This makes Java a good language for expressing high-level ideas without exhaustively working out every detail.

Disadvantages: The primary disadvantage of Java as a teaching language is that it hides too much complexity, somewhat misleading the beginner. For example, the Java Virtual Machine manages an application's memory without input from the user. This leads to an experience and intuition gap when students ultimately study memory management. Additionally, the Java Virtual Machine incurs performance overhead, so a program written in Java generally runs slower than the same program written in C.

MATLAB was invented in the late 1970s by Cleve Moler, who in 1984 cofounded The Mathworks that continues to develop and market MATLAB. It is widely used across academia and industry as a problem-solving environment and computation tool. Other numerical problem-solving environments include *Maple* and *Mathematica*.

Advantages: As shown throughout this book, MATLAB has an impressive repertoire of tools, including a rich library of mathematical functions and powerful graphical capabilities. Its user-friendliness makes it an excellent choice for first-time programmers, while its enormous collection of domain-specific packages accounts for its widespread use across the sciences and engineering. It also offers interfaces for interacting with other programming languages. For example, MATLAB can call functions written in C and FORTRAN and vice versa.

Disadvantages: Its behind-the-scenes treatment of data types and less-than-ideal support for object-oriented programming make MATLAB hard to use to master certain important features of advanced programming. A downside of its user-friendliness is that it distances the programmer from machine-level concerns such as memory management.

For the sake of comparison, we examine three solutions to the same problem—one written in MATLAB, one written in C, and one in Java. Consider writing a program to determine whether a linear combination $c_0 + c_1 x_1 + \cdots + c_n x_n = y$, evaluates to zero. Each solution consists of two parts:

- `evaluate` takes a list of x-values and returns the result of evaluating the combination given a list of corresponding coefficients and a constant term.

- main executes `evaluate`, tests the result to see if it equals zero, and prints the result. In our example, we use the following values: $c_0 = 0$, $c_1 = 1$, $c_2 = 2$, $c_3 = 3$, $x_1 = 1$, $x_2 = -2$, and $x_3 = 1$

Our MATLAB solution consists of two files. The first file, `evaluate.m`, is a function that evaluates a combination based on a scalar, a vector of coefficients, and a vector of x values. The script file `main.m` initializes our variables, calls the evaluation function, and prints the results.

The Function `evaluate`

```
function y = evaluate(constant, c, x)
% Evaluate a linear combination:
%    y = constant + c(1)*x(1) + c(2)*x(2) + ... + c(n)*x(n)
% where n is the length of real vectors c and x
% and constant is a real scalar.

y = constant;
for i = 1:length(c)
    y = y + c(i) * x(i);
end
```

The Script `main`

```
% Check if a linear combination evaluates to zero
constant = 0;   c = [1, 2, 3];   x = [1, -2, 1];

value = evaluate(constant, c, x);
if value==0
    fprintf('Evaluates to zero\n')
else
    fprintf('Evaluates to %f\n', value)
end
```

Our C solution mirrors MATLAB closely, and aside from a few syntactic differences, the correspondence is readily apparent. The main differences relate to C's "low level" qualities. Accessing the input/output (I/O) libraries requires a specific command (`#include "stdio.h"`), and arrays in C do not know their own length, so this information must be passed as a separate argument (hence the addition of the parameter `totalCoefficients`). Also observe that blocks in C are defined with curly braces, rather than end statements. Finally, notice that function declarations in C are more complicated than their MATLAB counterparts. These are largely the result of its "type system"—a system of automated checks that ensure the values passed to a function match the kinds of values the function expects.

The syntax of a Java program is similar to C—blocks are delineated with braces, declarations have types, semicolons terminate expressions, and so forth. But while MATLAB

The File `LinearCombination.c`

```c
#include "stdio.h"

/* Evaluate a linear combination */
double evaluate(double constant, int totalCoefficients,
                double* c, double* x) {
    double y = constant;
    int i;
    for (i=0; i<totalCoefficients; ++i) {
        y = y + c[i] * x[i];
    }
    return y;
}

/* Check if a linear combination evaluates to zero */
int main(int argc, char** argv) {
    double constant = 0;
    int totalCoefficients = 3;
    double c[] = {1, 2, 3};
    double x[] = {1, -2, 1};

    double value = evaluate(constant, totalCoefficients, c, x);
    if (value==0)
        printf("Evaluates to zero\n");
    else
        printf("Evaluates to %f\n", value);
}
```

and C programs are built from constituent functions, Java programs consist of interacting objects—programming structures that contain both data (called "fields") and a set of functions (called "methods") that operate on its fields. A class is a blueprint that describes what data an object will contain and what kinds of operations will be permitted on that data. In order to create an object from a class, its constructor, a function that has the same name as the class itself, is called. Once the constructor has created an object and initialized its fields, other functions in the class can access these fields in order to perform computation. This programming paradigm is called "object-oriented programming." Our solution uses a single class `LinearCombination`, which consists of two variables, called `constant` and `c`, as well as three methods: the constructor `LinearCombination`, the member function `evaluate`, and the entry point function `main`. In our example, `main` creates a `LinearCombination` object by calling the constructor, then calls the method `evaluate` on the newly created object, which computes the result using its parameter x and the object's fields `constant` and `c`.

All three languages share much of their structure and syntax, including conditionals expressed as `if-else` statements, `for`-loops and `while`-loops for iteration, functions with parameters and return values, and a wide variety of other fundamental programming components. As a consequence, regardless of which language is learned first, mastery of the second (and third) is less challenging. Indeed, most computational scientists find learning additional programming languages a necessity. An engineer might prototype a simulation in

The File `LinearCombination.java`

```
/* LinearCombination:
 * y = constant + c(1)*x(1) + c(2)*x(2) + ... + c(n)*x(n)
 */
public class LinearCombination {

    double constant;    /* c0 */
    double[] c;         /* coefficients c1, c2, ..., cn */

    /* Constructor: create a LinearCombination object */
    public LinearCombination(double constant, double[] c) {
        this.constant = constant;
        this.c = c;
    }

    /* Evaluate the linear combination */
    public double evaluate(double[] x) {
        double y = constant;
        for (int i=0; i<c.length; ++i) {
            y = y + c[i] * x[i];
        }
        return y;
    }

    /* Check if a linear combination evaluates to zero */
    public static void main(String[] args) {
        double[] c = {1, 2, 3};
        LinearCombination eqn = new LinearCombination(0, c);

        double[] x = {1, -2, 1};
        double value = eqn.evaluate(x);

        if (value==0)
            System.out.println("Evaluates to zero");
        else
            System.out.println("Evaluates to " + value);
    }
}
```

MATLAB but have to rewrite it in C in order to take advantage of a large, high-performance computing cluster. A scientist who programs in Java may find it easier to analyze results with MATLAB. A program written in C may need to call code written in MATLAB or interact with a server written in Java.

In the final analysis, every language has its strengths and weaknesses. By studying a variety of languages the practitioner can learn to deploy the best tool for each situation. In our opinion, MATLAB is a particularly solid, first-language choice. It sets the stage for more advanced programming and, equally important, it promotes the kind of intuitive thinking that is crucial to computational science and engineering.

Appendix D

Exit Interview

The Talking Points that conclude each section are an important part of this book's message. Here are some follow-up questions to ensure that you agree!

Q1.1 What is the difference between model error, measurement error, mathematical error, and roundoff error? Explain.

Q1.2 The manipulation of logical expressions that involve AND's, OR's, and NOT's has a strong similarity to the manipulation of arithmetic expressions that involve additions and multiplications. Explain.

Q2.1 A programmer working on a geometric problem complains about having to spend a lot of time figuring out how to handle situations near the boundary. Explain.

Q2.2 What steps should be followed to avoid making mistakes when designing a loop?

Q3.1 How is the big-O notation used to quantify the amount of work associated with a computation? Give examples.

Q3.2 What is the difference between an explicit formula and an implicit formula?

Q4.1 What does the term "granularity" mean when discussing the quality of a discretization?

Q4.2 How can interpolation be used to generate a succession of "equally spaced" colors in between two given colors?

Q4.3 Give several examples that illustrate the finiteness of floating point arithmetic.

Q5.1 Newton's method for finding a zero of a function $f(x)$ is an iteration that involves tangent lines. Explain with a picture.

Q5.2 When is it *not* advisable to write a function for a well-defined subcomputation?

Q5.3 Why is top-down design a valuable programming strategy?

Q6.1 Why are functions that generate random numbers referred to as "pseudorandom number generators"?

Q6.2 What is a random walk simulation?

Q6.3 Give a geometric example that demonstrates the power of repeated averaging.

Q7.1 What is a Markov chain simulation?

Q7.2 What makes the problem of grid generation challenging?

Q7.3 Explain the accuracy-versus-efficiency trade-off in the context of simulation on a grid.

Q8.1 What determines the efficiency of a computation such as the perfect shuffle, which involves no floating point arithmetic?

Q8.2 Why might one be more concerned about worst-case performance than average-case performance?

Q9.1 Linear search is applied to find the largest entry in an n-by-n array. By what factor would you expect execution time to increase if n is increased by a factor of 10?

Q9.2 Explain why the typical method for looking up a name in a telephone directory has features that are similar to both binary search and linear search.

Q9.3 Explain the similarities and differences between the method of binary search and the method of bisection.

Q10.1 What is meant by data abstraction and why is it important?

Q10.2 Give several examples of intersection problems that arise in computer graphics.

Q10.3 What is a "nearness" metric? Give several examples.

Q11.1 What skills are required to use an online data repository?

Q11.2 Give applications that require a megabyte, gigabyte, terabyte, and petabyte of storage.

Q12.1 Why are color maps important?

Q12.2 Describe some of the challenges associated with the image rendering problem.

Q12.3 How has the computer affected the field of font design?

Q12.4 What is meant by data compression?

Q13.1 Why is segmentation a hard problem in the context of acoustic data processing?

Q13.2 How are touch-tone signals deciphered?

Q14.1 What is the role of recursion in mesh generation?

Q14.2 Quantify the efficiency difference between merge sort and insertion sort.

Q14.3 Give an example of a recursive process that is terminated on the basis of a heuristic.

Q15.1 Why is the search space associated with the traveling salesperson problem so large?

Q15.2 Give an example of a constrained optimization problem.

Q15.3 Discuss the similarities between the process of model building in science and the process of design in engineering.

Index